THOMAS HARDY

COMING UP OXFORD STREET : EVENING

By THOMAS HARDY.

THE sun from the west glares back,
And the sun from the watered track,
And the sun from the plates of glass,
And the sun from each window-brass.

Sun-mirrorings, too, brighten
From show-cases beneath
The laughing eyes and teeth
Of ladies who rouge and whiten.

And the same warm god explores
Panels and chinks of doors;
Problems with chymists' bottles
Profound as Aristotle's
He solves, and with good cause,
Having been ere man was.

Also he dazzles the pupils of one who walks west,
Me, city-clerk, with eyesight not of the best,
Who see no escape to the very end of my days
From the rut of Oxford Street into open ways;
And I go along with head and eyes drooping forlorn,
Taking no interest in things, and wondering why I was
born.

(As seen July 4th, 18———.)

'Coming Up Oxford Street: Evening' as printed in
The Nation & the Athenaeum, 13 June 1925

THOMAS HARDY

HALF A LONDONER

MARK FORD

THE BELKNAP PRESS OF HARVARD UNIVERSITY PRESS

Cambridge, Massachusetts, and London, England

2016

DESIGN BY ANNAMARIE MCMAHON WHY

Library of Congress Cataloging-in-Publication Data

Names: Ford, Mark, 1962 June 24– author.

Title: Thomas Hardy : half a Londoner / Mark Ford.

Description: Cambridge, Massachusetts : The Belknap Press of Harvard
University Press, 2016. | Includes bibliographical references and index.

Identifiers: LCCN 2016014043 | ISBN 9780674737891 (hardcover : alk. paper)

Subjects: LCSH: Hardy, Thomas, 1840–1928—Homes and haunts—England—London. |
Hardy, Thomas, 1840–1928—Homes and haunts—England—Dorset. | Authors,
English—19th century—Biography. | Rural-urban relations in literature.

Classification: LCC PR4753 .F67 2016 | DDC 823/.8 [B]—dc23

LC record available at https://lccn.loc.gov/2016014043

For John and Joanna

1869. Spring . . . One of those evenings in the country which make the townsman feel: 'I will stay here till I die—I would, that is, if it were not for that thousand pounds I want to make, & that friend I want to envy me.'

The Personal Notebooks of Thomas Hardy (4)

What contrasting phases of existence he moved in—vibrating at a swing between the artificial gaieties of a London season and the quaintnesses of a primitive rustic life.

The Life and Work of Thomas Hardy (257)

I am quite sure he did not find all his queer characters hereabouts. He must have discovered a good many of them when he went to London.

Teresa Hardy (Thomas Hardy's cousin), *Interviews and Recollections* (241)

Contents

Note on Texts

The texts of Hardy's novels referred to are the editions published by Oxford University Press, with the exceptions of *The Hand of Ethelberta*, *A Laodicean*, and *The Well-Beloved*, where references are to the Penguin editions. All quotations from the poetry are taken from *Thomas Hardy: The Complete Poems*, edited by James Gibson and published by Palgrave Macmillan. (See Selected Bibliography for full publication details.)

What was effectively Hardy's autobiography was initially issued by Macmillan in two instalments, *The Early Life of Thomas Hardy, 1840–1891* (1928) and *The Later Years of Thomas Hardy, 1892–1928* (1930), under the name of his second wife, Florence Hardy. It was subsequently published in a single volume as *The Life of Thomas Hardy*. It emerged in due course, however, that, although the text was written in the third person, Hardy was himself responsible for all but the book's last chapters. An edition of the original typescript that Florence prepared from Hardy's longhand manuscript and from original sources such as letters and journal entries was published by Michael Millgate in 1984 under the title *The Life and Work of Thomas Hardy*. The textual apparatus in this edition includes details of all the alterations that Florence made to the typescript after Hardy's death. It is from Millgate's edition, its title shortened to the *Life*, that quotations are taken in this book. Quotations from passages deleted from the *Life* by Hardy but restored by Florence after his death are keyed both to Millgate's edition and to *The Life of Thomas Hardy* by Florence Hardy.

Abbreviations

AI	*An Indiscretion in the Life of an Heiress and Other Stories* (ed. Pamela Dalziel)
AL	*A Laodicean* (ed. John Schad)
CL	*The Collected Letters of Thomas Hardy*, 8 volumes (eds. Richard Little Purdy, Michael Millgate, and Keith Wilson)
CP	*Thomas Hardy: The Complete Poems* (ed. James Gibson)
DR	*Desperate Remedies* (ed. Patricia Ingham)
FFMC	*Far from the Madding Crowd* (ed. Suzanne B. Falck-Yi)
FH	*The Life of Thomas Hardy* by Florence Hardy
HE	*The Hand of Ethelberta* (ed. Tim Dolin)
JO	*Jude the Obscure* (ed. Patricia Ingham)
L	*The Life and Work of Thomas Hardy* (ed. Michael Millgate)
LLI	*Life's Little Ironies* (ed. Alan Manford)
LN	*The Literary Notebooks of Thomas Hardy*, 2 volumes (ed. Lennart A. Björk)
MC	*The Mayor of Casterbridge* (ed. Dale Kramer)
PBE	*A Pair of Blue Eyes* (ed. Alan Manford)
PM	*Thomas Hardy's 'Poetical Matter' Notebook* (eds. Pamela Dalziel and Michael Millgate)
PN	*The Personal Notebooks of Thomas Hardy* (ed. Richard H. Taylor)
PV	*Thomas Hardy's Public Voice: The Essays, Speeches, and Miscellaneous Prose* (ed. Michael Millgate)
PW	*Thomas Hardy's Personal Writings* (ed. Harold Orel)
RN	*The Return of the Native* (ed. Simon Gatrell)
SS	*Thomas Hardy's 'Studies, Specimens &c.' Notebook* (eds. Pamela Dalziel and Michael Millgate)
T	*Tess of the d'Urbervilles* (eds. Juliet Grindle and Simon Gatrell)
UGT	*Under the Greenwood Tree* (ed. Simon Gatrell)
W	*The Woodlanders* (ed. Dale Kramer)

WB   *The Pursuit of the Well-Beloved* and *The Well-Beloved* (ed. Patricia
         Ingham)
WT   *Wessex Tales* (ed. Kathryn R. King)

The following abbreviations are used to indicate the sources of quotations from
secondary sources and archives:

BL   British Library
CH   *Thomas Hardy: The Critical Heritage* (ed. R. G. Cox)
CT   *Thomas Hardy: The Time-Torn Man* by Claire Tomalin
DCM   Dorset County Museum
GT   *The Golden Treasury*, edited by Francis Turner Palgrave (ed. Christopher
         Ricks)
IR   *Thomas Hardy: Interviews and Recollections* (ed. James Gibson)
MM   *Thomas Hardy: A Biography Revisited* by Michael Millgate
RG   *Young Thomas Hardy* by Robert Gittings
RP   *Thomas Hardy: A Bibliographical Study* by Richard Little Purdy
         (ed. Charles Pettit)

Preface

Thomas Hardy is famous as the creator of Wessex. Anyone visiting the counties of Dorset or Wiltshire or Hampshire or Somerset will be struck by the plethora of businesses and enterprises making use of the term: Wessex Auctions, Wessex Building Services, Wessex Cars, Wessex Dental, Wessex Electrical, Wessex Fertility, Wessex Golf Centre. . . . You can stay in a Wessex Hotel in Bournemouth, in Winchester, and in Street, while in Dorchester itself you can stay in the Wessex Royale Hotel on High West Street, halfway between the Dorset County Museum, where Hardy's papers are housed and his study has been reconstructed, and the statue of Hardy by Eric Henri Kennington beside the Top o' Town roundabout.

It may have been, as Simon Gatrell suggests in *Thomas Hardy's Vision of Wessex*, the Dorset poet William Barnes's interest in the influence of Saxon Wessex on Dorset dialect that prompted Hardy to apply the term to the area of southern England where most of his novels are set.[1] While it was only gradually that Hardy became fully aware of the importance that the concept of Wessex might have for his imagination, as well as for his sales figures, once he'd embraced the notion that he could link his various novels and stories, and later his poems too, into an ongoing chronicle of a half-real, half-fictive region, he held on fast to the idea. The publication of collected editions of his work gave him the opportunity to revise his disparate early novels to make them fit with Wessex topography and nomenclature, enabling him to present himself as the preeminent regional writer of his era.

It is this book's contention that the focus on Wessex in critical responses to Hardy's work has obscured the importance of London to his career and development. Hardy spent five crucial years in the capital in his early twenties (1862–1867) and lived on and off in London and its suburbs until his early forties. His publishers, his editors, and most of his literary friends were based in London. In 1885 he and his wife, Emma, settled in Max Gate, a substantial red-brick villa that Hardy, who trained initially as an architect, designed, and had his father and brother (who were both in the building trade) construct on the outskirts of Dorchester. This by no means, however, signaled the end of Hardy and Emma's London lives, for they would spend several months each year in lodgings in the capital, attending fashionable parties, going to concerts, plays, and exhibitions, paying social calls, and visiting their clubs.

This is the first comprehensive account of Hardy as 'a London man', to borrow a phrase that he applied to himself in his autobiography (L 125). The idea of considering the metropolitan aspects of his life and work came to me while I was gathering material for my anthology *London: A History in Verse* (2012). I was surprised to find so many compelling poems by Hardy set in London, and I now regret not including in that volume pieces such as 'An East-End Curate', 'A Wife in London', and 'The Woman I Met'. In addition, during his five years in the city in his twenties, Hardy composed some of his most original and inventive poetry, and it occurred to me that it would be interesting to consider in depth the urban contexts of these early and, in my opinion, rather underrated poems whose place of composition, mainly Westbourne Park Villas (sometimes shortened to W.P.V.), Hardy often chose to indicate when they were eventually published many decades later. His residence in Tooting in South London between 1878 and 1881 resulted in a smaller batch of poems either written in those years, or written later but based on his Tooting experiences, while his flirtatious encounters in the city with various literary and Society women to whom he was attracted in the 1890s generated, as well as many fascinating diary entries and the drawing-room scenes in *The Well-Beloved*, a handful of urban poems that veer between the witty and the plangent.

Further stimulus to an exploration of Hardy's life and work through the prism of his time in the metropolis and its suburbs came from two excellent essays published in collections of Hardy criticism: Michael Slater's 'Hardy and the City' (1994) and Keith Wilson's 'Thomas Hardy of London' (2009) both posited the need for a fuller understanding of the role played by London in Hardy's evolution, personal and professional. Wilson even suggests that

London had for Hardy a significance 'that was in its way as important as that of Dorset'.[2]

This book pays particular attention to the traffic charted in Hardy's novels between Wessex and London, as well as to Hardy's shuttlings between his various Dorset homes and his residences in the capital. The isolated cottage in which he was born in 1840 in the tiny hamlet of Higher Bockhampton, about three miles from Dorchester, was near the old coaching road to London, but it was not until the arrival of the railways in 1847 that the secluded society of Hardy's childhood became vulnerable to the incursions of the metropolis. He made his first trip to London, as a nine-year-old boy, two years later.

Radical division and unsettling displacement are central features of Hardy's poetry and fiction. His oscillations as a young man between the routines and concerns of Higher Bockhampton and the excitements and dangers of London were crucial to the development of his profound personal sense of self-division, of being torn between worlds that were mutually dependent but often mutually uncomprehending. This self-division in turn motivates or underlies the explorations of change, loss, and uncertainty in much of his greatest writing. It helps explain, too, the diversity of Hardy's oeuvre, his willingness to explore and to experiment. Whereas some of the younger Hardy's depictions of London make use of the popular traditions of sensation fiction, revealing the influence of Wilkie Collins in particular, his later evocations of the city, especially those in *The Well-Beloved* and in his journal, are more radical and innovative, bringing to mind the metropolitan writings of such as Baudelaire, Rimbaud, Proust, Virginia Woolf, and James Joyce.

The complexity of Hardy's negotiations, both imaginative and practical, between the provincial and the metropolitan are also echoed in the responses of his contemporaries to his work: for if on one level Wessex proved popular with a mainly urban readership as a primitive region far removed from the daily quandaries of urban life, on another it appealed because the tragic narratives that Hardy set there dramatized the threat to a rural populace of precisely those anxieties that bedeviled city dwellers.

It is my hope that *Thomas Hardy: Half a Londoner* will demonstrate that the concept of Wessex itself evolved out of the dialogue between Dorset and

London that structured so many of Hardy's opportunities and experiences. Intertwining biographical accounts of Hardy's various sojourns in London with discussion of his dealings with his editors and publishers, it presents a multifaceted portrait of Hardy the 'London man'. It offers close readings of the poems that were written in London or are set there, as well as of the novels and short stories that make fullest use of the relationship between Wessex and the capital. While the Dorset-London axis is self-evidently important to the plots and themes of novels such as *Desperate Remedies*, *The Hand of Ethelberta*, *The Well-Beloved*, and Hardy's earliest attempt at fiction, *The Poor Man and the Lady*, my overarching argument is that all of Hardy's work benefits from being considered in the context of his pressing, at times almost obsessive need to make sense of the relationship between London and the provinces. It was in London that Hardy found fame, but it was also in London that he suffered his deepest anxieties and most troubling fits of self-doubt. Although the capital may not feature on the maps of Wessex that came to preface all his novels, it was in London that they were edited and published, and it was in London that judgement was passed on them by a class of person that Hardy came to detest—the metropolitan reviewer.

One can, of course, only speculate about the different turns that Hardy's life might have taken had he not set out for London on 17 April 1862, with a return ticket in his pocket, 'to pursue the art and science of architecture on more advanced lines' (L 40). He did indeed, to some extent, further his architectural career there. He also became a writer.

THOMAS HARDY

Hardy's residences in or near London from 1862 to 1881

1 1862: 3 Clarence Place

2 1863: 9 Clarence Place

3 1863–67: 16 Westbourne Park Villas

4 1870: 23 Montpelier Street

5 1872–74: 4 Celbridge Place

6 1875: St. David's Villa, Hook Road (Surbiton) *see inset*

7 1875: 18 Newton Road

8 1878–1881: 1 Arundel Terrace, Trinity Road (Tooting) *see inset*

Hardy's places of work in London

9 1862–63: 9 St. Martin's Place

10 1863–67: 8 Adelphi Terrace

11 1872: Bedford Chambers, Bedford Street

Hardy's residences in London during the Season

12 1884 and 1885: 29 Montague Street

13 1885: Montague Mansions, 56 Great Russell Street

14 1886: 23 Montague Street

15 1886: 14 Bedford Place

16 1886: 28 Upper Bedford Place

17 1887: 5 Campden Hill Road

18 1888, 1908 and 1909: West Central Hotel, 75–81 and 97-105 Southampton Row

19 1888 and 1901: Shirley's Temperance Hotel, 37 Queen Square

20 1888: 5 Upper Phillimore Place

21 1889: 20 Monmouth Road

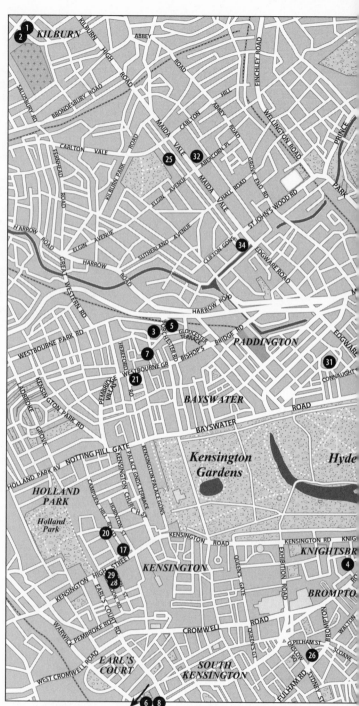

Hardy's London

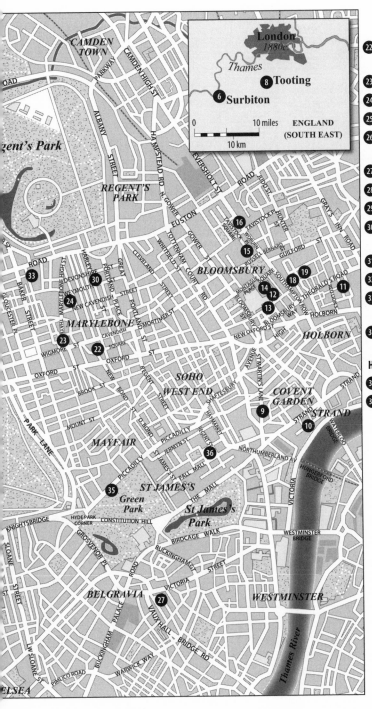

22 **1890:** 5 Chapel Place, Cavendish Square

23 **1891:** 12 Mandeville Place

24 **1892:** Beaumont Street

25 **1893:** 70 Hamilton Terrace

26 **1894 and 1896:** 16 Pelham Crescent

27 **1895:** 90 Ashley Gardens

28 **1898:** 9 Wynnstay Gardens

29 **1899:** 20 Wynnstay Gardens

30 **1900:** The Jeunes at 79 Harley Street

31 **1901:** 27 Oxford Terrace

32 **1904:** 13 Abercorn Place

33 **1905, 1906 and 1907:** 1-K Hyde Park Mansions

34 **1910:** 4 Blomfield Court

Hardy's Clubs

35 The Savile Club, 107 Piccadilly

36 The Athenaeum Club, 107 Pall Mall

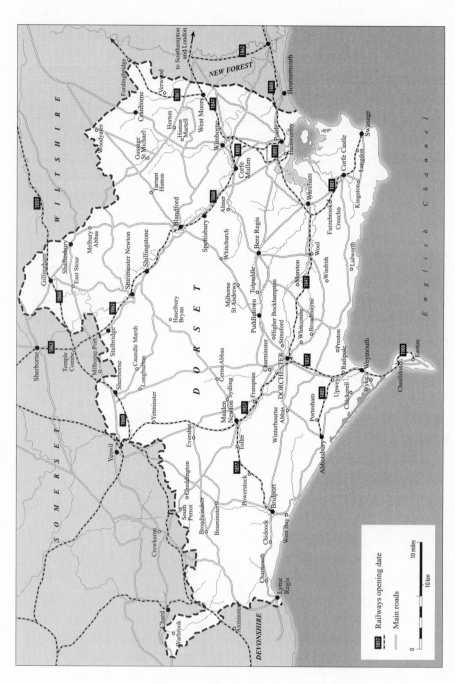

The development of the railway network in Dorset during the nineteenth century

Railways opening date
Main roads

Introduction: In Death Divided

Although he lost his religious faith towards the end of his five-year residence in London in the 1860s, Thomas Hardy remained 'churchy' (L 407), to use his own term, until the end of his life. He was particularly drawn to church-yards, and to the rituals and physical processes involved in church burial. In a late poem, 'The Six Boards', he even broods on the current state of the wood that will be used to make the coffin in which he will himself soon be interred:

> Six boards belong to me:
> I do not know where they may be;
> If growing green, or lying dry
> > In a cockloft nigh.

> Some morning I shall claim them. (CP 820–821)

Of course by the time he is ready to claim them he will be dead, and so un-able to assess their fitness for purpose. The poem goes on, nevertheless, to depict the very distinctive sort of intimacy that he anticipates enjoying with his six boards once they are safely underground together:

> Those boards and I—how much
> In common we, of feel and touch
> Shall share thence on,—earth's far core-quakings,
> > Hill-shocks, tide-shakings—

> Yea, hid where none will note,
> The once live tree and man, remote
> From mundane hurt as if on Venus, Mars,
> Or furthest stars.

'Hid where none will note'. Given the enormous fame that Hardy had enjoyed for decades by the time that this poem was published in his penultimate collection of poetry, *Human Shows* of 1925, one can't help wondering if he really thought it likely that his place of burial would attract no visitors. Droves of Wessex pilgrims had been seeking out the originals of the locations mentioned in his novels since the early 1890s, when *Tess of the d'Urbervilles* (1891) swept all before it. He must have known that his final resting place would be likely to feature in Hardy-themed itineraries of Dorset after his death.

Despite Hardy's decisive rejection of the Christian concept of an afterlife that resulted from his reading of Charles Darwin and Herbert Spencer in his early twenties, his poetry is insistently haunted by the posthumous. The spirit of place is nearly always crucial to these evocations of the departed, from the 'voiceless ghost' of his first wife Emma that leads him up and down the cliffs of Pentargan Bay in Cornwall in his great elegy 'After a Journey', to the ruminations of those buried in the graveyard of the church at Stinsford (the village nearest Higher Bockhampton) in poems such as 'Friends Beyond', 'Channel Firing', and 'Voices from Things Growing in a Churchyard'. In 'Her Haunting-Ground', another elegy for Emma inspired by the visit that he made in 1913 to the village of St. Juliot in Cornwall, where he had first met her forty-three years earlier, Hardy reflects uneasily on his decision to inter his wife in Stinsford, beside the graves of his own relatives, rather than on the Cornish coast where 'her life-parts most were played':

> And so, I ask, why, why should she
> Haunt elsewhere, by a slighted tomb,
> When here she flourished sorrow-free,
> And, save for others, knew no gloom? (CP 809)

Notwithstanding the fact that Emma spent only six years in Cornwall and well over thirty in Dorset, the poem presents Emma's spirit enduring a kind of posthumous exile from her true 'haunting-ground'. The poem asks us to picture her ghost pining in Stinsford churchyard, where her body was buried, and where Hardy in fact visited her grave on a regular basis, for the landscape where she most fully belongs, that around St. Juliot, her home from 1868 to 1874. In 'I Found Her Out There', one of the 'Poems of 1912–13' written shortly after Emma's death, Hardy vividly imagines her ghost escaping from Stinsford churchyard and making its way by subterranean means to the Cornish coast that she so loved in her youth:

> Yet her shade, maybe,
> Will creep underground
> Till it catch the sound
> Of that western sea
> As it swells and sobs
> Where she once domiciled,
> And joy in its throbs
> With the heart of a child. (CP 343)

In the light of this almost pagan obsession with the physical and imaginative afterlives of the dead, and the great significance that Hardy placed on being buried in the right place and beside the right people, it is hard to believe that he ever genuinely countenanced the idea that his mortal remains would not end up next to those of Emma, and of his parents and his grandparents and his sister Mary, in Stinsford churchyard. The tombstone that he designed for Emma was effectively for himself also, since it left room for his own name and details—and indeed for those of his second wife, Florence (née Dugdale), too. Hardy's elegies for Emma often figure her as eagerly anticipating his own burial beside her: 'So cold it is in my lonely bed,' he imagines her calling out in 'Something Tapped', 'And I thought you would join me soon!' (CP 464). In 'Rain on a Grave', composed two months after her death, and fifteen years before his own, he almost joyfully figures husband and wife as at last reunited in a shared grave—'folded away there / Exposed to one weather / We both' (CP 341).

Emma's was not, however, the only woman's body Hardy wished to lay his corpse beside. One of the most peculiar of the love poems that he wrote for Florence Henniker in the 1890s is called 'In Death Divided'. It wasn't, for obvious reasons, a poem that he chose to publish while Emma was still alive. 'I shall rot here,' it opens,

> with those whom in their day
> You never knew,
> And alien ones who, ere they chilled to clay,
> Met not my view,
> Will in your distant grave-place ever neighbour you. (CP 320)

In the wake of the success of *Tess*, and as his relations with Emma steadily worsened, Hardy found himself falling in love with a succession of sophisticated metropolitan literary women: Rosamund Tomson, Florence Henniker, and Agnes Grove all became highly charged figures of romance to the middle-aged Hardy, just as Elizabeth Bishop (the Lizbie Browne of a series of poems) and Louisa Harding had infatuated him in his youth. Hardy met Henniker in Dublin in May of 1893 and, over June and July, enjoyed a number of rendezvous with her that seem to have led him to believe that a physical affair between them might well develop. In the course of a visit to Winchester in August of that year, however, Florence, who had been married for over a decade to a professional soldier called Arthur Henniker-Major, made it clear that she had no intention of offering sexual solace to a 'time-torn man' (CP 136) (as Hardy self-pityingly styles himself in the reproachful 'A Broken Appointment'), no matter how deeply she admired his writing and valued his company. Unlike the adulterous lover of another graveyard poem, 'Her Late Husband', who on his death is buried next to his mistress by his tolerant widow, the couple of 'In Death Divided', despite their passionate bond, will moulder far apart:

> No shade of pinnacle or tree or tower,
> While earth endures,
> Will fall on my mound and within the hour
> Steal on to yours;
> One robin never haunt our two green covertures . . .
>
> And in the monotonous moils of strained, hard-run
> Humanity,

> The eternal tie which binds us twain in one
>> No eye will see
> Stretching across the miles that sever you from me. (CP 320–321)

Like so many of the poems that Hardy wrote that take place in, or reflect upon, churchyards, 'In Death Divided' reveals the unnerving literalism of his vision of life after death. At the same time, and somewhat in the teeth of the poem's ghoulish central conceit, the 'miles that sever' the corpses from each other in their respective burial spots come physically to embody the unbridgeable nature of the gulf between Hardy and Henniker, and indeed between Hardy and all the other well-bred London belles who were happy to flirt with a literary lion, but proved as maddeningly elusive, when pursued further, as the intense and nervy and sexually standoffish Sue Bridehead of *Jude the Obscure* (1895).

Despite the bitterness of some of his poems about her, and indeed the accusations of pusillanimity levelled in a couple of the letters that he fired off to her in the late summer of 1893, Hardy and Henniker ended up staunch friends. She predeceased him, finding her 'distant grave-place' in Eye, in Suffolk, in 1923. Hardy's own 'moils' ended five years later, just after nine o'clock on the evening of Wednesday, 11 January 1928. Did the title of this poem, one can't help wondering, flash into the consciousness of any of those pondering the peculiar decision eventually taken to give him not one but two funerals: to divide him in death between the grave that for over fifteen years had been awaiting him beside Emma at Stinsford and the hastily requested, and dubiously granted, niche in Poets' Corner in Westminster Abbey? The opening clause of Hardy's will (signed and witnessed on 24 August 1922) stated unambiguously his 'wish that I may be buried in Stinsford Churchyard Dorset near to the Grave of my parents and if possible in my wife Emma's Grave or close at the foot thereof according to consideration detailed in my directions to my Executors on a separate paper'.[1] This paper has never been found. It appears that the brash and bullying Sydney Cockerell alluded to it in his attempts to convince Hardy's surviving siblings, Henry and Kate, that their brother's body should be accorded a grand ceremonial funeral in the capital, but neither actually saw it. And surely the wording of the will suggests that, if it ever did come into existence, its purpose was to define the exact location of the 'next best' spot to that of Emma's grave. Favoured visitors to Max Gate in the last decades of Hardy's life were almost invariably taken to Stinsford churchyard, and there shown the graves of his wife and family, and the site where he intended his own body to come to rest. A letter written by J. M. Barrie (one of Hardy's closest literary friends) to Lady Cynthia Asquith during the course of a stay at Max Gate in June of 1920 neatly captures the almost compulsive aspect of Hardy's brooding on this topic: 'Hardy took me yesterday to the place where he is to be buried, and to-day he took me to see the place where he would like next best to be buried'.[2]

Nevertheless, when Cockerell—who was in fact only a *literary* coexecutor (with Florence), the testamentary executorship being assigned to legal officials at Lloyds Bank—peremptorily opened Hardy's will on the Max Gate dining-room table just hours after the writer's death, he found in this reference to a supplementary paper sufficient ambiguity to set in motion the events that would lead to the 'medieval butchery', as the writer Edmund Gosse later described it, of Hardy's body.[3] This butchery was the unsatisfactory compromise reached in a battle fought between the interests and convictions of London and Dorset. 'There is obviously a great feeling in London', Barrie wrote to Cockerell from the capital as he set about petitioning the great and powerful, 'that [Abbey burial] is the proper offer to one of her great ones'.[4] But back in Dorset, Hardy's relatives were dumbfounded at the possibility of Hardy not being buried in Stinsford: 'I am grieved', lamented his cousin Theresa to a reporter from the *Daily Telegraph*, 'that they are going to take poor Tom away to London. He wanted, I know, to lie with his own folk in the churchyard yonder' (IR 241). Henry Hardy, Cockerell dryly observed in his diary, was 'very emotional and strongly against the Abbey' when the plan was outlined to him, and most especially since the niche on offer in Westminster Abbey would entail cremation of his brother's body, a practice viewed with disgust in Dorset: 'Another staggering blow', recorded Kate in her diary, when informed of this.[5] Hardy's widow, Florence, whose consent to the abbey proposal Cockerell had to obtain, later also acknowledged that her husband 'would have been horrified at the idea of cremation'.[6] Indeed she came, as the other coexecutor, deeply to regret her failure to follow Hardy's clearly expressed intentions, a failure that would eventually mean that she and Emma would be buried either side only of her husband's heart.

'Wicked' is how she once described the funeral arrangements to the Hardy scholar Richard Purdy, although adding, in self-extenuation: 'One is not responsible at such a time. I never gave my consent, it never should have been done—it was contrary to Mr Hardy's wish'.[7]

Her guilt may have been compounded by the fact that she herself partially initiated this tussle between Wessex and the metropolis. As Hardy's end began to seem imminent on 9 January, she summoned Cockerell and Barrie to Max Gate. Both arrived that evening. Firmly believing that Hardy 'belonged to the nation' rather than to an obscure hamlet on the outskirts of Dorchester, they conferred the following day and came to the conclusion that the best way to engineer a Westminster Abbey funeral would be to present it as a fait accompli. Barrie returned to London and set about obtaining support for interment in Poets' Corner from the prime minister, Stanley Baldwin. With backing from such a source, he was in a strong position when he and the editor of *The Times*, Geoffrey Dawson, opened negotiations with the dean of Westminster, the Very Reverend W. Foxley Norris, the day after Hardy died. This meeting, Barrie was happy to inform Cockerell, had been 'immensely cordial', and it was determined that the abbey ceremony would take place on Monday, 16 January at 2:00 p.m.[8] It was the receipt of this news that finally enabled Cockerell to vanquish, although only temporarily, the much-pressured Florence's instinctive resistance, and to release to the press that very evening a statement declaring that 'Mrs Hardy, after profound consideration, has accepted the Dean's offer . . . although Mr Hardy had expressed a wish to be buried in Stinsford Churchyard, near his home, the nation's desire in the matter must be obeyed'.[9] Mission accomplished, Mrs Hardy's overbearing coexecutor left for London the next day to make arrangements for the cremation of Hardy's body.

When it arrived at the crematorium, however, it was missing a vital organ. Among those disappointed by Florence's acceptance of the dean's offer was the rector of Stinsford, the Reverend H. G. B. Cowley. Just over three years earlier, Hardy had directly raised with Cowley the prospect of his future burial in Stinsford, joking in the letter he sent on the issue: 'Regard me as a Parishioner certainly. I hope to be still more one when I am in a supine position some day' (CL 6:298). Cowley and his wife visited the grieving Florence on the day after Cockerell had informed the world that Hardy's funeral would be in London and his ashes interred in Poets' Corner in Westminster Abbey. In her conversation with the Cowleys, Florence evidently made it clear that she was already regretting her acquiescence in Cockerell and Barrie's scheme, while accepting that by this stage there was no going back. It is possible that Cowley's bizarre response to 'her dilemma', to borrow the title of a very early Hardy poem, was inspired by a talk given in December of 1926 by a local antiquary on the topic of heart burial in Dorset in the Middle Ages, although it is not known if Cowley was present at this. Hardy himself, however, would have no doubt connected the reverend's well-meaning but gruesome suggestion with the posthumous fate of his great hero, Percy Bysshe Shelley, whose heart was plucked by Edward Trelawny from the pyre on which the drowned poet was burnt on the beach at Viareggio in Italy, handed over to his widow, and decades later interred in the Shelley family vault in St. Peter's Church, Bournemouth, many miles severing it from the grave where the ashes of the rest of his body were buried in the Protestant Cemetery in Rome.

There is a great deal of difference between a symbolic heart and a real one. While the iconography of the Cowley plan had much to recommend it, it seems unlikely that its proponents fully visualized in advance the grisly violation of Hardy's body that it entailed. It's hard to disagree with Edward Clodd, who, in a letter of 14 January, described as 'very repellent' the 'division of [Hardy's] remains'.[10] Nevertheless, Florence saw in it a means both of doing justice to her husband's wishes and of placating his siblings and local sentiment. Weird and primitive as the notion must have sounded when first broached, the fact that it came from a rector of the Church of England—though Cowley himself acknowledged it was 'a very unusual course'—must have given it a veneer of official sanction.[11] Cockerell's permission was at once sought by telegram, and granted. Hence, later that evening, a local surgeon, Dr Nash-Wortham, and an operating theatre sister, Mary Eastment, found themselves being conducted by Dr Mann, Hardy's physician, up the stairs at Max Gate and into Hardy's bedroom, where the writer's body lay dressed in his Cambridge doctoral robes. There they removed his heart, wrapped it in a towel, but having forgotten in their haste to bring along a proper medical container, had to store it in a biscuit tin requisitioned from the kitchen at

Max Gate. For unspecified reasons, Dr Mann took Hardy's heart home with him that night, returning it the next day, when preparations for the twin funerals began in earnest: Hardy's heartless body was coffined and taken by hearse to a crematorium near Woking, and there consigned to the flames, enabling Barrie to deliver the urn containing his ashes to Westminster Abbey that evening. Meanwhile, the returned heart was transferred from the biscuit tin to a burial casket, ready for interment at Stinsford. In the event, therefore, Hardy needed the vividly imagined six boards of his coffin only for the few hours that it took to transfer his somewhat mutilated body from Dorchester to Woking.[12]

The anguished disagreements between his metropolitan friends and his Dorset-based family in the days after his death offer a telling reenactment of some of the most significant tensions that made Hardy into the kind of writer that he was. Hardy is so thoroughly identified with Wessex that to pay attention to the role played by London in his literary development and career can seem at best counterintuitive, at worst beside the point. J. M. Barrie's damning verdict in 1889 on Hardy's various attempts to write novels set anywhere other than Wessex, or even to introduce into his Wessex novels characters from other places, forcefully illustrates the concept of an authentic rural Hardy and an inauthentic—or at least ineffective—urban one:

> Rich as English literature is by his Wessex tales, it would have been richer had he not sometimes wandered abroad and astray for his chief characters. Never a careless writer, he has thrown away skill on books that have no value and little momentary interest. He is only on firm ground in the country, and not even then when he brings Society figures into it . . . London society and London professional life must be known to him, at least superficially, but they are strange to the Wessex he has by heart, and in attempting to draw them he fails absolutely. (CH 159)

By this stage in his career as a novelist, Hardy was himself also becoming increasingly conscious of the marketing potential of Wessex and of the appeal of this 'partly real, partly dream-country' (PW 9), as he characterized it, to his urban readership. The year before Barrie's essay appeared, for instance, Hardy wrote to his current publishers, Sampson Low, Marston & Co. with some shrewd advice:

> Could you, whenever advertising my books, use the words 'Wessex novels' at the head of the list? I mean, instead of 'By T.H.', 'T.H.'s Wessex novels', or something of the sort? I find that the name *Wessex*, wh. I was the first to use in fiction, is getting to be taken up everywhere: & it would be a pity for us to lose the right to it for want of asserting it. (CL 1:171)

From the outset of his literary career, Hardy was conscious that his work had to appeal to a predominantly metropolitan audience, and therefore, like the milk that Angel and Tess deliver to the train that will take it to the capital, that it needed to be tailored to the demands of the London market. Tess muses thoughtfully on the unknown city dwellers who will be consuming their milk the next morning as she and Angel drive from Talbothays Dairy to the nearest railway station:

> 'Londoners will drink it at their breakfasts tomorrow, won't they?' she asked. 'Strange people that we have never seen.'
>   'Yes—I suppose they will. Though not as we send it. When its strength has been lowered, so that it may not get up into their heads.' (T 205)[13]

There is surely a covert reference here to Hardy's prolonged and exasperating battles with the London publishing industry, whose editors were so often troubled by anything that might bring a blush to the cheek of a young person or challenge the status quo. Hardy's first novel, *The Poor Man and the Lady* (begun in 1867), which he later destroyed, was deemed by Chapman & Hall's reader, the poet and novelist George Meredith, to be so radical that its publication would fatally injure the young author's literary career before it had even begun. Magazine editors were more cautious still. Eventually, Hardy hit upon the ingenious, but time-consuming, solution of effectively writing two versions of the same novel: *Tess of the d'Urbervilles* and *Jude the*

Obscure were both serialized in radically bowdlerized forms (in *The Graphic* and *Harper's New Monthly Magazine,* respectively) and then restored by Hardy in accordance with his original intentions when published in book form.

The scene in *Tess* in which Talbothays milk is loaded onto a London-bound train is a good example of how in even his most regionally circumscribed novels Hardy finds ways to acknowledge the complex interplay between Dorset and London that formed the particular literary and social matrix in which his fiction evolved, and that so shaped his life and career. Indeed, an element in both the tragic pathos and the mythical resonance of Hardy's Wessex derives from the spectral presence of the city hovering over the region, threatening to render the culture that binds its communities together seem either humorously or disastrously obsolete. On occasion Hardy's letters suggest he was uneasily aware that his depictions of Dorset might themselves be seen as complicit with mocking or patronizing metropolitan perspectives on rural life: writing to his publishers about the illustrations for *Far from the Madding Crowd* (1874), for instance, he expresses the 'hope that the rustics, although *quaint*, may be made to appear *intelligent*, & *not boorish* at all' (CL 1:25). His anxiety on this score may have had a source extremely close to home, for anecdotal evidence suggests that Hardy's own mother felt a sense of betrayal in her son's '*quaint*' and comical depictions of relatives and locals to amuse an urban readership (CT 112–113).

It is difficult to overestimate the importance to Hardy's development of the five years that he spent in London as a young man. He set off for the capital at the relatively tender age of twenty-one, a classic mid-Victorian Dick Whittington, although one already Hardyishly ready for disappointment: 'With prudent forethought', he recounts in the *Life*, 'he bought a return ticket for the journey, so that he might be able to travel back to Dorchester did he reach the end of his resources. After six months {a subdued note of triumph perhaps inflecting the writing here} he threw away the unused half' (L 503/ FH 46).[14] The pride that Hardy felt in mastering the codes of the modern Babylon emerges somewhat more clearly in other passages in the *Life*. While reflecting, for example, on Meredith's verdict on the ill-fated *The Poor Man and the Lady*, he recalls:

It may be added that the most important scenes were laid in London, of which city Hardy had just had between five and six years' constant and varied experience—as only a young man in the metropolis can get it—knowing every street and alley west of St. Paul's like a born Londoner, which he was often supposed to be. (L 63–64)

Alas, the surviving record of these years is less complete than one would wish: just five letters from this period escaped Hardy's determination to head off the intrusions of prospective biographers by incinerating his correspondence, diaries, and some of his notebooks, once they'd been filleted for material for the composition of his autobiography, which, in a characteristic act of subterfuge, he wrote in the third person and had his second wife Florence issue under her name. And while twenty-nine poems dated 1865–1867 were eventually published, and two others found among his papers, Hardy suggests in the *Life* that these constituted only a selection of the verse that he composed in his Westbourne Park Villas lodgings, the rest of which he destroyed (L 51).

The Conquest of London—this was the subtitle used by Leon Edel for the second volume of his biography of Henry James. It's hard to think of a formulation less appropriate for Hardy's youthful years in the capital; during them he published just one item, a Dickensian skit entitled 'How I Built Myself a House', which appeared in the Edinburgh-based *Chambers Journal* in March of 1865. The poems that he sent out for publication in magazines were all rejected. While the well-connected James met, and impressed, everyone in the literary world who mattered, Hardy, or so he later claimed, never even considered making contact with other writers:

His unfortunate shyness—or rather aloofness, for he was not shy in the ordinary sense—served him badly at this period of his life. During part of his residence at Westbourne Park Villas he was living within half a mile of Swinburne, and hardly more than a stone's throw from Browning, to whom introductions would not have been difficult through literary friends of Blomfield's {owner of the architectural practice where Hardy worked}. He might have obtained at least encouragement from these, and, if he had cared, possibly have floated off some of his poems

in a small volume. But such a proceeding as trying to know these contemporaries seems never to have crossed his mind. (L 51–52)

When he returned to the parental home in Higher Bockhampton in ill health
in the summer of 1867, Hardy seemed, on the face of it, to have accomplished
nothing at all.

Yet had he not launched himself into a London life some five years earlier, it is hard to see how he could have gained, for all his intellectual precocity, the kinds of perspective on Dorset that would eventually enable him
to transform it into Wessex. London made Hardy into what *The Return
of the Native* (1878) calls, when introducing Clym Yeobright, 'a modern
type' (RN 165): deracination, thwarted idealism, distrust of established
religion, sexual anxiety (or indeed helplessness), a heightened sensitivity to
the complexities of class privilege and to the ruthless depredations of the
economic system, all are features of the 'ache of modernism' (T 140) that
afflicts Hardy's protagonists, and from which most find no escape. In his
first published novel, *Desperate Remedies* of 1871, Hardy presents a vivid
emblem of the incursions of both the city and modernity into the dream of a
rural idyll. Out walking in a lonely wood one dark night, Aeneas Manston is
startled in the course of a pleasing reverie by a 'sudden rattle':

There, before him, he saw rise up from among the trees a fountain of
sparks and smoke, then a red glare of light coming forward towards
him; then a flashing panorama of illuminated oblong pictures; then the
old darkness, more impressive than ever. (DR 143)

In one of the 'illuminated oblong pictures', which turn out to be the lighted
windows of railway carriages, he has glimpsed his estranged wife, on her way
down to Dorset from London by train to reclaim him.

It was in a letter to Edmund Gosse of 13 December 1916 that Hardy described himself as 'half a Londoner' (CL 5:190). He was referring to the habit
that he and Emma established after they moved in the summer of 1881 from
Tooting (a suburb of South London) back to Dorset, of returning to the capital for the roughly four months of the 'London Season', which ran from
April to July. A modern-style biographical note composed for the Hardy of

the next three decades would need, to be accurate, to describe him as 'dividing his time between Dorset and London'. The Hardys rented flats or houses at a variety of fashionable addresses in districts such as Bayswater, South Kensington, Holland Park, St. John's Wood, Marylebone, and Maida Vale, from which they sallied boldly forth to salons and soirées and crushes and dinners hosted by the beau monde. After the enormous financial success of *Tess*, they even experimented with bringing up their own servants from Max Gate so as to ensure that their domestic needs were fully catered to in their London lodgings. Anyone familiar only with the rural Hardy extolled by Barrie would be astonished to find pages and pages of the *Life* given over to his social exploits amongst the higher echelons of the London aristocracy, or to read his figurations in letters of Max Gate as a mere 'writing-box' in the country to which he retired when exhausted by the whirl of the metropolis.[15] Barrie strongly advised Florence to prune from the *Life*, as she prepared it for publication in the months following Hardy's death, paragraphs taken from his diary such as the following, from 1894:

> May 23. Dined at Mary Jeune's. Talked to people till my throat was tired [his throat was always weak]—namely Lady Brownlow, Mrs Adair, young Harcourt, Lady Charles Beresford, Lady Yarborough, Lady Wantage, Lord C. Beresford, Lord Wantage, Lord Wimborne. Took Lady Wimborne in to dinner. Afterwards went on to Lady Lewis's dinner to pick up Em. Met also a good many people there. (L 281)

Nevertheless, plenty of entries of a similar kind survived to drive home to the reader Hardy's easy familiarity with the nobility, and his ready access to London's most desirable and exclusive social circles.

Hardy was also a familiar presence in London's club land. Shortly after settling into the substantial suburban home that the Hardys rented at 1 Arundel Terrace, Trinity Road, Tooting, in March of 1878, Hardy joined the Savile Club, his first move in what the *Life* calls, perhaps slightly overdoing the tone of metropolitan world-weariness, the process of falling 'into line as a London man again' (L 125). From that point on, his clubs played a major role in the routines of Hardy's London life. He was a founding member of the Rabelais Club, inaugurated that same year by Sir Walter Besant to promote 'virility in literature' (L 136). In the summer of 1888 he embarked on a campaign to get elected to the more exclusive Athenaeum, for which Lord Carnarvon agreed to sponsor him, only to die before Hardy's application was ratified; he was eventually elected some three years later, on the grounds that he was a writer of 'distinguished merit'. Although, on its publication in 1895, *Jude the Obscure* was widely denounced by London reviewers as a scandalous attack on the central pillars of the establishment—on the institution of marriage, on the church, on the education system—there was nothing remotely bohemian or controversial about the behaviour of its author when performing his 'London man' persona. There is a striking separation between Hardy in his study at Max Gate, dreaming up novels that seemed to many unthinkably outrageous assaults on the orthodoxies of the day, and his conventional, professional demeanour as a London club man. Notoriously sensitive to criticism, he worried, on reading an anonymous negative article on *Tess* published in the *Saturday Review*, that this might make for some social awkwardness next time he visited his club:

> Now whenever I go to the Savile I meet a number of S. Reviewers—one of whom is probably my libeller . . . So that how can I go there again? Would you resign membership if you were in my place? Unfortunately I have just paid my year's subscription, & have no other place so convenient for lunching when I am in Town. (CL 1:252)

This was addressed to Besant, who wisely advised him to go there and act normally, as befitted a 'virile' writer.

None of Hardy's attempts to base himself in London could be called a success. His health was often poor in the city, and his six boards nearly had to be delivered prematurely to 1 Arundel Terrace in the winter of 1880–1881, during which he was bedbound for months and forced by his doctor to lie with his feet higher than his head. In the poem 'A Wasted Illness' he characteristically regrets his failure to reach 'the all-delivering door' on this occasion, since it means that he will have to journey through the 'grim chambers' that lead to it again at some point in the future (CP 152). Ill health was undoubtedly a major factor in his decision to move from Tooting to Wimborne Minster (a market town in East Dorset) as soon as he was well again, but in the *Life* Hardy also conceded that 'residence in or near a city tended to force mechanical and ordinary productions from his pen, concerning ordinary society-life and habits' (L 154). Certainly there are few readers who would consider the two novels that he produced in Tooting, *The Trumpet-Major* (1880) and *A Laodicean* (1881), as among his best. It was principally those that he composed after finally moving into Max Gate, situated on the outskirts of Dorchester, just over a mile from the first of the two Dorchester railway stations to open (now known as Dorchester South) and within walking distance of his family in Higher Bockhampton, that led to the dean of Westminster Abbey's offer to Mrs Hardy that her husband be accorded a niche in Poets' Corner: an offer, as Cockerell made plain to her, that she couldn't refuse.

Hardy's two funerals began simultaneously at two o'clock on the afternoon of Monday, 16 January 1928, five days after his death. The abbey was full long before the service commenced, and large crowds waited outside in the pouring rain. The urn containing Hardy's ashes had been placed for ceremonial purposes in a coffin that was carried by ten distinguished pallbearers: the Prime Minister Stanley Baldwin; the leader of the opposition, Ramsay MacDonald; the heads of Magdalene, Cambridge, and Queens, Oxford (where Hardy had been granted honorary doctorates); and six prominent writers—Rudyard Kipling, A. E. Housman, George Bernard Shaw, John Galsworthy, Edmund Gosse, and J. M. Barrie. 'It seemed absurd', Shaw's wife Charlotte wrote to T. E. Lawrence, then stationed in India, 'to have an immense bier and a great and splendid pall, white, embroidered with royal crowns and many other emblems, to enclose one small casket, but it made its effect' (CT 374). The choices taken by Hardy's siblings that day mirrored the peculiar division of their brother. Kate, who according to Cockerell believed that Hardy 'would never have refused Westminster Abbey', travelled with Florence up to London, while Henry attended the Reverend Cowley's service and burial of his heart in Stinsford.[16] Perhaps Kate wished she'd stayed with Henry and foregone the pomp and circumstance, and the dreadful weather, of the metropolis; for, she noted in her diary that evening, in marked contrast to the grand ceremony performed in the rainy capital, in Stinsford 'the good sun shone & the birds sang & everything was done simply, affectionately & well.'[17]

1

The Cries of London

I

If London offered Hardy social, sexual, and professional opportunities that would never have come his way had he remained, like Dorset's other great nineteenth-century writer, William Barnes, a lifelong resident of the county of his birth, it also evoked in him all sorts of phobias and anxieties that surely contributed to the illnesses that so often afflicted him there. The roughly equal mixture of attraction and repulsion in Hardy's relationship with the capital is one of the most striking features of the *Life*. Punctuating the roll calls of aristocrats met at this or that glittering social event are savage indictments of the lifestyles of the rich. Chapter 19, for instance, includes this entry made in his diary of 1891:

> 19 July. Note the weight of a landau and pair, the coachman in his grey great-coat, footman ditto. All this mass of matter is moved along with brute force and clatter through a street congested and obstructed, to bear the *petite* figure of the owner's young wife in violet velvet and silver trimming, slim, small; who could be easily carried under a man's arm, and who, if held up by the hair and slipped out of her clothes, carriage, etc. etc., aforesaid, would not be much larger than a skinned rabbit, and of less use. (L 249)

In the previous chapter he records taking Emma to a crush in honour of the Duke and Duchess of Teck:

Young Princess Mary also there. Duchess in black velvet with long black sleeves and a few diamonds. She bears a likeness to the Queen. The daughter is a pretty young woman in skim-milk-blue muslin, [afterwards Queen Mary.] Lady Burdett Coutts was in a head-dress that was a castellated façade of diamonds; she has strongly marked features. Met Mrs T. and her great eyes in a corner of the rooms, as if washed up by the surging crowd. The most beautiful woman present . . . But these women! If put into rough wrappers in a turnip-field, where would their beauty be? (L 235)[1]

Such entries illustrate how Hardy sought to gain satirical purchase on 'these women', whose beauty and wealth both stirred and troubled him, by imaginatively stripping them of their lavish accoutrements and introducing into the glamorous metropolitan scenes they inhabited the elemental rigours of country life. This is the Hardy characterized by the novelist and playwright Somerset Maugham as preserving, even when dressed in a 'boiled shirt and high collar', a 'strange look of the soil' (IR 89).

Lady Burdett Coutts and Princess Mary would no doubt have been horrified to know that the famous writer seeming to admire them was in fact reconfiguring them in his mind as turnip hackers on a farm like that of Flintcomb-Ash, on which Tess and Marian and Izz suffer bitter cold and ill treatment in *Tess of the d'Urbervilles*. The vituperative aspect of Hardy's transposition of Society women to his rural world probably reflects his own unease about his ability to perform effectively in their urban one. An entry of 16 April 1892 suggests that he at times found the 'boiled shirt and high collar' as gruelling as they would have found hacking swedes in 'rough wrappers': 'Am glad I have got back from London and all those dinners:— London, that *hot-plate* of humanity, on which we first sing, then simmer, then boil, then dry away to dust and ashes!' (L 260). Nevertheless, as regularly, and at roughly the same time, as the swallows arrived in Dorset from Africa each spring, so he and Emma performed their annual migration from Max Gate to London.

In a passage that he decided to cut from the *Life*, but which Florence restored, Hardy revealed that he had a powerful aversion to being touched: 'to the end of his life he disliked even the most friendly hand being laid on his arm or his shoulder. Probably no one ever observed this' (L 502/FH 32). This condition must have rendered London's seething crowds particularly daunting. One of the few diary entries included in the chapter in the *Life* devoted to his early years in London records his ill-fated attempt to participate in the celebrations for the wedding of the Prince of Wales and the Princess of Denmark on 10 March 1863. Hardy finds himself dangerously buffeted by the great mass of people surging through the overflowing streets, and almost crushed in the throng at the bottom of Bond Street, 'where my waistcoat buttons were torn and my ribs bent in before I could get into a doorway' (L 42). While Dickens revelled in the anarchic energies of Londoners en masse, Hardy seems to have been profoundly disturbed by the loss of individuality entailed in becoming part of a crowd. In November of 1879 he took Emma to the top floor of the offices of the magazine *Good Words*, who were about to begin serialization of *The Trumpet-Major* and were based in Ludgate Hill in the City, or financial district of London, in order to give her a superior view of the Lord Mayor's Show. Neither, however, seems to have been favourably impressed by the urban pageant unfolding beneath them. Emma observed that the surface of the crowd resembled 'a boiling cauldron of porridge', while Hardy was inspired to a nightmarish comparison of the masses filling the streets to a single, inhuman, voracious, primal monster:

> As the crowd grows denser it loses its character of an aggregate of countless units, and becomes an organic whole, a molluscous black creature having nothing in common with humanity, that takes the shape of the streets along which it has lain itself, and throws out horrid excrescences and limbs into neighbouring alleys; a creature whose voice exudes from its scaly coat, and who has an eye in every pore of its body. The balconies, stands, and railway-bridge are occupied by small detached shapes of the same tissue, but of gentler motion, as if they were the spawn of the monster in their midst. (L 134)

Some five months later the image of the city's population as a weird and terrifying creature made up of multiple heads and eyes keeps him awake for an entire night. This monster's nearness to him is what he finds most unsettling:

'The following note on London at dawn occurs on May 19, a night on which he could not sleep, partly on account of an eerie feeling which sometimes haunted him, a horror at lying down in close proximity to "a monster whose body had four million heads and eight million eyes" ' (L 141).

Among the few books owned by Hardy to have survived from his child-hood, which are all now stored in the Dorset County Museum, is *Cries of London*, a chapbook of woodcuts and rhymes for children. He is reputed to have read this book by the age of three: 'Come buy, come buy, for sell I must', it opens, 'Rosemary and briar so sweet'. Like this herb seller, Hardy the novelist understood what he calls in the *Life* 'the pecuniary value of a repu-tation for a speciality' (L 105). The titles of his two most successful early novels, *Under the Greenwood Tree* (1872) and *Far from the Madding Crowd*, signal, with all the vigour and clarity of the herb seller's cry, their offer of an escape from the urban maelstrom into the traditions of pastoral summoned up by Hardy's borrowings from *As You Like It* and Thomas Gray's 'Elegy Written in a Country Churchyard': 'Far from the madding crowd's ignoble strife, / Their sober wishes never learn'd to stray; / Along the cool sequester'd vale of life / They kept the noiseless tenor of their way' (l.73–76). The fre-quent comparisons by reviewers of *Far from the Madding Crowd* with George Eliot's *Adam Bede* (1859) further consolidated in the novel-reading public's mind the figuration of Hardy as a purveyor of rosemary and thyme. No doubt when Leslie Stephen, editor of the *Cornhill* magazine in which *Far from the Madding Crowd* was serialized, offered to run its successor too, he expected, and certainly hoped for, more of the same. What Stephen had not reckoned with was the streak of resistance, amounting here almost to perversity, that so strongly characterized Hardy's responses to the expecta-tions of literary London. Hardy presents in the *Life* his decision 'to put aside a woodland story he had thought out (which later took shape in *The Woodlanders*)' and plunge, instead, 'in a new and untried direction', as primarily motivated by his desire to expose the 'fooleries of critics', and to wrong-foot his readers:

> He had not the slightest intention of writing for ever about sheep-farming, as the reading public was apparently expecting him to do, and as, in fact, they presently resented his not doing. Hence, to the

consternation of his editor and publishers, in March he sent up as a response to their request the beginning of a tale called *The Hand of Ethelberta—A Comedy in Chapters*, which had nothing whatever in common with anything he had written before. (L 105)

Hardy's daring, even wilful determination to embark 'in a new and untried direction' is refracted in all manner of ways in the novel that he wrote instead of the pastoral woodland story. Ethelberta, the daughter of a butler and a domestic nurse and the sister of carpenters and servants, must conceal her humble provincial origins, just as Hardy liked to conceal his: success for both involves improvising a sophisticated metropolitan identity. And just as Hardy needed to prove himself 'a good hand at a serial' (L 102) in order to generate a regular income, so Ethelberta depends for her livelihood on her ability to hold the attention of her London audience with her stories— stories which, although based on her own experiences, must never reveal the true facts of her situation. But perhaps she most significantly resembles her creator, or at least as he characterizes himself in his autobiography, in setting herself on the path of ascent through the ranks of London society, yet without particularly believing in the worth or virtue of the life to which she aspires. 'Experimentally,' she explains to her impoverished and eventually discarded provincial admirer Christopher Julian, 'I care to succeed in society; but at the bottom of my heart, I don't care' (HE 128).

When dividing up his fiction for the Wessex Edition of 1912, Hardy consigned *The Hand of Ethelberta* (1876), along with *Desperate Remedies* and *A Laodicean*, to the category of 'Novels of Ingenuity'. Its ingenuity takes many forms, including the encoding of a private family reference into its title: Hardy's mother, who was born Jemima Hand, had, the *Life* tells us, resided in London 'for some months' in her early twenties (L 22). Like the fictional Ethelberta's sisters Gwendoline and Cornelia, Jemima had been sent into service at an early age, being employed by the Reverend Charles Redlynch Fox-Strangeways, the rector of Maiden Newton (a village about eight miles northwest of Dorchester), and then the Reverend Edward Murray, the vicar of Stinsford. It seems that, like Hardy and Emma decades later, both families would take their servants to London with them for the Season. Hardy is characteristically vague in the *Life* about the reason for Jemima's time in

London—at times the *Life* might itself be categorized as a masterpiece of 'ingenuity'—but the likelihood is that it was as a servant accompanying a rich family that Jemima first came to the capital. Clearly she enjoyed city life, for we also learn that she resolved to apply for a job as a cook in a London club-house; 'but her plans in this direction', Hardy continues, 'were ended by her meeting her future husband, and being married to him at the age of five-and-twenty'—a marriage that took place in Melbury Osmond (a village about fourteen miles northwest of Dorchester) when she was already three and a half months pregnant, and aged twenty-six rather than twenty-five (L 12).[2]

The Dorset-London axis so crucial to Hardy's development, and most fully explored in fictional terms in *The Hand of Ethelberta*, can be traced back, therefore, to Jemima's accounts of the experiences that she had in London some years before her eldest child's birth. That Hardy saw himself as to some extent following in her footsteps, or even as fulfilling her metro-politan ambitions for her, is obliquely suggested in chapter 19 (which covers 1891) of the *Life*: here he records how he used to attend services at St. James's Piccadilly in honour of his mother's earlier attendance at the same church. When considered in the context of the previous paragraph, which vividly evokes the chaos and temptations of life in the West End, this memory of his mother's London churchgoing registers as a treasured ideal of family conti-nuity, indeed almost as a means of warding off the perils of urban life by ob-serving a tradition established some six decades earlier by Jemima:

> Piccadilly at night.—'A girl held a long-stemmed narcissus to my nose as we went by each other. At the Circus among all the wily crew of har-lots there was a little innocent family standing waiting, I suppose for an omnibus. How pure they looked! A man on a stretcher, with a bloody bandage round his head, was wheeled past by two policemen, stragglers following. Such is Piccadilly.'
>
> He used to see Piccadilly under other aspects however, for the next day, Sunday, he attended the service at St. James's—as he did off and on for many years—because it was the church his mother had been ac-customed to go to when as a young woman she was living for some months in London. 'The preacher said that only five per cent of the in-habitants entered a church, according to the Bishop of London. On

coming out there was a drizzle across the electric lights, and the paper-
boys were shouting, not "Go to church!" but, "Wee-naw of the French
Oaks!" ' (L 247) [3]

The collaging of third-person narrative with journal excerpts makes the sar-
donic diary entry with which the second paragraph concludes seem to ema-
nate jointly from Hardy and his mother, although there would of course have
been no electric lights in the 1830s. Hardy invested the equally unillusioned
Ethelberta not only with his mother's gift for oral storytelling, but with her
fierce determination to improve the social and material lot of her family, whatever the personal cost. Jemima was the possessor, Hardy wrote when introducing her in the *Life*, 'of unusual ability and judgement, and an energy that
might have carried her to incalculable issues' (L 12)—a character assessment
that could easily be transposed to Ethelberta. Somewhat less happily, Jemima's intense clannishness, or family loyalty, served, to a large extent, to insu-
late Hardy and his siblings from the dangers of too close contact with outsiders
(Hardy was the only one of the four to marry, and that in the face of strong
opposition from his mother), rather as the innocent family waiting for an
omnibus amid the prostitutes and brawlers of Piccadilly Circus is enclosed
in a familial cocoon that allows it to remain 'pure' amid squalor and vice.
Ethelberta's mixture of iron will, ingenuity, and intrepidness drives the somewhat picaresque plot of the novel in a way that makes it come to seem, when
viewed from the biographical angle hinted at in the private pun buried in its
title, a peculiar fusion of both mother and son's actual and fantasy London
adventures.

Hardy first heard the cries of London when he accompanied Jemima, in
the autumn of 1849, on a trip to Hatfield in Hertfordshire for an extended
visit with his Aunt Martha, who was in the late stages of her fifth pregnancy
in seven years. Martha, born three years after Jemima, was the youngest of
the Hand family. In 1841 she had left Puddletown (a village about six miles
northeast of Dorchester), where many of Hardy's uncles and aunts and
cousins were based, after marrying John Brereton Sharpe, who, it has been
argued, was the 'original' of *Far from the Madding Crowd*'s Sergeant Troy
(MM 47), while Hardy himself identified Martha as a model for Bathsheba
Everdene.[4] When the Hand sister in between Jemima and Martha, Mary, had

visited her younger sister in Hatfield in December of 1846, her complex journey had involved taking a coach from Dorchester to Andover, a train from Andover to London, and then, the following day, a coach from London to Hitchin. But when, three years later, Jemima and her nine-year-old son set off on what seems to have been the only substantial journey that they ever took together, their itinerary was considerably less convoluted; for the railway had at last reached Dorchester.

In a speech that Hardy gave on being granted the Freedom of the Borough of Dorchester (the highest award that a municipal council can bestow) on 16 November 1910, he reflected, in tones at once rueful and stoical, on the many changes that the town had undergone within his own memory: 'Dorchester's future will not be like its past', he asserted, 'we may be sure of that. Like all other provincial towns, it will lose its individuality—has lost much of it already. We have become almost a London suburb owing to the quickened locomotion, and, though some of us may regret this, it has to be' (L 380–381). By 'locomotion' he is referring primarily to the advent of the railways, though by 1910 a few cars were also beginning to appear on the highways of Dorset. Hardy's native county was by no means the first of the English regions to be transformed by the burgeoning spread of the rail network, which reached an early peak during the railway boom of the mid-1840s.[5] The first line operative in the county was opened to the public on the day before Hardy's seventh birthday, that is on 1 June 1847. It ran from Dorchester to Southampton, from where passengers could catch a train to London. In the first section of the *Life*, Hardy poignantly, and characteristically, registers the changes that followed the arrival of this new means of locomotion in a lament for the disappearance of certain favourite old ballads from the communal repertoire. Towards the end of a description of a harvest-supper that he attended when he was ten, he pauses to reflect: 'It may be worthy of note that this harvest-home was among the last at which the old traditional ballads were sung, the railway having been extended to Dorchester just then, and the orally transmitted ditties of centuries being slain at a stroke by the London comic songs that were introduced' (L 25).

Hardy is obviously exaggerating for effect when he describes the railways transforming Dorchester into a mere 'London suburb', or declares that the London comic songs obliterated the old Dorset ballads 'at a stroke'. Such exaggerations are an interesting index of his occasional determination to present himself as a sophisticated and clear-eyed observer of technological progress—'it has to be'—and its impact on the culture into which he was born. But, as is often pointed out, there are no railways marked on the maps of Wessex, drawn by Hardy himself, first included in the 1895–1896 Osgood, McIlvaine & Co. edition of his fiction, although trains feature prominently in *Desperate Remedies*, *A Pair of Blue Eyes* (1873), *The Hand of Ethelberta*, *A Laodicean* (whose heroine, Paula Power, owes her wealth to the railways, and is nearly struck, along with the hero, George Somerset, by a train in a railway tunnel), *Jude the Obscure*, and *The Well-Beloved* (1897). Indeed, only the texts of *Under the Greenwood Tree*, *The Return of the Native*, and *The Trumpet-Major* make no mention at all of trains or railways.[6]

The divided nature of Hardy's attitude to the spread of the rail network can be illustrated by contrasting the narrator's reference in *A Pair of Blue Eyes* to the 'monotony of life we associate with people of small incomes in districts out of the sound of the railway whistle' (PBE 102), with the figuration of the train that takes the Talbothays milk up to London in *Tess*, which Hardy presents in terms that recall the diary entry comparing a London crowd to a primeval monster: 'Modern life stretched out its steam feeler to this point three or four times a day, touched the native existences, and quickly withdrew its feeler again, as if what it touched had been uncongenial' (T 204). To increase still further the opposition between the 'secluded world' of the novel's Wessex and all that the railway represents, Hardy adds to the scene a poignant tableau of Tess momentarily caught in the glare of the train's headlamps:

> The light of the engine flashed for a second upon Tess Durbeyfield's figure, motionless under the great holly-tree. No object could have looked more foreign to the gleaming cranks and wheels than this un-sophisticated girl with the round bare arms, the rainy face and hair, the suspended attitude of a friendly leopard at pause, the print gown of no date or fashion, and the cotton bonnet drooping on her brow. (T 205)

It is striking that the unforgettable simile likening Tess to 'a friendly leopard at pause' occurs in a passage in which her physical palpability is heightened by comparison with a London-bound train, as if the contrast between her 'round bare arms' and the 'gleaming cranks and wheels' of the engine afforded Hardy a particularly intense awareness of the otherness, as well as the desirability, of his heroine.

Trains speed from town to town, and to and from London, carrying characters and plot, on a regular basis in Hardy's novels and short stories, as well as in numerous poems such as 'Midnight on the Great Western', 'Faintheart in a Railway Train', 'On the Departure Platform', and 'After a Romantic Day'. Yet, as the passage above from *Tess* dramatizes so powerfully, the railway is also seen as antithetical to certain aspects of Hardy's vision of Wessex, aspects that need, like Tess's gown, to be of 'no date or fashion' to be effective. This division within Hardy's oeuvre, and within Hardy himself, is mirrored in some of the paradoxes of his reception. The hand-drawn maps of Wessex, for instance, included since the Osgood, McIlvaine & Co. edition in nearly all reprintings of Hardy's fiction, may not have been much practical use to readers planning an excursion from London by rail to see Little Hintock or Egdon Heath, and yet the very absence of railways from these cartographical representations of Hardy country, however unjustified, played no insignificant part in inspiring the desire to jump on a train and experience at first hand the 'unsophisticated' preindustrial rural life described in novels such as *Under the Greenwood Tree* and *Far from the Madding Crowd*.

More even than in most other parts of Britain, the railway network in Dorset developed in a stop-start, piecemeal fashion. Throughout the 1840s and 1850s, proposals for all manner of routes and lines were launched, but most were abandoned, before or after being authorized by Parliament. Bids for routes were complicated further by what was known as the Battle of the Gauges, which raged between companies such as the Great Western, which used Isambard Kingdom Brunel's broad gauge, while most of the others competing for franchises in Dorset were committed to the narrower standard gauge. At issue also was the route to be chosen for the line that would be the major rail thoroughfare from London to the West Country: one proposal involved an extension of the line from Southampton to Dorchester on through Bridport and Axminster, and thence to Exeter (known as the 'coastal route'), but this eventually lost out to the Salisbury and Yeovil Railway's 'central route', operated by the London and South Western Railway, which passed only through northern Dorset, and towns such as Gillingham and Sherborne and Yeovil. So while the various major lines and branch routes built during Hardy's childhood and adolescence made the county as a whole far more accessible and, accordingly, vulnerable to the influence of metropolitan culture, it's also worth pointing out that had the 'coastal route' been chosen and Dorchester become an important hub through which quantities of passengers and freight passed between London and the West Country, the town would surely have been far more quickly and thoroughly modernized and expanded, making it rather less susceptible to presentation as the remote and secluded Casterbridge of the novels and short stories in which it features.[7]

II

If Hardy's Wessex emerges from his fiction as both a pastoral 'dream-country' and as a region culturally shaped by many of the dominant features of Victorian industrialization, such as the 'railways, the penny post, mowing and reaping machines, union workhouses, lucifer matches', to quote from the catalogue of nineteenth-century innovations to be found in 'modern Wessex' given in the 1895 preface to *Far from the Madding Crowd* (PW 9), then it is surely possible to read this duality as reflecting mid-century Dorset's uncertainty about the extent to which progress was embracing or rejecting it, invading or ignoring it.[8] The battle between the old ways and the new is most directly staged in the struggle for supremacy between Michael Henchard and Donald Farfrae in *The Mayor of Casterbridge* (1886). Hardy sets their duel in the mid-1840s, shortly before the Southampton line's extension to Dorchester had been completed—in chapter 37 we learn that the 'railway had stretched out an arm towards Casterbridge at this time, but had not reached it by several miles as yet' (MC 245). Accordingly, the 'royal personage' whose visit to Casterbridge is described in this chapter has to travel in the 'old fashion', that is, by carriage, from the nearest railway junction, whereas in fact, Prince Albert, on whose 1849 trip to Dorset this episode is based, arrived in the county's capital by rail. Rather than flocking to the train station to await the arrival of the regal dignitary, the excited population of Casterbridge fix their expectant gaze on 'the far-stretching London highway' (MC 245).

This highway passed quite close to Hardy's childhood home, as he points out in his account, in the notebook 'Memoranda I', of Kenfield, the guard of the mail-coach that plied this route in the 1830s. Kenfield lived in Higher Bockhampton, 'the reason probably being that the spot lay near the London Road, so he could take small packages to London on his own account, by collusion with the coachman' (PN 16). The entry, composed in 1874 when Hardy was back living in the family home and writing *Far from the Madding Crowd*, communicates a characteristic fascination with life in the era immediately before his birth, and its details no doubt derive from his paternal grandmother, Mary Hardy (née Head): Kenfield carried two pistols, a cutlass and a blunderbuss when on duty, as well as a supply of mulled ale. The description of the mail-guard's illicit, small-scale trading evokes Hardy's oft-expressed admiration for smugglers, as developed, say, in the short story 'The Distracted Preacher' (1879), and, although elliptically written, the entry as a whole suggests a lively interest in the vanished rituals of coaching. These rituals are invested with a romance that 'this travelling without horses that's getting so common' (MC 298), as an anonymous character describes journeying by train in *The Mayor of Casterbridge*, rarely has in Hardy's fiction.

It was by rail, however, that Hardy made that first trip to London with his mother in 1849. Although their journey was less complex than Mary's, it was still impossible to get from Dorchester to Hatfield in one day, and they were obliged to stay overnight in the capital. In the *Life* Hardy suggests that one of the reasons that his mother wanted him to accompany her was as a safeguard against the unwanted attentions of men—' "for protection", as she used to say—being then an attractive and still young woman' (L 21). It was, indeed, notoriously difficult for even unimpeachably respectable women walking down Haymarket or Regent Street to communicate to those in search of sex that they were not prostitutes. The nine-year-old Hardy is, of course, unlikely to have understood that his mere presence would have protected the 'attractive and still young' Jemima from the nuisance and embarrassment of being propositioned. His description in the *Life* of his first experiences of London emphasizes the imaginative connection that the trip allowed him to

forge with the high romance conducted between Shelley and Mary Godwin—
with no mention of the unhappy Harriet whom Mary supplanted, and who
drowned herself in the Serpentine many months pregnant with an illegitimate child, having, or so Shelley suggested in a letter written after her death,
herself 'descended the steps of prostitution'.[9] The glimpse subliminally offered in ' "for protection" ' of what the life of an unprotected young woman
on the streets of London might have been like, offers a less alluring vista of
love in the city than that of the legendary poet and the seventeen-year-old
Mary enjoying a rendezvous in the attic of the Cross Keys coaching-inn in
Clerkenwell, the very inn where Hardy and his mother stayed on their journey
back from Hatfield:

> Their return from this visit was marked by an experience which be-
> came of interest in the light of after events. The Great Northern Railway
> to London was then only in process of construction, and it was neces-
> sary to go thither by coach from Hertfordshire in order to take the train
> at Waterloo Station for Dorchester. Mrs Hardy had not been to London
> since she had lived there for some months twelve years earlier. The
> coaching-inn was The Cross-Keys, St. John Street, Clerkenwell, and
> here mother and boy put up for the night. It was the inn at which Shelley
> and Mary Godwin had been accustomed to meet on week-ends not two-
> score years before, and was at this time unaltered from its state during
> the lovers' romantic experiences there—the oval stone staircase, the
> skylight, and the hotel entrance being untouched. As Mrs Hardy and
> her little boy took a room rather high up the staircase for economy, and
> the poet had probably done the same from impecuniousness, there is a
> possibility that this may have been the same as that occupied by our
> most marvellous lyrist. (L 22)[10]

'Ah, did you once see Shelley plain?' exclaims the star-struck speaker of
Robert Browning's 'Memorabilia', 'And did he stop and speak to you?' Something of Browning's speaker's awe of Shelley accompanies nearly all of Hardy's references to 'our most marvellous lyrist'. In his account in chapter 3 of
the *Life* of the differences between the London of 1862 and the London of
the time of writing (1917), he refers to the now demolished Skinner Street,

with 'Godwin's house yet standing in it, at which Shelley first set eyes on Mary' (L 44). In 1879 he was introduced at the painter William Powell Frith's studio to the poet's son, Sir Percy Shelley, and the meeting triggers that misty-eyed sense of the sublime so characteristic of acolytes' responses to contact, at whatever remove, with a sainted hero:

> Hardy said afterwards that the meeting was as shadowy and remote as were those previous occasions when he had impinged on the penumbra of the poet he loved—that time of his sleeping at the Cross Keys, St. John Street, and that of the visits he paid to Old St. Pancras Churchyard.[11] He was to enter that faint penumbra twice more, once when he stood beside Shelley's dust in the English cemetery at Rome, and last when by Mary Shelley's grave at Bournemouth. (L 134–135)

On the subject of dust, the poem 'Shelley's Skylark' describes a visit made in 1887 to the Livorno region of Italy, where Hardy broods on the where-abouts of 'the pinch of unseen, unguarded dust', secreted somewhere in the landscape, that is all that remains of the skylark that had enraptured the pro-phetic bard, back in June of 1820, inspiring him 'to win / Ecstatic heights in thought and rhyme': 'Go find it, faeries,' he urges,

> go and find
> That tiny pinch of priceless dust,
> And bring a casket silver-lined,
> And framed of gold that gems encrust;

> And we will lay it safe therein. (CP 101)

Hardy's Shelley-worship took a range of forms: to Elliot Felkin he con-fessed, in a conversation of August 1919, that Shelley 'was the only man whose steps he had ever cared to trace', and he suggested to Felkin that on his next trip to London he 'go and see Millicents [i.e., St. Mildred's Church], Bread Street [which is in the City], where P.B.S and Mary were married' (IR 116). Sir George Douglas, who met Hardy in 1881, recalls accompanying him on a visit to this church for precisely this purpose, 'to inspect the registry signed by Shelley and Mary after their marriage' (IR 17). When describing this pilgrimage, which took place in late June of 1899, in the *Life*, Hardy again assumes the reverential tones of the speaker of 'Memorabilia', stressing the fact that, like the Cross Keys in 1849, St. Mildred's had not been renovated since it was hallowed by the presence of Shelley and his bride: 'The church was almost unaltered since the poet and Mary had knelt there, and the vestry absolutely so, not having even received a coat of paint as it seemed' (L 327). In the Cross Keys, in St. Mildred's, Hardy figures himself connecting with Shelley through the very fabric of the buildings in which crucial episodes in the poet's life were enacted—the unchanged oval stone staircase and skylight, the unrepainted church vestry—with all the fervour of a disciple. For many of Shelley's Victorian admirers (including his widow), Shelley's extreme political beliefs and initiatives were best passed over in silence, but it's clear that his firebrand activism was a central part of his heroic appeal to Hardy: 'I have been thinking', he wrote to Florence Henniker on 24 January 1897, 'that of all men dead whom I should like to meet in the Elysian fields I would choose Shelley, not only for his unearthly, weird, wild appearance & genius, but for his genuineness, earnestness, & enthusiasms on behalf of the oppressed' (CL 2:144).

A more sophisticated kind of homage is, of course, developed in the prose and verse: Shelley is the writer most often quoted from in the fiction, while the 'penumbra' of Shelley's poetry can be traced, explicitly or obliquely, at various levels of Hardy's own. Although generally reluctant to acknowledge the influence of anyone's work on the evolution of his literary sensibility or writings, Hardy made of Shelley a dramatic exception, stressing his affiliation to the 'matchless singer' (CP 104) on numerous occasions. It is unlikely that when Hardy actually slept at the Cross Keys at the age of nine that Shelley's poetry, or even name, meant much to him; the coincidence could only have struck him retrospectively. His raising, nevertheless, of the 'possibility' that he and his mother may have spent a night in the same room as Shelley and Godwin serves almost as a foundation myth for the 'after events' of his career as a writer. What's more, this 'possibility' enables him to incorporate Jemima into the narrative of his moment of literary election in the capital, rather as his attendance at St. James's Piccadilly created a sense of shared experience of London some forty years later.

Hardy was exhilarated by Shelley's transgressive behaviour and scorn for conformity, as he was by the outspokenness and defiance of the contemporary poet who most excited him in his early twenties, Algernon Charles Swinburne. The two are brought together at the end of 'A Refusal', a monologue delivered by an outraged dean of Westminster in response to a public campaign to have Byron honoured in the cathedral:

> 'Twill next be expected
> That I get erected
> To Shelley a tablet
> In some niche or gablet.
> Then—what makes my skin burn,
> Yea, forehead to chin burn—
> That I ensconce Swinburne! (CP 803)

But if, as a writer, he shared with them the ability to arouse controversy, the appeal of these two Eton- and Oxford-educated poets might also be construed as an aspect of Hardy's fantasy of escape from his utterly different social circumstances. Shelley's 'impecuniousness', after all, which may, Hardy speculates, have led him to rent the cheapest room in the Cross Keys, was of a quite different kind from that of Jemima, whose mother, Betty Hand, had been so destitute that she had often had to apply for poor relief (MM 15). In claiming as his literary godfather the tall, sexually compelling, supremely confident, sublimely irresponsible son of a baronet, Hardy was demonstrating the belief that he imbibed from Shelley's poetry in the power of the imagination to liberate from all social conventions and *'petty'* inhibitions—*'petty'* (his italics) being the damning adjective Hardy used in his letter of 17 August to Florence Henniker in the wake of her refusal to consummate their love during the trip they made to Winchester (CL 2:28).[12]

Hardy may not have read 'Epipsychidion' or *Prometheus Unbound* when he and Jemima broke their journey from Hatfield to Higher Bockhampton at the Cross Keys, but he was already an ardent admirer of Harrison Ainsworth, and in particular of his historical romance *Old St. Paul's* (1841). In June of 1913 he was introduced, at a lunch given by Florence Henniker at Southwold House, to Stewart Ellis, whose *William Harrison Ainsworth and*

His Friends had been published some two years earlier. Ellis was delighted
to find a fellow Ainsworth devotee:

> Mr Hardy said that Ainsworth was the most powerful literary influence
> of his boyhood, and *Old St. Paul's* his favourite romance, so much so
> that when he paid his first visit to London as a boy of nine, in 1849, he
> procured a map of the City, marked out all the streets, lanes, and pur-
> lieus described by Ainsworth, and then made a personal tour, first going
> to Wood Street, thence following the movements of Leonard Holt as
> depicted in the story. (IR 110)

It is unlikely that he had time to follow all of Leonard Holt's very extensive
peregrinations, which include, in a fever of activity caused by a bout of the
plague, swimming across the Thames and back, but Hardy clearly found in
the young, upwardly mobile apprentice a hero with whom he could identify.
Set in the years 1665–1666, *Old St. Paul's* draws heavily on *Journal of the
Plague Year* by Daniel Defoe, and may indeed have pushed Hardy to read
Defoe, whose 'affected simplicity', to use his own phrase, he used as a model
for the style of *The Poor Man and the Lady* (L 63). No one could accuse Ainsworth of 'affected simplicity', his writing being so turgid and inept and
repetitive as to be almost unreadable. Yet *Old St. Paul's* clearly sparked
Hardy's interest not only in London but in the layers of history encoded in
its buildings, an interest dramatized in poems such as 'The Coronation'
and 'A Spellbound Palace' and 'In St Paul's a While Ago'.

    In the figure of Ainsworth's Rochester, a libertine loosely based on the
Restoration poet but drastically simplified to fit the Victorian template of the
melodramatic villain, Hardy might be said to have encountered his idealized
Shelley's evil twin—a sexually driven proto-Alec d'Urberville to balance the
ethereal, harp-playing, 'Shelleyan' Angel Clare ('Though not cold-natured
he was rather bright than hot; less Byronic than Shelleyan', T 211). Robert
Gittings argued in his *Young Thomas Hardy* of 1975 that Ainsworth's callous but smoothly irresistible seducer, who is also a master of disguise, lurks
in particular behind the ageless, demonic (but wholly asexual) William Dare
of *A Laodicean*, and indeed that, in the light of Hardy's own 'childlike features', 'Dare-Rochester was [Hardy's] own fantasy self' (RG 201). Gittings's

distaste for his subject is more than usually apparent in this far-fetched spec-
ulation: Hardy's Dare, it is true, is not a lot more convincing or plausible
than Ainsworth's Rochester, but if Hardy's 'fantasy self' had not found expression in more interesting ways than in *A Laodicean*'s scheming photog-
rapher, then his writings would have languished as unread as those of the
novelist through whose historical romance he first explored London as a
child.

Despite the protection offered by the presence of her eldest son, Jemima
carefully searched every corner of the room in the Cross Keys before going
to bed.[13] No sinister Rochester was found lurking in the cupboard or behind
the curtains. Hardy's memories of what he saw in the hours that he and his
mother spent wandering through the city together are brief, but revealing in
the light of his later sensitivity to the plight of animals, a sensitivity passed
on to such as Tess and Sue and Jude, and shared with Emma, even when
they came to disagree about everything else:

> They stayed but a short time in London, but long enough for him to
> see and remember some of the streets, the Pantheon, then a fashion-
> able Pantechnicon {a bazaar}, Cumberland Gate into Hyde Park, which
> then could boast of no Marble Arch, and the pandemonium of Smith-
> field {London's meat market}, with its mud, curses, and cries of ill-
> treated animals. Also, that when passing through the city on the way
> up, they stopped at the point now called Swiss Cottage, and looked
> back at the *outside* of London creeping towards them across green
> fields. (L 22)

The peculiar image of the '*outside*' of London 'creeping towards them across
green fields' again evokes Hardy's vision of the city as a monster, here, as in
the train episode in *Tess*, stealthily exploring, with the aim of exploiting or
appropriating, its antithesis, the rural. The passage also, however, registers
the ruthless manner in which the city imports and consumes the country-
side's products, in this case its livestock: the anguished lowing and bleating
of animals as they are driven through the streets of the city for slaughter in
the chaos of Smithfield affords Hardy a glimpse of London as an urban hell.
His striking visualization of London uncannily pursuing them as their coach
journeys beyond the city's clutches has the primal, haunted clarity of a Word-

sworthian spot of time, as well as being sound social history, for it neatly encapsulates the relentless processes of urban expansion that accelerated to a new pitch in the almost seven decades between Hardy's first experience of London, and his recounting of this visit in his autobiography.

Hardy had a cousin as well as an aunt called Martha. Martha Sparks, the third daughter of Jemima's sister Maria, was six years older than Hardy, and, like her carpenter brothers James and Nat, thought to try her luck in London, where she worked as a lady's maid (MM 59). Hardy's first surviving letter, written to his sister Mary a few months after his own arrival in the city, relates meeting up with Martha and going to the International Exhibition of 1862 in South Kensington with her. It is perhaps surprising, given his precocity and curiosity, that the eleven-year-old Hardy was not taken on a day trip to its predecessor, the Great Exhibition of 1851, which attracted some six million visitors to its compendious display of scientific exhibits and technological developments, as well as crafts and wonders from around the world, including the largest known diamond, the famous Koh-i-Noor. Excursion trains were laid on from Dorchester, and were indeed described in detail by Hardy in 'The Fiddler of the Reels' of 1893. In this, one of Hardy's finest short stories, Car'line and her illegitimate daughter make a trip to visit the stolid and steady Ned Hipcroft, whose proposal of marriage Car'line had rejected some four years earlier, prompting Ned to set off for London, where he finds steady employment as a mechanic. Seduced and abandoned by the eponymous Fiddler of the Reels, Mop Ollamoor, Car'line writes to Ned, and he replies suggesting that she come up and visit the Great Exhibition with him on what he hopes will be a sunny June day. This being a story by Hardy, it turns out wet and cold, allowing him to re-create in full the discomforts of an early train journey from Dorchester to London, and to put on record the fascination this new form of locomotion inspired in Dorset in its infancy:

The 'excursion-train'—an absolutely new departure in the history of travel—was still a novelty on the Wessex line, and probably everywhere. Crowds of people had flocked to all the stations on the way up to witness the unwonted sight of so long a train's passage, even where they did not take advantage of the opportunity it offered. The seats for the humbler class of travellers in these early experiments in steam-locomotion were open trucks, without any protection whatever from the wind and rain; and damp weather having set in with the afternoon, the unfortunate occupants of these vehicles were, on the train drawing up at the London terminus, found to be in a pitiable condition from their long journey: blue-faced, stiff-necked, sneezing, rain-beaten, chilled to the marrow, many of the men being hatless; in fact, they resembled people who had been out all night in an open boat on a rough sea, rather than inland excursionists for pleasure. The women had in some degree protected themselves by turning up the skirts of their gowns over their heads, but as by this arrangement they were additionally exposed about the hips, they were all more or less in a sorry plight. (LLI 145)

The Great Exhibition opened in May, some eight months after Hardy began walking the three miles from Higher Bockhampton into Dorchester each day to attend the British School, a Nonconformist institution run by the much-admired Isaac Last. This commute from a rural hamlet to the county capital was Hardy's first experience of making a regular transition between, as he put it in the *Life*, 'a world of shepherds and ploughmen . . . where modern improvements were still regarded as wonders' (as instanced by the crowds gathered at rural stations to watch an excursion train pass), and a provincial town 'which had advanced to railways and telegraphs and daily London papers' (L 36). The 'old gentleman' who introduces the narrative of 'The Fiddler of the Reels' identifies the Great Exhibition as a crucial, even decisive factor in the history of the county, presenting it, like the advent of the railways, as a watershed or, to use his own geological term, a 'fault': 'For South Wessex', he ruminates, the year of 1851

formed in many ways an extraordinary chronological frontier or transit-line, at which there occurred what one might call a precipice in Time. As in a geological 'fault,' we had presented to us a sudden bringing of ancient and modern into absolute contact, such as probably in no other single year since the Conquest was ever witnessed in this part of the country. (LLI 137)

Indeed, he describes the Great Exhibition as almost a form of metropolitan soft power or cultural invasion, diffusing its influence into the remotest regions, places such as Stickleford, Mellstock, and Egdon, and even altering the population's habits of speech:

> The Great Exhibition of 1851, in Hyde Park, London. None of the younger generation can realize the sense of novelty it produced in us who were then in our prime. A noun substantive went so far as to become an adjective in honour of the occasion. It was 'exhibition' hat, 'exhibition' razor-strop, 'exhibition' watch; nay, even 'exhibition' weather, 'exhibition' spirits, sweethearts, babies, wives. (LLI 137)

It is not known if the young Hardy experienced Exhibition-fever of the kind described by the old gentleman, but clearly he came to believe in the 1890s, when he adopted most explicitly the role of the historian of Wessex, that the first Great Exhibition, which was visited by roughly a third of Britain's population at that date, played a significant part in breaching the county's insularity and diluting its distinctiveness. It is, in addition, a telling coincidence that 'the chronological frontier or transit-line' attributed to the Great Exhibition occurred at roughly the time of his own first important break from home. And although, perhaps on account of the fact that his mother was six months pregnant with his younger brother Henry when it opened, he never himself marvelled at the Great Shalimar and all it contained, it was in the early 1850s that, under the tutelage of Isaac Last, Hardy found his intellectual horizons really beginning to widen, and the 'bringing of ancient and modern into absolute contact' asserted its grip on his imagination.

2

⎯⎯⟨⎯⟨⟨⎯⟨⎯⎯

Only Practical Men Are Wanted Here

I

Hardy's enduring pride in the verse that he wrote in London during his first residence there can be gauged from the prominence given to these early poems in his first collection, *Wessex Poems* of 1898. Thirteen of the book's first sixteen poems are explicitly dated to the years 1865—1867. No date is given for the book's opening poem, 'The Temporary the All', but it seems reasonable to assume that it too was composed while Hardy was living in Paddington and working as an architect's clerk in an office just off the Strand in the mid-1860s.[1]

Hardy's decision to introduce himself as a poet to his vast readership with this particular sample of his experiments in metre and diction can, I think, be seen as another illustration of the strain of perversity in his temperament that led him to respond to Leslie Stephen's offer to publish a follow-up to *Far from the Madding Crowd* with a satirical novel set mainly in London. The first poem in the current standard edition of all of Hardy's poetry, James Gibson's of 1976, is 'Domicilium', transposed from the *Life*, where it is printed in a footnote and introduced as 'the earliest discoverable of young Hardy's attempts in verse' (L 8). Gibson uses the bucolic and 'Wordsworthian'—to borrow Hardy's own adjective—'Domicilium' as a kind of preface to the eight volumes that follow. The more rebarbative 'The Temporary the All' was the opening salvo, however, not only of *Wessex Poems* but of the two editions of Hardy's *Collected Poems*, published in 1919 and 1923, that he himself saw through the press.[2] The blank verse 'Domicilium' describes the cottage in which Hardy grew up in Higher Bockhampton and is certainly a gentler and more appealing introduction to his poetic oeuvre than 'The Temporary the All', which is composed in Sapphics, a complex, even somewhat outlandish metre for anyone writing in English. Nevertheless, this was the poem chosen by Hardy to initiate his thirty-year campaign to persuade his followers that, the popularity of recent novels such as *Tess of the d'Urbervilles* and *Jude the Obscure* notwithstanding, his true gift was for verse.

The bracketed subheading 'Sapphics' was added only when the poem was reprinted in Hardy's *Selected Poems* of 1916. Hardy's interest in the metre was no doubt sparked by Swinburne's poem, simply entitled 'Sapphics', published in 1866 in *Poems and Ballads*. In a notebook that he kept from 1865 to 1867, which he headed 'Studies, Specimens &c.', Hardy copied out numerous lines from Swinburne's *Poems and Ballads*, a volume that had an electrifying effect on him. In a letter of 1897 to Swinburne he recalled 'the buoyant time of 30 years ago, when I used to read your early works walking along the crowded London streets, to my imminent risk of being knocked down' (CL 2:158). This image of Hardy utterly absorbed in *Poems and Ballads* as he makes his way through the streets of London recurs in the third stanza of his elegy for Swinburne, 'A Singer Asleep':

> O that far morning of a summer day
> When, down a terraced street whose pavements lay
> Glassing the sunshine into my bent eyes,
> I walked and read with a quick glad surprise
> New words, in classic guise. (CP 323)

Swinburne's 'Sapphics' blends the new and the classic in a fluent, charged, hypnotic lyricism ('Only saw the beautiful lips and fingers, / Full of songs and kisses and little whispers') that makes one almost forget the formidable prosodic challenge the poet has set himself. Not so Hardy's 'The Temporary the All', which opens in his most cranky and contorted alliterative mode, every line encrusted with verbal gargoyles:

> Change and chancefulness in my flowering youthtime,
> Set me sun by sun near to one unchosen;

Wrought us fellowlike, and despite divergence,
        Fused us in friendship. (CP 7)[3]

Hardy greatly admired Swinburne's virtuosity as a mediator of the classical, and his ability to infuse versions of such as Sappho with a striking theatrical intensity.[4] But, if one thinks of 'The Temporary the All' as establishing a surreptitious dialogue with Swinburne's 'Sapphics', then Hardy seems, in this opening poem, also to be trying to make us aware of how far removed his classical education was from that of Swinburne, and of the vast gulf that lay between their ways of bringing the 'ancient and modern into absolute contact'.

In 1852, when Hardy was twelve and in his second year at Isaac Last's school, his parents arranged for him to learn Latin, at the cost of an extra five shillings per term. He began teaching himself Greek shortly after starting work, in the summer of 1856, as an apprentice architect in the office of John Hicks in Dorchester. (Both Hardy's parents were keen for their gifted oldest son to continue in the family trade, but as an architect rather than a builder.) Midway though his pupillage, Hardy inquired of his friend and mentor Horace Moule if he thought he should continue with his Greek studies, with the aim of applying for a place at Cambridge, and then entering the church or becoming an academic scholar. Eight years older than Hardy, the brilliant but unstable Moule, who was the fourth son in the family of the Reverend Henry Moule, the vicar of Fordington, replied in the negative, much to Hardy's chagrin:

> Moule's reluctant opinion was that if Hardy really had (as his father had insisted, and as indeed was reasonable since he never as yet had earned a farthing in his life) to make an income in some way by architecture in 1862, it would be hardly worth while for him to read Aeschylus or Sophocles in 1859–61. He had secretly wished that Moule would advise him to go on with Greek plays, in spite of the serious damage it might do to his architecture; but he felt bound to listen to reason and prudence. (L 38)

This instance of 'divergence' in the relationship of Hardy and Moule had far-reaching consequences, and might even be said to have made inevitable his move to London a few years later. By 1862 Hardy had learned all that he could from Hicks and was more or less obliged, if he was to advance any further in his architectural career, to find a position in the capital. But Moule's advice that he abandon Greek, without which he would never be accepted as an undergraduate into Oxford or Cambridge, clearly rankled, as the next paragraph in the *Life* makes clear:

> It may be permissible to ponder whether Hardy's career might not have been altogether different if Moule's opinion had been the contrary one, and he had advised going on with Greek plays. The younger man would hardly have resisted the suggestion, and might have risked the consequences, so strong was his bias that way. The upshot might have been his abandonment of architecture for a University career, his father never absolutely refusing to advance him money for a good cause. Having every instinct of a scholar he might have ended his life as a Don. (L 38)

At stake in his discussion with the man with whom he was most firmly 'fused in friendship' in his early life, were all manner of tangled issues: Moule, who was 'a fine Greek scholar' (L 38), had studied at both Oxford and Cambridge, although he'd graduated from neither. While his reply to Hardy's inquiry was undoubtedly more thoughtful and courteous than that of the Biblioll College master who advised Jude Fawley in *Jude the Obscure* that he had 'a much better chance of success in life by remaining in [his] own sphere and sticking to [his] trade' (JO 110), the burden of it was more or less the same: Greek was a luxury that he, or rather his family, couldn't afford. Moule's image of Hardy's father was clearly not of a man in a position to advance the amounts of money needed for such a scheme, which Hardy himself once characterised as 'highly visionary' (L 52). Yet Moule is hardly to blame for being unable to offer a satisfactory practical response to a problem that would loom over much of his friend's early manhood and would not be resolved until Hardy and Emma kept finding themselves surrounded by women reading *Far from the Madding Crowd* whenever, in the winter of 1874, they took the train from the London suburb of Surbiton up to Waterloo Station.

Hardy's account of his disappointing discussion with Moule about Greek is placed at the end of chapter 2 of the *Life*, which covers his five years with

Hicks. Had he successfully pursued this 'visionary scheme', which he didn't fully abandon until 1866, Hardy might have ended up with a life similar to that of William Barnes (who in 1862 was appointed to the living of Winterbourne Came)—that is as a curate in a country village, writing poetry on the side.[5] Hardy presents his decision to abandon Greek as his 'road not taken', and, like the narrator of Robert Frost's poem, he ends 'with a sigh' and the fatalistic formula that he was so fond of: 'But this was not to be, and it was possibly better so' (L 38). Instead, he went to London, where he spent his evenings composing poems such as 'The Temporary the All', whose outré diction foregrounds his virtuoso transposition of a complex Greek meter into English, but whose overall theme is putting up with what circumstances send one's way—which was, of course, precisely the tenor of Moule's advice: ideals and dreams must give way to 'reason and prudence'.[6] The narrator of the poem meets, as well as the friend from whom he has some 'divergence', a damsel 'unformed to be all-eclipsing', but decides that she'll have to do until 'arise my forefelt / Wonder of women'. He also finds himself in a tenement 'uncouth', but accepts that it too will have to serve ('"Let such lodging be for a breath-while," thought I, / "Soon a more seemly"') until he is able to move into his 'visioned hermitage'. As for the 'high handiwork' that he plans to make his 'life-deed', alas, that too has to be postponed, 'the ripe time pending'. In the last stanza, these various provisional choices, or accommodations with necessity, are revealed to be all that life will ever grant him:

> Mistress, friend, place, aims to be bettered straightway,
> Bettered not has Fate or my hand's achievement;
> Sole the allowance those of my onward earth-track—
>   Never transcended! (CP 7)

While the poem's classical meter might be read as signalling Hardy's self-taught familiarity with the language that Moule advised him to drop, its utterly unclassical diction points to the expertise that he gained by accepting his mentor's advice, and, like Jude, 'sticking to [his] trade': the skills that Hardy acquired as a 'young Gothic draughtsman' (L 41) not only kept him financially afloat until the success of *Far from the Madding Crowd* allowed him to think of himself as a professional novelist, but profoundly affected many aspects of his writing, in particular his poetry. If Swinburne's 'Sapphics' offers 'new words in classic guise', 'The Temporary the All' advertises the Gothic fecundity of Hardy's poetic resources, his love of the freakish, the extravagant, the convoluted, the discordant. In later life he occasionally expressed regret for his part in 'the craze for indiscriminate church-restoration' (Preface to PBE 3) inspired by the Gothic Revival, and he was always modest about his architectural talents.[7] He was eloquent, however, on the importance of the training that he received while working under Hicks in Dorchester, and then Arthur Blomfield in London, on the development of his poetry:

> He knew that in architecture cunning irregularity is of enormous worth, and it is obvious that he carried on into his verse, perhaps unconsciously, the Gothic art-principle in which he had been trained—the principle of spontaneity, found in mouldings, tracery and such-like, resulting in the 'unforeseen' (as it has been called) character of his metres and stanzas. (L 323)

It was the 'Gothic art-principle' that enabled him to evolve a poetic idiom far more distinctive and various and expressive than Swinburne's classicism, however extreme the emotions it dramatized, could ever be.

On starting in July of 1856 in Hicks's office at 39 South Street in Dorchester, Hardy was introduced to two fellow architectural pupils: Herbert Fippard, the son of a Fordington grocer, and Henry Bastow, an earnest Baptist who was eager to persuade Hardy to follow his lead and undergo adult Baptism—a topic taken up in the opening chapters of *A Laodicean*. Until the London-educated Bastow left Dorchester to take up a position in an architect's office in the capital in 1860, from where he later emigrated to Australia, he and Hardy enjoyed sessions construing passages from classical texts together, reading the New Testament in Greek, and engaging in scholarly jousting with Hicks. Fippard, who was six years older than Hardy, and whose articles were about to expire when Hardy arrived, lodged in Hardy's memory for less high-minded reasons: this 'comet-like young man' (L 39) had made a number of visits to London, or so he claimed, and dazzled Hardy with accounts of dancing in the Argyle Rooms, an entertainment venue just off Regent Street, and on the platform of the Cremorne Pleasure Gardens on the north bank of the Thames in Chelsea:

> Hardy would relate that one quadrille in particular his precursor Fippard could whistle faultlessly, and while giving it would caper about the office to an imaginary dance-figure, embracing an imaginary Cremorne or Argyle *danseuse*. The fascinating quadrille remained with Hardy all his life, but he never could identify it. (L 38–39)

Soon after his own arrival in London, Hardy visited both places of entertainment in the hope of tracking down this mysterious tune, which lodged in his consciousness, rather in the way Vinteuil's *petite phrase* is presented as haunting Marcel in *À la recherche du temps perdu*. Alas, it had 'vanished like a ghost' (L 45), and he failed to unearth it in any of the city's second-hand music shops or even in the library of the British Museum. The only time that he ever heard it again was in Tooting in 1878, when played by a passing organ-grinder: Hardy leaped up from his desk, dashed out of the house, and pursued the organ-grinder down the street, only to discover that he spoke hardly any English, and knew it simply as 'Quad-ree-ya!'. 'It was possibly one of Jullien's', Hardy concludes, 'then gone out of vogue—set off rather by the youthful imagination of Hardy at sixteen than by any virtue in the music itself' (L 126–127). The lost time he seems to be attempting to recover in his dogged quest for the song in the dance halls and music shops and library catalogues and streets of London is, paradoxically, the vision of the capital that it evoked for him when he first heard it whistled by his 'jaunty young' fellow apprentice in 39 South Street in Dorchester.

Chapter 2 of the *Life* artfully concludes with Hardy's recollection of Fippard's note-perfect rendition of the nameless quadrille, and all that it summoned up of the excitement and glamour of the city's nightlife when operated upon by Hardy's 'youthful imagination'. The opening sentence of chapter 3 records with precision the date on which he himself embarked on his *vita nuova* in the city, with a hint of mockery at the solemnity of his ambitions: 'On Thursday, April 17, 1862, Thomas Hardy started alone for London, to pursue the art and science of architecture on more advanced lines.' The first encounter that he records with a denizen of the city was not, however, an encouraging one:

> Hardy used to relate humorously that on the afternoon of his arrival he called to inquire for lodgings at a house where was employed a bachelor some ten years older than himself, whose cousin Hardy had known. This acquaintance, looking him up and down, was sceptical about his establishing himself in London. 'Wait till you have walked the streets a few weeks', he said satirically, 'and your elbows begin to shine, and the hems of your trousers get frayed, as if nibbled by rats! Only practical men are wanted here.' Thomas began to wish he had thought less of the Greek Testament and more of iron girders. (L 40)

Clearly Hardy had not fixed up even temporary lodgings in advance, believing that the leads he'd gathered from Dorset friends and contacts would be sufficient for him to gain a foothold in the city. It's likely that this sceptical bachelor was himself part of the Dorset-London diaspora that Hardy was now joining, and whose numbers his Sparks cousins had already swelled; and that, like Nathaniel and James and Martha, this acquaintance who was 'employed' at a house—in service? as a carpenter?—belonged to the class from which the London publishing industry, as well, of course, as his own talent, would eventually enable Hardy to escape. Although we get only the barest glimpse of this bachelor in his early thirties, like the city clerk so memorably depicted in the poem 'Coming Up Oxford Street: Evening' who 'sees no escape to the very verge of his days / From the rut of Oxford Street into open ways' (CP 717), he embodies for Hardy a vision of the London life that he was desperate to evade: unmarried, in low-paid employment, aware not of the riches on offer in the shop windows or 'show-cases' of the city streets but of rats nibbling the hems of ragged trousers. With hindsight Hardy can 'humorously' relish the irony that the intellectual curiosity that led him to read the New Testament in Greek proved, in the long run, of more 'practical' use than his knowledge of 'iron girders'; but at this stage it was only his training with Hicks, and the letters in his pocket recommending him to the attention of two London architects, Benjamin Ferrey and John Norton, that elevated him above the prospect of a life in service or as a manual labourer.

In a speech that Hardy wrote in 1908 to commemorate the fifth anniversary of the founding of The Society of Dorset Men in London, he noted the 'cohesive feeling' that unites people from the county when 'away from home' (PW 218). This talk (which was never actually delivered) captures more vividly than the *Life* his initial need to locate reassuring *points de repère* that would allow him to make sense of the confusion that threatens to engulf anyone new to the city.[8] He asks us to imagine

> a young man just arrived in London from Dorchester, with a half-formed intention of making the capital the scene of his life's endeavours. He pauses, maybe, on Waterloo Bridge, and, Dorset people being impressionable, he experiences as he gazes at the picture before him a vivid sense of his own insignificance in it, his isolation and loneliness. He feels himself among strangers and strange things. Being, however, though impressionable, also a very thorough sort of person, he means to explore the town, and leaning against the parapet of the bridge he looks at his new map to find out his bearings. He perceives that, despite the first strangeness, there are three 'Dorset' Streets, a 'Dorset' Square, and one or two 'Dorset' roads in the wilderness of brick and stone encampments about him. Also a 'Weymouth' Street, a 'Blandford' Square and Street, a 'Bryanston' Square, Place and Street, a 'Sherborne' Lane, a 'Cranbourne' Street, a 'Melbury' Road, a 'Bridport' Place, and even a 'Bindon' Road. (PW 220)

The Dorchester to London train would also have deposited Hardy at Waterloo, but he probably crossed the Thames, like Ethelberta's younger sister Picotee in *The Hand of Ethelberta*, on Westminster Bridge (HE 134), which was free, whereas a toll of a half-penny was levied on foot passengers using Waterloo Bridge. Picotee makes for Ethelberta's house, located in the original version in Connaught Crescent, a name later altered to Exonbury Crescent—like many of his revisions, the change serves to heighten the interactive relationship developed in the novel between the capital and Wessex, for Exonbury was Hardy's Wessex name for Exeter.[9] The Thames before the construction of the Embankment was noxious-smelling at the best of times, and Picotee, a newcomer to London, notices pedestrians holding 'handkerchiefs to their mouths to strain off the river mist from their lungs' (HE 135). Picotee is a timid and limited character, but her first impressions of London are given with a complexity and vividness that suggests that she is here serving as a vehicle for Hardy's own initial responses to the city. Crossing the Thames, she

> saw a luminous haze hanging over each well-lighted street as it with-
> drew into distance behind the nearer houses, showing its direction as
> a train of morning mist shows the course of a distant stream when the
> stream itself is hidden. The lights along the riverside towards Charing
> Cross sent an inverted palisade of gleaming swords down into the
> shaking water. (HE 134–135)

While the urban haze of street lamps is rendered somewhat less alien by its comparison with mist above a hidden rural stream, the Thames itself seems the site of conflict, as if encroached upon by the martial energies required to succeed 'In the Great Metropolis', to borrow the title of a poem by Arthur Hugh Clough, which succinctly captures the laissez-faire capitalist spirit of mid-Victorian London: 'Each for himself is still the rule, / We learn it when we go to school—/ The devil take the hindmost, o!'. Picotee has to inquire for directions, whereas the young man of the address to The Society of Dorset Men in London is imagined consulting a 'new map'. Hardy's own would probably have been new in both senses, Stanford's map of London and its suburbs having been published in February of 1862.

Not only do the names of numerous London squares and streets derive from Dorset, Hardy continues in his speech, warming to his theme, but so does the fabric of many of its most famous landmarks. The young man has only to raise his eyes to St. Paul's Cathedral, and he will be gazing on a building 'almost as much Dorset as he is':

> To be sure, it has been standing here in London for more than two hun-
> dred years, but it stood, or rather lay, in Dorset probably two hundred
> thousand years before it got here. How thoroughly metropolitan it is;
> its façade thrills to the street noises all day long, and has done so for
> three or four human lifetimes. But through what a stretch of time did it

thrill all day and all night in Portland to the tides of the West Bay,
particularly when they slammed against the island during south-west
gales, and sent reverberations into the very bottom quarry there. (PW
220–221)

Slabs squared and ready for use in the construction of the cathedral, but
never in the end required, Hardy adds, still litter the Portland cove from
which the stone was transported to London. From Portland also came the
stone used to build Somerset House, Whitehall Banqueting House, the
Horse Guards, the General Post Office, as well as most of Wren's churches,
while the paving stones of the city's streets were furnished by the quarries
of Swanage and the Isle of Purbeck.[10]

All such observations are calculated to inspire a warming 'cohesive feeling'
among Dorset men in London, to 'stouten their hearts and set them girding
their loins anew' (PW 224). And yet Hardy can't help offering in his concluding remarks a glimpse into the loneliness of his five years in London,
into 'that feeling of gloomy isolation to which young men of Dorset stock are
peculiarly liable in an atmosphere not altogether exhilarating after their own
air'. Hardy was particularly ruthless in his destruction of letters and diaries
from this period, which would culminate, like his spell in Tooting, in a crisis
both physical and mental. London would never become his 'true locality and
anchorage', to quote from the speech's final sentence, which advises men of
Dorset to find out 'where what they can do best can best be done'. This can
be read as an oblique defence of his eventual return to Dorset, but it was a
return made only after London had proved the catalyst for his discovery of
what it was he himself could do best, and the means of making a living
from it.

It is not known where he spent his first few nights. On 20 April he moved
into 3 Clarence Place just off the Kilburn High Road.[11] Kilburn was at that
time some distance from London proper, and when Egbert Mayne, the hero
of the novella 'An Indiscretion in the Life of an Heiress' (published in 1878
but largely quarried from Hardy's first unpublished novel, *The Poor Man and
the Lady*, composed ten years earlier), walks there after failing to persuade
the heiress Geraldine Allenville to meet him at midnight outside her Park
Lane mansion, he is almost in the country, 'wandering among some fields

by a way he could never afterwards recollect', and brooding morosely on the lights of London from afar (AI 89–90). Mayne is a successful writer, by this stage, but his prototype, Will Strong of *The Poor Man and the Lady*, came to the city, like his creator, to further his career as an architect.

Putting out of his mind the doubts sown by the bachelor, Hardy at once set about searching for a suitable berth in the capital and found himself, far from being blocked by 'Crass Casualty', to borrow his phrase for bad luck from the early poem 'Hap', to be in this instance the favourite of 'dicing Time' (CP 9). Although Benjamin Ferrey, for whom his father had worked and who seemed the more promising source of employment, was polite but unhelpful, John Norton, who was a friend of Hicks, took the 'pink-faced youth' (his own description of himself, L 41) under his wing, allowing him to set up base in his Old Bond Street office and then highly recommending him to Arthur Blomfield when Blomfield was casting around for a young draughtsman with experience of ecclesiastical architecture. 'Here was indeed as good a thing as could have happened', Hardy acknowledges in the *Life* (L 41). Just two and a half weeks after his arrival he began work for Blomfield at 9 St. Martin's Place (just off Trafalgar Square) on a salary of £110 a year. He was able to share his Clarence Place rooms with Philip Shaw, a trainee architect also employed by Blomfield. Shaw seems to have come from a somewhat superior social and financial background, and he was clearly keen to widen Hardy's artistic interests: in Hardy's first extant letter, written to his sister Mary on 17 August 1862, he records that 'P.S. is reading extracts from Ruskins "Modern Painters"' out loud to him as he writes to her (CL 1:1).

Hardy was therefore somewhat exaggerating when he characterized, in retrospect, his life in the city as that 'of an isolated student cast upon the billows of London with no protection but his brains—the young man of whom it may be said more truly than perhaps of any, that "save his own soul he hath no star"' (L 51)—the quote is from Swinburne's 'Prelude', collected in *Songs Before Sunrise* of 1871. But the emphasis that he puts on his life in the city being like that of a student devising his own programme of study without pedagogical guidance very accurately captures the overall shape of the years from 1862 to 1867. The dedicated, intense, wide-ranging self-education that he undertook while in London laid the foundation for his subsequent adoption in his novels of the role of the connoisseur of culture able to observe that 'those who remember Greuze's "Head of a Girl" in one of the public picture-galleries have an idea of Cytherea's look askance at the turning' (DR 56), or to suggest of the inebriated rustics staggering in the wake of a whistling Sergeant Troy that 'the whole procession was not unlike Flaxman's group of the suitors tottering on towards the infernal regions under the conduct of Mercury' (FFMC 251). His use of such allusions has been construed as the irritating compulsion of an autodidact to show off his painfully earned knowledge.[12] Certainly, as in 'The Temporary the All', the awkwardness makes us aware of the labour involved in acquiring such knowledge, as well as of the gap between Hardy's somewhat self-conscious deployment of cultural references in his writing and the ease and confidence with which a poet like Swinburne or a novelist like Henry James address a reader automatically assumed to be as well-educated as themselves. Probably the most striking image that the *Life* offers us of Hardy's determination to make himself into a classical scholar on the level of a Horace Moule or the character that Moule inspired, Henry Knight of *A Pair of Blue Eyes*, is of his rising at four in the morning in the cottage at Higher Bockhampton to read the *Aeneid* and the *Iliad* before walking into work in Dorchester, but it was in London that his autodidacticism reached an almost dangerously manic pitch. He found there no equivalent to Bastow, with whom he could exchange notes and queries, and indeed his strenuous labours seem eventually to have developed into a lonely addiction that threatened his health: in the summer of 1867 he found himself much 'weakened' after a prolonged period in which 'he had been accustomed to shut himself up in his rooms in Westbourne Park Villas every evening from six to twelve reading incessantly, instead of getting out for air after the day's confinement' (L 54).

There were various strands to this project for self-improvement. Some months before Hardy left for London, Horace Moule made him a present of a copy of Francis Turner Palgrave's best-selling anthology, *The Golden Treasury of the Best Songs and Lyrical Poems of the English Language*, published the previous year. Palgrave's anthology was instrumental in shaping and defining Victorian taste in verse, and it certainly had an extraordinary impact on Hardy.[13] 'His only ambition', Florence records him remarking some six weeks before he died, 'so far as he could remember, was to have some poem or poems in a good anthology like the *Golden Treasury*' (L 478). In a letter to Edmund Gosse of 1883 he recalled how Thomas Lodge's 'Rosaline' (XIX in Palgrave's Book I) 'awakened in [him] a true, or mature, consciousness of what poetry consists in—after a Dark Age of five or six years which followed that vague sense, in childhood, of the charms of verse that most young people experience' (CL 1:122). 'Mature' may perhaps seem an odd word to associate with a poem that includes lines such as 'Her paps are centres of delight, / Her breasts are orbs of heavenly frame' (GT 25), but, as his 'Studies, Specimens &c.' notebook reveals, Hardy's enthusiasm for poetry in general, but particularly that of the Elizabethans anthologized by Palgrave, was intimately bound up with the simultaneous awakening of his erotic consciousness. In the opening pages of this notebook, started in 1865, Hardy would excerpt phrases from poems that impressed or delighted him, creating a series of fractured poetic collages that might well appeal in their own right to a devotee of avant-garde poetry of a century later. His extracts from, say, Lodge's 'Rosaline' suggest that copying out such poems was a means for Hardy to experience a richly textured verbal sensuality, a way of voicing through the words of another—and through words made respectable by their inclusion in the Tennyson-sanctioned *Golden Treasury*—his own 'mature' erotic cravings:

> her lips are like two <u>budded</u> roses
> whom <u>ranks</u> of lilies <u>neighbour</u>
> <u>nigh</u> / <u>centres</u> of delight / orbs /
> feed perfection = keep perfect what
> is already so / with orient pearl, with
> sapphire blue with marble white, with
> ruby red her body every way is fed
> yet soft in touch & sweet in view (SS 10)

So voracious grew his appetite for poetry that during his last two years in London he gave up, or so he claimed, reading prose altogether, aside from an occasional glance at a daily newspaper or weekly review. By this stage he had arrived at the 'Quixotic opinion' that poetry was the most efficient way of gaining the knowledge that he needed, and thus a kind of fast track to the truth and, by implication, success: 'as in verse was concentrated the essence of all imaginative and emotional literature, to read verse and nothing else was the shortest way to the fountain-head of such for one who had not a great deal of spare time' (L 51). The bachelor's stern warning that 'Only practical men are wanted here' achieves a dizzying fusion with Hardy's rampant po-etical enthusiasms in this peculiar line of argument, which tries to apply a pragmatic business model to his desire to be a poet-prophet. It would be over forty years before the results of Hardy's impassioned self-education in verse in his twenties would assume a 'practical' form in the publication of *Wessex Poems*, but then—having abandoned prose once again to devote himself to poetry—he would find himself with three decades of 'spare time' in which to pursue his primary vocation.

II

In the *Life* Hardy suggests that the timing of his arrival in the capital was influenced by the imminent opening of the Great Exhibition of 1862. Housed in an enormous purpose-built twin-domed construction in South Kensington, on the site later occupied by the Natural History Museum, it was not as excitedly remembered as its predecessor, but attracted similarly large crowds. It ran from 1 May to 1 November and clearly had a huge fasci-nation for Hardy: he visited not only with his cousin Martha Sparks but with Horace Moule, with a former pupil of Hicks called Ellis, and with his sister Mary, to whom he wrote: 'I generally run down to the Exhibition for an hour in the evening two or three times a week, after I come out I go to the reading room in the Kensington Museum' (CL 1:1). Hardy the polymath, so in evidence to anyone who peruses Lennart Björk's two-volume edition of his *Literary Notebooks*, worked his way steadily through the vast, to many overwhelming, displays of inventions and artefacts and materials and art-works gathered from Britain and around the world. Unless he visited the National Gallery first, it would have been his first opportunity to experi-ence paintings in a museum setting, and it initiated a life of gallery going. Moule may have helped foster this interest; among the pictures that they saw together was Jean Leon Gérôme's *Roman Gladiators*, which inspired Moule to write a poem called 'Ave Caesar' that was published in the maga-zine *Once a Week* in September of 1862.[14] The following year Hardy began his earliest surviving notebook, entitled *Schools of Painting*, which records the names of almost 200 painters, with brief comments: 'Paolo Uccello—corrected perspective errors'; 'Raphael—b. 1483. ideal beauty, loftiness, & volupts . . . the rival of M. Angelo'; 'Gerard Douw—gentle & humorous' (PN 105, 107, 112). Such entries were the result of frequent sessions in the National Gallery, and possibly his half-hearted quest for a means of escaping the 'monotonous and mechanical' tedium of his working life, which mainly involved copying out senior architects' designs. Casting around for alternative ways of making a living, Hardy briefly considered trying to turn himself into an art critic, with a specialisation in architectural art. This notion, however, like the subsequent and even more unlikely schemes that he mooted, such as becoming a metropolitan columnist for a provincial newspaper or writing popular plays in blank verse, never took root. When we next hear in the chapter on London in the *Life* of his self-education in the work of the Old Masters, he is keen to insist on the purely aesthetic nature of his engagement with the pictures selected for prolonged contemplation:

> His interest in painting led him to devote for many months, on every day that the National Gallery was open, twenty minutes after lunch to an inspection of the masters hung there, confining his attention to a single master on each visit, and forbidding his eyes to stray to any other. He went there from sheer liking, and not with any practical object; but he used to recommend the plan to young people, telling them that they would insensibly acquire a greater insight into schools and styles by this means than from any guide books to the painters' works and manners. (L 53)

The mixture of pleasure ('sheer liking') and the enforcement of a regime ('forbidding his eyes to stray to any other') is characteristic of Hardy's need at once to gratify himself and to improve and to police himself. Such divisions reflect an inner conflict between a Samuel Smiles-inflected concept of striving ('The battle of life is, in most cases, fought uphill; and to win it without a struggle were perhaps to win it without honour'), and a longing for a private aesthetic experience that is untrammelled by anxiety about what the *Life* calls 'ways and means' (L 49), by public approval or the need to be 'practical'.[15] Egbert Mayne, the hero of 'An Indiscretion in the Life of an

Heiress', finds himself similarly torn between looking at paintings for pleasure and his sense of their value to him as social capital:

> He had not the old interest in them for their own sakes, but a breath-
> less interest in them as factors in the game of sink or swim. He entered
> picture galleries, not, as formerly, because it was his humour to dream
> pleasantly over the images therein expressed, but to be able to talk on
> demand about painters and their peculiarities. He examined Correggio
> to criticise his flesh shades; Angelico, to speak technically of the pink
> faces of his saints; Murillo, to say fastidiously that there was a certain
> silliness in the look of his old men; Rubens for his sensuous women;
> Turner for his Turneresqueness; Romney was greater than Reynolds
> because Lady Hamilton had been his model, and thereby hung a tale.
> Bonozzi Gozzoli was better worth study than Raffaelle, since the for-
> mer's name was a learned sound to utter, and all knowledge got up about
> him would tell. (AI 80–81)

Sink or swim . . . The earnestness that Hardy brought to these years of
self-education probably made him something of a fish out of water in Blomfield's office, where the talk was of the romantic adventures of the celebrity
beauties of the day. Before turning his attention exclusively to poetry, he read
widely in Auguste Comte and Charles Fourier, in J. S. Mill and Charles
Darwin and John Henry Newman and Marcus Aurelius (a selection of whose
writings was another present from Moule). When he attended Shakespeare
plays, it was book in hand. Of his visits to the Cremorne Pleasure Gardens
and the Argyle Rooms, in search of the entrancing lost quadrille, he records
that he did not dance 'much himself, if at all' (L 45)—though that may have
been because he realized that most of the single women there were prostitutes. He taught himself shorthand; he took lessons in French at King's
College with Professor Leonce Stièvenard, to whose 'Lectures Françaises' he
alludes in The Well-Beloved (WB 309); he read the Saturday Review (as he
had done in Dorchester), and passed on back-issues to his sister Mary, asking
her to store them in case he needed them again; he bought a second-hand
violin so that he could keep up his music; he went regularly to the opera,
and to church. When his father visited him at the end of October of 1862,

Hardy avoided accompanying him on a trip to the Brunels' great feat of engineering, the Thames Tunnel, it being situated, he notes with a touch of hauteur in a letter to Mary, in 'one of the lowest and most crowded parts of London'. He goes on to describe his father's unsophisticated enthusiasm for London sights such as the Monument with a somewhat patronizing humour that calls to mind Pip's attitude to Joe Gargery when he appears in his London rooms in Dickens's *Great Expectations*. Recounting his father's ascent of the Monument, he pokes gentle fun at Thomas Hardy Senior's Dorset accent—'He said he shd not have gone up only "he zid a lot of other voke guane up"' (CL 1:2/CL 7:171). The letter suggests that Hardy, who, certainly when at home, probably spoke pretty much like his father up until he left Dorset, had within six months managed to 'obliterate his local colour' so as to 'merge himself in the type Londoner as quickly as possible'. This is from his address to The Society of Dorset Men in London, where he reminisces about the London of fifty years ago, a time when 'an unfamiliar accent was immediately noted as quaint and odd, even a feature of ridicule' in metropolitan circles, and accordingly it was 'the aim of every provincial, from the squire to the rustic, to get rid of his local articulation at the earliest moment' (PW 219).

Arthur Blomfield, who was the son of the Bishop of London and had been educated at Rugby and Cambridge, had no accent to lose. Hardy presents him as a 'lithe, brisk man' (L 41), and their friendship lasted until Blomfield's death in 1899. His practice specialized in building churches, work no doubt aided by his father's connections and influence. Blomfield's pupils tended to be 'Tory and Churchy young men' (L 43), and Hardy records the pranks they played on members of the radical Reform League, who occupied the ground floor of 8 Adelphi Terrace, into which, in February of 1863, Blomfield moved his business. Recalling the antics of his colleagues over half a century later, Hardy maintains a tone of amused neutrality, and Blomfield's office comes across from the *Life* as easy-going and somewhat philistine and a little blasé, as more interested in japes than in encouraging the kind of idealism that animated such as Bastow—although for many the Gothic Revival was intimately bound up with hopes for a more general spiritual awakening. Hardy's architectural *confrères* seem to have tolerated rather than been enthused by his delivery of 'short addresses or talks on poets and poetry'

(L 49) on afternoons when there wasn't much going on, but one fears might have rebelled had he read out loud to them extracts from an early poetic project, his peculiar attempt to rewrite the book of Ecclesiastes in Spenserian stanzas.

The wilful oddness of such a scheme—though soon abandoned since the original proved 'unmatchable' (L 49)—might be seen as symbolic of Hardy's resistance to the pressure to conform to the orthodoxies that surrounded him. One of the reasons that a spell in London was deemed crucial to an ambitious young architect's prospects was the introduction that it afforded to social circles and contacts vital to the development of a successful career. Hardy, however, discovered in himself 'neither the inclination nor the keenness for getting into social affairs and influential sets which would help him start a practice of his own' (L 49). Accordingly, he reverted to his 'literary pursuits'. It's worth pointing out, however, that among the first results of these 'literary pursuits' was a novel that would have appealed far more to members of the Reform League, whose vast demonstrations of 1866 and 1867 helped bring about the 1867 Reform Act's extension of suffrage, than to the Tory and Churchy young men on the floor above. *The Poor Man and the Lady* was, in Hardy's words,

> a sweeping dramatic satire of the squirearchy and nobility, London society, the vulgarity of the middle class, modern Christianity, church restoration, and political and domestic morals in general, the author's views, in fact, being obviously those of a young man with 'a passion for reforming the world'—those of many a young man before and after him, the tendency of the writing being socialistic, not to say revolutionary. (L 63)

In other words, far from choosing to model himself on Blomfield, from seeking to overcome his straitened provincial background and work his way into a niche in the current hierarchy, Hardy was radicalized by his years in London into believing that the Establishment, despite the fact that it had offered him a foothold on the lowest rung of its ladder, ought to be swept away on a tide of revolution.

Adelphi Terrace was a neoclassical terrace of twenty-four houses between the Strand and the Thames, designed by the Adam brothers and built between 1768 and 1772 (it was demolished in the 1930s). From the first-floor windows of number 8 Hardy could see 'right across the Thames', he wrote to his sister shortly after starting work there, 'and on a clear day every bridge is visible'. On the day on which this letter was composed, however (19 February 1863), London was suffering weather to rival the opening of Dickens's *Bleak House*—'It was almost pitch dark in the middle of the day, and everything visible appeared of the colour of brown paper or pea-soup' (CL 1:3). Joseph Bazalgette's new drainage system was in its infancy, and during the years that Hardy worked in Blomfield's riverside office the Thames remained, to all intents and purposes, an open sewer. Picotee, or Hardy, may have been indulging in a flight of fancy when seeing 'swords' in its quivering waters, but death from 'miasma' stalked the imagination of every Londoner—hence the handkerchiefs across the mouths of the pedestrians whom Picotee observes. Work on Bazalgette's other great project, the Thames Embankment, was begun the year of Hardy's arrival in London, and from Adelphi Terrace he had a bird's-eye view of its progress. Just up river, construction was also under way of Charing Cross Station and the Charing Cross Hotel, which opened in 1864 and 1865, respectively, on the site formerly occupied by Hungerford Market.[16]

'It may be hardly necessary to record', Hardy writes in the *Life*, 'that the metropolis into which he had plunged at this date differed greatly from the London of even a short time after' (L 43). The pace of change in the period of his first residence in London was indeed ferocious, and must have appeared especially so to one of Hardy's origins, experience, and temperament. The railways were the principal reason, for the 1860s saw the invasion of district after district by new lines and stations. The decade has been called among 'the most destructive and the most creative' in the history of the city.[17] It is not surprising that Hardy's nostalgic cast of mind, which found the sources of tragedy in the changes brought about by technological progress in Dorset and saw modern figures such as *The Mayor of Casterbridge*'s Donald Farfrae as the nemesis of those associated, like its protagonist Michael Henchard, with a vanishing way of life, led Hardy to add an occasional wash of sepia to an account of London in the 1860s that was largely composed in the middle of the First World War.

It was the London of Dickens and Thackeray . . . No bridge across
Ludgate Hill disfigured St. Paul's and the whole neighbourhood . . .
There was no underground railway, and omnibus conductors leaving
'Kilburn Gate', near which Hardy lived awhile, cried 'Any more pas-
sengers for London!' The list of such changes might be infinitely ex-
tended. (L 43-44)

On the other hand, his studious attendance at the Great Exhibition suggests
that in his twenties Hardy was far from immune to the scientific optimism
of the age, and he was in fact among the first to use the pioneering line of
the Underground, the Metropolitan Railway, which ran from Paddington
to Farringdon Street: 'Everything is excellently arranged' (CL 1:4), he reported approvingly to Mary after trying it in December of the year that it
opened, 1863.

As an architect, he was particularly sensitive to alterations in the fabric of
the city, although his own tasks involved restoration rather than experimenting with the new building materials that made possible constructions
such as the 1862 Great Exhibition buildings or the Royal Albert Hall (1871),
both designed by Francis Fowke. Blomfield was pleased enough with his new
draughtsman to propose him for membership of the Architectural Association within six months of his commencing work, and, in the spring of 1863,
Hardy won first prize in two competitions that he entered, one for the
design of a country mansion, the other for an essay 'On the Application of
Colored Bricks and Terra Cotta to Modern Architecture', a topic of absolute centrality to Victorian architects such as Fowke and Sir George Gilbert
Scott and Norman Shaw. One wonders if Hardy's research for this topic, conducted mainly in the Reading Room at South Kensington, led him to loiter
outside 2 Palace Green, the house that Thackeray (with whose daughter,
Anne, Hardy would become good friends) had built between 1860 and 1862
near Kensington Palace Gardens, and which was faced in Queen Anne-
style red brick. 'Sir John Millais used to laugh, and declare that my father
first set the fashion for red brick, of which the crimson floods have undoubtedly overflowed in every direction since those days', Anne wrote in one of
her introductions to a complete edition of her father's novels published in
1899.[18] Hardy's own Max Gate is itself prima facie evidence of the far-

reaching extent of the crimson floods that Thackeray, or so Millais claimed, had initiated.

Hardy's essay does not, alas, survive. Although awarded the Royal Institute of British Architects' (RIBA) Silver Medal for his submission, the prize of £10 (somewhat more than a month of his current salary) was held back on the grounds that he had not addressed 'that portion referring to moulded and shaped bricks'. As this aspect of the topic had not been part of the prize's original rubric, it is easy to see why Hardy was disgruntled to learn that he would not receive the money. He kept the medal, which was presented to him at a General Meeting of the RIBA on 18 May 1863, to the end of his days, but must have received it with mixed feelings. Michael Millgate, Hardy's most diligent and exhaustive biographer, believes an exasperated Hardy may himself have removed his semi-prize-winning essay from the institute's library (MM 78).

Adelphi Terrace was not far from Holywell Street, which ran parallel to the Strand just beyond Somerset House. Holywell Street was for long the centre of Victorian London's pornography trade, and was the first street to be raided after the passing of the Obscene Publications Act in September of 1857. In the wake of a concerted, but not entirely successful, attempt by the authorities to sanitize the area, it was renamed 'Booksellers' Row', but Hardy preferred the earlier name, or so he told Edmund Blunden in a conversation that took place in July of 1922: 'T.H. acknowledged himself a book-hunter; in the pre-Kingsway days he had haunted Bookseller's Row, which he would have properly named Holywell Street' (IR 171).[19] It's clear from the *Life* that, notwithstanding his unwillingness to accompany his father to Wapping and Rotherhithe, he did not avoid the less salubrious parts of the city. His walk to work would have taken him through the rookeries of Soho and Seven Dials, and the Hoxton scenes of *Desperate Remedies* register the kinds of poverty that so appalled 1860s visitors to London such as Dostoyevsky and Gustave Doré and Hippolyte Taine: 'Only for one short hour in the whole twenty-four' do Mrs Higgins and her unemployed carpenter husband, who inhabit squalid lodgings near Old Street, 'taste genuine happiness. It was in the evening, when, after the sale of some necessary article of furniture, they were under the influence of a bottle of gin.' The novel's hero, Edward Springrove, finds Mrs Higgins 'helpless' and only half-dressed, and ignoring the cries of six or seven children 'small enough to be covered by a washing tub' (DR 296).

Hardy did not, however, come to London in search of material or experiences that would enable him to develop into an urban social realist. Both the fantasy and—eventually—the actual trajectory of his London life might be captioned by the title of the novel that he wrote in the immediate aftermath of his formative five years in the city: *The Poor Man and the Lady*. The novella that he salvaged from the rejected manuscript, and published in 1878 as 'An Indiscretion in the Life of an Heiress', describes a romance that begins in the village of Tollamore (one of Hardy's pre-Wessex names for Stinsford) in Dorset, moves for its central episodes to London, and then reaches its tragic finale in Tollamore House, which is based, like Knapwater House in *Desperate Remedies*, on Kingston Maurward, a stately home about a mile from the Hardys' cottage at Higher Bockhampton.

Kingston Maurward was the young Hardy's equivalent of Pip's Satis House in Dickens's *Great Expectations*. Like Miss Havisham, the lady of the manor, Julia Augusta Martin, had no children of her own (although unlike Miss Havisham she was married), and, as Hardy tells it, she developed a longing to take young Tommy under her wing to a greater extent than his mother Jemima was willing to countenance. A veritable tug of war ensued. Jemima's decision to remove Hardy from the Bockhampton National School, in which Julia Martin was heavily involved, and send him to Last's Nonconformist British School in Dorchester, was undoubtedly in part influenced by Jemima's desire to remove her precocious son from the influence of her rival. Given Hardy's guardedness when recounting—or not recounting—so many aspects of his life, it is surprising, and even unnerving, to read his recollections of his relationship with a woman thirty years his senior, but whom he thought of in the most intimate and adult of ways:

> She had grown passionately fond of Tommy almost from his infancy—said to have been an attractive little fellow at the time—whom she had been accustomed to take into her lap and kiss until he was quite a big child. He quite reciprocated her fondness. . . . In fact, though he was only nine or ten and she must have been nearly forty, his feeling for her was almost that of a lover. (L 23–24)

Aggrieved by the departure of her favourite from her school, Julia Martin took revenge on Hardy's father (as the lady of 'An Indiscretion' retaliates for the hero's stolen kiss by dispossessing Egbert Mayne's grandfather of his land and farmhouse), peremptorily dismissing him from the building work that he was accustomed to carry out on the Kingston Maurward estate. Despite the potentially serious financial consequences of the dispute for his family, Hardy 'secretly mourned' the loss of the caresses and attentions of a woman who combined the erotic desirability of Estella with the wealth and status of Miss Havisham. He found that he 'had grown more attached than he cared to own' (L 24) to Mrs Martin, the first of many ladies of superior social status who would haunt his imagination, in spite of his mother's displeasure at his romantic hankering after a class of women that she clearly scorned. The battle over her son that she joined with Julia Martin would metamorphose into the unending hostilities of her campaign against the less grand, but more formidable—since Hardy had married her—Emma.

Infatuated young Hardy managed just one more surreptitious meeting with Julia Martin at a harvest supper, in the course of which he declared, lover-like, that he would never desert her, before she and her husband sold the estate and moved to London, settling in Bruton Street in wealthy May-fair. Shortly after his arrival in the city, to Bruton Street Hardy bent his foot-steps, and there paid what was probably the first social 'call' of his life on 'the lady of his earlier passion'. He recognized the butler who opened the door and looked 'little altered' by the ten years that had elapsed since the family left Kingston Maurward . . . 'But the lady of his dreams—alas!' (L 43). Rather than Estella, he found himself facing Miss Havisham. 'Love is lame at fifty years', concludes, somewhat uncharitably, the narrator of 'The Revisitation', a poem that has its origins in this moment of erotic disillu-sionment and his horrified recognition of the physical effects of 'Time's transforming chisel'. Perceiving her former lover's physical recoil from her 'wasted figure', the spurned woman in the poem bursts out:

> 'Can you really wince and wonder
> That the sunlight should reveal you such a thing of skin and bone,
> As if unaware a Death's-head must of need lie not far under
>   Flesh whose years out-count your own?' (CP 194)

Yet, twelve years on from what turned out to be their final meeting, Hardy was still prone to erotic fantasies about her. In 1874 she wrote to congratulate him on the popular success of *Far from the Madding Crowd*:

> She was now quite an elderly lady, but by signing her letter 'Julia Augusta' she revived throbs of tender feeling in him, and brought back to his memory the thrilling 'frou-frou' of her four grey silk flounces when she had used to bend over him, and when they brushed against the font as she entered church on Sundays. He replied, but, as it appears, did not go to see her. Thus though their eyes never met again after his call on her in London, nor their lips from the time when she had held him in her arms, who can say that both occurrences might not have been in the order of things, if he had developed their reacquaintance earlier, now that she was in her widowhood, with nothing to hinder her mind from rolling back upon her past. (L 104–105)

Hardy's penchant for speculating on what might have been is taken to bewildering heights here, especially since he would have received this letter only a short time after his marriage to Emma—and is recalling his responses to it many decades later. Michael Millgate is surely right to suggest that the autobiographical intensity informing the pages that Hardy recycled from *The Poor Man and the Lady* and used in 'An Indiscretion' derive in part from his feelings for a woman the mere sight of whose name triggers such an expansive erotic reverie.

The swing from the actuality of her elderliness to the memory of the sound of her flounces in church, which in turn begets thoughts of the physical intimacy they might have shared together, is interestingly reversed in the opening scene of 'An Indiscretion', which is set in Stinsford or Tollamore Church. Egbert is overwhelmingly conscious of the beautiful young Geraldine Allenville, whose life he'd saved from the wheel of a threshing machine a few days earlier, alone in her private pew, while he sits with the rest of the congregation:

> Over her head rose a vast marble monument, erected to the memory of her ancestors, male and female; for she was one of high standing in the parish. . . . As the youthful schoolmaster gazed, and all these details

became dimmer, her face was modified in his fancy, till it seemed almost to resemble the carved marble skull immediately above her head. The thought was unpleasant enough to arouse him from his half-dreamy state, and he entered on rational considerations of what a vast gulf lay between that lady and himself, what a troublesome world it was to live in where such divisions could exist, and how painful was the evil when a man of his unequal history was possessed of a keen susceptibility. (AI 44)

It is by moving to London and writing novels that Egbert Mayne sets about bridging the 'vast gulf' between himself and Geraldine. Poetry, initially anyway, was to be Hardy's route to improving his 'unequal history'.[20] His visit to Bruton Street inspired the earliest of the London poems to survive, 'Amabel', which, although less trenchant and cruel than 'The Revisitation', is also about a woman felled by 'Time the tyrant'.[21]

> I marked her ruined hues,
> Her custom-straitened views,
> And asked, 'Can there indwell
> My Amabel?'
>
> I looked upon her gown,
> Once rose, now earthen brown;
> The change was like the knell
> Of Amabel.
>
> Her step's mechanic ways
> Had lost the life of May's;
> Her laugh, once sweet in swell,
> Spoilt Amabel. (CP 8)

When Hardy eventually came to publish 'Amabel', which follows 'The Temporary the All' in *Wessex Poems*, he included an illustration of an hourglass with most of the sand run out, either side of which are two butterflies, symbols of transience, one perched on the lower half of the hourglass (with Hardy's initials directly below it), the other on the ground. The attack on

her 'custom-straitened views' makes Amabel seem, like Florence Henniker
and Sue Bridehead, one of Hardy's gallery of women who have betrayed the
Shelleyan ideals of free love they seemed to espouse, while 'mechanic' is a
word he often associated with the effect of London on the imagination. A
further, and specifically London-related, irony lurks in the name chosen for
the woman whose 'earthen brown' gown suggests that, while she is not yet
quite dead, she is, like the left-hand butterfly, no longer likely to fly. For
Amabel is the name of the young heroine of Harrison Ainsworth's *Old
St. Paul's*.[22] Although the daughter of a grocer, this Amabel is so beautiful
that the evil Rochester is for a time converted from his nefarious ways by
marriage to her—a marriage that he thought, and intended to be, a fake one,
but which actually turns out, after a number of preposterous plot turns, to
be legal. The apprentice Leonard Holt, with whom Hardy identified, is as
devoted to Amabel as the child Hardy was to Julia Augusta, but is eventually bested by the cunning earl and forced, to quote from the poem 'Amabel', to 'leave her to her fate', which turns out to be the gruesome one of
being deliberately infected with the plague and dying with neither the
faithful Holt nor the repentant Rochester by her side. By giving the ageing
Amabel of the poem the name of the desirable young heroine of the novel
that made such an impression on him when young, Hardy again combines
female freshness and beauty with an awareness of the skull beneath
the skin.

A perspective somewhat antithetical, however, to the poem's overall tone
of romantic lament also briefly emerges. In the *Life* Hardy recalls attending
the funeral of Charles Darwin in Westminster Abbey on 26 April 1882 and
adds: 'As a young man he had been among the earliest acclaimers of *The Origin of Species*' (L 158), which was published in 1859 when Hardy was nineteen. No one has ever discovered exactly how this acclaiming was done, but
a glimpse is surely offered into the impact of Darwin on Hardy's thinking in
stanza five of 'Amabel':

> Knowing that, though Love cease,
> Love's race shows no decrease;
> All find in dorp or dell
>   An Amabel.[23]

From his early passion for Julia Augusta Martin, thirty years his senior, to his infatuation as an old man with Gertrude Bugler (the Wessex Players' Tess) who was born fifty-seven years after him, Hardy's power to fall in love is undoubtedly one of the most striking aspects of his life and central to the vitality and longevity of his imagination. The glance at Darwinian theories of the compulsive propagation of the species allows the battle between instinct and convention played out in Hardy's work to register as itself a testimony of love showing 'no decrease'. However impossible the loves that Hardy pursued, the 'throbbings of noontide' (CP 81) that animate his writing are, in light of the discoveries of Darwin, evidence of the most practical drive of all: the urge to 'traverse old love's domain' (CP 352), however often he abjured it, yet again.

3

Crass Clanging Town

I

After over a year of sharing lodgings in Kilburn, Hardy moved to 16 West-bourne Park Villas, a street parallel to the Great Western Railway line running west out of Paddington. There he rented a room of his own, at the back, on the top floor. It had a pleasant view over gardens and the roofs and chimneys of the houses on Westbourne Park Road as well as, off to the right, the spire of St. Stephen's Church. Hardy made an ink sketch from his window on the evening of 22 June 1866, including, on what must be his desk in the foreground, a couple of books. The caption records precisely the time the drawing was made: '1/2 past 8 evening'.[1] It was in this room, after work and on weekends, that he accomplished the extensive course of reading that he set himself and transcribed, occasionally with his own reformulations, into his notebook headed 'Studies, Specimens &c.' lines and passages from *The Golden Treasury* and the Bible as well as the work of favourite poets such as Scott and Swinburne and Shelley.[2] And here he embarked on his own lit-erary career, writing poems and dispatching them to the editors of various unidentified magazines. All, he tells us in the *Life*, were returned.

It's a great shame that no traces survive in the archives of any poetry-publishing newspapers or journals of the 1860s indicating what pieces Hardy submitted and the reasons for their rejection. Although in various ways anomalous and distinctive, the poems written by Hardy in London in his twenties are at nowhere near as acute an angle to the dominant conventions of the day as those of, say, Gerard Manley Hopkins or Emily Dickinson. The influence of both Robert and Elizabeth Barrett Browning, as well as of George Meredith's *Modern Love*, published in 1862, is at times clear. It is also uncertain in what state he sent them out—or to put it another way, how much he rewrote these poems before publishing them in *Wessex Poems* (where the majority appear) and subsequent volumes. In the *Life* he tells us 'it was by the mere change of a few words or the rewriting of a line or two' that he made them 'quite worthy of publication' (L 49). It was often Hardy's habit to destroy the original manuscript after finishing a revised version, making it impossible to know exactly what words or lines were changed. In reflecting on the rejection slips that he accrued over these years in the *Life*, he declares himself grateful for being 'saved from the annoyance of seeing his early crude effusions crop up in later life', but his disappointment also on occasion creeps through; like many a young poet, it didn't take him too long to arrive at the conclusion that the editors of the magazines who rejected his work 'did not know good poetry from bad' (L 51).

The only poet mentioned in the *Life* in relation to these early 'effusions' is John Donne: 'It is somewhat unusual that he was not so keenly anxious to get into print as most young men are found to be, in this indifference, as in some qualities of his verse, curiously resembling Donne' (L 51). It was the conventions of manuscript culture rather than indifference that kept Donne, for the most part, out of print, but the connection is an interesting one. Donne was by no means a popular poet in the mid-Victorian era: he had no poems at all selected for inclusion in the 1861 edition of *The Golden Treasury*, and indeed his work has often been seen as completely antithetical to Victorian poetic ideals.[3] In his influential essay of 1921, 'The Metaphysical Poets', T. S. Eliot championed the 'intellectual poet', exemplified by Donne, of the golden age before the 'dissociation of sensibility' set in, over the merely 'reflective poet' of the Victorian era: 'Tennyson and Browning think; but they do not feel their thought as immediately as the odour of a rose. A thought to Donne was an experience; it modified his sensibility.'[4] Donne does not feature in Hardy's 'Studies, Specimens &c.' notebook, while quite a lot of *In Memoriam* gets copied out, but his poetry of the 1860s is undoubtedly much closer to that of Donne than that of Tennyson. Like the poetry of Donne, Hardy's early verse makes serious, indeed strenuous attempts to digest the implications of new scientific discoveries that, if accepted, call into question the entire metaphysical belief-system of the day; like many of Donne's *Songs and Sonnets*, Hardy's early love poems are disputatious, dramatic, sceptical, self-conscious, antilyrical, and obsessed with ways of defining separation rather than the possibilities of 'junctive law fulfilling', to use a Donnean phrase from 'Revulsion' (CP 14). Further, Donne's brilliance, his need to dazzle the reader with the ingenuity of his conceits and the 'masculine persuasive force' ('Elegy 11: On His Mistress') of his arguments, channel and refract the anxieties generated by the specifically urban contexts in which the poems happen, and were written. Hardy is rarely as directly aggressive or hectoring as Donne can sometimes be, but the analogy is useful in suggesting the extent to which the idiom and concerns of his early poetry can be seen as shaped by his experience of city life, and in particular by the heightened tensions that the 'crass clanging town' ('From Her in the Country', CP 234) induces between private emotions and public display.

Surveying the capital by night from the hill beyond Kilburn in 'An Indiscretion in the Life of an Heiress', Egbert Mayne observes what these days would be called 'light pollution'—'the vast haze of light extending to the length and breadth of London' (AI 89). Hardy's early poem 'In Vision I Roamed' raises the eyes above the bewildering, dwarfing spectacle of the illuminated modern city to the even more bewildering and dwarfing spectacle of the modern night sky. Both inculcate in the protagonist, like the crowds observed from Waterloo Bridge by the new arrival in Hardy's speech to The Society of Dorset Men in London, 'a vivid sense of his own insignificance', of 'isolation and loneliness' (PW 220). 'In Vision I Roamed' is Hardy's earliest poetic response to the 'New Astronomy', a term of Johannes Kepler's revived by certain nineteenth-century astronomers to emphasize how their discoveries were changing the concept of space as radically as Kepler's *Astronomia Nova* of 1609 had altered the attitudes to the heavens of such as Donne.[5] While Darwin and Spencer were showing the Earth to be far older than had been assumed, astronomers like John Herschel were proving the universe to be far larger than had previously been thought. Hardy may have come across or read about Herschel's *General Catalogue of Nebulae and Clusters of Stars*, which was published in 1864, and vastly expanded the number of entries included in his father William Herschel's earlier *Catalogue of*

Nebulae and Clusters of Stars. Hardy would explore the implications of the discovery of 'outer space' (a term coined in the Victorian era) most fully in *Two on a Tower* of 1882. Like the novel, 'In Vision I Roamed' is concerned not only with developments in astronomy but with the effects that an awareness of the dizzying vastness of the universe can have on human relations. It's a sonnet dedicated to an unspecified person ('To—'), leading one to expect a love poem. Like so many of Donne's love poems, however, it's not afraid to baffle before delivering its compliments:

> In vision I roamed the flashing Firmament,
> So fierce in blazon that the Night waxed wan,
> As though with awe at orbs of such osténit;
> And as I thought my spirit ranged on and on
>
> In footless traverse through ghast heights of sky,
> To the last chambers of the monstrous Dome,
> Where stars the brightest here are lost to the eye:
> Then, any spot on our own Earth seemed Home!
>
> And the sick grief that you were far away
> Grew pleasant thankfulness that you were near,
> Who might have been, set on some foreign Sphere,
> Less than a want to me, as day by day
> I lived unware, uncaring all that lay
> Locked in that Universe taciturn and drear. (CP 9–10)

Of the fifteen sonnets that Hardy preserved from the years 1865–1866, seven are in the voice of a woman. The elliptical dedication creates the impression that 'In Vision I Roamed' is spoken by a man, and indeed derives from an actual relationship, but its argument is certainly of the kind that would appeal to the Elizabeth-Jane of the end of *The Mayor of Casterbridge*, who is described as finding happiness to 'consist in the cunning enlargement by a species of microscopic treatment, of those minute forms of satisfaction that offer themselves to everybody not in positive pain' (MC 309). The comfort that the poem posits for the 'sick grief' of separation is that the beloved

was not born on some 'foreign Sphere' in a remote part of the universe, since
that would have left the speaker wholly 'unware' that she had ever come into
being. It's a conceit that serves to increase rather than minimize the distance
between the lovers, marooning them in the poem's final lines on different
planets, and picturing them completely ignorant of each other's existence.
The fear of contingency that drives the ingenious metaphors with which
Donne tries to imagine his lovers united, even if only as a bracelet of hair
around the wrist of a skeleton, is surely one of the 'qualities' that links early
Hardy with the Renaissance poet. Rather than a love poem, 'In Vision I
Roamed' comes to seem a meditation on randomness and incomprehensi-
bility; indeed the very notion of 'Home' feels absurd in relation to the inter-
stellar vistas explored by its imagery.[6]

The poem's discomforting subjection of the conventions of the love sonnet
to the cosmic perspectives opened up by the new astronomy is answered in
part by a poem of the same year, 'The Musing Maiden'. Like so many of the
poems that Hardy composed in London, it rings changes on the conceit of
separation. The maiden, like the speaker of 'From Her in the Country', is
explicitly located in a rural district, and her musings concern fantastical ways
of connecting with her London-based lover, although its last line rather calls
into question the degree to which her passion is reciprocated. Rambling over
the 'hog-backed down', she allows herself to 'think the breeze that stroked
his lip / Over my own may slip', and that the highway she walks 'reaches to
his feet: / A meditation sweet':

> When coasters hence to London sail
> I watch their puffed wings waning pale;
> His window opens near the quay;
>   Their coming he can see.
>
> I go to meet the moon at night;
> To mark the moon was our delight;
> Up there our eyesights touch at will
>   If such he practise still. (CP 903)

The moon here is a comforting token that is shared—or at least possibly
shared—by the parted lovers, rather than one of the innumerable 'orbs' that

make the night sky of 'In Vision I Roamed' attract words such as 'footless', 'ghast', and 'monstrous'. If the poems are read as antithetical companion pieces in the mysterious, shadowy dialogue between Her and Him developed in Hardy's early poems, then once again doubting Thomas seems to be taking evasive action, while the musing and much more enthusiastic maiden has no qualms about directly declaring herself, as in the opening line of 'She, to Him III': 'I will be faithful to thee; aye, I will!' (CP 15).

Although in many ways a pretty generic lyric, 'The Musing Maiden' may well be Hardy's most explicit poetic acknowledgement of his relationship with Eliza Bright Nicholls, with whom he seems to have been involved, although how deeply it's impossible to say, during his years in London. She spent much of her childhood in Kimmeridge Bay, on the east Dorset coast, where her father was a coastguard. The first 'She, to Him' sonnet is illustrated in *Wessex Poems* by a picture of an appropriately nebulous couple walking a winding path up a hill towards a tower that has been identified as Clavell Tower, a cliff-top Tuscan-style folly that was erected just above Kimmeridge Bay in 1830. Hardy was certainly in this region in early September of 1863, for he made dated sketches, now in the Dorset County Museum, of nearby Gad Cliff and Worbarrow Bay. Eliza's parents had moved by then to Findon, just north of Worthing in Sussex, where Hardy visited over Whitsun of 1866, a trip recorded by a sketch he made of the village church. It's not clear where the 'coasters' of 'The Musing Maiden' set sail from, but in both Findon and Kimmeridge Eliza was close to the sea, while Hardy's window in 8 Adelphi Terrace offered a fine view of boats docking at quays on both banks of the Thames.

Evidence of Eliza's importance to Hardy is so vague and circumstantial that she escaped the attention of his first modern biographer, Robert Gittings, altogether. It is indicative of the complexity of the relationship between the private and the public in Hardy's life and writing that he should, on the one hand, have erased all traces of her presence from the record, and yet, when it came to publishing the poems written under her aegis, feel compelled to introduce them with a clue to the experiences from which they emerged. The picture is itself in conflict with the couple depicted in the poems, who are never side by side, let alone hand in hand. Indeed, in just one poem are they actually in each other's company, the desolate 'Neutral Tones', which functions as a bleak finale to the sequence and offers instruction merely in romantic disillusionment—'keen lessons that love deceives, / And wrings with wrong' (CP 12).

Like his cousin Martha Sparks, Eliza was in service. She worked as a lady's maid to Emma Hoare, who lived with her barrister husband in Orsett Terrace, a couple of streets east of Westbourne Park Villas. Prayer book annotations reveal that Hardy attended services at St. Stephen's Church in Paddington, where she worshipped, on several occasions while he was still living in Kilburn. 'Do you ever write to Eliza?' he questions his sister Mary in his letter of 3 November 1863 (CL 1:2), which would indicate, if it's indeed Eliza Nicholls that he is referring to, that Hardy introduced her to at least one other member of his family. Hardy gave her his photograph (now in the Beinecke Library in Yale) taken in 1862 or 1863. By all accounts Eliza was extremely pious, whereas in the course of his London residence Hardy's faith gradually but steadily weakened. While there may, as Nicholls family traditions hold, have been an 'understanding' or even an engagement between them, their relationship must have been carried out mainly by letter, for she moved from London to Godstone in Surrey sometime in the latter part of 1863 to care for her employer's father, Archdeacon Hoare, in his final illness and after his death moved back into the family home in Findon. Hardy last visited her there in early 1867, the year that he wrote 'Neutral Tones', which describes a pond that has tentatively been identified by Michael Millgate as one just west of Findon near Tolmare Farm (MM 96).

In the passages describing his childhood and adolescence in the *Life*, Hardy freely admits to falling in love with all and sundry: after Mrs Martin there was a pretty girl on horseback whose name he never learned; another who'd lived in Windsor but was disappointingly uninterested in Harrison Ainsworth's *Windsor Castle* (1842); there was Elizabeth Bishop, the gamekeeper's daughter; and the farmer's daughter, Louisa Harding. Some of these infatuations would eventually beget tripping lyrics such as 'To Lizbie Brown' and 'To Louisa in the Lane' (L 29–30). The sequence that Hardy wrote in London about a relationship between the poet and a nameless woman derives, instead, from the complex rhetoric of Donne's love poems and Shakespeare's sonnets, and from the anatomy of a marriage heading for divorce so unsparingly dramatized by Meredith in the fifty sixteen-line sonnets of *Modern Love*. The difficult emotions brought into play make taxing demands of the language at Hardy's command: 'Love is lovelier / The more it shapes its moans in selfish-wise' ('She, to Him IV', CP 16). 'Neutral Tones' itemizes in painful, draining detail the couple's mutual exhaustion of all the signifiers with which they'd attempted to express and exchange their love: 'Your eyes on me were as eyes that rove / Over tedious riddles of years ago'; 'The smile on your mouth was the deadest thing / Alive enough to have strength to die' (CP 12). Indeed, this exhaustion is all they still share. The poem marks some kind of loss of innocence presented, in its final verse, as a decisive initiation into a world whose laws are inflexible and inescapable, making it hard to imagine that such a devastating analysis of love's failure was wholly invented. Alas, no names or details of the women that Hardy met, or even admired from afar, surface in his autobiographical account of his London years. Louisa Harding, whom he used to visit in Dorset on his trips down from the city until he was twenty-three or twenty-four, is the last woman mentioned as having caught his evidently roving eye until his trip in March of 1870 to St. Juliot Rectory, where he met Emma. With his arrival in London in April of 1862 and his dispiriting *rencontre* with the lady of his dreams that occurred soon after, the *Life* falls silent on the subjects of erotic attraction and romantic disappointment.

Of course Hardy's thoughts didn't fall silent too; the only glimpse, however, that we get of them is the entry that he made in his diary on his twenty-fifth birthday: 'Wondered what woman, if any, I should be thinking about in five years' time' (L 52). At Blomfield's office he was surrounded by metropolitan chatter of the fashionable beauties occupying the attention of the popular press. 'Any spice in the papers?' was often the opening query of the day. Hardy was probably not the one who responded: 'The ladies talked about by the architect's pupils and other young men into whose society Hardy was thrown were Cora Pearl, "Skittles", Agnes Willoughby, Adah Menken, and others successively, of whom they professed to know many romantic and *risqué* details, but really knew nothing at all' (L 43). His somewhat tart comment on their ignorance makes clear that he was not drawn to following the adventures of demi-mondaines such as Catherine Walters (aka 'Skittles'), although her ascent through the echelons of society would in some respects resemble his own: her much-celebrated horseback appearances on Rotten Row in Hyde Park, where the beau monde paraded

on horses and in carriages, attracted large crowds in the 1860s. Hardy undoubtedly on occasion joined the throng gawping at the stream of vehicles
and equestrians in Hyde Park on late afternoons in the Season, for he has
Mrs Swancourt take Elfride there in chapter 14 of *A Pair of Blue Eyes* and
instruct her in the semiotics of High Society's self-display. The satire of the
episode is genial rather than caustic, yet it also offers a good instance of
Hardy's fascinatingly conflicted feelings about the parts played by artifice
and nature in women's power to attract. 'And what lovely flowers and leaves
they wear in their bonnets!' artlessly exclaims Elfride of some passing
ladies:

> 'O yes,' returned Mrs. Swancourt. 'Some of them are even more striking
> in colour than any real ones. Look at that beautiful rose worn by the
> lady inside the rails. Elegant vine-tendrils introduced upon the stem
> as an improvement upon prickles, and all growing so naturally just over
> her ear—I say *growing* advisedly, for the pink of the petals and the pink
> of her handsome cheeks are equally from Nature's hand to the eyes of
> the most casual observer.' (PBE 131)[7]

Jude's disgust at Arabella's hairpiece is faintly foreshadowed here, while
Elfride's innocent admiration resembles that of the country girl in the poem
'The Ruined Maid', written in 1866:

> 'I wish I had feathers, a fine sweeping gown,
> And a delicate face, and could strut about Town!'—
> 'My dear—a raw country girl, such as you be,
> Cannot quite expect that. You ain't ruined,' said she. (CP 159)

The music-hall humour of the poem, like the knowing mockery of Mrs Swancourt's observations, allow Hardy a firm grip on the performance of the
erotic in relation to the social codes of the city.

Hardy's own profound personal reluctance to accept or engage in such
public codifications of desire is captured, paradoxically of course, in the love
sonnet, or rather antilove sonnet, 'Revulsion' (1866), which explores the Laodicean, or lukewarm, aspects of Hardy's sensibility, in particular in rela-

tion to his ability to commit himself to love. It offers another demonstration
of what he calls in the *Life* his 'lack of social ambition', his unwillingness to
'grow up' and 'be a man' (L 20):

> Though I waste watches framing words to fetter
> Some spirit to mine own in clasp and kiss,
> Out of the night there looms a sense 'twere better
> To fail obtaining whom one fails to miss.
>
> For winning love we win the risk of losing,
> And losing love is as one's life were riven;
> It cuts like contumely and keen ill-using
> To cede what was superfluously given.
>
> Let me then feel no more the fateful thrilling
> That devastates the love-worn wooer's frame,
> The hot ado of fevered hopes, the chilling
> That agonizes disappointed aim!
> So may I live no junctive law fulfilling,
> And my heart's table bear no woman's name. (CP 14)

The highly unnatural taboo that Hardy's mother placed on her children's
relations with members of the opposite sex was surely a powerful influence
on the erratic fluctuations of Hardy's responses to women, so vividly evoked
in his depictions of the sexual frustrations endured by such as Jude and Giles
Winterborne of the *The Woodlanders* (1887). It was Jemima's hope that her
four children would live as sibling couples, Thomas and Mary together and
Henry and Kate together. Only Thomas summoned up the courage required
to defy her in this. 'Revulsion' obliquely suggests how Jemima's deeply en-
grained distrust of 'junctive law' battled in her son with the 'fateful thrilling'
and 'fevered hopes' inspired by falling in love. The borrowing of terms from
Hamlet ('the proud man's contumely' [III, 1, l. 70]) and Sonnet 24 ('in table
of my heart' [l. 2]) emphasizes the literariness of the poet's refusal to risk
suffering the pangs of despised affection, a literariness that comes to seem
a deliberately deployed sublimation of the urge to 'clasp and kiss'. It is,

nevertheless, somewhat surprising to find in this sonnet, so replete with echoes of Shakespeare, no *volta*, no 'and yet' followed by a rejection of its rejection of love. It persists, one might say, in its commitment to detachment, to lukewarmness, with impassioned fervour. Its final lines would certainly have pleased Jemima, who passed on to her son an unremitting determination to be one of the less deceived; in a notebook entitled 'Memoranda I' Hardy made this entry for 30 October 1870: 'Mother's notion, & also mine: That a figure stands in our van with arm uplifted, to knock us back from any pleasant prospect we indulge in as probable' (PN 6–7).

'Where do these / Innate assumptions come from?' asked Philip Larkin, Hardy's successor to the role of laureate of the less deceived. It is 'out of the night' that the philosophy articulated in 'Revulsion' 'looms', while that of Larkin's 'Dockery and Son' is figured as 'sand-clouds, thick and close'.[8] Both poems are concerned with what it means 'to fail obtaining whom one fails to miss'; 'To have no son, no wife, / No house or land still seemed quite natural', broods Larkin's narrator, as entrenched as Hardy's in his determination to remain unattached. The instinct behind 'Revulsion' can, I think, be profitably expanded beyond the realm of love to include a more general unwillingness to enter the public arena, an unwillingness strong in the 'assumptions' of both Hardy and Larkin. In both poets, this reluctance, however voluntarily or involuntarily communicated, contributes significantly to the appeal of their work to the vast audiences that they acquired. 'A certain man', Hardy observed in a notebook entry from 1866–1867 included at the end of the London chapter of the *Life*, 'He creeps away to a meeting with his own sensations' (L 56). However often he translated these sensations, which had to be dealt with cautiously in privacy rather than acted on in the social moment, into fictions and poems that were then successfully brought to the public's attention, the spirit of 'Revulsion' that loomed out of the night as Hardy worked away on his sequence of love sonnets (most of which he later destroyed) in the 'waste watches' in his room in Westbourne Park Villas was never entirely quelled. It re-emerged, for instance, in the oft-quoted remark that he made to Florence shortly before his death: 'He said that if he had his life over again he would prefer to be a small architect in a county town, like Mr Hicks at Dorchester, to whom he was articled' (L 478).

II

In a number of the sonnets that escaped the cull, Hardy presents himself in the act of reading or writing. 'I lingered through the night to break of day', he reports in 'Her Definition', about a *nuit blanche* spent trying to find an epithet that will do justice to the beloved, though he ends up only with the 'homely wording' of 'That maiden mine!' (CP 220). Such self-figurations bolster the image of Hardy as 'an isolated student' that is put forward in the *Life*, one more often to be found in his garret than out breasting 'the billows of London' (L 58). This is the complaint of the woman in 'Her Reproach', whose opening lines set up a contrast between the poet busy at his books indoors and her endurance of inclement weather outside, although it's possible that these 'biting blasts' may also be a metaphor for malicious gossip. This sonnet is a good example of Philip Larkin's contention that every Hardy poem has 'a little spinal cord of thought' that keeps one interested, however idiosyncratic its vocabulary or argument.[9]

> Con the dead page as 'twere live love: press on!
> Cold wisdom's words will ease thy track for thee;
> Aye, go; cast off sweet ways, and leave me wan
> To biting blasts that are intent on me.
>
> But if thy object Fame's far summits be,
> Whose inclines many a skeleton overlies
> That missed both dream and substance, stop and see
> How absence wears these cheeks and dims these eyes!
>
> It surely is far sweeter and more wise
> To water love, than toil to leave anon
> A name whose glory-gleam will but advise
> Invidious minds to eclipse it with their own,
>
> And over which the kindliest will but stay
> A moment; musing, 'He, too, had his day!' (CP 135)

In the first quatrain the cold words he pores over in his room are contrasted with her bitter outdoor suffering, and the dead page that he reads is contrasted with her live love, while in the second quatrain the skeletons of failed would-be writers are played off against the skeletal appearance that she is assuming as a result of his neglect of her. While not as spectacular as Donne, the connections and contrasts are deftly made and testify to Hardy's absorption of metaphysical deployments of imagery. The wider interest of the poem, however, derives from its attempt to triangulate the three competing but interlocking narrative strands of Hardy's London years. The first is the narrative of his private life, spent in rigorous self-education, the 'toil' of reading and writing undertaken principally for its own sake but possibly with the distant hope of future fame. The second is the narrative of his social and amative life, in this case his relations with a woman who begs him to 'water love', an image conjuring up the 'sweet' and 'wise', if bourgeois, ideal of a marriage that might put an end to his studies and destroy his imagined literary career, but who is also necessary to him, since she is the inspiration of the poem, and indeed its speaker. The third is the narrative of public fame that might result from his studies and literary experiments but whose 'glory-gleam' is imagined as turning, if not quite to ashes, to tepid approbation that barely justifies the sacrifices required to achieve it, especially given that pursuit of this fame will involve him in competition with 'invidious minds', that is, entry into the public sphere of the literary rat race. The dramatic framing of the sonnet enables Hardy to use it to juggle and rehearse rather than resolve these divided aims, and to ponder rather than heal his fragmented, uncertain sense of both his present self and his possible futures. The question to which the poem, in its oblique way, seems to be seeking an answer can perhaps best be summed up by the title of a Wallace Stevens poem: 'How to Live, What to Do'.

Hardy's use of a female speaker in his early poetry looks forward to the extraordinary powers of imaginative sympathy that he brought to bear on the creation of characters such as Tess, Elizabeth-Jane, Viviette of *Two on a Tower*, and *The Woodlanders*'s Grace Melbury. Indeed one of the 'She, to Him' sonnets is 'prosed' almost directly in *Desperate Remedies* into a speech by Cytherea Graye, lending credence to the claim made by Eliza Nicholls, according at any rate to her niece, that she was the model for the heroine of

Hardy's first published novel (Cytherea's character and the novel's plot are discussed in detail in Chapter 4).[10] 'She, to Him II' imagines her long-departed beloved being reminded of her by the features or accent of another woman, and murmuring to himself 'Poor jade!':

> And thus reflecting, you will never see
> That your thin thought, in two small words conveyed,
> Was no such fleeting phantom-thought to me,
> But the Whole Life wherein my part was played;
> And you amid its fitful masquerade
> A Thought—as I in your life seem to be! (CP 15)

The emotional complexity of the poem arises from the disjunction between the private 'Thought' and the public 'masquerade'. The momentary expression of sympathy, 'Poor jade!', has the same status as the dismissive critical judgement, 'He, too, had his day!', in 'Her Reproach', or indeed the epithet 'That maiden mine!', which is all that emerges from a whole night of composition in 'Her Definition'. Hardy seems to be marvelling at the radical, one might say outrageous, incompatibility between the inner life and the outer forms that that inner life assumes both in one's own words and in those of others. 'But ah, Owen', Cytherea muses miserably to her brother just before giving her prose version of the sonnet, 'it is difficult to adjust our outer and inner life with perfect honesty to all! Though it may be right to care more for the benefit of the many than for the indulgence of your own single self, when you consider that the many, and duty to them, only exist to you through your own existence, what can be said?' (DR 236).

The question, like that posed in 'Her Reproach', is unanswerable. The pathos of Cytherea's outburst is given perspective in the context of the novel by the reader's knowledge of the social pressures and plot convolutions that have brought her to wed the reckless and scheming, but erotically charged, Aeneas Manston, while the conventions of sensation fiction allow one to feel fairly confident that her distress is the darkest hour before the dawn, rather than a recognition of a terrible and irreversible event of the kind that ruins the life of Tess. The poem's exploration of these ideas has no such steadying guy ropes, and its sadness can only be deepened by the knowledge that

Eliza Nicholls never married, and twisted deeper still if the story told by her niece is true—that she called at Max Gate after Emma's death in the hope that the internationally famous writer would now make good on the 'understanding' that he had entered into some fifty years earlier (MM 96).

It is the concluding sentence of the speech delivered by Cytherea, and Owen's response to it, that express most directly the mixture of sensitivity and indifference operative in 'She, to Him II':

'And they will pause just for an instant, and give a sigh to me, and think, "Poor girl," believing they do great justice to my memory by this. But they will never, never realize that it was my single opportunity of existence, as well as of doing my duty, which they are regarding; they will not feel that what to them is but a thought, easily held in those two words of pity, "Poor girl," was a whole life to me; as full of hours, minutes, and peculiar minutes, of hopes and dreads, smiles, whisperings, tears, as theirs: that it was my world, what is to them their world, and they in that life of mine, however much I cared for them, only as the thought I seem to them to be. Nobody can enter into another's nature truly, that's what is so grievous.' (DR 236)

To which Owen answers, 'Well, it cannot be helped.' Something of Hardy's horror at the thought of going to sleep in a city harbouring 'four million heads and eight million eyes' (L 141) can be discerned here: Cytherea is able to generalize, as the poem can't, on the limits of imaginative sympathy, but her experience of these limits as frustrating or 'grievous' aligns her impulses with those of her imaginative, and consequently vulnerable, creator. Owen, on the other hand, responds in the 'mechanic' or 'practical' way that Hardy discovered to be necessary for success in the struggle for survival amidst the overwhelming tide 'of hopes and dreads, smiles, whisperings, tears' experienced by the 4 million around him.

If Eliza did indeed visit Hardy between the death of Emma and his marriage to Florence in the hope of resuming relations, then she would have caught up in life with her poetic avatar: the first of the 'She, to Him' sonnets imagines the pair meeting up in old age, and her asking in its concluding lines: 'Will you not grant to old affection's claim / The hand of friendship down Life's sunless hill?' (CP 15). The lines shadow forth the notion of 'lov-ingkindness' (CP 136) that Hardy came to see as the most valuable counter-weight to misery and wrongdoing, a quality he accuses Florence Henniker of lacking in the poem in which he uses the term, 'A Broken Appointment', which describes her failure to show up to a rendezvous at the British Museum. And, looking yet further forward, they would acquire a characteristically caustic spin when rewritten by Philip Larkin as the concluding couplet of 'Toads Revisited' of 1962: 'Give me your arm, old toad; / Help me down Cemetery Road.'[11] But then Hardy himself dreamt up an even more morbid and extreme image of helpless mutuality in a poem that he set five years after Larkin's was composed: '1967', written in 1867, attempts to picture life a hundred years in the future and, in melioristic fashion, tries to anticipate the twentieth century as showing 'at its prime, / A scope above this blinkered time'; 'Yet what to me', he interrupts himself,

> how far above?
> For I would only ask thereof
> That thy worm should be my worm, Love! (CP 220)

As old people holding hands, as bodies eaten by the same worm—these im-ages are as far as Hardy could get when it came to figuring reciprocal phys-ical relations between his 'lovers'.

The most explicitly erotic of the sonnets is 'She, to Him IV', a poem of jealousy possibly inspired by a flirtation between Hardy and Eliza's sister Jane.[12] It stands out from the other 'She, to Him' sonnets in being propelled by an impassioned energy sufficient to overcome caution and social mores, and prefigures the heart-rending account of the sexual attraction to Angel suffered by the Talbothays milkmaids in chapter 23 of *Tess*, which leaves them 'writh[ing] feverishly under the oppressiveness of an emotion thrust on them by cruel Nature's law—an emotion which they had neither expected nor desired', reducing each to a 'portion of one organism called sex' (T 162). Jealousy frequently drives desire into action in Hardy's fiction and poetry. In 'She, to Him IV' Hardy's language turns explicitly Donnean in its attempts to record the transformation of identity wrought upon one's 'separateness' by a love that obliterates all previously held or conventional perspectives on life:

How much I love I know not, life not known,
Save as one unit I would add love by;
But this I know, my being is but thine own—
Fused from its separateness by ecstasy. (CP 16)

The infatuation of the milkmaids Izz and Retty and Marian is described as 'ecstasizing them to a killing joy', even though they know that they have no hope of winning Angel as a husband. While Donne's 'extasie', in the poem of that name, is a conceit that enables a complex dialogue between man and woman and body and soul, for both the Talbothays milkmaids and for the woman of 'She, to Him IV', 'ecstasy' is solitary and corporeal, the physical, involuntary symptom of ungratified desire. 'Lovingkindness' has no purchase on 'cruel Nature's law', and clearly Hardy's reading of Darwin had, as early as the mid-1860s, shaped his sense of an irresolvable antagonism between sexual compulsions and what *Tess* calls 'the eye of civilization'. Yet there is also an unnerving, even Gothic element in the passion of the speaker of the poem, who curses her rival and prays for her death. Like Lady Macbeth, she 'puts all humanity' from her and articulates in the poem's final lines a vision of love at quite the opposite end of the spectrum from, say, the happy companionship we are invited to imagine Gabriel and Bathsheba enjoying at the end of *Far from the Madding Crowd*. The speaker's passion is closer to that of the *amour fou* of Boldwood:

Believe me, Lost One, Love is lovelier
The more it shapes its moan in selfish-wise. (CP 16)

While there is no explicit endorsement of this proto-Lawrentian view of desire, the lines suggest that, like the Tennyson of 'Mariana', Hardy found both expressive freedom and poetic originality, as well as, perhaps, a measure of psychic relief, in the use of a female poetic speaker abandoned by her lover.

Some of the more peculiar entries in the 'Studies, Specimens &c.' notebook also register as attempts to channel the pressures of the erotic through the kind of word-spinning performed in the last lines of 'She, to Him IV', which bring to mind, in their alliterative intensity, some of the verbal experiments that Gerard Manley Hopkins embarked on roughly ten years later.

Hardy would take passages from Old Testament prophetic books such as Isaiah, Jeremiah, Ezekiel, and Habakkuk, and use them as the basis for passages of free association that often deploy the vocabulary of love: 'Woe unto them', opens Isaiah X, which Hardy transforms into 'woe unto kisses'. Verse 2 of this chapter is an attack on the greed of tyrants (the words in bold are those picked up by Hardy): '**To turn aside** the **needy** from judgment, and to take away the right from the poor of my people, that widows may be their prey, and that they may rob the **fatherless!**' 'To turn aside', runs Hardy's 'concoction', to use his own term, based on this verse, 'a tear, fondness, thought of me : needy / lips, her needy eyes, glance, my needy / lips, her needy beauty : my hope died / childless' (SS 48). Hardy's freewheeling word clusters are perhaps no more than the equivalent of a pianist's scales, a way of savouring language; but they also imply a somewhat less than reverential attitude towards the Bible. 'O Lord', exclaims Habakkuk, 'how long shall I cry, and thou wilt not hear! even cry out unto thee of **violence**, and thou wilt not save! Why dost thou **shew** me iniquity . . . Therefore the law is **slacked**'. What Hardy calls his 'Concoc: from Hab^k.' uses the trigger words to launch all manner of sensual, even Swinburnian imagery: 'violent kisses : delight / too <u>violent</u> for me : violent days : she <u>showed</u> / <u>me</u> smiles : I thought what the turned years / had <u>showed</u> me : her red spoilt eyes : her / lips slack with sorrow : if time would slack / a little : his love is slacked : the fall of mouth / upon mouth' (SS 70–71). In this particular riff the words are a mere jumping-off point for Hardy rather than a scaffold to which he returns—there are no mouths falling on mouths in Habakkuk.

It is revealing that, even in a private notebook with 'To be <u>destroyed</u>' written above its title, Hardy often reverted to the symbols of the shorthand that he'd acquired to disguise references to parts of the body and to acts relating to sex, while also making use of abbreviations such as 'k–', 'n–k', 'l–p' for *kiss*, *neck*, and *lip* (SS 60–61). Nevertheless, in the passages 'inspired' by runs of words taken from a thesaurus or dictionary, Hardy pushes towards an erotic explicitness that makes certain pages into an abecedarian list of Victorian terms for sexual dalliance. These examples are taken from a section subtitled '<u>Thes.</u>' [i.e., Thesaurus]:

sweet <u>agonies, alert</u> flush, beating kisses, <u>beck</u> of eye, <u>bend</u> of mouth, sweet <u>bends</u> of neck, brim of thy mouth, <u>calms</u> between rushing kisses,

capering thrills, catch of lip by lip, long kisses & short ceasings, sweet
chafe, eager cleavings together, the close of arms ab^t me, slow closes of
thy lips on . . . , long low close of a k–, coil of arms ab^t me, fair curves,
white curves, long dance of sweets, deep dells of thy hair, dip of thy lip
into mine, dip into thy neck, as thy bosom dipped & filled, soft ends
of thy hair, this dear evil. (SS 61–62)

He even set about distorting phrases from Thomas Rickman's *An Attempt
to Discriminate the Styles of Architecture in England, from the Conquest
to the Reformation* into various unarchitectural locutions. Rickman's
'fine hollow mouldings' become 'fine-drawn kisses', his 'flowered capitals'
'flowered braids', and the architectural term 'dripstone', 'drip of tears'. Rickman's 'sweep of mouldings' begets 'sweep of lip', and an erotic rhapsody of
Hardy's own contriving: 'soft suck of thy mouth / (lip) on mine, suck k–s
from my mouth' (SS 62–63 and 142). It is indeed, as its editors observe, remarkable that this notebook escaped being thrown into one of the many
bonfires that consumed Hardy's private papers in the garden at Max Gate,
given his determination to obliterate all records and diaries once they had
been consulted for what they could contribute to the *Life*.

The choice of passages from Rickman's sober and scholarly tome for conversion into the language of the love lyric might be seen as emblematic of the
struggle raging in Hardy, in the years 1865–1867, between his dutiful pursuit
of his career as an architect and his sense that poetry was his true vocation.
The conflict between them is stylized in a poem written not at Westbourne
Park Villas but at his workplace, 8 Adelphi Terrace, and dedicated to his employer, Arthur Blomfield. There is no record of Blomfield's response to
'Heiress and Architect', which restages the battle between the imagination
and scientific truth rehearsed in romantic poems such as Keats's 'Lamia'. The
architect is here the remorseless Apollonius-figure who unweaves the rainbow
of the heiress's visioned hermitage, dismissing all her expansive plans and
insisting, like Apollonius, on 'rule and line' (l. 235). In alternating verses she
propounds her dreams of high halls, wide windows, and ornate interior dec-
orations, and he then vetoes them. Her last request is for a 'narrow winding
turret' in which to grieve at the loss of all her illusions, yet even this receives
short shrift:

> 'Such winding ways
>   Fit not your days,'
> Said he, the man of measuring eye;
> 'I must even fashion as my rule declares,
> To wit: Give space (since life ends unawares)
> To hale a coffined corpse adown the stairs;
>   For you will die.' (CP 76)

If not quite a coded letter of resignation, the poem certainly expresses Hardy's frustration with the 'mechanical' nature of his day-to-day activities, as well as his belief (a belief that the *Life* acknowledges to be a strange one) that 'architecture and poetry—particularly architecture in London—would not work well together' (L 52). His sense of the impossibility of achieving a workable balance between the two in the capital in particular reflects not only his understanding of the social and class hierarchies that he'd have to set about infiltrating to succeed as an architect in London but his disappointment at the absence of higher aims animating those directing, and profiting from, the Gothic Revival in metropolitan architectural practices. The mass construction of churches undertaken by such as Blomfield evoked for him the term used by the architect in the poem, 'prudent fashionings' (CP 75), rather than the kinds of visionary exaltation that inspire the heiress, or drove such as Bastow.

III

Blomfield's office was, however, the catalyst for Hardy's first-ever publication, the jeu d'esprit, to use his own term, 'How I Built Myself a House' (L 50). This somewhat Dickensian sketch, written for the amusement of Blomfield's pupils, is delivered in the first person by a comically hen-pecked but indubitably middle-class, even affluent, family man and leads one to ponder the extent to which Hardy revealed his origins to his colleagues. The fact that he mentioned the possibility of his roommate at Clarence Place, Philip Shaw, visiting Higher Bockhampton over Christmas of 1863, suggests that he was not initially as defensive on this score as he later became. One wonders, further, if his family read this squib, and, if so, what they made of it.

The hardships endured by the narrator and his wife, Sophia, in their Highly-Desirable Semi-detached Villa in a suburb of London, could hardly be further from those suffered by the various branches of the Hand and Hardy clans:

> If we managed to squeeze a few acquaintances round our table to dinner, there was very great difficulty in serving it; and on such occasions the maid, for want of sideboard room, would take to putting the dishes in the staircase, or on stools and chairs in the passage, so that if anybody else came after we had sat down, he usually went away again, disgusted at seeing the remains of what we had already got through standing in these places, and perhaps the celery waiting in a corner hard by. (AI 3)

If the sketch was indeed perused in Higher Bockhampton or Puddletown, it may have been with the hard-pressed maid, rather than the householder and his demanding wife, that Hardy's relatives identified.

The story describes a move from suburbia to outer suburbia. The plot on which the new home is to be built has to be 'easily accessible by rail', and Hardy has some fun with the way estate agents' maps emphasize the rustic—sketches of cabbages in rows indicating trees, blue patches showing fishponds and fountains—while cunningly siting the railway station in a corner, 'as if it would come within a convenient distance, disguise the fact as the owners might' (AI 4). Hardy also somewhat presciently captures the nondescript nature of the commuter belt, for the couple end up buying a lease on a plot 'rather convenient, and rather healthy, but possessing no other advantage worth mentioning'. Slight as it is, and replete with urbanely told in-jokes, the narrative presents an interesting account of London actively in the process of creeping 'across green fields' (L 22), expanding by erecting just the kinds of villa that Hardy and Emma would inhabit in Surbiton and Tooting, and then build on the outskirts of Dorchester. And with its jocular focus on the price of various extras indispensable to bourgeois domestic life—'a sink in the scullery, a rain-water tank and a pump, a trap-door into the roof, a scraper, a weather-cock and four letters, ventilators in the nursery, same in the kitchen, . . . patent remarkable bell-pulls; a royal letters extraordinary kitchen-range' (AI 9)—it graphically depicts the cost and responsibilities attendant upon agreeing to 'water love' (CP 135).

For most of his first residence in the capital Hardy was what the poem 'Dream of the City Shopwoman' (1866) calls a 'garreteer'. She, like the clerk of 'Coming Up Oxford Street: Evening', longs to escape London and 'city people's snap and sneer' (CP 609), fantasizing about a rustic life with a husband and brood of children in 'a cot of thatch and clay' in 'some snug solitary glen'. As for the clerk, however, there seems no escape from a solitary, gruelling existence in the city, where she is condemned, like Ixion in a pea-souper, to 'writhe on this eternal wheel / In rayless grime' (CP 609–610).[13] Her antithesis, in Hardy's early London poems, is the speaker of 'From Her in the Country', a sonnet that reverses the direction of most Victorian representations of contrasts between the rural and the urban. While the city shopwoman nurtures a wholesome Wordsworthian vision of happiness in nature, the speaker of 'From Her in the Country', despite her best efforts, can find in herself no 'zest for bird, and bud, and tree'.

> I thought and thought of thy crass clanging town
> To folly, till convinced such dreams were ill,
> I held my heart in bond, and tethered down
> Fancy to where I was, by force of will.
>
> I said: How beautiful are these flowers, this wood,
> One little bud is far more sweet to me
> Than all man's urban shows; and then I stood
> Urging new zest for bird, and bush, and tree;
>
> And strove to feel my nature brought it forth
> Of instinct, or no rural maid was I;
> But it was vain; for I could not see worth
> Enough around to charm a midge or fly,
>
> And mused again on city din and sin,
> Longing to madness I might move therein! (CP 234)

There seems, indeed, a strong element of parody of the Wordsworthian in play here. Certainly this sonnet emphasizes the 'dramatic and personative' (to quote from the preface to *Wessex Poems*, CP 6) aspects of Hardy's work, and it might even be said to perform, like a Gothic gargoyle, a wry and mocking grimace in its niche in the edifice of 'Hardy the Regional Writer'. It also, however, conveys facets of the ambivalence that marks Hardy's responses to the city, and the directions in which it pushed him: if the stylized and unstimulating imagery of bud and bird and bush and tree debunks the curative properties attributed to nature by Wordsworth, there is nothing utopian in the poem's figuration of the city—indeed the opposite. It draws, instead, on the satirical tradition of London as Babylon, a 'crass clanging town' whose hollow and deceptive 'urban shows' betray newcomers, such as Luke in Wordsworth's 'Michael', into 'evil courses' (l. 445). The poem's London is indeed Wordsworth's 'dissolute city' (l. 444), a dangerous, addictive, dizzying pandemonium of 'din and sin'. In a further, telling twist, the woman's dreams of hedonistic transgression there are presented very much as a 'spontaneous overflow of powerful feelings', to borrow Wordsworth's famous phrase. These dreams defeat all attempts at repression and triumph over the artificial, reductive, moralizing dictates of the merely rational, just as the nature-inspired imagination is so often presented as doing in Wordsworth. This 'rural maid' is as 'tethered', as 'in bond' to her limited rural surroundings, as the city shopwoman to her counter: she must 'by force of will' try to make her 'fancy' respond to woods and flowers, while the poem's third quatrain exhibits an almost gleeful relish at the paradoxes implicit in her self-conscious, unnatural attempts to feel in tune with nature.

In wit and conception, 'From Her in the Country' is much closer to 'The Ruined Maid' than to the other sonnets that Hardy composed in Westbourne Park Villas. Both run extravagantly counter to Victorian conceptions of the angel in the house, so influentially propounded by Coventry Patmore, whose long narrative poem of that name was completed in 1862, as well as of the weeping Magdalen or repentant fallen woman, of which Tess is a variant. For both the speaker of the sonnet and the courtesan bedecked in her finery are happy, indeed eager, to assume a role in 'urban shows' and to participate in the capital's 'din and sin', although it's also worth noting that their self-dramatizations depend on interaction with the rural to be performed:

'O 'Melia, my dear, this does everything crown!
Who could have supposed I should meet you in Town?

And whence such fair garments, such prosperi-ty?'—
'O didn't you know I'd been ruined?' said she.

—'You left us in tatters, without shoes or socks,
Tired of digging potatoes, and spudding up docks;
And now you've gay bracelets and bright feathers three!'—
'Yes: that's how we dress when we're ruined,' said she.

—'At home in the barton you said "thee" and "thou",
And "thik oon", and "theäs oon", and "t'other"; but now
Your talking quite fits 'ee for high compa-ny!'—
'Some polish is gained with one's ruin,' said she. (CP 158–159)

The poem's relationship to mid-Victorian popular culture, and in particular to the music hall, has been thoughtfully analysed by two of Hardy's most
enterprising critics, Keith Wilson and Richard Nemesvari.[14] In 1866, the date
of the poem's composition, London boasted between 200 and 300 small
music-hall venues, and thirty large ones with a capacity ranging from 1,500
to 3,000 seats.[15] The induction of a rustic girl into the mysteries of city life
was a popular item in the repertoire, and indeed, as Wilson points out, a version of Hardy's poem itself became part of Elsa Lanchester's revival of old
music-hall numbers the following century. Despite his dismissive attitude
to the tittle-tattle circulating through Blomfield's office about the modish
filles de joie who featured in gossip columns and headlines, the poem suggests that Hardy also found something liberating in the kinds of self-invention
that the city made possible. He undoubtedly witnessed the performances of
real-life ruined maids in London dance halls such as Willis's Rooms or pleasure gardens such as the Cremorne, and although he doesn't mention visiting music halls in the 1860s in the *Life*, it's more than likely that he did so.[16]
He certainly patronized them later. In a letter to Florence Henniker of 25 July
1899 he follows a complaint about the quality of the new plays that he'd seen
performed in recent years on the English stage with the observation: 'I find
far more interesting forms of art at the music halls' (CL 2:225).[17]

Although harder to quantify, Hardy's experiences of the kinds of public
performance on offer in London, from supper-room songs to Shakespearean
tragedies, from melodrama to opera, from public readings by such as Dickens

to raucous music-hall entertainments, were just as crucial to his formation as a writer as the hours devoted to solitary study and composition each evening in his room in Westbourne Park Villas—in some ways more so, for he could have read just as widely in a garret in Dorchester as one in Paddington. Further, the music hall's stereotype of the ruined maid exemplified, like the careers of 'Skittles' and the other courtesans admired by Blomfield's pupils, the increasing porousness of class boundaries, particularly in cities, where less rigid attitudes to social and moral conventions were making themselves felt in popular culture. The comedy of Hardy's poem resides in the fallen woman's sublime indifference to all the standard implications of being fallen, and the innocence of the amazed responses of her old friend from the village:

> 'Your hands were like paws then, your face blue and bleak
> But now I'm bewitched by your delicate cheek,
> And your little gloves fit as on any la-dy!'—
> 'True. One's pretty lively when ruined,' said she. (CP 159)

The complex, and eventually thwarted, narrative of upward mobility that drives the plot of *The Poor Man and the Lady* and its offshoot, 'An Indiscretion in the Life of an Heiress', is here accomplished in a trice. The poem's burlesque succeeds by inviting the knowing reader to ignore, for the moment, the reality of the life of a prostitute or kept woman in mid-Victorian London and to savour, instead, her triumphant self-performance. The country girl's bewilderment at 'Melia's transformation achieves its counterbalancing tragic echo in Angel's surprise when he advances to embrace Tess in the front room of the elegant lodging house The Herons in Sandbourne—Hardy's name for Bournemouth:

> She was loosely wrapped in a cashmere dressing-gown of grey-white, embroidered in half-mourning tints, and she wore slippers of the same hue. Her neck rose out of a frill of down, and her well-remembered cable of dark-brown hair was partially coiled up in a mass at the back of her head, and partly hanging on her shoulder, the evident result of haste.
> He had held out his arms, but they had fallen again to his side. (T 400)

'These clothes are what he's put upon me', Tess tells her baffled husband. Her passive acquiescence in the role of mistress leads to the opposite of 'Melia's theatrical self-display: 'his original Tess', the stunned Angel reasons to himself as he makes his way to the railway station, 'had spiritually ceased to recognize the body before him as hers—allowing it to drift, like a corpse upon the current, in a direction dissociated from its living will' (T 401).

Hardy's nuanced but persistent fascination with both the legitimate and the illegitimate theatre had its origins in his early years in London.[18] He appeared on stage himself one night in the Christmas pantomime season of 1866–1867, having arranged to take a walk-on part in Gilbert À Beckett's *Ali Baba and the Forty Thieves; or, Harlequin and the Genii of the Arabian Nights!*, which opened at Covent Garden on 26 December. This was to be the first step in a scheme even more visionary than training to be a country curate: making his living by composing blank-verse drama. Like Dickens's Nicholas Nickleby, who is for a time employed to write melodramatic plays (which must always include a water pump and two washtubs recently acquired as props by the company) for the enthusiastic actor-manager and impresario Vincent Crummles, Hardy descried in the theatre an escape from his current difficulties, that is the impasse that he felt that he had reached in his architectural career and his repeated failure to get published as a poet. He approached the stage manager of the Haymarket with the notion of working as an extra for six months or a year in order to gain 'technical skill' in dramatic construction. Perhaps fortunately, rather than fuelling Hardy's ambition, the highly un-Crummlesian stage manager took it upon himself to nip in the bud his theatrical ardour, quoting some dispiriting sayings of the actor Charles Mathews—'that he would not let a dog of his go on the stage, and . . . would rather see a daughter of his in her grave than on the boards of a theatre' (L 55).

It does seem, though, that for a while visions of himself as a Victorian Shakespeare danced before Hardy's eyes. In a letter of 13 August 1916 to J. W. Mackail he revealed that he read Shakespeare 'more closely from 23 to 26' than he had ever done since (CL 5:174). In 1867 he composed two excited sonnets in praise of Mrs Mary Francis Scott-Siddons (great-granddaughter of the famous Mrs Siddons) after witnessing her West End debut as Rosalind in *As You Like It* at the Haymarket. Like the elegy for Swinburne, 'To

an Actress' offers a glimpse of Hardy on the streets of London, glancing at
adverts, blankly registering multitudes of names clamouring for his attention, passing hers 'vacantly' in that numb state caused by information over-
load so characteristic of city dwellers:

> I read your name when you were strange to me,
> Where it stood blazoned bold with many more;
> I passed it vacantly, and did not see
> Any great glory in the shape it wore. (CP 235)

In the sestet he presents himself as suddenly changed by her, as if he had
absorbed her 'nature's essence' and, like a thespian, become a fresh character:
his 'old world of then is now a new', for she has unblocked 'springs' in him
that were formerly 'sealed up utterly'. 'Could *that* man be this I', he wonders,
marvelling at his own metamorphosis and the transformation of life from 'a
thing of formal journeywork' into something completely different. It is probably no coincidence that he saw Scott-Siddons perform in the most pastoral
of Shakespeare's plays. Further, *As You Like It* not only furnished him with
the title of his second published novel, but its comic exchanges offered the
most influential template for the humorous dialogue that he put into the
mouths of the rustic characters in his early fiction. These frankly admiring
sonnets addressed to a public figure stand in striking contrast to the secre-
tive, anguished intensities of the 'She, to Him' sequence and to the coded,
private erotica of the 'Studies, Specimens &c.' notebook. The 'crass clanging
town' certainly drove Hardy in on himself for long stretches, but it also encouraged him to be 'dramatic and personative', pushed him to imagine
himself as more than the dutiful performer of the 'journeywork' allotted him.
'To an Impersonator of Rosalind' and 'To an Actress' themselves 'woo,
parley, plead', like their inspirer, and register as declarations of love as public
and unashamed as the poems that *As You Like It*'s Orlando inscribed on
trees.

   Nevertheless, even with his 'springs' unsealed, as important to the welling
up of his ambition to become a successful writer as the lure of 'great glory'
or the dream of featuring in adverts like Mary Scott-Siddons, was dismay at
the 'mechanical' indifference, and poverty, of the millions of Londoners in

whose midst he anonymously moved. 'The world', he bleakly observed in a diary entry included in his chapter on 'the city of din and sin' in the *Life*, 'does not despise us; it only neglects us' (L 50). Not until he was back under the greenwood tree, and away from the neglectful, and neglected, multitudes, did Hardy find a literary mode commensurate with this new public self, launching his career as a writer of fiction with a 'socialistic novel' (L 58) that attacked political inequality and the class system, and whose hero, Will Strong, denounces the landed classes at radical meetings held in Trafalgar Square. It fell on stony ground, just like his early poems, but its successors not only 'blazoned bold' his name—they enabled the poor man, for better, for worse, to win the lady.

4

Power & Purpose

I

The division between the rural and the urban dramatized in poems such as 'From Her in the Country' and 'The Ruined Maid' can be seen as part of a debate pursued throughout Hardy's oeuvre about the relationship between the metropolis and the provinces. That Hardy's London experiences tend to figure minimally in accounts of the evolution of Wessex is testimony to the power of the popular image of Hardy as a celebrant of rural practices and traditions, as spokesperson for the ideal of an organic community living in harmony with nature. One of the most resonant figurations of Hardy as a repository and expounder of country lore is Seamus Heaney's 'The Birthplace', which I here adduce in order to contrast it with the Australian poet Peter Porter's more anomalous meditation on the deracinated and much less familiar urban Hardy of the mid-1860s.

'The Birthplace' describes a visit to Hardy's cottage in Higher Bockhampton. 'The deal table where he wrote, so small and plain', the poem opens, 'the single bed a dream of discipline'; downstairs 'mote-slants // of thick light' illuminate the 'flagged kitchen'. Rural virtues and pleasures, the slow passing of time and weather, and the oral tradition from which Hardy derived so many of his stories ('the unperturbed, reliable / ghost life he carried, with no need to invent'), are all skilfully evoked in the poem, and prompt the reader to consider the similarities between Hardy's childhood and that of Heaney growing up on a farm in Northern Ireland. Although he goes on to question the kinds of rural nostalgia embodied by terms such as *'birth-*

place, roofbeam, whitewash, /flagstone, hearth', which are compared to 'un-
stacked iron weights // afloat among galaxies', in the poem's concluding
lines Heaney is able to finesse the postmodern anxiety about placelessness
by recalling an occasion when he stayed up all night to finish a novel by
Hardy:

> was it thirty years ago
> I read until first light
>
> for the first time, to finish
> *The Return of the Native?*
> The corncrake in the aftergrass
>
> verified himself, and I heard
> roosters and dogs, the very same
> as if he had written them.[1]

The continuity established is vivid and personal, 'verified' by the connections that the poem makes between Hardy's writing, the young Heaney
reading, and the older Heaney remembering the shared experience of the
natural world that resulted.

Peter Porter's 'Thomas Hardy at Westbourne Park Villas', collected in
Preaching to the Converted of 1972, offers a very different perspective on the
concept of nature in Hardy's writing: 'each house knows', he muses of the
street where Hardy lived in Paddington,

> As many stories as in the iron sublime we call
> Victorian. Suicide, lost love, despair are laws
> of a visiting Nature raging against proof and practice and changing all.[2]

It is not continuity that this 'visiting Nature' fosters, but radical disjunction:
the stories told in Hardy's writing chart the ungovernable eruption of
irrational compulsions that conflict with existing conventions ('proof and
practice') and lead to disaster. The Victorian 'iron sublime', Porter's lines
imply, is as unforgiving and inexorable, and as neglectful of individuals'

hopes for happiness, as the plot of *Jude the Obscure*, of which Hardy himself observed, in a letter to Edmund Gosse: 'It is really sent out to those into whose souls the iron has entered, & has entered deeply, at some time of their lives' (CL 2:93). Hardy was responding here to Gosse's complaint in a review in *Cosmopolis* that the story the novel told was 'abnormal', a 'shriek of discord' (CH 268, 270); but Jude's experience of 'the contrast between the ideal life' that he wished to lead and 'the squalid life he was fated to lead', Hardy argued in a postscript to his letter, was by no means abnormal, and could indeed be 'discovered in *every* body's life'. It was, Porter's poem goes on to suggest, in the course of his first residence in London that Hardy imbibed the laws of the iron sublime, that he first weighed up 'the worst of all possible odds' in a manner akin to Father Time's assessment that 'It would be better to be out o' the world than in it' (JO 322).

> Here, rather than in death-filled Dorset, I see him,
>   The watchful conspirator against the gods
> Come to the capital of light on his own grim
> Journey into darkness; the dazzle would tell
>   Him these were the worst of all possible odds—
> ordinary gestures of time working on faces the watermark of hell.

It is the secular hell of the city clerk of 'Coming Up Oxford Street: Evening', who finds no comfort in the dazzling sunset, but 'goes along with head and eyes flagging forlorn', that is here limned by Porter. If the dazzle begets its opposite, a 'grim / Journey into darkness', then London rather than 'death-filled Dorset' initiated Hardy into the art of being less deceived, because the dazzle promised so much. Only a very 'watchful conspirator' could set to one side the entrancing, shimmering surfaces of the first section of 'Coming Up Oxford Street', to concentrate, in the second, on a passing face stamped with the 'watermark of hell'. Further, in the light of Porter's figuration of Hardy's London as an everyday *Inferno*, it is worth pointing out that the distance between the city clerk and Hardy himself was considerably elided when the poem was first published in *The Nation & the Athenaeum* in June of 1925 (see Frontispiece), for in this printing, its second section was in the first person, making its last lines read: 'And I go along with head and eyes drooping forlorn, / Taking no interest in things, and wondering why I was born.'[3] In this version one hears more clearly the echo of Father Time's expostulation on the night before the catastrophe in *Jude the Obscure*: 'I wish I hadn't been born!' (JO 323).

One of the most peculiar stages of what Porter calls Hardy's 'grim / Journey into darkness' brought him face to face with metropolitan disruption in the most literal of ways. As the respected son of a former bishop of London, Hardy's employer, Arthur Blomfield, was deputed by the current bishop to oversee the removal of coffins and corpses from city churchyards whose land had been requisitioned by railway companies as they constructed new lines into London in the 1860s. Although these companies were supposed to arrange dignified reinterring of the bodies, one of the reburial sites that Blomfield visited showed no signs of having been disturbed, and he heard rumours of bags full of mysterious contents: 'I believe those people are all ground up!' Hardy reports his employer exclaiming on his return to the office (L 46).

In the autumn of 1866 work began on the approach of the Midland Railway line into St. Pancras, and since it would run through a section of Old St. Pancras Churchyard, Blomfield was again in the position of having to oversee the respectful relocation of hundreds of coffins and loose bones. This was the labour of men and shovels, horses and carts, and a considerable undertaking, for by the time the work finished in 1867 an estimated 8,000 corpses had been moved to new resting places. To avoid alarming passers-by, all removals of human remains were carried out at night behind hoardings, and it became Hardy's duty to appear in the churchyard periodically each evening to make sure that these exhumations were being carried out 'decently'. Given that this task was allotted him at the height of his Shakespeare mania, it is hard not to imagine him as a latter-day Hamlet brooding on skulls and worms, and certainly something of Hamlet's saturnine humour invigorates the poem 'The Levelled Churchyard', which was written in the Dorset town of Wimborne Minster in 1882. While this poem primarily refers to the 'improvements' of the Wimborne Minster churchyard carried out by T. H. Wyatt in the mid-1850s, it also reflects the gruesome sights that he and his employer shared in London. When Hardy and Blomfield met up after fifteen years of separation, among Blomfield's first questions was: 'Do you remember how we found the man with two heads in St. Pancras?'—a reference to a coffin

that they were carrying that fell apart to reveal a skeleton and two skulls
(L 47).

> 'O passenger, pray list and catch
>   Our sighs and piteous groans,
> Half stifled in this jumbled patch
>   Of wrenched memorial stones!
>
> 'We late-lamented, resting here,
>   Are mixed to human jam,
> And each to each exclaims in fear,
>   "I know not which I am!"' (CP 157–158)

The image of 'human jam' allies the jumbled-up dead with Emma's vision of
the crowd attending the Lord Mayor's Show as 'porridge', and indeed with
Hardy's comparison of the masses in the streets with the tissue and spawn
of a 'molluscous black creature' (L 134). The poem goes on to extract from
the afterlife of body parts the kind of macabre jocosity that Hamlet displays
when imagining Alexander as a plug for a beer-barrel, or Caesar as clay stop-
ping a hole in a wall:

> 'Here's not a modest maiden elf
>   But dreads the final Trumpet,
> Lest half of her should rise herself,
>   And half some sturdy strumpet!' (CP 158)

In the *Life* Hardy leaves it to the reader to picture the thoughts aroused in
him by the 'mournful processions' that he witnessed each night (L 47). Although it has never been proved that he played any part in the stacking of
'wrenched memorial stones' around an ash sapling planted in what was left
of St. Pancras Churchyard after the incursions of the Midland Railway, this
tree, its roots writhing among dozens of weathered, mossy gravestones, is
now known as the Hardy Tree.

It is, no doubt, a coincidence that an ash tree features in Hardy's most successful and celebrated early poem. 'Neutral Tones' was composed in West-

bourne Park Villas in 1867 and refracts many aspects of his last months in London. By midsummer of that year his health had deteriorated so badly that 'on sitting down to begin drawing in the morning he had scarcely physical power left him to hold the pencil and square' (L 54). The sapping 'enervation of London', and the 'fitful yet mechanical and monotonous existence' that he led there, had left him 'much weakened' (L 65). His 'languor increased month by month', until friends were 'shocked at the pallor which sheeted a countenance formerly ruddy with health' (L 54). Although set in winter, 'Neutral Tones' mirrors almost exactly the state of emotional and physical exhaustion that overwhelmed Hardy that summer: its sun is 'white, as though chidden of God', its ash leaves are grey and fallen and lifeless, and its 'sod' is 'starving'. No better terms can be found for the couple's pitiful emotional state and exchanges than Hardy's—weakened, languorous, enervated, mechanical, monotonous, fitful.

More fortunate than his city shopwoman and his city clerk, Hardy was able to escape the paralysis brought on by the 'rayless grime', the 'rut' of London routines, although only by beating a somewhat ignominious retreat to the family home. In the *Life* he is keen to assure us that his years of experience 'as a young man at large in London' meant that, like *The Return of the Native*'s Clym Yeobright, he was a native returning with 'very different ideas of things' (L 57). But one also intuits the disarray and disappointment in which Hardy's first London campaign ended: when he decamped from the city that summer, he could boast of only modest progress in his architectural career and had little concrete to show from his intensive literary studies. His indecisiveness at this juncture, his lack of 'power & purpose', to borrow a phrase used by the publisher Alexander Macmillan in the letter that he wrote to Hardy after reading the manuscript of *The Poor Man and the Lady*, can be deduced from the fact that he left behind in his lodgings in London not only his belongings and books, but his papers, even those on which he'd copied out his early poems, including 'Neutral Tones', an enigmatic and withdrawn poem about withdrawal, an antilove lyric that laments the loss of all feeling and belief. Like the miserable couple whose parting it depicts, it found itself abandoned.

As John Hughes has remarked in a subtle and illuminating essay, 'Neutral Tones' is frequently discussed as Hardy's 'first signature poem, one of those early pieces by which a poet's sensibility appears unaccountably to arrive on the page'.[4] Samuel Hynes, Robert Gittings, John Bayley, and Claire Tomalin all, for instance, present it as the first definitive example of echt Hardy, the real thing: reading 'Neutral Tones', 'we recognize and acknowledge one man's sense of the world' (Hynes); 'this poem is uniquely Hardy's own' (Gittings); ' "Neutral Tones', dated 1867, is already a complete Hardy poem' (Bayley); 'with this poem Hardy establishes himself as a poet with a voice of his own, to be taken seriously' (Tomalin).[5] Hughes compares its status to that of totemic early poems such as Tennyson's 'Mariana' and T. S. Eliot's 'The Love Song of J. Alfred Prufrock', but goes on to make the point that rather than initiating further excited exploration of the themes and tones and techniques discovered in its composition, Hardy more or less turned his back on poetry for several decades after completing it. 'The poem's achievement', as Hughes puts it, 'paradoxically signals both Hardy's arrival as a poet, and his departure.'[6] There is undoubtedly a buried link between the suspension of energy and meaning depicted in the poem and the renunciation that Hardy made soon after composing it of the art that, as he later told it, had struck him in his mid-twenties with the force of a revelation: 'A sense of the truth of poetry, of its supreme place in literature, had awakened itself in me. At the risk of ruining all my worldly prospects I dabbled in it . . . was forced out of it' (L 415). While 'Neutral Tones' is never explicitly a poem about poetry, it is hard not to make a comparison between the leaves of paper on which it and Hardy's other early poems were drafted, and which in the summer of 1867 were left behind in Westbourne Park Villas, and the 'few leaves' strewn on the 'starving sod' at the foot of the ash tree in the poem's first stanza.

When Hardy describes himself as 'forced out of' poetry, one assumes that he is referring to the rejection slips that he received from editors, and his reluctant acknowledgement that he would never make a living by writing poems, even ones as good as 'Neutral Tones'. 'Almost suddenly he became more practical', he writes of his decision, on his return to Dorset, to attempt 'to achieve some tangible result from his desultory yet strenuous labours at literature' by writing a novel (L 58). The 'force' separating the lovers in 'Neutral Tones' is nothing if not 'desultory' and in this reflects Hardy's understanding of the random operations of 'Crass Casualty'; but whereas 'Hap' registers a protest at the forces of contingency that it anatomizes, the authorial voice of 'Neutral Tones' is dissolved by, and into, the desultoriness that it surveys. And yet, although the poem's mise en scène is unambiguous and conventional enough, and its details are delivered with what R. W. King called, in 1925, 'acrid clarity', some unformulated 'riddle' still seems to 'rove' beneath its enervated surfaces and the numbing nondrama that it presents.[7]

We stood by a pond that winter day,
And the sun was white, as though chidden of God,
And a few leaves lay on the starving sod;
　　—They had fallen from an ash, and were gray.

Your eyes on me were as eyes that rove
Over tedious riddles of years ago;
And some words played between us to and fro
　　On which lost the more by our love.

The smile on your mouth was the deadest thing
Alive enough to have strength to die;
And a grin of bitterness swept thereby
　　Like an ominous bird a-wing. . . .

Since then, keen lessons that love deceives,
And wrings with wrong, have shaped to me
Your face, and the God-curst sun, and a tree,
　　And a pond edged with grayish leaves. (CP 12)

The Donnean ingenuity and drive that makes the 'She, to Him' sonnets resemble a set of cunningly woven knots is here replaced by a relatively sequential narrative mode: five of its sixteen lines begin 'And', while its last two lines reconfigure its opening images in a fairly standard romantic model of recapitulation; we begin and end like Keats's knight-at-arms in 'La Belle Dame Sans Merci', palely loitering by a wintry lake where no birds sing. As a poem of four quatrains depicting the separation of an unhappy couple, it summons up also the ghost of Meredith's sixteen-line sonnet sequence

Modern Love, but perhaps only to emphasize its own lack of the bravura and dramatic impetus that propels Meredith's narrative and self-figurations. An even more famous precursor that 'Neutral Tones' seems to want—if 'want' is not too strong a word for a poem so in thrall to the states of paralysis that it denotes—to neutralize is *In Memoriam,* whose *abba* rhyme scheme it adopts, while stripping it of all its consoling powers of connection and continuity. And while the poem's painterly title seems to promise to frame the remembered scene like a recurrent traumatic memory liable to replay itself whenever triggered by subsequent failures in love, the poem intimates that the experience, however haunting in its mundane particulars, was merely an induction into the way things are. This means there is nothing cathartic in the recollection of the scene of parting, or exceptional about the scene itself; it is useful only as an instance of the truth that Hardy shared with his mother—that 'a figure stands in our van with arm uplifted, to knock us back from any pleasant prospect we indulge in as probable' (PN 6–7). The poem's 'lesson', then, reverses that customarily derived from the recreation of traumatic experience or transgression or loss, the kind of moral, for instance, with which Coleridge's Ancient Mariner concludes his tale:

> He prayeth best who loveth best
> All things both great and small:
> For the dear God, who loveth us,
> He made and loveth all. (l. 614–618)

Something of the grandiloquent negativity of *The Mayor of Casterbridge*'s dying Michael Henchard perhaps flickers in the image of the 'God-curst sun', but, staggering under the weight of its own staginess, it fast succumbs to the entropy that is nature's 'neutral' way of collapsing and exhausting and dispersing, reducing all to disbelief and repetition and inertia, to a series of neutral tones, to 'a tree, / And a pond edged with grayish leaves'. Its chiding God is less a blasphemous repudiation of the Ancient Mariner's loving deity than a fretful absence, sceptically invoked for want of any more credible authority.

The iconography of the poem's final image is a striking illustration of the freedom from sexual self-consciousness enjoyed by pre-Freudian poets. In this instance, however, the male tree, the female pond, the chiding father-sun lend themselves to a psychosexual reading whose banality is in keeping with the banality of the scene itself. The mysterious potency of the poem resides not in the business of decoding its imagery but in the 'neutral' spaces it creates between the tree and the pond and the sun and the man and the woman. Porter's phrase 'laws / of a visiting Nature' captures something of the dislocation and homelessness that Hardy manages to convey through the poem's crumbling anticlimaxes, which serve to translate the unnerving vistas of distance and separation of 'In Vision I Roamed' to a mundane scene of parting by a pond and an ash tree. It is the 'laws / of a visiting Nature' that metamorphose a 'grin of bitterness' into an 'ominous bird a-wing', or allow a smile to be defined as 'Alive enough to have strength to die'. And the divorce, as the late John Bayley first argued in his compelling discussion of 'Neutral Tones' in *An Essay on Hardy* of 1978, is not only between the man and the woman and the tree and the pond and the sun, but also between Hardy's 'sense of, and use of, nature, and that of the English romantic poets and their Victorian successors'—and, one might add, of their postmodern successors like Seamus Heaney too.[8]

The separations 'played' out in the poem, in other words, can be extended to Hardy's relationship with the poetry that 'awakened' such deep passions in him that in the course of the previous two years he willingly ran 'the risk of ruining all [his] worldly prospects' by dabbling in it. Like a bankrupt gambler expelled from a casino, Hardy here grimly confronts the banality of life after having been 'forced out' of the poetic realm that so excited and enchanted him. And although he would eventually discover all manner of poetic possibilities in the world of the posthumous first shadowed forth in 'Neutral Tones', in the context of his early London years the poem comes to stand as an elegy lamenting the failure of any number of things—love, poetry, faith in God, belief in a benign or meaningful nature, and confidence in his own social, sexual, and literary future.[9] Hughes is surely right to wonder if Hardy was 'personally equipped' at this stage of his life to cope with the implications of a prognosis so bleak and the recognition that his muse differed from that of both loved predecessors and admired contemporaries in being 'so relentlessly unsparing, dissociative, and agnostic'.[10] Of British poets, only James Thomson, whose 'The City of Dreadful Night' (first published in 1874) was to have such an influence on T. S. Eliot's *The Waste Land*, matches Hardy in the rigour of his negations.

II

'A dolt', Hardy observed in the bitter quatrain 'A Young Man's Epigram on Existence' of 1866, 'is he who memorizes / Lessons that leave no time for prizes' (CP 299). With the exception of Tennyson, the ratio between the effort expended on mastering the lessons required to write poetry and the prizes with which its Victorian practitioners were rewarded was not an encouraging one. Hardy resolved to be a dolt no longer; 'abandoning verse as a waste of labour' (L 58), he responded positively to a request from his first employer Hicks, who was suffering badly from gout and needed an assistant with experience of church restoration in his Dorchester architectural practice.[11] Blomfield advised him that 'to stay permanently in the country would be a mistake' (L 54), but Hardy had decided, somewhat ironically, given his later hobnobbing with the rich and powerful, that his ineptitude in 'the business of social advancement' meant that he was unlikely ever to develop a successful career as an architect in London. He was granted a temporary leave of absence and returned home in July. Once he'd escaped the stench of the Thames in summer and the miasma infecting the city's air, his health quickly recovered, and by late summer he had resumed his former routines, living in Higher Bockhampton and walking each day to 39 South Street in Dorchester.

The Return of the Native's Clym Yeobright set about putting into effect the 'very different ideas of things' that he had developed during his years in a metropolis (in his case Paris) by launching a scheme to raise the educational attainments of the heath-dwellers that he had grown up amongst; Hardy did so by writing. In the intervals of his duties at Hicks's practice, and in his bedroom at home, on the 'deal table, so small and plain', Hardy set to work on his 'sweeping dramatic satire of the squirearchy and nobility, London society, the vulgarity of the middle class, modern Christianity, church restoration, and political and domestic morals in general'. This wide-angled satire's 'most important scenes', he added, 'were laid in London' (L 63), and reflected what he called his 'years of London buffeting' (L 76). Initially, vestiges of his heady poetic enthusiasms were to be allowed to leaven a genre that he had often publicly disparaged during the literary lectures that he gave on slow afternoons at Blomfield's: his original title for the novel was *The Poor Man and the Lady. A Story with no plot; Containing some original verses.* These verses were possibly dissolved into the novel in a manner akin to that of *Desperate Remedies,* and it was not until *The Dynasts* that Hardy evolved a hybrid project that effectively combined poetry and prose. His title was eventually abridged to one with a more politically combative feel: *The Poor Man and the Lady; By the Poor Man* (L 58). In October he made a flying visit to London to gather up from 16 Westbourne Park Villas his books and what he drily calls 'other impedimenta': his poetic manuscripts now reduced to the status of cast-off encumbrances, so many fallen, 'grayish leaves'.

The first draft of *The Poor Man and the Lady* was completed by January of 1868. Hardy spent a further six months revising and making a fair copy and on 25 July dispatched the 440 pages of his first novel to Alexander Macmillan, the cofounder (with his brother Daniel) in 1843 of the firm that would eventually acquire the rights to all of Hardy's fiction and poetry. He included a letter of introduction from Horace Moule and a covering letter in which he attempted to suggest that the book's attacks on the upper classes were oblique and subtle rather than direct: the poor man's feelings about the circles in which the high-born lady moves had been 'inserted edgewise', 'half concealed beneath ambiguous expressions, or at any rate written as if they were not the chief aims of the book (even though they may be)' (CL 1:7). Further, the novel was topical, dealing with upward mobility and class conflict, for 'now a days, discussions on the questions of manners, rising in the world, &c (the main incidents in the novel) have grown to be particularly absorbing'. In addition, although in telling a love story Hardy conceded that he may have sacrificed originality for commercial appeal, he was keen to point out that his *donnée* gave the book a certain freshness. Like 'How I Built Myself a House', *The Poor Man and the Lady* was written in the first person, and in allowing the poor man's perspective so to dominate, Hardy was venturing into new terrain: 'That novelty of *position* and *view* in relation to a known subject, is more taking among the readers of light literature than even absolute novelty of subject' (CL 1:8). Conscious of the gap between his class status and that of the upper echelons depicted, he freely admitted that he was a 'comparative outsider' to the rituals and mores of London Society, but made the ingenious claim that in that lay the novel's interest and appeal.

Macmillan's reply was prompt. A mere two and a half weeks after submitting the book, Hardy received a letter outlining the publisher's personal responses, as well as a reader's report by John Morley. Macmillan's opening paragraph spoke, alas, of 'fatal drawbacks to its success'—'another rejection', Hardy must have muttered to himself—but sugared the pill with a thoughtful and detailed critique that reveals the extent to which the novel engaged his attention. He seems not to have agreed with Hardy's assertion that the book's attacks on the upper classes had been 'inserted edgewise':

> Your pictures of character among Londoners and especially the upper classes are sharp clear incisive and in many respects true, but they are wholly dark, not a ray of light visible to relieve the darkness & therefore exaggerated & untrue in their result. Their frivolity heartlessness, selfishness are great & terrible, but there are other sides, and I can hardly conceive that they would do otherwise than what you seek to avoid 'throw down the book in disgust.' Even the worst of them would hardly I think do things that you describe them as doing. . . . The utter heartlessness of *all* the conversation you give in drawing rooms and ball rooms about the working-classes, has *some* ground of truth I fear, and might justly be scourged as you aim at doing, but your chastisement would fall harmless from its excess. Will's speech to the working men is full of wisdom—(though by the way would he have told his own story in public, being as you describe him a man of substantially good taste?—) and you there yourself give grounds for condemning very much that is in other parts of the book. Indeed, nothing could justify such a wholesale blackening of a class but large & intimate knowledge of it. Thackeray makes them not greatly better in many respects, but he gave many redeeming traits & characters, besides he did it all in light chaffing way that gave no offence—and I fear did little good, and he soothed them by describing the lower class which he knew nothing of & did not care to know, as equally bad when he touched them at all. He meant fair, you '*mean mischief*'.

Three times Macmillan alludes to the 'power' of Hardy's writing: 'your really admirable handling often gives a certain dignity and power'; 'the scene in Rotten Row, seen as it is & described *by an outsider* is full of real power & insight'; 'You see I am writing to you as to a writer who seems to me of, at least potentially, considerable mark, of power & purpose. If this is your first book I think you ought to go on. May I ask if it is? and—you are not a lady so perhaps you will forgive the question—are you young?'[12]

Morley's report conveys a similar mixture of admiration for the 'real feeling' in the writing and unease at how far Hardy took his satire:

> A very curious & original performance: the opening pictures of the Christmas Eve in the tranter's house are really of good quality, much of the writing is strong & fresh. But there crops up in parts a certain rawness of absurdity that is very displeasing, and makes it read like some clever lad's dream: the thing hangs too loosely together. There is real feeling in the writing, though now & then it is commonplace in form as all feeling turning on the insolence and folly of the rich in face of the poor is apt to sound. . . . If the man is young, there is stuff and promise in him: but he must study form & composition, in such writers as Balzac & Thackeray, who would I think come as natural masters to him.[13]

Macmillan's letter and Morley's report are the only first-hand accounts of the novel that survive. In April of 1915, however, Hardy responded to Edmund Gosse's interest in his first attempt at fiction by recollecting what he could of it. Gosse transcribed Hardy's reconstruction of its characters and plot in his diary, which he then used as the basis for an article on Hardy's 'lost novel' that appeared in the *Sunday Times* shortly after Hardy's death.[14] The account given to Gosse of the book that inaugurated Hardy's fictional career almost fifty years earlier runs as follows:

> The scene was laid in Dorsetshire, and the hero was the son of peasants working on the estate of the great local squire. This squire had a beautiful and spirited daughter, who was a great heiress. The hero showed remarkable talent, and was patronized by the people of the great house, who had him educated, and attached to an architect's office. He

proved to be a very capable draughtsman, and when he was just grown up he was thrown with the squire's daughter, who took a romantic interest in him. Her parents, discovering this, forbade all communication with him, and he was sent up to London, where he got on in his profession. The lovers, however, kept up some correspondence with each other. He was very bitter against the father, and became a bitter stern radical. The great Wessex family came up to their town house, and the Lady and the architect contriving to meet, their engagement was secretly renewed. But he took to addressing public meetings, and once when he was speaking angrily against the landed classes to a crowd in Trafalgar Square, the Lady drove by in her carriage, recognised [him], and stopped to hear what he was saying. . . . The Lady was greatly offended by this radical speech, and broke off all relations with the architect. A short time afterwards, however, there was given a concert, at which the Lady happened to be seated alone at the last row of the expensive places, and the architect immediately behind her in the front row of the cheap places. Both were extremely moved by the emotion of the music, and as she chanced to put her hand on the back of her seat, he took it in his, and held it till the end of the performance. They walked away together, and all their affection was renewed. She asked him to call on her openly, at the great town house, and he did so. Unfortunately the Lady was out, and her mother received him, with great anger and arrogance. He lost his temper, and they both became so excited that the Mother fainted away. He found some water, and flung it over her face, with the result that the rouge ran on her cheeks. On coming to, she discovered this, with redoubled rage, and the Squire himself coming in, a footman turned the architect out at the front door. The family returned to Dorsetshire, and no more letters passed. In the course of time, however, the architect learned from his relations that the Squire's daughter was just about to marry the heir of a great neighbouring landowner. On the night before the wedding, hanging about the churchyard, the church being still open, he saw a muffled figure steal into the church, and, following her, found himself alone with her. They had a very emotional interview, she being at first very angry, and then confessing that she had never loved any man but him. The story then ended, but Hardy could not remember whether she married the proposed bridegroom or not. He racked his brains to recollect, but in vain: he could not tell at all.[15]

The Lady (Miss Allancourt) undoubtedly did die in the original, as in the spin-off, 'An Indiscretion in the Life of an Heiress', for Hardy wrote to Martha Sparks's brother-in-law, George Brereton Sharpe, who had trained as a doctor, inquiring about a suitable cause for a short sharp death that would leave the character's faculties unimpaired to the last and received the recommendation of 'hemorrage of the lungs' (MM 101).[16] Both Geraldine Allenville in 'An Indiscretion' and Cytherea Aldclyffe of *Desperate Remedies* die this way also. Sharpe also assured Hardy that it was feasible that his architect hero might suffer a spell of temporary blindness brought on by studying too much too late.

To the précis set down by Gosse can be added Hardy's own description in the *Life* of a minor character, the music-hall dancer, who sounds like a prototype for *Jude the Obscure*'s Sue Bridehead. Will Strong, the novel's hero, is introduced

> to the kept mistress of an architect who 'took in washing' (as it was called)—that is, worked at his own office for other architects—the said mistress adding to her lover's income by designing for him the pulpits, altars, reredoses, texts, holy vessels, crucifixes, and other ecclesiastical furniture which were handed on to him by the nominal architects who employed her keeper—the lady herself being a dancer at a music-hall when not engaged in designing Christian emblems—all told so plausibly as to seem actual proof of the degeneracy of the age. There is no doubt that this scene, if printed, would have brought down upon his head the cudgels of all the orthodox reviews. (L 63)

Hardy seems to be reprising the architect and his music-hall mistress's unorthodox working relationship when Jude loses his contract to renew the faded lettering of the Ten Commandments above the altar in a church near Aldbrickham upon discovery by church officials that Sue is assisting him with the task. By the time of *Jude* it is, of course, the cudgels brought down upon the heads of the protagonists, rather than the fact that they are 'living in sin', that is presented as proof of the 'degeneracy of the age'.

Hardy later claimed that *The Poor Man and the Lady* was 'the most original thing (for its date) that I ever wrote' (CL 4:130).[17] The divided responses of both Macmillan and Morley testify to the confrontational aspects of the book, as well as to its power and unusualness; 'curious and original' is Morley's opening assessment, and his characterization of the novel as some 'clever lad's dream' suggests, if in somewhat patronizing terms, the youthful idealism animating it—an idealism that inspires, however, potentially disruptive notions and actions. Unlike the social criticism of the genial Thackeray, that of *The Poor Man and the Lady* is intended to inspire political change, or as Macmillan trenchantly put it, 'you *"mean mischief"*'. In the *Life*, Hardy described the 'tendency of the writing' as 'socialistic, not to say revolutionary' (L 63), and undoubtedly his immersion in the work of political theorists such as Mill and Fourier, and in the political poetry of Shelley, influenced its action and ideas. In the summer of 1866 Hardy was reading *The Revolt of Islam*, Shelley's nearly 5,000-line poem in Spenserian stanzas, and wrote around the title in his own recently purchased copy of the book the words 'Hyde Park—morning'. Claire Tomalin has suggested that in doing so he was making a connection between Shelley's political epic about revolution and the rally that took place in Hyde Park on 23 July organized by the recently founded Reform League, whose principal aim was the extension of suffrage to working class men (CT 76). This demonstration was declared illegal by the government, who ordered the park gates to be locked, only for the protestors to break down sections of the railings and pour in through the gaps, initiating three days of confrontation between activists and the police. And in having his bitter, radical hero speak at rallies in Trafalgar Square, Hardy surely intended another reference to the political activities of the occupants of the ground floor of 8 Adelphi Terrace: John Bright and Charles Bradlaugh addressed a massive demonstration organized there by the Reform League on 29 June 1866, and a second meeting also held there on 2 July resulted in rioting in the West End. We don't know if Hardy braved the mockery of his colleagues and attended any of these events, but he certainly witnessed John Stuart Mill address an outdoor crowd almost exactly a year earlier, in Covent Garden on 10 July 1865. The speech was part of Mill's campaign, supported by the Reform League, for the parliamentary seat of Westminster, and the experience made such an impression on Hardy that he was able to recall it with startling clarity fifty years later: in a letter to the *Times* of May 1906, the centenary of Mill's birth, he depicted his hero, whose *On Liberty* 'we students of that date knew almost by heart', conveying both 'personified earnestness' and 'a curious sense of perilous exposure', as if he were 'a man out of place' (PV 239). One suspects that these phrases relate also to Hardy's attitude to his first fictional hero, Will Strong, as he rose to address protestors at a rally in Trafalgar Square.

The architect hero of *The Poor Man and the Lady* is given a name, Will Strong, that transparently conveys his creator's yearning for the 'power & purpose' exemplified by the work of such as Shelley and Mill, and that Alexander Macmillan felt Hardy's own writing might one day achieve. Strong is clearly determined and resilient, one might almost say hardy: 'I was a striver with deeds to do / And little enough to do them with', reflects one of the many descendants of Hardy's original self-projection, the speaker of the poem 'A Poor Man and a Lady' (published in *Human Shows* of 1925), a poetic version of an episode from the novel to which Hardy appended an explanatory note: 'The foregoing was intended to preserve an episode in the story of "The Poor Man and the Lady", written in 1868, and, like these lines, in the first person; but never printed, and ultimately destroyed' (CP 792).

Edward Springrove (*Desperate Remedies*), Stephen Smith (*A Pair of Blue Eyes*), George Somerset (*A Laodicean*), Swithin St. Cleve (*Two on a Tower*), Jude Fawley, as well, of course, as Egbert Mayne (who is also hardy, strong, full of might and main) of 'An Indiscretion in the Life of an Heiress', all derive from Hardy's sense of himself as a young man 'with deeds to do / And little enough to do them with', though rarely do their battles result in the direct political action of the kind taken by Will Strong. It is intriguing that Hardy made at least one of the speeches that he delivered in Trafalgar Square to some extent autobiographical, an aspect of *The Poor Man and the Lady* objected to by Macmillan: 'Would he have told his own story in public, being as you describe him a man of substantially good taste?' The importance of keeping the personal and the public separate that, in later life, Hardy liked to assert whenever asked to espouse a particular political cause, was evidently reversed in his first embodiment of himself in a public role; it is by speaking personally that Will Strong looks to shape the political views of the working men that he addresses. *The Poor Man and the Lady* was not only a portrait of the artist as a young man but showed how the experiences that fuelled its writing could be translated into effective political oratory—and subsequent political action.

Ralph Pite is probably right to suggest in his biography of Hardy that the romance at the heart of the novel was a reworking of Hardy's childhood passion for Lady Julia Martin.[18] In its later incarnation in 'An Indiscretion in the Life of an Heiress', the excitement derives principally from the crossing of class boundaries, and there is little sense of direct and explicit sexual feelings of the kind evoked in Bathsheba by Troy, or in Boldwood by Bathsheba in *Far from the Madding Crowd*. The most graphic illustration of the thrill of surreptitiously reaching across the class divide occurs in the scene set in the concert hall in London at a performance of the *Messiah*. Egbert manages to secure a seat just behind Geraldine's, although a 'red cord' (AI 85) separates her superior seats from his bench. Just as Hardy remembered the 'thrilling "frou-frou"' of Julia Martin's 'four grey silk flounces when she had used to bend over him' (L 104), so Egbert listens in 'half-pleasant misery' to 'the rustle of her garments' as she settles in her seat. As the oratorio builds, she becomes symbolic to him of everything absent from the world of 'Neutral Tones', seeming 'to absorb all the love and poetry that his life had produced, to pour it upon that one moment, and upon her who stood so close at hand' (AI 86). The writing fuses her with the music, until the 'storm of sound now reached its climax, and Geraldine's power was proportionately increased' (AI 87). 'My love!' he whispers:

> 'Oh, Egbert!' she said; and her countenance flagged as if she would have fainted.
> 'Give me your hand,' he whispered.
> She placed her hand in his, under the cord, which it was easy to do without observation; and he held it tight.
> 'Mine, as before?' he asked.
> 'Yours now as then,' said she. (AI 87)

They arrange to meet at midnight, outside her town house in Chevron Square, just off Park Lane, but instead of appearing she leaves a letter for him, in which she explains that her residence in London has made her 'complicated, exclusive, and practised' (IA 89); to accept his addresses would be to accept 'an entire loss of position' that would be intolerable. Like Will Strong, Egbert Mayne makes a disastrous subsequent social call, though Hardy cut the angry, arrogant mother whose rouge runs when she faints and he pours water over her. Again the hero is dismissed, and, like Hardy in the summer of 1867, finding life in London 'depressing' (AI 93) and dangerous to his health, he returns to his native Tollamore, where the novella's climax is set.

In both novel and novella, the lady dies and the male protagonist survives. In the episode versified in the poem 'A Poor Man and a Lady', however, this narrative vengeance on the upper classes is withheld. Instead, Hardy works up the contrast between the lovers in their innocent early raptures and the sophistications and worldly wisdom that they acquire from life in London. In the first stanza, they enter into a private faux marriage, depicted in terms that evoke the rural setting in which both Will Strong and the Lady and Egbert Mayne and Geraldine fall in love:

> We knew it was not a valid thing,
> And only sanct in the sight of God
> (To use your phrase), as with fervent nod
> You swore your assent when I placed the ring
> On your pale slim hand. Our whispering
> Was soft as the fan of a turtledove
> That round our heads might have seemed to wing;
> So solemn were we; so sincere our love. (CP 791)

This presumably sexual relationship must, of course, be kept secret. As in novel and novella, the Lady soon after embarks on a life in upper-class metropolitan circles. Absorbed in her 'town campaigns', she grows, like Geraldine, increasingly 'complicated, exclusive, and practised'. Eventually the poor man reads in the newspapers that she is to marry a man 'of illustrious line and old'. Whereas the man and woman in *The Poor Man and the Lady* and 'An Indiscretion' run into each other the night before her wedding in the church in Tollamore, in the poem, their final rendezvous is in a church in London:

We met in a Mayfair church, alone:
(The request was mine, which you yielded to).
'But we were not married at all!' urged you:
'Why, of course we were!' I said. Your tone,
I noted, was world-wise. You went on:
' 'Twas sweet while it lasted. But you well know
That law is law. He'll be, anon,
My husband *really*. You, Dear, weren't so.'

'I wished—but to learn if—' faltered I,
And stopped. 'But I'll sting you not. Farewell!'
And we parted.—Do you recall the bell
That tolled by chance as we said good-bye? . . .
I saw you no more. The track of a high,
Sweet, liberal lady you've doubtless trod.
—All's past! No heart was burst thereby,
And no one knew, unless it was God. (CP 792–793)

Unlike the fervent Will Strong and Egbert Mayne, the speaker of the poem tells his tale from a knowing, resigned perspective. In fashioning this episode into an illustration of sophisticated town manners and social realpolitik, it is as if Hardy is directly acting on Morley's advice to him to read Balzac. The poem's attempt at wry and worldly humour makes it difficult to relate back to its original fictional source, its 'hard brio', to use a phrase of John Bayley's, being in complete contrast to the enraptured helplessness of his first novel's hero.[19] What is most interesting about the poem's narrative is what it reveals of Hardy's ability to derive a different kind of 'power & purpose' from his fantasy of an affair between a poor man and a lady: the narrator's magnanimity in the final stanza suggests the conversion of class resentment into what is almost its opposite, a demonstration of the gentlemanly independence and elegant savoir faire that he has developed as a result of his involvement with a 'comely woman of noble kith'. The allusion to the tolling bell is exquisitely in keeping with the sentimental education as to what makes a 'sweet, liberal lady', and what she can and can't do, that the poem records. The 'clever lad' has metamorphosed into an experienced and well-bred man about town.

Hardy must have taken Macmillan's letter and Morley's report as not quite adding up to a definitive rejection. Macmillan had, after all, said he ought to 'go on', and had even offered to find someone more familiar than he was with upper-class London life to give Hardy pointers on his representation of the beau monde. On 10 September 1868 Hardy wrote again, asking for clarification and advice:

> I wonder if your friend [i.e., Morley, whose report had been anonymous] meant the building up of a story, & not English composition, when he said I must study composition. Since my letter, I have been hunting up matter for another tale, which would consist entirely of rural scenes & humble life; but I have not courage to go on with it till something comes of the first. (CL 1:8)

In a postscript he added, either ingenuously or desperately, or both: 'Would you mind suggesting the sort of story you think I could do best, or any literary work I should do well to go on upon?' This reads as an almost embarrassingly frank request to Macmillan to take him under his wing, as Moule had earlier done, and illustrates the other side of the streak of stubbornness or perversity that so often led Hardy to confound expectations: his, on occasion, almost disarming openness to advice. He gave up the study of Greek, and all that it might have made possible, because Moule advised him to do so, and here seems to be asking Macmillan to decide what sort of writer he should try to be. Macmillan advised him to 'go on'; therefore he would 'go on', just as soon as he'd learned from the publisher what he should 'go on upon'. And yet although the letter may, as Michael Millgate has posited, reveal Hardy's 'professional and emotional vulnerability at this period' (MM 104), it also suggests his undiminished confidence in his own cleverness: once the topic of his homework has been set, there is no reason why he shouldn't come top of the class, as he had always done at school.

Macmillan was not to be drawn. In December of 1868 Hardy went up to London in person for an interview and learned that while *The Poor Man and the Lady*, 'if printed, might create a considerable curiosity, it was a class of book which Macmillan himself could not publish' (L 60). In the modern book trade's parlance, it was 'not quite right for our list'. Macmillan passed him on to Chapman & Hall, the publishers of Dickens. 'I fear the interview was an unfortunate one', noted Hardy in his diary after handing over his manuscript to Frederick Chapman in person in their offices at 193 Piccadilly (L 60). He had again to endure much shilly-shallying. Hearing nothing well into the New Year, on 17 January of 1869 he returned to London, thinking he might be able to expedite matters by being on the spot. He met again with Macmillan and was introduced to Morley; both suggested he find himself a niche in mid-Victorian Grub Street by contributing, like his friend Horace Moule, to publications such as the *Saturday Review*. Although a great ad-mirer of the *Saturday Review*, Hardy wisely resisted that particular route into the metropolitan literary industry, perhaps realizing that his only chance of launching and sustaining a literary career was by developing the profile that he had offered of himself in his first letter to Macmillan, that of 'a compara-tive outsider'. Further, as Charles Morgan put it in his account of Hardy's dealings with the firm, 'he was at heart a poet and a story-teller, not a con-troversialist'.[20] Both adrift and on tenterhooks, he spent his days 'studying pictures at the South Kensington Museum, and other places, and reading desultorily' (L 62). On 8 February he learned that Chapman & Hall's reader felt that the book lacked an 'interesting story', a failure that left its various episodes 'fatally injured'.[21] However, when Hardy was summoned to their offices, presumably thinking he was to have his manuscript returned to him, it was to be informed that the firm *would* publish his novel provided that he offered a £20 guarantee against loss. He returned to Higher Bockhampton, where proofs were to be sent, in the expectation that he would soon be making his literary debut, only to receive in early March a further summons to the offices of Chapman & Hall, this time to meet in person 'the gentleman who read your manuscript' (L 62).

'Forty years back,' opens Hardy's *terza rima* elegy of May 1909 for George Meredith,

> when much had place
> That since has perished out of mind,
> I heard that voice and saw that face.

> He spoke as one afoot will wind
> A morning horn ere men awake;
> His note was trenchant, turning kind. (CP 297–298)

There is a light irony in this vision of Meredith as a fearless Shelleyan prophet awakening mankind, for what he advised Hardy was, essentially, caution: *The Poor Man and the Lady* was so incendiary that publication might well ruin Hardy's literary career before it had started. Like the bachelor whom Hardy met on his first day in London, Meredith warned him of the importance of being 'practical'. Lecturing the novice 'in a sonorous voice', Meredith 'strongly advised' him 'not to "nail his colours to the mast" so definitely in a first book, if he wished to do anything practical in literature; for if he printed so pronounced a thing he would be attacked on all sides by the conventional reviewers, and his future injured' (L 62). Meredith was speaking from bitter experience. His first novel, *The Ordeal of Richard Feverel* (1859), had been deemed too sexually explicit by Mudie's Circulating Library, who cancelled their order of 300 copies—indeed it was partly the loss of revenue that followed Mudie's ban that meant Meredith had to supplement his income by working as a reader for Chapman & Hall. When Meredith's *Modern Love* was published in 1862, the *Saturday Review* pronounced it 'an elaborate analysis of a loathsome series of phenomena'.[22] Similar 'bludgeonings', to borrow a term used by Hardy in a posthumously published centenary tribute to Meredith written shortly before his own death (PV 469), would undoubtedly, the older novelist argued, greet the publication of *The Poor Man and the Lady*. Self-censoring revision was possible, but, in Meredith's opinion, the tyro author would be better off starting afresh, attempting 'a novel with a purely artistic purpose, giving it a more complicated "plot"' (L 64).

Even with such heartfelt advice ringing in his ears, Hardy could not quite bring himself to abandon all hopes of seeing his book in print. On 15 April he sent it to Smith, Elder & Co.—and on 30 April wrote to them arranging for the rejected manuscript to be deposited at Dorchester Station until he found time to collect it. The last firm he tried was Tinsley Brothers, who had established themselves as the leading purveyors of sensation fiction with

Mary Elizabeth Braddon's *Lady Audley's Secret* of 1862 and Wilkie Collins's *The Moonstone* of 1868. It seems that Moule acted as an intermediary for Hardy in negotiations with this firm, who were certainly the least prestigious of the four publishers that Hardy approached. They kept the manuscript for three months and then requested financial guarantees that must have exceeded those demanded by Chapman & Hall: in a letter of 14 September Hardy thanked them for communicating to his friend the terms on which they would publish his novel, but conceded the sum required was 'rather beyond me just now' (CL 1:10). His well-travelled and by now no doubt somewhat dog-eared manuscript was to be packaged up and sent by rail to the end of the line—'to be left at Weymouth Station till calld for'. The poor man at last gave up on *The Poor Man and the Lady.*

III

Well, not quite. It is perhaps ill-judged to figure a book that caused Hardy such grief and humiliation as a supernova, but his first three published works of fiction all contain significant amounts of material displaced from this lost ur-novel, and its influence can even be detected in as distant a star as *Jude.*[23] Retrieved from Weymouth Station, the manuscript must have been on or beside his desk as he set about conjuring up a novel with a complex plot (*Desperate Remedies*), in accordance with Meredith's advice, as well as when he went 'hunting up matter' for a tale that 'would consist entirely of rural scenes & humble life' (CL 1:8), a tale that turned into *Under the Greenwood Tree*. It was even drawn upon for the London scenes of *A Pair of Blue Eyes*, and possibly *The Hand of Ethelberta* too, before finally emerging in truncated form as 'An Indiscretion in the Life of an Heiress' in 1878. While never the *succès de scandale* it might have been if published in the late 1860s, it undoubtedly enjoyed a rich and complex afterlife. 'The varying strains shook and bent him to themselves as a rippling brook shakes and bends a shadow' (AI 86), Hardy observed of the effect of the *Messiah* on Egbert Mayne. He must have forgotten that he had already cannibalized the London concert scene in *Desperate Remedies*; listening to Aeneas Manston's performance of an oratorio on his organ, Cytherea is similarly overcome: 'The varying strains—now loud, now soft; simple, complicated, weird, touching, grand, boisterous, subdued; each phase distinct, yet modulating into the next with a graceful and easy flow—shook and bent her to themselves, as a gushing brook shakes and bends a shadow cast across its surface' (DR 131–132). What we don't know is if the extra material was also copied directly from the manuscript of *The Poor Man and the Lady*, or added only as he composed *Desperate Remedies*. There must have been some consolation for Hardy, and perhaps even an element of mischievous pleasure, in getting passages from a novel that had been so often rejected at last into print.

The toing and froing between London and Dorset of the manuscript of Hardy's first novel was replicated not only in the action of *The Poor Man and the Lady* itself, but in the convoluted plot that Hardy devised for his second assault on the London publishing industry. Reading the runes, he came to understand that it was the translation of his youthful aggression into an outspoken satirical attack on the ruling classes and the political regime over which they presided that had unsettled prospective publishers. There existed, however, a genre that, although it frequently provoked outrage in conservative quarters, not only channeled many of the disruptive energies that propelled *The Poor Man and the Lady* but attracted widespread attention and sold well too. Indeed, playing that June at the Theatre Royal in Weymouth was a stage version of the Tinsley brothers' first great success, *Lady Audley's Secret*. Sensation fiction, as developed by Mary Elizabeth Braddon and Wilkie Collins and Ellen Wood (whose highly popular *East Lynne* Meredith had also advised Chapman & Hall to turn down), allowed the transgressive excitements of the Gothic novel to invade that most sacred of Victorian spaces—the family hearth and home.[24] The challenge it posed to social conventions was not that of a man on a soapbox addressing like-minded protestors at a rally in Trafalgar Square, or the monstrosity of the son of peasants aspiring to the hand of the daughter of the local squire; more insidious, more exciting, more uncanny, it explored its readers' yearning to indulge in fantasies of violence and lawlessness, of liberation from all that 'proof and practice', to borrow Porter's terms, suppressed. The reader was not, of course, directly encouraged to condone bigamy and murder; rather the genre permitted the thrill of imaginatively participating in such crimes and the dissolution of customary restrictions that resulted, knowing that the narrative, in its final chapters, would reaffirm the moral and social status quo.

An outspoken foe of sensation fiction, it is unlikely that Meredith intended Hardy to follow in the footsteps of such as Collins and Braddon. In the *Life*, Hardy confesses that he put 'too crude an interpretation' on Meredith's words (L 87) when he 'set about constructing the eminently "sensational" plot of *Desperate Remedies*' (L 64), going on to suggest that the whole sensation genre went 'quite against his natural grain' (L 87).[25] Since an element of the sensational operates in nearly all of Hardy's novels, this reads like the attempt of a grand old man of letters, and one more proud of his poetry than his prose, to distance himself from the popular fiction market into which he was so eager to force his way in his youth. There is no doubting, however, his honesty when he reflected on the motives that prompted him, in the teeth of Meredith's views on the genre, to make use of it: 'finding himself in a corner, it seemed necessary to attract attention at all hazards' (L 87).

'At all hazards' . . . Meredith, Morley, Macmillan had already told Hardy that he pushed things too far—and critics of *Jude the Obscure*, from contemporaries such as Edmund Gosse to those who study the novel these days at school or university, often make the same point. In a characteristic fit of immoderation, Hardy decided that his first attempt at a sensation novel, a genre in which, to quote from his preface to the 1889 edition, 'mystery, entanglement, surprise, and moral obliquity are depended on for exciting interest' (DR 388), should have its plot set in motion by an incident of such extreme 'moral obliquity' that he must surely have known that every publisher in London would instantly blue-pencil it. The action of *Desperate Remedies* opens in Bloomsbury in 1835 with the arrival of Ambrose Graye, a young architect who has just joined a practice in the Midlands, to stay for Christmas with an old Cambridge friend who now lives in the capital. In the course of this visit Ambrose Graye is introduced to a retired naval officer called Bradleigh, and to his wife and daughter, who live in a small street near Russell Square. Ambrose rapidly falls in love with the daughter, Cytherea, and she seems to reciprocate his passion, only, for some unexplained reason, suddenly to cast him off. In Hardy's original version, this unexplained reason was that the previous year she had been raped at an evening party, and subsequently given birth to a son. For Morley, who again acted as a reader for Macmillan, this 'disgusting and absurd outrage' was 'too abominable to be tolerated as a central incident from which the action of the story is to move'.

It put the book categorically beyond the pale: 'Don't touch this', he counseled Macmillan, although again he found much in the novel that was impressive, conceding that Hardy's writing 'shows *power*—at present of a violent and undisciplined kind'; 'beg the author', he added, ' to discipline himself to keep away from such incidents as violation'.[26]

Sensation fiction operated on the premise that criminality was to be found where it was least expected, but in making the rape of a seventeen-year-old girl at a London evening party the origin of his novel's mystery, Hardy had again produced an unacceptable 'shriek of discord'. In the revised version the rape is dropped, and Cytherea is seduced and betrayed by a cousin, 'a wild officer of six and twenty' (DR 372), who then goes off to India and dies. Cytherea gives birth in Germany, and then returns to London. One night, anxious to be rid of her disgrace, she wraps up her infant, pins to his chest an envelope containing all the money that she can muster and a letter explaining that he must be called Aeneas (the son, in Virgil's *Aeneid*, of Venus/ Cytherea), and walks to Clapham: 'Here in a retired street she selected a house. She placed the child on the doorstep and knocked at the door, then ran away and watched. They took it up and carried it indoors' (DR 372). Soon regretting this precipitate disposal of her infant, she secretly arranges to have him brought to her at various hotels and coffee houses in Chelsea and Pimlico and Hammersmith, before paternal decree makes her sever all further contact. Decades later, having inherited a fortune, and hired as her lady's maid the daughter of the recently deceased Ambrose Graye—also named, in melancholy tribute to her, Cytherea—she resolves to engineer a match between her illegitimate son Aeneas and the beautiful young daughter of the only man she had ever loved . . .

Desperate Remedies was mainly composed in Hardy's lodgings at 3 Wooperton Street in the seaside town of Weymouth, where he lived for the second half of 1869. Hicks had died in February of that year, and Hardy found himself employed by his successor, George Crickmay, to direct the rebuilding of a church in a village some twenty miles north of Weymouth (where Crickmay's practice was based) called Turnworth. In *Desperate Remedies*, Weymouth becomes Creston (changed in accordance with Wessex nomenclature to Budmouth in the 1896 edition), Turnworth becomes Palchurch, and Stinsford becomes Carriford—having been Tollamore in

The Poor Man and the Lady. Whereas Hardy's first novel presented a fairly straightforward use of locations, opening in Dorset, moving to London, returning to Dorset, *Desperate Remedies* is shaped by a complicated and unsettling sense of mobility that refracts the enormous changes wrought in the county by the spread of the railways. Trains are vital to its plot, as indeed is *Bradshaw*, the railway guide first published in 1839, which Manston on one occasion crucially misreads; his failure to differentiate between the arrival times of second- and third-class trains from London to Carriford contributes significantly to the events leading up to his murder of his wife.

The novel also, on occasion, explores the damage inflicted by the railways on everyday rural life. The Three Tranters Inn, for instance, owned by the father of the novel's hero, Edward Springrove, was a vibrant staging post in the coaching era, but is now sinking into dereliction: 'The railway had absorbed the whole stream of traffic which formerly flowed through the village and along by the ancient door of the inn', the narrator explains, before picturing the deserted, silent stables:

> Next to the general stillness pervading the spot, the long line of outbuildings adjoining the house was the most striking and saddening witness to the passed-away fortunes of the Three Tranters Inn. It was the bulk of the original stabling, and where once the hoofs of two-score horses had daily rattled over the stony yard, to and from the stalls within, thick grass now grew, whilst the line of roofs—once so straight— over the decayed stalls, had sunk into vast hollows till they seemed like the cheeks of toothless age. (DR 118)

In this description of the decay afflicting the former staging inn, Hardy unwittingly broached exactly the kind of 'literary work', to borrow the terms of the postscript of his letter to Macmillan, that he 'should do well to go on upon': the pastoral under threat, a preternaturally astute editor might have advised him, would be what metropolitan audiences wanted, and would prove the key to commercial success.

The plot of *Desperate Remedies* is too involved and intricate, however, to allow much time for the pathos of rural obsolescence. Like that of *The Hand of Ethelberta*, it involves frequent shuttling between Dorset and London. Edward Springrove sets off for the capital in order to advance his career as an architect, as does, eventually, Cytherea's brother Owen, although only when all tribulations have been resolved. The two Cythereas travel up to London for the interviews held in Lincoln's Inn Fields for the stewardship of the Knapwater Estate. Aeneas Manston's wife travels down to Dorset from the capital, as does her double, Anne Seaway, a prostitute whom Aeneas hires to pretend to be his wife when it begins to be suspected that he murdered the first Mrs Manston. Letters between Cytherea and Springrove (who finds lodgings near Charing Cross—and works at Adelphi Place) and to Manston from his first wife Eunice (who lives for a time in impoverished Hoxton) are also used by Hardy to forward the London-Dorset axis of the plot. 'London N!' exclaims Cytherea Aldclyffe, pondering an envelope that contains a letter threatening blackmail from Manston's wife; 'It is the first time in my life I ever had a letter from that outlandish place the North side of London' (DR 152). Although no representative of rural innocence, Cytherea Aldclyffe here reflects the novel's general wariness of communications, and intruders, 'creeping across green fields' from the city to the country. London is figured in the novel as either the source of or location for many of the more sensational, or criminal, turns in the narrative. It is there that Aeneas Manston disguises himself and tails Edward Springrove, and afterwards spies on him through the window of his lodgings. From a fictitious address in London—79 Addington Street, Lambeth—Manston receives a fake letter, in fact composed by himself, purporting to be a reply from his wife to the adverts that he has been placing in London newspapers (DR 271). The epistolary traffic between London and Dorset is central to an extended sequence towards the end of the book in which Manston takes the early morning mail train from Waterloo to a station just short of Dorchester (here called Froominster) in order to track and intercept a letter written by Springrove (who has been pursuing amateur detective–style enquiries in the capital) to the Graye siblings. This letter contains evidence decisively proving that the supposed Mrs Manston is an impostor.

Hardy uses the reflections of the murderous, bigamous Aeneas Manston, as he idles around town before catching his night train from Waterloo back to Dorset, to convey the novel's sense of the deceitful uncertainties inherent in city living. Manston finds himself pondering the paradoxical

aspects of 'the individuals about him in the lively thoroughfare of the
Strand':

> Tall men looking insignificant: little men looking great and profound:
> lost women of miserable repute looking as happy as the days are long:
> wives, happy by assumption, looking careworn and miserable. Each and
> all were alike in this one respect, that they followed a solitary trail like the
> inwoven threads, which form a banner, and all were equally unconscious
> of the significant whole they collectively showed forth. (DR 299)

It is the occluded, and potentially treacherous, nature of the relationship between the individual and the collective in the city that Manston here articulates, and that he and his mother introduce into the rural community of
Carriford.

Desperate Remedies boasts no fewer than three young trainee architects—
or four if one includes the young Ambrose Graye. Edward Springrove is the
closest of these to his creator, and indeed appears to have imbibed the jaundiced, satirical perspective on the capital developed in *The Poor Man and
the Lady* even before attempting to better his fortunes there. The evening
before he leaves Creston for London he explains to Cytherea why he will not
prosper in the city: he shrinks from what Hardy called in the *Life* 'the business of social advancement' (L 54):

> 'Worldly advantage from an art doesn't depend upon mastering it. I
> used to think it did; but it doesn't. Those who get rich need have no
> skill at all as artists.'
>   'What need they have?'
>   'A certain kind of energy which men with any fondness for art pos-
> sess very seldom indeed—an earnestness in making acquaintances, and
> a love for using them. They give their whole attention to the art of dining
> out, after mastering a few rudimentary facts to serve up in conversa-
> tion.' (DR 44)

As Egbert Mayne's 'town campaign' leads him to expound the virtues of
Bonozzi Gozzoli rather than those of Raphael, so Edward Springrove is

already pondering the gap between a love of art and the acquisition and display of cultural capital. At times the poor man's outrage infiltrates the narrator's observations too: when the Cythereas alight in the middle of August from a cab in Waterloo Place, a contrast is offered between the idle lives of London's rich and those of its working population: 'they went along Pall Mall on foot, where in place of the usual well-dressed clubbists—rubicund with alcohol—were to be seen in linen pinafores, flocks of house-painters pallid from white lead' (DR 104). While the wealthy summer in the country, artisans, like Hardy's cousins Nat and James Sparks (later to be used as models for Sol and Dan Chickerel in *The Hand of Ethelberta*) repaint their expensive, exclusive clubs.

The struggle between Manston and Springrove for Cytherea is an archetypal pitting of the metropolitan libertine against the honest provincial.[27] Manston, as Robert Gittings first pointed out (RG 201), is modeled primarily on Ainsworth's Rochester from *Old St. Paul's*: 'He is a voluptuary with activity' (DR 109) the London lawyer Mr Nyttleton is able to declare after interviewing him, and Anne Seaway finds much evidence of his dissipation when she breaches his secret cabinet and discovers 'letters from different women, with unknown signatures, Christian names only; (surnames being despised in Paphos)' (DR 327)—Paphos being the kingdom of love and the birthplace of Venus or Aphrodite or Cytherea. As with Ainsworth's Rochester, it is, paradoxically, effeminacy that is the facial signifier of libidinous extremes:

> These [his lips] were full and luscious to a surprising degree, possessing a woman-like softness of curve, and a ruby redness so intense, as to testify strongly to much susceptibility of heart where feminine beauty was concerned—a susceptibility that might require all the ballast of brain with which he had previously been credited to confine within reasonable channels. (DR 128)

Hardy, who himself visited a phrenologist shortly after he arrived in London, uses the same cross-gendering formula to denote the transgressive desires of Cytherea Aldclyffe, who—in this luckier than her son—does get to spend a night kissing and fondling her namesake: 'There was a severity about the lower outlines of the face which gave a masculine cast to this portion of her countenance. Womanly weakness was nowhere visible save in one part—the curve of her forehead and brows—there it was clear and emphatic' (DR 55).

Mother and son's physiognomies are neatly complementary, for Manston's masculinity is concentrated in his forehead and eyes, which are 'penetrating and clear' (DR 128). Their easily established sexual mastery over Cytherea, which occurs almost instantly in both cases, is that of urban sophisticates over a defenceless ingénue, and matches that of Rochester over Amabel. As owner and steward of the Knapwater Estate, their economic advantage is also never in doubt, although, intriguingly, Hardy doesn't allow into the equation the kind of class superiority with which Ainsworth's evil rake taunts the low-born Leonard Holt. Elevated to be mistress of Knapwater House, Cytherea Aldclyffe behaves in the haughty, peremptory manner of an aristocrat, but as Cytherea Bradleigh she would, in her youth, have been delighted to marry a young architect with a job in the Midlands. And it transpires that the kind hands that lifted the infant Aeneas from a doorstep in Clapham belonged to the widow of a schoolmaster. Only a freak turn of fortune has granted them power over such as Cytherea and Owen Graye, who are looking to regain the rank and economic status lost by their improvident father, or over Edward Springrove, for whom architecture is to be the means to a secure position in the professional middle classes, and an escape from the threat of rural dispossession and poverty.

As well as providing the ingredients for a novel rich in 'mystery, entanglement, surprise, and moral obliquity', the battle fought for control of Cytherea by Manston (so aided and abetted by his mother that they are almost a double act), by Springrove, and by her brother Owen also, was Hardy's imaginative way of pondering the divisions created in him by his five years' residence in London. He returned 'with very different ideas of things' (L 57), and these ideas were destabilizing and disruptive. Indeed, the very act of choosing to set a novel in such a contemporary and highly controversial genre largely in the rural backwater near the place in which he had grown up was itself destabilizing and disruptive—the cultural equivalent of opening a railway line from the region to London. The scheming Manston and his mother serve as the alien but potent embodiments of these ideas, and while they end up suitably punished by its narrative, which concludes with Carriford cleansed and restored, for much of the novel it seems that Hardy has himself fallen under their spell. Although both are sensually greedy and deceitful, they are also glamorous, erotically mesmerizing, unpredictable, swayed by strong emotions, and between them inspire many of the novel's most memorable scenes: powerful and purposeful themselves, it is they, exotic, dangerous foreign bodies, geographic and generic transplants, who drive Hardy to demonstrate the 'power & purpose' of which his writing was capable.

The most obvious way in which *Desperate Remedies* refracts the destabilization effected by London on the returned native is Hardy's splitting of himself into three different architect figures. If Owen Graye evokes the pre-London Hardy, an affectionate brother rather than an aspirant lover, lame for much of the book, economically ineffective and easily bribed by Manston to hand over his sister; and Springrove is a version of the Will Strong/Egbert Mayne Hardy, who returns to Dorset from London having won his spurs (although through his detective rather than architectural or literary feats); then Manston is the Hardy made dangerously, even unassimilably sophisticated and ambitious by London, a daring artist who introduces into Dorset the tumultuous passions inspired by the *Messiah* in the breasts of Egbert Mayne and Geraldine Allenville by playing an oratorio on an organ of his own devising. The effect of the performance on Cytherea during a ferocious thunderstorm is as emotionally and erotically overwhelming as Hardy's 'awakening' to poetry in the years 1865–1867; the music exposes her to a whole new order of sensation and possibility: 'She was swayed into emotional opinions concerning the strange man before her; new impulses of thought came with new harmonies, and entered into her with a gnawing thrill. A dreadful flash of lightning then, and the thunder close upon it. She found herself involuntarily shrinking up beside him, and looking with parted lips at his face' (DR 132). 'O, how is it that man has so fascinated me!' she wonders, walking back to Knapworth House. As in the London concert hall scene in 'An Indiscretion', which it remodels, Hardy here allows his narrative to dilate self-reflexively on the power of art. Both Morley and Macmillan had commented on the power of *The Poor Man and the Lady*, and, although recommending the rejection of *Desperate Remedies* also, Morley's report couldn't help conceding the '*power*' of Hardy's writing. Macmillan concurred: a letter of 4 April 1870 conveyed his admiration for the book's 'very decided qualities, & very considerable power', although he quickly added that it was 'of far too sensational an order for us to think of publishing', and pointed out that the central incident of the story was 'such as greatly to endanger the success of any novel'.[28]

This verdict was delivered on a work of fiction that was actually unfinished, for, somewhat bizarrely, given its genre, Hardy chose to dispatch his manuscript to Macmillan on 5 March 1870, before he had composed its final few chapters, although he must have included the '*précis*' of its denouement mentioned in the *Life* (L 79). Two days later he set off, on another commission from Crickmay, to assess the repairs needed to a church in St. Juliot in Cornwall. When Emma Gifford opened the front door of the rectory on the evening of 7 March, to set eyes on her future husband for the first time, she noticed a blue paper sticking out of the young architect's pocket and was delighted when it proved not to be a drawing of the church, as she had assumed, but the manuscript of a poem. To deepen the alliance of power with purpose in his art, Hardy required a woman to woo and to win; and having gained the hand of the lady, the poor man would also need to earn enough from his writing to support her according to the expectations of her class.

Hardy's coffin leaving Max Gate for cremation in Woking

The urn containing Hardy's ashes in the crematorium at Woking

Wreaths in Poets' Corner after Hardy's Westminster Abbey funeral

The burial of Hardy's heart in Stinsford

Hardy's gravestone in Westminster Abbey

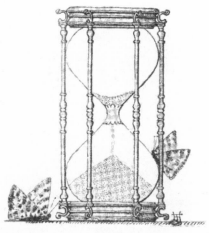

Hardy's illustration for 'Amabel' in *Wessex Poems*

16 Westbourne
Park Villas

Holywell Street

Sketch of view from Westbourne Park Villas, 22 June 1866

Sketch of St. James's Park, 28 April 1863

Hardy's illustration for 'She, to Him I' in *Wessex Poems*

Eliza Nicholls's photograph of Hardy (c.1862)

The Hardy Tree in St. Pancras Churchyard

St. Giles Cripplegate Church

1 Arundel Terrace, Trinity Road, Tooting

Mr Hardy and Mr Comyns Carr are not admiring Mr Stare's acting. They have brought Mr George Lewis to see whether it will be possible to imprison Mr Pinero.

Sketch of Hardy, J. Comyns Carr, and George Lewis in a box at
St. James's Theatre watching Pinero's *The Squire* (*The Illustrated
Sporting and Dramatic News*, 7 January 1882)

5

The Hand of E. (I)

I

Four years before he embarked on his fateful trip to St. Juliot, Hardy composed a short lyric entitled 'Postponement':

Snow-bound in woodland, a mournful word,
Dropt now and then from the bill of a bird,
Reached me on wind-wafts; and thus I heard,
    Wearily waiting:—

'I planned her a nest in a leafless tree,
But the passers eyed and twitted me,
And said: "How reckless a bird is he,
    Cheerily mating!"'

'Fear-filled, I stayed me till summer-tide,
In lewth of leaves to throne her bride;
But alas! her love for me waned and died,
    Wearily waiting.

'Ah, had I been like some I see,
Born to an evergreen nesting-tree,
None had eyed and twitted me,
    Cheerily mating!' (CP 11)

The poem's lilting rhymes and alliterations and refrains, and its use of a stylized pastoral setting, serve almost as camouflage for the anguished social, political, and personal dilemma that Hardy here articulates. The importance to him of the marriage question can hardly be overestimated; it looms large in nearly all of his fiction, and as a motive for the writing of that fiction as well. 'Postponement' reveals him as both frankly envious of those born into such affluence that they can wed when- and whomever they want, and as clear-eyed about the social humiliations risked by anyone attempting to enter the marriage market without such class and economic privileges; the eyeing and the twitting of the mocking passers-by are experienced as more galling even than the loss of the bird's projected mate. Hardy's pursuit of the hand of Emma, despite the *Life*'s protestations to the contrary, ended up exposing him to precisely the kinds of ridicule and scorn anticipated in this poem: 'a low-born churl who has presumed to marry into *my* family' is how Emma's father, John Attersoll Gifford, taking the role of the outraged paterfamilias of melodrama, on one occasion described his illustrious son-in-law.[1] What was undoubtedly clear to Hardy by the end of his first residence in London was that the composition of lyrics such as 'Postponement' was not going to enable him to change from one 'wearily waiting' to one able to provide his spouse with an adequately furnished nest.

Hardy and Emma's courtship lasted from March of 1870 to September of 1874. The four novels that he published during these years all present, like 'Postponement', a competition for the right to set about 'cheerily mating'. Indeed, in its depiction of the battle between Manston and Springrove for Cytherea, *Desperate Remedies* established the template roughly adhered to in the majority of Hardy's subsequent novels: two or more male protagonists compete for the right to marry the heroine. Hardy was particularly drawn to the formula of three different kinds of suitor pursuing the same woman from different social and economic angles: Dick Dewy, Farmer Shiner, and Reverend Maybold are the contrasting rivals for the hand of Fancy Day in *Under the Greenwood Tree*; Stephen Smith, Henry Knight, and Lord Luxellian for that of Elfride Swancourt in *A Pair of Blue Eyes*; Gabriel Oak, Farmer Boldwood, and Sergeant Troy for that of Bathsheba in *Far from the Madding Crowd*; Bob Loveday, John Loveday, and Festus Derriman for that of Anne Garland in *The Trumpet-Major*. The picaresque storyline of *The Hand of Ethelberta* throws up four candidates for the heroine's affections (Christopher Julian, Eustace Ladywell, Alfred Neigh, and Lord Mountclere), while the plots of *The Return of the Native*, *A Laodicean*, *The Mayor of Casterbridge*, *The Woodlanders*, and of *Tess* and *Jude* require only two. It might well be argued that the most crucial compositional decision that Hardy ever made was to split his ur-hero Will Strong of *The Poor Man and the Lady* into the three competing architect figures of *Desperate Remedies*, for it was this initial act of self-triangulation that ended up furnishing him with a seemingly inexhaustible set of narrative possibilities. Only *Two on a Tower* and *The Well-Beloved* develop plots that do not make use of the dynamics of male rivalry.

As far as one can tell, Hardy himself had no serious competitors for Emma's hand, although much was made in the rectory at St. Juliot of various attentions that had been paid to her by a local farmer (MM 113). While the contending males of Hardy's early novels refract the class and professional and economic uncertainties by which he was so acutely riven during the years of his courtship of Emma, his unstable conception of his identity and future can also be traced in his repeated and erratic shifting of quarters from Dorset to London and back. In the poem 'In the Seventies', collected in *Moments of Vision*, he reflects on the construction put by his neighbours and a single friend (presumably Horace Moule) on the seeming aimlessness of his life at this time. Unlike the bird of 'Postponement', who rashly makes public his dreams, only to be eyed and twitted by caustic observers, the poem's speaker rather proudly records how he kept 'penned tight' in his breast the 'starry thoughts that threw a magic light' on his inner sense of purpose. This reticence, however, led onlookers back then to assume that he was merely drifting, and likely to go to the bad:

> In the seventies when my neighbours—even my friend—
> > Saw me pass,
> Heads were shaken, and I heard the words, 'Alas,
> For his onward years and name unless he mend!'
> In the seventies, when my neighbours and my friend
> > Saw me pass.

In the seventies those who met me did not know
    Of the vision
That immuned me from the chillings of misprision
And the damps that choked my goings to and fro
In the seventies; yea, those nodders did not know
    Of the vision. (CP 459)

The poem's epigraph from Job, however, somewhat undermines the radiant confidence that Hardy here asserts underlay his apparent indecisiveness. *Qui deridetur ab amico suo sicut ego* ('I am as one mocked by his neighbour'). Hardy inscribed the dates 1868–1871 beside this verse in one of his bibles (MM 106), suggesting that his inner belief in his own election was not consistently able to dispel anxiety about those eyeing and twitting his unsteady pursuit of his 'starry thoughts'.

'Goings to and fro' neatly captures the restlessness and randomness of Hardy's early courtship years. Some two months after he returned to Dorset from St. Juliot, with magic in his eyes, Hardy set off again for London. The initial spur to this particular flitting was the welcome news that Tinsley was willing to publish *Desperate Remedies*, provided Hardy himself contributed £75 up front to defray expenses. While not exactly a munificent offer, it was enough to make the much-rejected author feel like trying his luck in the capital again. This time he found lodgings at 23 Montpelier Street, just off the Brompton Road in Knightsbridge. It was perhaps his hope that the energies of the city would instil in him a measure of drive and purposefulness, but it appears that instead he found himself almost unnervingly rudderless, becalmed, as he put it, in a 'backwater' (L 80). Certainly there is precious little evidence of the visionary conviction depicted in 'In the Seventies' in his account of his metropolitan summer of 1870 in the *Life*: 'He seems to have passed the days in Town desultorily and dreamily—mostly visiting museums and picture-galleries, and it is not clear what he was waiting for there' (L 79). He did odd jobs for Blomfield, as well as for the architect and architectural writer Raphael Brandon, whose chambers at 17 Clement's Inn on the Strand would later serve as a model for Henry Knight's chambers in *A Pair of Blue Eyes*. He met up with Moule. He wrote letters to Emma, and the poem 'Ditty' that is dedicated to her. He read Auguste Comte. Seven days after his thirtieth birthday he saw the announcement of the death of Charles Dickens but was inspired to no further comment by the passing of the era's greatest novelist. Hardy must surely have been puzzled that summer to find himself, despite Tinsley's firm offer, stubbornly incapable of composing the final four chapters of *Desperate Remedies* (these chapters are, perhaps unsurprisingly, by far the least convincing part of the book). He was able to turn his hand to the task only on his return to Dorset after his August holiday in Cornwall, and it was not until early December that he eventually dispatched to Tinsley the final version of the manuscript, much of which was in 'the hand of E.', having been fair-copied by Emma.

The book was published in three volumes, in an edition of 500 copies, on 25 March 1871. Among the most excruciating of the 'chillings of misprision' that Hardy was ever to experience came the following month: 'This is an absolutely anonymous story', opened the review in the *Spectator*,

> no falling back on previous works which might give a clue to the authorship, and no assumption of a *nom de plume* which might, at some future time, disgrace the family name, and still more, the Christian name of a repentant and remorseful novelist—and very right too. By all means let him bury the secret in the profoundest depths of his own heart, out of reach, if possible, of his own consciousness. The law is hardly just which prevents Tinsley Brothers from concealing their own participation also. (CH 3)

Punning on the novel's title, the reviewer went on to call it a desperate remedy for 'an emaciated purse'. Far from feeling himself 'immuned' by his vision from all such slurs, Hardy was cut to the quick; in a passage intended for the *Life*, but which he eventually decided to omit, he recorded the devastating effect on him of the *Spectator*'s attack: 'He remembered, for long years after, how he had read this review as he sat on a stile leading to the eweleaze {sheep pasture} he had to cross on his way to Bockhampton. The bitterness of that moment was never forgotten; at the time he wished that he were dead' (L 507/FH 111). Although he eventually decided to remove this particular example of his sensitivity to the scornful jibes of metropolitan reviewers, the *Life* offers an extensive and detailed litany of Hardy's complaints at the various injustices that he endured in the pages of London's newspapers and magazines. The image of an embattled provincial writer suffering the slings and arrows wantonly hurled at him by the urban reviewing industry is so persistent in his autobiography as to become almost a leitmotif—and it might be said, on its own plane, to echo the duel between Manston, the urban dandy, and the honourable rural Springrove. Even in the years of his greatest acclaim, Hardy found that the whole business of London reviewers delivering their judgements of his work provoked in him an irritation that often bordered on outrage. Certainly it was to this damaging review that Hardy attributed the speedy remaindering of *Desperate Remedies*, which he was aghast to find on sale at Smith and Son's on Exeter Station platform for a mere two shillings and sixpence only three months after its publication. The *Spectator*, he decided, had 'snuffed out the book' (L 87).

Hardy probably met his first publisher William Tinsley for the first time in January of 1871, when he made a flying visit to London to hand over in cash the £75 required to underwrite the publication of *Desperate Remedies*. Although the firm that he founded with his brother Edward (who died in 1866) was held in much lower esteem than publishers such as Macmillan, Chapman & Hall, and Smith, Elder & Co., William Tinsley deserves considerable credit for the role he played in launching Hardy's novelistic career. Over the summer of 1871 Hardy set about expanding the tranter scenes that Morley had praised in his report on *The Poor Man and the Lady* into *Under the Greenwood Tree* (subtitled, perhaps in tribute to his dreamy hours in London's galleries, 'A Rural Painting of the Dutch School'), which was submitted to Macmillan in August. There it elicited yet another thoughtful and largely positive reader's report from Morley, who was charmed by its humour and its characters, but questioned the book's likely profitability: 'I don't prophesy a large market for it', he warned, 'because the work is so delicate as not to hit every taste by any means. But it is good work, and would please people whose taste is not ruined by novels of exaggerated action or forced ingenuity'—that is novels such as *Desperate Remedies*![2] Macmillan intimated to Hardy that he would probably be willing to publish it the following year, but his letter suggesting as much seems to have been interpreted by Hardy as a rejection. Immediately he turned again to Tinsley, only to find that he too was unwilling to commit himself to publishing

Hardy's 'little rural story' (CL 1:13). That the book ever saw the light of day was the result more of chance than Hardy's inner belief in his own literary destiny, or his trust in the 'magic light' that he kept 'penned tight' in his breast in the seventies:

> In the seventies nought could darken or destroy it,
>> Locked in me,
> Though as delicate as lamp-worm's lucency;
> Neither mist nor murk could weaken or alloy it
> In the seventies!—could not darken or destroy it,
>> Locked in me. (CP 459)

But locked in him it might well have remained, or so the *Life* would have us believe, had Hardy not happened to run into Tinsley in the Strand in late March of 1872.

The year 1872 was undoubtedly the pivotal year in Hardy's literary career. That spring he embarked on yet another London sojourn, resolutely determined to succeed there—as an architect. Despite Emma's urgings that he should persist with his 'true vocation' of literature, Hardy was this time 'fully bent on sticking to the profession which had been the choice of his parents for him rather than his own'; all he allowed himself was 'a faint dream at the back of his mind that he might perhaps write verses as an occasional hobby' (L 89). Just as in the summer of 1867 he left behind in Westbourne Park Villas the poems composed during his first residence in London, so he returned to the capital five years later without the manuscript of *Under the Greenwood Tree*, which lay abandoned in a box in the family home. With it lay Hardy's hopes of making a living from his writing.

In this grimly realistic mood he moved into lodgings in his old stomping ground of Paddington, at 4 Celbridge Place, only a couple of hundred yards from 16 Westbourne Park Villas. He found employment with T. Roger Smith, one of the judges of the Architectural Association prize that Hardy had won some nine years earlier. Smith's offices were in Bedford Street just off the Strand, and Hardy was hired to assist with designs for a series of new London schools that Smith planned to enter into a competition organized by the London Schools Board. Like his namesake in *A Pair of Blue Eyes*,

Smith had spent a number of years in Bombay, where his designs were used for the grandiose, Ruskin-inspired post office, and for the British Hospital. Living in Paddington, working in an architectural office off the Strand, there must have been an element of Groundhog Day for Hardy as, mornings and evenings, he trudged across town, no doubt wondering, like the clerk of 'Coming Up Oxford Street', if he'd ever escape the 'rut' of such routines. Like this clerk, he too was worried about his eyesight. Soon after arriving in London, Hardy bumped into Horace Moule just off Trafalgar Square. He revealed to his mentor that, Moule's belated but laudatory response to *Desperate Remedies* in the *Saturday Review* notwithstanding, he had decided to abandon literature once and for all:

> Moule was grieved at this, but merely advised him not to give up writing altogether, since, supposing anything were to happen to his eyes from the fine architectural drawing, literature would be a resource for him; he could dictate a book, article, or poem, but not a geometrical design. This, Hardy used to say, was essentially all that passed between them; but by a strange coincidence Moule's words were brought back to his mind one morning shortly after by his seeing, for the first time in his life, what seemed like floating specks on the white drawing-paper before him. (L 90)

One is put in mind of Owen Graye's lameness, which is so clearly a physical embodiment of his social and economic powerlessness. As Hardy had learned on his very first day in the city, only practical men were wanted in London.

This moment of feared visual impairment registers as the nadir of Hardy's fortunes, as they are reconstructed, at any rate, by the narrative of the *Life*, and the affliction is subliminally evoked in the dazzle blinding the city clerk whose eyesight, we learn, is 'not of the best', but whose livelihood self-evidently depends on being able to see. (It is perhaps worth pointing out that the previous year Hardy had listed his occupation in the national Census as 'architect's clerk', just as he had in the Census of 1861, MM 123.) The specks dancing before his eyes may well have been a psychosomatically induced ailment that served to justify his 'keeping a hand on the pen' (L 91), but they must also have filled him with the bleak terror that makes his city clerk wonder why he was born. It is striking, further, that in his triumphant re-configuration of his life in the seventies in the retrospective poem of that name, he stresses the power of his 'vision', which neither 'mist nor murk could weaken or alloy'.

It was, in the event, or at least as he tells it, a chance encounter on the Strand with Tinsley that was to save Hardy from his city clerk's fate, and allow him to convert the oppressive urban dazzle of 'Coming Up Oxford Street' into the 'magic light' of 'In the Seventies'. The son of a gamekeeper, Tinsley had grown up in Hertfordshire and never acquired the metropolitan polish and authority of establishment literary figures such as Hardy's next editor, Leslie Stephen. In his account of their meeting in the *Life*, Hardy feels free to reproduce phonetically Tinsley's uncouth speech, making him into a stage Cockney. The publisher's offices were in Catherine Street, near the Royal Opera House in Covent Garden, and it was while musing on a poster advertising the Italian Opera that Hardy felt a heavy hand on his shoulder. When, its owner peremptorily demanded, was Hardy going to give him another novel? Although he was pleased to have recently learned that he'd lost only £15 of his original £75 stake in *Desperate Remedies*, Hardy firmly replied 'Never'.

'Wot, now!' said Tinsley. 'Haven't you anything written?'

Hardy remarked that he had written a short story some time before, but didn't know what had become of the MS., and did not care. He also had outlined one for three volumes; but had abandoned it. He was now doing better things, and attending to his profession of architect.

'Damned if that isn't what I thought you wos!' exclaimed Mr Tinsley. 'Well, now, can't you get that story, and show it to me?'

Hardy would not promise, reminding the publisher that the account he had rendered for the other book was not likely to tempt him to publish a second.

''Pon my soul, Mr Hardy,' said Tinsley, 'you wouldn't have got another man in London to print it! Oh, be hanged if you would! 'twas a blood-curdling story! Now please try to find that new manuscript and let me see it.'

Hardy could not at first recollect what he had done with the MS., but recalling at last he wrote to his parents at home, telling them where to search for it, and to forward it to him. (L 90–91)

Hardy had in fact undertaken to call at Tinsley's offices, as detailed in a letter that predates this encounter (CL 1:16), so he may be overplaying the serendipitous aspect of this sudden turn of events. But sudden it certainly proved to be, for in under three months *Under the Greenwood Tree* was in print, and by the end of the year its publication had prompted Leslie Stephen to write to Hardy asking if he would contribute a serial to the prestigious *Cornhill* magazine. The irony that Hardy seems to be relishing in the *Life* is that, whereas he had gained nothing from his previous attempts to forward his literary fortunes by coming up to London in order to be 'on the spot', it was while doggedly pursuing his architectural career in the city that his literary ambitions received this decisive fillip.

Hardy, afterwards always so canny in his dealings with publishers, sold the copyright of *Under the Greenwood Tree* for a mere £30. The novel was, as Tinsley recalled in his autobiography, 'one of the best press-noticed books' that his firm ever published, though sales were unimpressive.[3] The *Athenaeum* was pleased to see that the author of *Desperate Remedies* had exchanged his 'explorations into the dark ways of human crime and folly' for rustic humour, 'that vein of his genius which yields the best produce' (CH 9). On 5 July the *Pall Mall Gazette* commended its 'freshness and originality', although, like many subsequent reviewers of Hardy's novels, doubted the veracity of the shrewd eloquence put into the mouths of its yo-kels.[4] Horace Moule came through, although again belatedly, declaring in the *Saturday Review* that Hardy had written 'the best prose idyl [*sic*] that we have seen for a long while past', one 'full of humour and keen observation, and with the genuine air of the country breathing throughout it' (CH 11, 14).

II

It was 4 July, the day before the *Pall Mall Gazette* review appeared, that Hardy dated his observation of his hapless doppelganger on Oxford Street:

The sun from the west glares back,
And the sun from the watered track,
And the sun from the sheets of glass,
And the sun from each window-brass;
Sun-mirrorings, too, brighten
From show-cases beneath
The laughing eyes and teeth
Of ladies who rouge and whiten.
And the same warm god explores
Panels and chinks of doors;
Problems with chymists' bottles
Profound as Aristotle's
He solves, and with good cause,
Having been ere man was.

Also he dazzles the pupils of one who walks west,
A city-clerk, with eyesight not of the best,
Who sees no escape to the very verge of his days
From the rut of Oxford Street into open ways;
And he goes along with head and eyes flagging forlorn,
Empty of interest in things, and wondering why he was born.

As seen 4 July 1872 (CP 717)

The date 4 July of 1872 was a Thursday, and it was no doubt on his homeward journey from Bedford Street to Celbridge Place that Hardy noted
down the details of the street scene that inspired this two-part poem. The
contrast between its first and second sections vividly embodies the conflicted
polarities of Hardy's feelings about the city. The first is almost a hymn to
some urban Apollo, a paean to a 'warm' metropolitan god of light and
plenty, and erotic possibility. Like the 'conspiring sun' of Keats's 'To Autumn',
Hardy's pagan deity is impartially everywhere, linking all that he explores,
solving whatever he touches, penetrating even the layers of the city's evolution
and history, 'Having been ere man was'. A number of the attributes associated
with Apollo are lightly evoked—in addition to sun and light there are glancing
allusions to medicine ('chymists' bottles') and knowledge (Aristotle), while

the section's fourteen rhymed lines register as a celebration of poetry's own sunlike powers of connection. The 'sun-mirrorings' unify the precise, if fragmented, details that the poem records into a kaleidoscopic whole, at the same time dissolving all the judgements that would impose divisions between, say, the manmade and the natural, between the 'laughing eyes and teeth' of the ladies, and their rouge and whitener. Are they bourgeois women out shopping, or prostitutes at work? This is one of the 'problems' that would confront anyone attempting to interpret the human traffic on Oxford Street on a summer evening in 1872, but one that the indifferent sun renders meaningless through its beneficent impartiality, liberating all that is observed into a sublime unity with the warm primal god who presides over the scene.

Urban oppression is often conveyed in Hardy's London poems by absence of light: the city shopwoman longs to escape the 'rayless grime' of the metropolis, while the wife in 'A Wife in London', who is about to learn that her husband has been killed in the Boer War, is enveloped in a murky pea-souper—'the tawny vapour / That the Thames-side lanes have uprolled' (CP 91). The Clement's Inn tree addressed in 'To a Tree in London' is 'swarthy', 'black, blind', unaware 'That far hence / Air is sweet in a blue immense' (CP 868), while Hardy's equally sun-starved East End curate lives in a 'small blind street off East Commercial Road' (CP 713). His city clerk is tormented, in contrast, by the irrelevance to him of the sunlit abundance and variety on display in the shops and in the street; or, to put it another way, by the social anxieties and pressures that make it impossible for him to inhabit the high romantic genre of the hymn to the 'warm god'. The sun may render material conditions of no moment to the rhapsodic, free-floating consciousness of the first section, but the lodgings-bound commuting city clerk belongs to a different genre, that of social realism—as do the shopwoman, the soon-to-be-bereaved wife, and the selfless curate. His condition might be read as the antithesis of that of the poet of 'In the Seventies', who, however menaced by 'mist and murk' without, feels irradiated by his own inner 'magic light'. Hardy's clerk, surrounded on all sides by dazzle, is inside 'Empty of interest in things'. The long lines and heavy rhymes (west / best, days / ways, forlorn / born) convey the melancholy monotony of a life lacking what 'In the Seventies' calls 'vision'. In other words, the second wing of this asymmetrical urban diptych dramatizes, like 'Neutral Tones', Hardy's fear of a life deprived of both romance and poetry.

The disjunction between the two sections' metres and genres reflects the personal Rubicon that Hardy reached in the summer of 1872, and it may have been to deflect attention from the poem's relevance to his own biography that he altered the pronouns from the first to the third person when he collected it in *Human Shows*. That summer Hardy stood, as he later put it in a letter, 'at the parting of the ways' (CL 4:83). On 8 July Tinsley wrote inquiring about the novel in three volumes to which Hardy had alluded in the course of their discussion on the Strand, and in an earlier letter (CL 1:14). Would he consider submitting it to run as a serial in *Tinsley's Magazine*, commencing in September? While Hardy claimed to have 'abandoned' this project when he mentioned it to the publisher in late March, his nervous response of the following day makes it clear that he hadn't really begun it: 'I have nothing ready I am sorry to say. . . . On looking over the MS. I find it must have a great deal of re-consideration. Thanks for your offer to give it your attention. I shall leave town on the 27th & will take an opportunity of giving you a call before I go' (CL 1:17). Even its title had not been settled on, Hardy initially intending to call it *A Winning Tongue Had He*. A sly humour permeates what may well be the largely fictitious account given in the *Life* of his jousting with Tinsley at their meetings in Catherine Street, meetings that Robert Gittings doubts ever took place (RG 227). Having worked out, Hardy recounts, what he might earn from architecture in the six months that he reckons it will take him to write the novel, he doubles the figure and presents it to Tinsley: ' "All right, all right, Mr Hardy—very reasonable," said the friendly publisher, smacking Hardy's shoulder. "Now come along into the office here, and we'll sign the agreement, and the job will be off our minds." ' Eager to prove himself no longer a country rube, Hardy tells us that he smelled a rat and backed off. On his return the next day, having read up on copyright, he made it clear to Tinsley that he would not repeat the blunder of signing away future rights. Both Hardy and Tinsley, who came from roughly similar rural socio-economic backgrounds, emerge from the account in the *Life* sounding more like a pair of hard-bargaining horse-traders than an author and his publisher:

'Well, I'm damned!' Tinsley said, with a grim laugh. 'Who the devil have you been talking to, Mr Hardy, if I may ask, since I saw you yesterday?'

Hardy said 'Nobody'. (Which was true, though only literally.)

'Well, but—Now, Mr Hardy, you are hard, very hard upon me! However, I do like your writings; and if you'll throw in the three-volume edition of the novel with the magazine rights I'll agree.'

Hardy assented to this. (L 92)

Whether or not this conversation took place, Hardy's assent, confirmed in a letter of 27 July, proved to be the moment that he committed himself to a literary career. He was to receive £200, at the rate of £15 a month, and agreed to deliver the first instalment (chapters 1–5) by 7 August, with publication scheduled to commence the following week. This brutal deadline led him to wonder if he had not done 'a rash thing' (L 93), especially since his contract with Smith ran up to the end of July. In the evenings after work, and in the first week of August, Hardy sat down in his lodgings in Celbridge Place and set about discovering if he could become, in his own phrase, 'a good hand at a serial' (L 102).

III

It took him a while to get going. The first two paragraphs of the version of *A Pair of Blue Eyes* printed in *Tinsley's Magazine* and then in the first edition of 1873 (these paragraphs were cut in 1877) reveal Hardy at his most laborious and periphrastic:

Concerning the beings categorised above [a reference to the cast list of characters given] it may be premised that of the aim and meaning of their appearance upon the earth, of what, in its highest sense, they came into the world to do—if much, if little, or whether to be only lookers-on and do nothing at all—no analysis will be given. Even from their social life—a congeries of significant phenomena—we sip but a sweet or bitter here and there in flying along. In other words, on the subject only of some nodes in the orbits of their lives is it the province of this narrative to be diffuse. (PBE 355)

Oh dear oh dear, Tinsley must have thought on reading this, and he could hardly have been cheered up by Hardy's second paragraph, which delivers the same ungainly mix of defensiveness and pompous throat clearing. Then we meet Elfride Swancourt, who is introduced to us reading a romance. This section of *A Pair of Blue Eyes* appeared only in the magazine version, Hardy perhaps deeming its gentle mockery of her tearful response to the fictional hero's death likely to undermine the pathos of Elfride's own premature demise. The passage is interesting, however, in its depiction of his heroine on the cusp of a decisive change, a change that can be construed as an inverted reflection of the moment of transition through which Hardy was himself passing: 'She never forgot that novel, and those minutes of sadness', the narrator observes:

> Not that the story was the most powerful she had ever read; not that those tears were the bitterest that had ever flowed. But for this reason: that it was the last time in her life that her emotions were ever wound up to any height by circumstances which never transpired; that the loves and woes, expectations and despairs, of imaginary beings were ever able so much to emulate her own experiences as to make a perceptible difference to her state of mind for a whole afternoon. (PBE 356)

Hardy's acceptance of Tinsley's offer meant that he was effectively committed to jumping the other way through the looking glass: 'imaginary beings', and his ability to interest readers in their 'loves and woes, expectations and despairs', were to become crucial to the ways in which his real-life 'circumstances', such as his chances of marrying the original of Elfride, 'transpired'.

On 7 August Hardy boarded a steamship bound for Plymouth at London Bridge. Aware that the journey might furnish him with useful material for the novel on which he had embarked, he paid detailed attention to the docklands scene on the Thames, as well as to the journey itself; chapter 39 in instalment nine of *A Pair of Blue Eyes* duly describes Elfride, Knight, and Mr and Mrs Swancourt travelling across the city to London Bridge and then making exactly this voyage. From Plymouth, Hardy travelled to Kirland House near Bodmin in Cornwall, whither he had directed Tinsley to send proofs of the first instalment of *A Pair of Blue Eyes*, care of Mr Gifford, Emma's father. If the intention was that the arrival of a substantial packet of proofs from a London publisher would dispose the irascible, alcoholic, and highly class-conscious ex-solicitor to look favourably on the tyro novelist's request for his daughter's hand in marriage, then Hardy's gambit miserably failed. All mention of this presumably disastrous interview has been wiped from the record, although traces of it surely found their way into Mr Swancourt's outraged response to Stephen Smith's declaration of his desire to marry Elfride. An elliptical reference to the 'evil wrought at Rou'tor Town' (CP 517—Rough Tor is not far from Bodmin) was the only allusion that Hardy ever allowed himself to his ill-judged attempt to gain the blessing of his future father-in-law.

Like its predecessors, *A Pair of Blue Eyes* drew heavily on *The Poor Man and the Lady*, fusing this pre-existing material with Hardy's fictional recreation of his courtship of Emma in the rectory at St. Juliot, where Emma lived with her younger sister Helen and Helen's much older husband, the Reverend Caddell Holder. Although Hardy had made his initial journey to Cornwall on 7 March from Higher Bockhampton as the employee of an architectural firm based in Weymouth, it is as a 'London man' (PBE 8) that Stephen Smith is anxiously awaited by Elfride, while her father suffers, as Emma's brother-in-law had on the evening of Hardy's arrival, an attack of gout. How, Elfride wonders to her ailing father, should she receive this 'strange London man of the world' (PBE 9)? The discomfiting joke played by Hardy on the inhabitants of the fictional rectory at Endelstow, and to some extent on those of the real one at St. Juliot, was that this 'strange London man of the world' turns out, like his creator, to be the son of a mason—in the magazine version and first edition a mere journeyman mason, although in later editions Hardy elevated his status to that of a master-mason (PBE 68). More excruciating still, Smith was born and bred in a humble cottage not far from the rectory, where his parents and siblings still live.

In developing the arc of its plot and the themes that emerge from it, *A Pair of Blue Eyes* is as dependent as *The Poor Man and the Lady* and *Desperate Remedies* before it on transitions between London and its rural setting, a region of Cornwall peopled by rustics who bear a suspicious resemblance to the inhabitants of Tollamore and Carriford and Mellstock. Smith's situation is so closely modelled on that of his creator that Hardy's claim to have invested none 'of his own personality' (L 76) in the young architect's clerk, basing the character on a mason employed by his father, registers as one of his least convincing attempts to fend off biographical inferences. The novel almost transparently uses Smith as a vehicle for Hardy's feelings of deracination and the issues raised by his ill-defined, intermediate social status. Smith, we learn, received, like Hardy, a good education (with Knight playing the role of Horace Moule), was apprenticed to a provincial architect at the age of fifteen (a year younger than Hardy), and then found employment in a London architectural office (PBE 71).

Among the questions tacitly raised by Hardy's depiction of Stephen Smith in *A Pair of Blue Eyes* was one of pressing personal significance: to what extent can the opportunities for upward mobility made available by commercial London effect the kind of class transformation that would allow the son of a mason to be deemed an appropriate suitor for the daughter of a rector— or a solicitor? Once apprised of his guest's background, the Reverend Swancourt directs his rage not only at Smith's imposture, but at the deception of his employer, Mr Hewby (of Percy Place, Charing Cross), in presenting his low-born deputy as a professional London man. Swancourt and Elfride engage in a heated debate that dramatizes the clash between the rural landed gentry's commitment to an immutable class hierarchy and the mercantile imperatives that allow a London professional to break free of inherited class identity. It was the professional language used by Hewby, Swancourt complains, that pulled the wool over his eyes:

> 'Let me speak, please, Elfride! "My assistant, Mr. Stephen Smith, will leave London by the early train to-morrow morning . . . *many thanks for your proposal to accommodate him . . . you may put every confidence in him*, and may rely upon his discernment in the matter of church architecture." Well, I repeat that Hewby ought to be ashamed of himself for making so much of a poor lad of that sort.' (PBE 80)

To which Elfride replies with a lecture on the freedom that professional success in the city offers from all such distinctions, although it is a freedom, she goes on to acknowledge, that comes at a price: ' "Professional men in London," Elfride argued, "don't know anything about their clerks' fathers and mothers. They have assistants who come to their offices and shops for years, and hardly even know where they live. What they can do—what profits they can bring the firm—that's all London men care about"' (PBE 81). But there is no convincing her father, who, indeed, blames the city generally for allowing the education made available by its various cultural institutions and its entertainment industry to disguise 'the cloven foot of the upstart' (PBE 81). When Elfride points out how graceful Stephen's manners are, her father denounces the meretricious nature of the urban polish that Hardy had himself so laboriously acquired during his first residence in London: 'Ay; anybody can be what you call graceful, if he lives a little time in a city, and keeps his eyes open. And he might have picked up his gentlemanliness by going to the galleries of theatres, and watching stage drawing-room manners' (PBE 79). The fact that Swancourt is here acting the part of the never-darken-my-doors father in a stage melodrama only enriches the probing ironies of the scene.

The future that Smith can offer Elfride, in practical terms, is that of 'the wife of a London professional man' (PBE 80). It is interesting that, although this was effectively what Hardy was hoping that the success of the book would enable him to offer Emma, overall the novel itself generates little enthusiasm for this particular outcome. Despite the seclusion of her life in the remote backwater of Endelstow, Elfride is confident that the anonymity offered by the city will cut the Gordian knot of the class complications that make her father shudder at the thought of a union with the son of a local cottager. It is surely a tribute to Emma that her fictional counterpart is so remarkably un-fazed when her wooer breaks to her the news of his background: 'Stephen, why do we trouble? Why should papa object? An architect in London is an architect in London. Who enquires there? Nobody. We shall live there, shall we not? Why need we be so alarmed?' (PBE 72). She seems familiar, too, with the entrepreneurial self-help ethos that made the story of Dick Whittington so popular on the Victorian stage: 'It has become a normal thing', she reminds her self-doubting lover, 'that millionaires commence by going up to London with their tools at their back, and half a crown in their pockets.' In a fleeting moment of optimism, Stephen also allows himself to entertain this uplifting fantasy of their future: 'I will make a fortune, and come to you, and have you. Yes, I will!' (PBE 90) he enthusiastically declares after being banished from the rectory. Although he never quite becomes a millionaire, his architectural successes in

India do, eventually, mean he fulfils his part in this envisioned narrative, although his return in triumph comes far too late.

It is telling that Hardy presents Elfride's love for Stephen as melting away so easily after she is introduced to a more intellectually confident denizen of the city, the London literary man Henry Knight. Her love for Knight is of a quite different order, pushing her, like Tess after her rejection by Angel, to the brink of despair. As in *Desperate Remedies*, Hardy's self-division results in a schematically patterned contest for the heroine's hand, but his burgeoning novelistic career prompted him to make one of the rivals into a metropolitan man of letters. Knight is not, of course, a novelist—indeed his demolition in a review of the Arthurian romance that Elfride publishes shows him to be a fearsome enemy of the genre. Like Moule, Knight is impressively educated, and although he appears to devote little time to his nominal profession of lawyer, he suffers none of the class and career and financial anxieties that bedevil his protégé. He is unlike Stephen, also, in being too rarefied ever to discuss with Elfride, or even to consider privately, the practicalities of married life.

The pivot of both their suits is Stephen and Elfride's mad dash to London and back in chapter 12. The journey functions in the novel rather like the break between sections in 'Coming Up Oxford Street', for it effects a radical transition from romance to realism. Their plan was to marry in Plymouth, but Stephen greets her at the station there with the distressing news that the licence that he'd applied for in his parish in London could only be used in a church in that parish:

> 'What shall we do?' she said blankly.
> 'There's only one thing we can do, darling.'
> 'What's that?'
> 'Go on to London by a train just starting, and be married there tomorrow.'
> 'Passengers for the 11.5 up-train take their seats!' said a guard's voice on the platform.
> 'Will you go Elfride?'
> 'I will.'

In three minutes the train had moved off, bearing away with it Stephen and Elfride. (PBE 105)

This initiates the first of the ghastly episodes of disillusionment towards which so many of Hardy's novels inexorably move: a change occurs, as decisive as the eating of the fruit of the tree of knowledge in *Paradise Lost*. 'You don't seem the same woman, Elfie, that you were yesterday' (PBE 111), Stephen remarks on their return to St. Launce's the next day, anticipating Angel's devastating response to Tess's account of her history: 'You were one person: now you are another' (T 248).

It is interesting to contrast Stephen and Elfride's ill-considered journey to London with the station scene presented in a somewhat elliptical poem called 'The Change' (dated Jan.–Feb. 1913). In this poem, which gathers together various episodes from Hardy's courtship of Emma, he figures himself waiting for his beloved in a crowded London station that was no doubt Paddington, since that was where Great Western Railway trains from Plymouth arrived:

> In a crowd uncaring what time might fate her,
> Mid murks of night I stood to await her,
> And the twanging of iron wheels gave out the signal that she was come.
>
> She said with a travel-tired smile—
>   Who shall lift the years O!—
> She said with a travel-tired smile,
>   Half scared by scene so strange;
> She said, outworn by mile on mile,
> The blurred lamps wanning her face the while,
> 'O Love, I am here; I am with you!' . . . Ah, that there should have come
>   a change! (CP 455)

Emma's arrival is presented in the poem as a triumph of love over doubt and adversity, although one later overtaken by an unspecified 'doom' that is mysteriously visited on the couple. As in *A Pair of Blue Eyes*, a bold, even reckless, commitment to love is shown collapsing, and ending in 'bale'.[5]

The strangeness of London not only scares Elfride, it makes her panic and flee. She and Stephen spend only about fifteen minutes in Paddington, the station beside which Hardy lived for so many years. As the train nears its destination, she peers out of the window and sees 'the lamps, which had just been lit, blinking in the wet atmosphere, and rows of hideous zinc chimney-pipes in dim relief against the sky' (PBE 106). This is Babylon the Second, as it is called earlier in the novel (PBE 14), a hideous monster blinking in the wet and gloom. The self-alienation induced in Elfride is at once visceral and uncanny: 'She writhed uneasily', the narrator observes, as the train makes its way through the 'maze of rails' at the entrance to the station, as if she were already in the grip of the monster, and the moment that she steps onto the 'strange ground' of the platform, she realizes the extent to which she has betrayed herself:

> She looked at her betrothed with despairing eyes.
> 'O Stephen,' she exclaimed, 'I am so miserable! I must go home again—I must—I must! Forgive my wretched vacillation. I don't like it here—nor myself—nor you!' (PBE 106)

Stephen, who finds himself equally depressed, outlines the risks to her reputation involved in returning unmarried, and indeed it is the revelation of this aborted elopement that eventually pushes the puritanical Knight to cast her off. Beneath the narrative implications of the episode, however, lurks a more fundamental and disturbing sense of irrevocable transformation. After their breathless scramble for the return train they hear a passer-by comment: 'Those two youngsters had a near run for it, and no mistake!' (PBE 107). The poignancy of the remark lies in its ironic inappropriateness; after this trip to London they are no longer youngsters, and Elfride has no hesitation in agreeing with Stephen's observation the morning after that she no longer seems the same woman: 'Nor am I', she replies decisively.

It is not known if the episode is a fictional reworking of an incident in Hardy and Emma's courtship, of the kind obliquely gestured towards in 'The Change'. Composing his first serial rapidly and on the hoof in London, in Cornwall, in London again, and then in the family home, Hardy found himself making much direct use of personal experience. His desultory summer

in London of 1870, particularly the weeks spent working for Raphael Brandon
in Clement's Inn, proved useful when it came to hitting off Knight's habitat:
the tables in his chambers are crowded with books and folios, while prints
and paintings are heaped against its walls 'like roofing slates in a builder's
yard' (PBE 121)—a simile neatly capturing the distance between an architectural assistant and a London man of letters. Knight's study represents for
Stephen the intellectual life to which his friend has opened his eyes, and
which indeed served as a catalyst for his rise in status and earning potential,
but from which the exigencies of his life as an urban professional man now
effectively debar him. 'Have you kept up your Greek?' Knight peremptorily
demands as soon as he has polished off the piece that he is writing and can
turn his attention to his young friend. 'No', Stephen replies:

> 'How's that?'
> 'I haven't enough spare time.'
> 'That's nonsense.' (PBE 122)

There may be a covert reference here to Moule's pragmatic recommendation
to Hardy that he give up Greek in order to concentrate on his architectural
career. Moule led Hardy to consider the life of an independent, university-
educated intellectual as that most to be desired, but he also suggested that it
was not for the likes of a son of a mason. The conflicted feelings aroused by
this attitude emerge in Hardy's characterization of Knight in *A Pair of Blue
Eyes*, and in the contest that develops between the man of letters and his
protégé. On this first occasion that we see them together, in Bede's Inn,
Stephen is still in thrall to the ideal of learning embodied for him by Knight:
'What a heap of literature!' he exclaims when about to leave, taking 'a final
longing survey round the room, as if to abide there for ever would be the great
pleasure of his life, yet feeling that he had almost outstayed his welcome-
while' (PBE 126).

    Hardy's description of Knight in his chambers astutely reflects the mix-
ture of self-importance and marginality that prevailed in the chambers of Raphael Brandon, who expended his energy on various 'strange projects and
hopes, one of these being a scheme for unifying railway fares on the principle
of letter postage' (L 80). Knight strikes Stephen as worldly and authoritative,

and he is certainly never short of an opinion, but the narrator's presentation of his rooms, particularly in relation to the 'crowded and poverty-stricken' network of alleys that they are perched above, stresses the gulf between 'shirtless humanity's habits and enjoyments' (PBE 120) and the littérateur's privileged pursuits. Knight's dandyish characterization of the cut and thrust of city life unfolding beneath his windows as 'my Humanity Show' (PBE 125) has a coolness that approaches the callous. He has only to look down from his back window to witness the struggles for survival from which, insulated in his chambers, 'immuned' by his class, he is exempt:

> Crowds—mostly of women—were surging, bustling, and pacing up and down. Gaslights glared from butchers' stalls, illuminating the lumps of flesh to splotches of orange and vermillion, like the wild colouring of Turner's later pictures, whilst the purl and babble of tongues of every pitch and mood was to this human wildwood what the ripple of a brook is to the natural forest. (PBE 126)

The evocation of Turner, and the comparison of competing voices to the ripple of a brook, show how, to an experienced and detached observer, the urban jungle can be aestheticized, and made into a delightful pageant: '"There!" said Knight, "where is there in England a spectacle to equal that? I sit there and watch them every night before I go home."' The narrative also, however, makes clear that such aesthetic appreciation depends on the firm division that exists between the cloistered inn and those foraging for sustenance in the swarming streets below. If Knight occasionally hears 'the echo of a blow or a fall, which originates in the person of some drunkard or wife-beater', he can yet be sure that his own secluded nook is not under threat: 'Characters of this kind frequently pass through the Inn from a little foxhole of an alley at the back, but they never loiter there' (PBE 120).

It is, ironically, the time that Elfride spends in London under the tutelage of her wealthy stepmother, whom her father secretly married while she was failing to get married to Stephen, that makes her receptive to Knight's more complex appeal. 'A mere season in London with her practised stepmother had so advanced Elfride's perceptions, that her courtship by Stephen seemed emotionally meagre, and to have drifted back several years into a childish past' (PBE 140), the narrator observes. Knight's withering review in the London paper *The Present* of her historical romance, *The Court of King Arthur's Castle*, increases her awareness of the limitations of her provincial outlook—for she shares with Stephen a desire to expand her horizons beyond the stratified class markers that determine the views of their parents. If, in different ways, Knight fails both of them, the failure is implicit in the portrayal of his chambers as an intellectually well-provisioned but self-enclosed, even stifling, garrison. This failure, in turn, obliquely reflects Hardy's restless uncertainty in his courtship years of the niche that he might plausibly occupy should he marry Emma and set up as a professional writer in London. What the novel doesn't, of course, foresee is that he would end up a habitué of the circles of those who parade up and down in carriages in Rotten Row—although it might be argued that Elfride's eventual marriage to neither Stephen nor Knight but to Lord Luxellian offers a prophetic glimpse into the dramatic feat of upward mobility that Hardy would himself accomplish.

Elfride's rash journey to the capital to plead with Knight in his Bede's Inn chambers provides the climax to their courtship, echoing her reckless visit to London with Stephen. It is dark and raining again, reducing the noise made by the Humanity Show to mere 'clatter and quick speech', and leaving the 'footway and roadway slippery, adhesive, and clogging to both feet and wheels' (PBE 314). Elfride, in the novel's most famous scene, had managed to save Knight from plunging to his death on the slippery slope of the nameless cliff by peeling off her underclothes and making from them a rope. Now Knight, challenged in his London lair to unwind his protective prejudices and throw her a lifeline, miserably fails to rise to the occasion. 'It is ruin to your good name to run to me like this!' (PBE 315) he exclaims in response to her impassioned declarations of love. In *The Poor Man and the Lady* Hardy had clearly, indeed—by his own account—brazenly evoked neo-bohemian mores and lifestyles, and in Manston in *Desperate Remedies* dramatized, more censoriously, Paphian excesses. Knight finds himself marooned at the opposite end of the spectrum, in an idealism that is as obsessive as Manston's libertinism. In a fine irony, the narrator notes that Knight's high-minded views end up consigning him to 'a worse state of things than any he had assumed in the pleasant social philosophy and satire of his essays' (PBE 317).

And just as Stephen watched Elfride disappear on her pony from St. Launce's 'with the agonizing sensation of a slow death' (PBE 111), so his mentor is drained, at the crucial moment, of vitality and the power to act: berated by a furious Mr Swancourt, who has come up to London to retrieve his errant daughter, 'Knight, soul-sick and weary of his life, did not arouse himself to utter a word in reply' (PBE 316).

It is highly appropriate, in terms of the geography of the novel, that in its final chapters Elfride's ex-lovers, now jealous rivals, should journey by train down from London to Cornwall in pursuit of her. The formal patterning of the book, its elaborate symmetries and self-reflexive narrative structure, extend to Hardy's portrayal of the relationship between the primary site of his courtship and the metropolis where his success or failure as a writer would be decided. Towards the very end we learn that Elfride died in London (PBE 346), making her stay in the capital with Lord Luxellian the culminating disaster to her trips there with Stephen to get married, and alone to Knight's chambers to beg for forgiveness. The excited pair leave Paddington, unaware of the other's purpose, each determined to win the heroine's hand; but she has not only already married somebody else: she has died of a miscarriage, and her body is being transported from London to Cornwall at the back of the very train on which they are travelling.

6

—◦/◦/◦—

The Hand of E. (II)

I

A Pair of Blue Eyes was the last of Hardy's novels that Tinsley would publish. On 30 November of 1872, Leslie Stephen wrote from 15 Waterloo Place, the offices the *Cornhill* magazine shared with its parent company, Smith, Elder & Co, to Hardy in Higher Bockhampton, having obtained his address from Horace Moule. Stephen was familiar with neither *Desperate Remedies* nor the first three instalments of *A Pair of Blue Eyes*, but *Under the Greenwood Tree* had been brought to his attention by Frederick Greenwood, the editor of the *Pall Mall Gazette*. He had read the story, he informed Hardy, 'with very great pleasure indeed': 'I think the descriptions of country life admirable and indeed it is long since I have received more pleasure from a new writer . . . If you are, as I hope, writing anything more, I should be very glad to have the offer of it for our pages' (RP 336). Hardy must have been particularly buoyed by Stephen's assertion at the conclusion of the letter, that, should he be able to furnish the *Cornhill* with a serial, the novelist would find arrangements 'satisfactory in a pecuniary point of view' (RP 337). The *Cornhill*, and Smith, Elder & Co, were, indeed, able to double what Tinsley paid for *A Pair of Blue Eyes*, offering £400 for the right to publish Hardy's next novel, *Far from the Madding Crowd*, first in the magazine, then in a two-volume edition.

This letter, which proved so important to Hardy's success, was nearly, or so the *Life* tells us, never delivered. Just as he stressed the fortuitous nature of his encounter in the Strand with Tinsley, which led to the publication of

Under the Greenwood Tree and his contract to write *A Pair of Blue Eyes*, so he was keen for readers to appreciate the workings of chance when it came to this second decisive upward turn in his literary career. Vital letters often go astray in his fiction, and this one, from the most highly esteemed editor of the day inviting him to contribute to a prestigious magazine that was also popular, almost ended up, like the one from Tess to Angel that remains hidden beneath the carpet of Angel's bedroom, unread.[1]

> It was, indeed, by the merest chance that he had ever got the *Cornhill* letter at all. The postal arrangements in Dorset were still so primitive at this date that the only delivery of letters at Hardy's father's house was by the hands of some friendly neighbour who had come from the next village; and Mr Stephen's request for a story had been picked up in the mud of the lane by a labouring man, the schoolchildren to whom it had been entrusted having dropped it on the way. (L 98)

Such incidents are used by Hardy in the *Life* to link the randomness and contingency central to his fiction with the blind forces that, in this instance, furthered his literary fortunes, but might just as easily have stymied them. Further, it reinforces our sense of the gap between Hardy's remote and inaccessible place of origin and the leading figure in the epicentre of culture who was now wooing him.[2]

When he found out that Hardy had been poached by an upmarket rival, Tinsley was aggrieved enough to accuse him of a 'breach of courtesy' (CL 1:24). Inept and ephemeral as much of the material published in *Tinsley's Magazine* was, his assessment of Hardy's talent showed considerable astuteness, and the encouragement that he offered came at a vital moment: 'I *shall lose my reputation* as a judge of good fiction if you don't do great things' (RP 333), he had written on receiving the second instalment of *A Pair of Blue Eyes*, and in a letter of a couple of years later, the one in which he offered Hardy back the copyright of *Under the Greenwood Tree* for the exorbitant sum of £300, he even averred: 'I think your genius truer than Dickenses [*sic*]'; 'but you want', he added, 'a monitor more than the great Novelist ever did' (RP 335). Tinsley had never himself adopted this role, but his successor, Hardy came to discover, was more than willing to do so. Stephen was acutely sensitive to what might offend readers of his magazine, and although in private he called them the 'stupid public' (RP 339), it was he who initiated Hardy into the mysteries of the fine line between the acceptable and the offensive that mid-Victorian upholders of morality policed so vigorously.

What correspondence survives suggests that Hardy acceded with good grace to Stephen's excisions and anxieties. While it has been argued that these interventions materially altered Hardy's intentions for *Far from the Madding Crowd*, the case can also be plausibly advanced that Stephen's editing improved the novel, and that even those cuts that were made—like that of the description of the corpse of Fanny Robbin's baby beside its dead mother in the coffin—to ward off the 'Grundian cloud' (L 101), can be justified aesthetically.[3] It is hard to know Hardy's real feelings about Stephen's use of his blue pencil; certainly not all of his cuts were reversed in later editions. It is a shame that the original of his letter to Stephen about wanting to be considered a good hand at a serial has disappeared. His quotation from it in the *Life* fits in with his biography's overall determination to convince the reader of the superiority of his poetry to his prose, and, as Robert Gittings has pointed out (RG 277), was clearly a calculated move in his attempts to keep on the right side of Stephen at a time when his literary and marital prospects depended on the serial being successfully promoted by its editor. 'The truth', he wrote to Leslie Stephen, 'is that I am willing, and indeed anxious, to give up any points which may be desirable in a story when read as a whole, for the sake of others which shall please those who read it in numbers. Perhaps I may have higher aims some day, and be a great stickler for the proper artistic balance of the completed work, but for the present circumstances lead me to wish merely to be considered a good hand at a serial' (L 102). Certainly this must have reassured Stephen, who was particularly concerned that Troy's seduction of Fanny should be presented in 'a gingerly fashion' (RP 338).

It was also under the aegis of Stephen that Hardy began moving in select echelons of London literary society. During 1873 and 1874 he appears to have enjoyed an arrangement with his Celbridge Place landlady, Mrs Williams, the wife of a tailor, that enabled him to take up residence at will. From this base, during various stays in the capital, he made forays into new social territory.[4] It was in the course of a visit in December of 1873 that he called on

Stephen, who lived at 8 Southwell Gardens in South Kensington. The meeting was a success, and Hardy was invited back for lunch on the following day (9 December), an occasion recalled in the memoir of Stephen that he wrote in 1906:

> I . . . arrived in a yellow fog which ate into the very bones. Mrs Stephen [Harriet—known as Minny—the daughter of Thackeray] and Miss Thackeray [her sister, Anne] were present in shawls. We sat over the fire after lunch, and the closeness of the printers in the rear of my pen led Stephen to remark that *Vanity Fair* was written at the rate of five pages a day, *The Newcomes* at the rate of ten, and *Esmond* (I think) at the rate of three. We also talked of Carlyle. (PV 261)

Such conversation was considerably more than Tinsley could offer, and Hardy was clearly delighted to be taken up in this manner. He was by now impressively bearded, as befitted a mid-Victorian man of letters. At a dinner he attended at the Stephens' in May of 1874 he was introduced to the illustrator of *Far from the Madding Crowd*, Helen Paterson. It is perhaps an indication of the febrile state induced in Hardy by the success of his serial and the social doors in London that were opening for him because of it that he allowed his imagination to dwell on other marital prospects than union with Emma. In the poem 'The Opportunity' (dedicated to 'H.P.') he ponders 'the tide of chance' that meant that later in the year Paterson would marry the Irish poet William Allingham, and Hardy would be joined to Emma.

> Had we mused a little space
> > At that critical date in the Maytime,
> One life had been ours, one place,
> > Perhaps, till our long cold claytime. (CP 621)

Perhaps . . . but no evidence has come to light suggesting that Helen Paterson also mused in this manner. At the same dinner Hardy met the editor of the *Pall Mall Gazette*, Frederick Greenwood, and Mrs Procter, who was married to Bryan Procter (aka the poet Barry Cornwall) and was famous for her anecdotes of the numerous writers that she had met. With these stories she 'charmed Hardy' (L 103), and he would in due course become a regular at her salon.

It was in these years, too, that the gulf between Hardy as purveyor of regional pastoral and Hardy as literary man about town had its origins. Stephen's letter praising *Under the Greenwood Tree*'s 'descriptions of country life' had perhaps influenced his decision to set *Far from the Madding Crowd* in a rural district not yet transformed by the railways. This allowed him to make innovative use of the traditions of pastoral, and of epic as well, but these the novel fuses with the less hallowed genres of sensationalism and stage melodrama. Indeed Hardy himself clearly recognized the novel's inherent theatricality, in 1879 adapting it into a play entitled *The Mistress of the Farm—A Pastoral Drama*.[5] Although *Far from the Madding Crowd* excludes obtrusive references to modern life and, in certain scenes and passages, directly evokes the ideal of a natural rural community, some of its early reviewers were alert to the sleight of hand whereby Hardy embedded a story that belonged to the very contemporary genres of melodrama and sensation fiction in a setting that gratified mid-Victorian fantasies of the idyllic and timeless. In this lay his 'cleverness'—a term that crops up time and again in reviews of his early work. Henry James went one step further, complaining of Hardy's 'artifice' in a highly critical piece in the *Nation*:

> This is Mr. Hardy's trouble; he rarely gets beyond ambitious artifice—the mechanical simulation of heat and depth and wisdom that are absent. Farmer Boldwood is a shadow, and Sergeant Troy an elaborate stage-figure. Everything human in the book strikes us as factitious and insubstantial; the only things we believe in are the sheep and the dogs. But, as we say, Mr. Hardy has gone astray very cleverly, and his superficial novel is a really curious imitation of something better. (CH 31)

By Jamesian standards of realism, *Far from the Madding Crowd* is merely an unconvincing set of stage tricks. It was its sensationalism as well as its phony theatricality that most forcibly struck the anonymous writer who assessed it for the *Westminster Review*: 'In *Far from the Madding Crowd* sensationalism is all in all. If we analyse the story we shall find that it is nothing else but sensationalism, which in the hands of a less skilful writer than Mr. Hardy, would simply sink the story to the level of one of Miss Braddon's earlier performances' (CH 33).

If *Desperate Remedies* almost explicitly dramatized the process of importing into rural Dorset the anxieties and deceits of mid-Victorian urban culture that motivated the writing of, and taste for, sensation fiction, then *Far from the Madding Crowd* 'cleverly' obscured the connection of its narrative and characters to the staples of the metropolitan entertainment industry. Yet, however 'skilful' his erasure of these links, Hardy failed to deceive the author of the piece in the *Westminster Review*: 'The scene in which Troy woos Bathsheba with his sword is a piece of mad extravagance, fit only for the boards of some transpontine theatre.' By 'transpontine' he means south of the River Thames, deeming Hardy's soldier unsuited even to appear in a West End burlesque of the kind that Hardy had himself performed in, fit only for a South London music hall or pantomime or melodrama. Of course the novel itself 'cleverly' plays on Troy's theatrical antecedents by making him into the Great Cosmopolitan Equestrian and Roughrider in a travelling circus, and then, in a further layer of theatrical fiction, having him perform the role of the highwayman Dick Turpin. Indeed, the *Westminster* reviewer goes on to suggest that, like Troy's performance in the role of Dick Turpin, the novel is deliberately and self-consciously ersatz, a 'curious imitation', to use James's phrase, of 'the real thing': 'Of course Mr. Hardy has had good reasons for dealing us such a dose of sensation. He knows what true art is, but he prefers in this story at least to give his readers a bastard substitute' (CH 33).

These sceptical responses to his great popular success may go some way to explaining Hardy's decision to move in his next novel, *The Hand of Ethelberta*, in completely the opposite direction: instead of transplanting theatrical artifice and the performance of the sensational into a bucolic setting, he would dramatize the exploits of a provincially reared heroine inventing herself in High Society in the capital, in the process deploying every artifice at her command. So, rather than appropriate and adapt stereotypes, he would, too bluntly for many, ridicule them; and while *Far from the Madding Crowd* conceals, or at least allows to be untroubling, the disjunctions between its various genres, *The Hand of Ethelberta* foregrounds both the social and the literary inauthenticities that constitute its diagnosis of metropolitan life.

II

'The day we were married', wrote Emma in her memoir *Some Recollections*, 'was a perfect September day—the 17th, 1874—not brilliant sunshine, but wearing a soft, sunny luminousness; just as it should be.'[6] Just as it should be—if one overlooks the absence that morning in the newly built St. Peter's Church on Elgin Avenue in Maida Vale of all relatives from Hardy's side of the family, of her own parents, and of her sister and brother-in-law, who had, initially at least, encouraged the match. Her uncle, the Reverend Edwin Hamilton Gifford, Canon of Worcester, officiated. On his promotion to Archdeacon of London, he would become Emma's most oft-cited claim to the social distinction of her family, although, alas, the respect was far from mutual. Also present as witnesses were her brother Walter, who lived in nearby Chippenham Road, where Emma had been staying, and Sarah Williams, the daughter of Hardy's Celbridge Place landlady. Festivities were probably limited to a lunch at the Palace Hotel on what is now Queensway. The next day Hardy sent a short letter from Brighton to his brother Henry informing him that the ceremony had taken place, and alerting him to a notice that would appear in the 'Marriages' section of the *Dorset County Chronicle*: in it he described himself as 'of Celbridge-place, Westbourne Park, London'. The entry also acknowledged the social divide between the two families that the marriage in theory united: 'the son of Mr. T. Hardy, of Bockhampton' had been joined in matrimony with the 'younger daughter of J.A. Gifford, Esq., of Kirland, Cornwall' (MM 151). Hardy's hopes of bridging the divide between 'Mr.' and 'Esq.' rested in the profession that he entered in the marriage register: 'Author'.

The Hardys arrived back from their two-week honeymoon in Paris and Rouen on 1 October. They had nowhere to live. 'Dirty London. Very wet—', observed Emma in her diary entry for that day.[7] They had decided to settle in what Mrs Procter called in a letter to Hardy of August 1874 that is excerpted in the *Life*, 'stony-hearted London', where the 'great fault is that we are all alike. . . . We press so closely against each other that any small shoots are cut off at once, and the young tree grows in shape like the old one' (L 103–104). Despite the success of *Under the Greenwood Tree* and *Far from the Madding Crowd*, Hardy suggests in the *Life* that he now became convinced that to sustain a career as a novelist he needed to start taking an interest 'in ordinary social and fashionable life as other novelists did'. The 'circulating-library subscriber', he asserted, cared only for 'pictures of modern customs and observances', and material for such novels had to be gathered at 'dinners and clubs and crushes', a business 'not much to his mind' but 'necessary meat and drink to the popular author' (L 107). Hardy was obviously right to be conscious of the enormous importance to the professional author of circulating libraries such as W. H. Smith's or Mudie's, but it is difficult to work out exactly how or why he developed the conviction, if he really did, that subscribers to them were interested only in society novels. His airing of this belief in the *Life* makes it sound like an excuse for the perverse turn taken in *The Hand of Ethelberta*. Further, it contradicts his declaration a couple of pages earlier that by writing a satirical social comedy set largely in London he was not only making 'a plunge in a new and untried direction', but risking his commercial future, for he was fully 'aware of the pecuniary value of a reputation for a speciality', and his speciality was country life (L 105). All that he adduces as evidence that novels had to be about 'social and fashionable life' to be popular was Anne Thackeray's response to his discussion with her of his dilemma: 'Certainly; a novelist must necessarily like society!' (L 107).

After five days of house hunting in districts of South London such as Wimbledon and Denmark Hill, Hardy and Emma opted for the more remote Surbiton, taking half of a large detached house called St. David's Villa on Hook Road, which they shared with a family and their dog. They stayed there under six months, for Hardy soon found himself repeating the peripatetic habits of the years between his first residence in London and his marriage. In March of 1875 he wrote to his publisher George Smith that he and Emma were 'coming to Town for three months on account of Ethelberta, some London scenes occurring in her chequered career which I want to do as vigorously as possible' (CL 1:35). On 22 March they moved into 18 Newton Road, which was, like Celbridge Place, just a few streets from Westbourne Park Villas. Their 'entire worldly goods', which could be fitted into four packing cases (two and a half of them taken up with books), were put into storage (L 106). By the time that the first instalment of *The Hand of Ethelberta* appeared in the *Cornhill* in July of 1875, they had again upped sticks. After an unsatisfactory stay in Bournemouth, commemorated in the poignant poem 'We Sat at the Window', they settled in the small town of Swanage on the Dorset coast, remaining there until March of 1876, when the delights of Yeovil beckoned, but proved illusory. By July of that year they had again moved, this time to Sturminster Newton in the Blackmore Vale area of Dorset, about fifteen miles north of his native Higher Bockhampton.

If Hardy was heartened by the number of women that he and Emma saw reading *Far from the Madding Crowd* on their train journeys between Surbiton and Waterloo, he was deeply uncertain as to how next to appeal to the readership that he had gained. His intention to write something more cosmopolitan can be inferred from the letter that he sent to his brother Henry from Brighton, in which he presented his honeymoon as a research trip: 'I am going to Paris for materials for my next story' (CL 1:31). In fact, Rouen rather than Paris proved to be the location to which he dispatched Ethelberta and her various suitors, for no particularly good reason other than to add some continental colour. Pressed, perhaps before he was ready, by Leslie Stephen for details of his next project, in January of 1875 Hardy submitted a rough draft of its opening, and in a letter of 27 February announced himself ready to open negotiations for the rights to *The Hand of Ethelberta: A Comedy in Chapters*. The popularity of *Far from the Madding Crowd*, whose first edition had just sold out, put him in a strong position. This time he was offered £700 for the serialization and first edition, to which he was able to add a further £550 by the sale of the American rights.

Leslie Stephen himself served as a rough model for Alfred Neigh, one of the four men in pursuit of the hand of Ethelberta. About half of the novel is set in the capital. The two principal London locations are the Doncastles' house in 'a moderately fashionable square' (HE 56) in West London, where Ethelberta's father is the butler, and the house in Connaught Crescent, the last two years of whose lease is all that Lady Petherwin bequeaths to Ethelberta, along with its furniture, after cutting her daughter-in-law out of her will for publishing a volume of 'ribald verses' (HE 85). Ethelberta's daring plan to move her mother and most of her siblings into this town house, and there have some of them pretend to be her domestic staff, allows Hardy to dramatize the operations of social distinctions within the same family living under the same roof. Her older sisters Gwendoline and Cornelia become her cook and housemaid, while her younger brother Joey is dressed in livery and given the role of page. On his first visit to Ethelberta there, the novel's pallid, and eventually sidelined, leading man, Christopher Julian, meets her brothers Sol and Dan in their work clothes busy painting the house: 'you'd better not bide here', Sol tells his sister and her suitor, 'talking to we rough ones, you know, for folks might find out that there's something closer between us than workmen and employer and employer's friend . . . if we baint company for you out of doors, you baint company for we within . . . you keep to your class, and we'll keep to ours' (HE 126). Ethelberta attributes Sol's touchiness to incipient political radicalization, suggesting that her brother has imbibed 'a few town ideas from his leaders'. Hardy is vague, however, on the extent to which she shares these town ideas; 'strange accidents', she reflects to Christopher, 'have split us up into sections as you see, cutting me off from them without the compensation of joining me to any others' (HE 127). Her eventual resolution of the dilemma caused by these 'strange accidents', marriage to a seedy old viscount, in fact only increases her separation from her family. One of the more interesting paradoxes of Ethelberta's situation is that it is precisely the intensity of her tribal commitment to her family's welfare that most drives her away from them.

The 'strange accidents' that set up Hardy's peculiar plot are described in the novel's opening paragraphs with quite bewildering concision:

> She was a respectable butler's daughter, and began life as a baby christened Ethelberta after an infant of title who does not come into the story at all, having merely furnished to Ethelberta's mother a means of occupying herself as head nurse. She became teacher in a school, was praised by examiners, admired by gentlemen, not admired by gentlewomen, was touched up with accomplishments by masters who were coaxed into painstaking by her many graces, and, entering a mansion as governess to the daughter thereof, was stealthily married by the son. He, a minor like herself, died from a chill caught during the wedding tour, and a few weeks later was followed into the grave by Sir Ralph

Petherwin, his unforgiving father, who had bequeathed his wealth to his wife absolutely.

These calamities were a sufficient reason to Lady Petherwin for pardoning all concerned. She took by the hand the forlorn Ethelberta—who seemed rather a detached bride than a widow—and finished her education by placing her for two or three years in a boarding-school at Bonn. Latterly she had brought the girl to England to live under her roof as daughter and companion, the condition attached being that Ethelberta was never openly to recognize her poor relations. (HE 11)

However, when Lady Petherwin discovers that her daughter-in-law is the author of a much talked-about volume of verse called 'Metres by Me' ('Metres by E.' in later editions), she flies into a rage, summons her lawyer, and promptly disinherits her. Although Lady Petherwin later changes her mind, she fails to alter her will again before she dies, leaving Ethelberta stranded, like Hardy himself, between different social classes. Ethelberta can keep living in the large, furnished town house in Connaught Crescent rent-free for two years, but after that, for all her beauty and graces and accomplishments, she will be no better off than her nine siblings.

Hardy's resourceful narrative presents his equally resourceful heroine prosecuting two successive 'town campaigns' (CP 792). She attempts initially to support herself and her numerous family dependants with the money that she makes as a professional storyteller. Her act is simple: she sits on a chair 'as if she were at her own fireside, surrounded by a circle of friends. By this touch of domesticity a great appearance of truth and naturalness was given' (HE 118–119). Having converted her own home into a theatrical set and her family into characters in a play, it is fitting that she should appear in public as if contentedly chatting beside that quintessential icon of the Victorian private life, the hearth. It is also consonant with the book's ironies that the great anxiety of this skilful manipulator of artifice is 'a fear of seeming artificial', of failing to convince her auditors of her 'naturalness'. Hardy clearly relished spinning a covert analogy between Ethelberta's career as a performer in London's great public halls and his as a novelist appearing in one of London's most renowned magazines. When the novelty of Ethelberta's act starts to wear off and her audiences dwindle, it is almost as if Hardy were worrying that his novel was also losing its grip on the public's attention, or was in danger of exhausting the possibilities inherent in its highly original premise. In his discussion of the waning of Ethelberta's appeal as a performer he explicitly ponders the loss of 'freshness' and 'unique charm' entailed in becoming an experienced professional, or, to apply the case to himself, 'a good hand at a serial'. It was her 'being out of place', the spectacle that she presented of 'a beautiful woman on a platform, revealing tender airs of domesticity which showed her to belong by character to a quiet drawing room' that won her so many admirers. Alas, the more experienced she becomes, the less effective her performance: 'custom was staling this by improving her up to the mark of an utter impersonator, thereby eradicating the pretty abashments of a poetess out of her sphere' (HE 169).

Hardy is evidently exploring here an acute personal anxiety: to what extent did his assumption of the role of a professional metropolitan novelist, one interested in 'modern customs and observances' (L 107), involve lopping off the 'small shoots', to borrow Mrs Procter's phrase, of his own originality? From this perspective, the novel as a whole can be seen as a coded attempt by Hardy to articulate his troubling sense of the cost of allowing himself to move, as both a writer and a man, 'out of [his] sphere'. Might he, like Ethelberta, end up as a mere 'impersonator'? And for how long would the public be interested in his writing should it lose the 'freshness' and 'unique charm' that his early work derived from his provincial awkwardness, but that the 'custom' of being a professional purveyor of fiction was now threatening to erode?

Fascinating self-referential issues of this kind flicker intermittently but intriguingly beneath the novel's narrative. *The Hand of Ethelberta* also, however, delivers one of Hardy's most disconcerting and unsentimental examinations of the marriage question. When, despite her great initial success, the income from Ethelberta's performances slows to a trickle, Hardy's heroine casts around for a more reliable means of securing her financial and social future. It is only, she decides, by wedding a rich husband, preferably one who will be indifferent to her lowly birth and connections when eventually apprised of them, that she can make permanent her transition from the working to the upper classes.

III

Wessex first appears in Hardy's fiction in the opening sentence of chapter 50 of *Far from the Madding Crowd*—'Greenhill was the Nijnii Novgorod [a city in central Russia famous for its large annual fair] of South Wessex' (FFMC 327). It was, however, somewhat paradoxically, in *The Hand of Ethelberta* that Hardy really began to make use of the term: it occurs fourteen times in the novel, or sixteen if one includes references to the newspaper that the region acquires, the *Wessex Reflector*. Wessex, this suggests, emerged initially for Hardy as a useful concept in his quest to dramatize the relationship between the country and the city.[8] The *Wessex Reflector*, it is worth noting, has its own 'London Correspondent', and it is from his gossip column that Christopher Julian, who is living at the time in Sandbourne (Bournemouth) and scratching a living as a music teacher, learns that the author of 'Metres by Me' is indeed, as he suspected, the woman with whom he fell in love when she was a governess called Ethelberta Chickerel. The interpenetration of London and Wessex is greater in *The Hand of Ethelberta* than in any of Hardy's other novels—and was heightened by revisions such as the one that renamed Connaught Crescent Exonbury Crescent. The maiden name of Hardy's upwardly mobile heroine, who so dazzles metropolitan society, itself encrypts a reference to her provincial Dorset origins, Chickerell being a small town just north of Weymouth.

In the chapter that follows Christopher's discovery in his local newspaper of Ethelberta's triumphant debut in London literary circles with a volume of verse that clearly recalls Hardy's own 'She, to Him' sonnets, the traffic flows the other way. Attending a party at a home on the north side of Hyde Park, Ethelberta is requested to sing the most successful of the musical settings made of her poems: the best, she declares, reached her that morning by post from a place in Wessex, its composer being 'an unheard-of man who lives somewhere down there' (HE 78), this 'unheard-of man' of course being Christopher. She performs it to great acclaim, and Hardy seems to be encouraging the notion that together Ethelberta and Christopher might establish a working union comparable to that of Oak and Bathsheba, and thereafter 'conquer' London. But this one performance proves their only shared triumph. It is revealing that it occurs when they are far apart, she in London and he in

Wessex, as if the happy marriage of her acquired metropolitan sophistication and his authentic provincial talent depended on maintaining a firm geographical divide. Certainly we hear no more of Christopher's musical compositions after he pursues her to the capital. Hardy's refusal to develop the narrative that the scene shadows forth is of a piece with the book's overall determination to outwit its readers and create a fictional world that is unpredictable, even topsy-turvy: 'The times have taken a strange turn', observes Mrs Doncastle after Ethelberta's butler father sets off for Knollsea to prevent her marriage to Lord Mountclere, 'when the angry parent of the comedy, who goes post-haste to prevent the undutiful daughter's rash marriage, is a gentleman from below stairs, and the unworthy lover a peer of the realm!' (HE 338).

How much, one can't help wondering, did Hardy want readers to connect Ethelberta's anomalous situation with his own? Plenty of his relatives had been employed in service: his mother as a cook, his cousin Martha as a lady's maid, his cousin Emma as a servant, while James and Nathaniel Sparks had worked as carpenters in London. The links between Ethelberta's numerous siblings and Hardy's numerous cousins are on occasion quite explicit: both Emma and Martha, for instance, ended up emigrating to Australia, as do two of Ethelberta's sisters, Gwendoline and Cornelia. When Ethelberta almost reveals the secret of her lowly origins to the guests assembled at Lord Mountclere's Wessex country seat, Lychworth Court, her aim, the narrator informs us, is to 'get rid of that self-reproach which had by this time reached a morbid pitch, through her over-sensitiveness to a situation in which a large majority of women and men would have seen no falseness' (HE 298). Hardy's own confessional impulse is heavily disguised by the dispassionate tone in which the story is narrated, and by the ingenuity of the twists and turns that he gives it; but at such moments one seems invited to guess at the 'sensitiveness' lurking beneath its satirical jibes and the not entirely 'genteel' class comedy that its plot provokes.[9]

The concept of writing a novel in one of whose episodes a butler waits on his own daughter may have come to Hardy after he attended a dinner given by the Reverend Reginald Smith and his wife Geneviève in the rectory at West Stafford (two miles from Higher Bockhampton) in early 1874. The Smiths' butler was James Pole, and some years earlier Hardy had 'walked out' with his daughter Cassie Pole.[10] *The Hand of Ethelberta* transposes the

scene to London and adds several extra layers of complication: Ethelberta's
sister Picotee has persuaded Ethelberta and her father to let her observe the
evening's festivities in secret; accordingly she is smuggled into the Doncastles' London house shortly before the grand dinner begins, and it is through
her eyes that we are given a glimpse of Ethelberta in her pomp, 'the chief
figure of a glorious pleasure-parliament of both sexes, surrounded by whole
regiments of candles grouped here and there about the room' (HE 224). Picotee is delighted to note that her sister is acting brilliantly—'her eyes were
bright, and her face beaming, as if divers social wants and looming penuri-
ousness had never been within her experience'. It soon emerges, however,
that Hardy is much more interested in recording the antics of those below
stairs than in recreating the chit-chat of the beau monde. While the guests
feast and carouse in the dining room—'Ha—ha—ha—ha—ha—ha!' is all we
get of their conversation—the servants engage in games and dancing in the
front drawing room, directly above the diners:

> 'Now let's have a game of cat-and-mice,' said the maid-servant
> cheerily. 'There's plenty of time before they come up.'
> 'Agreed,' said Menlove promptly. 'You will play, will you not, Miss
> Chickerel?
> 'No, indeed,' said Picotee, aghast.
> 'Never mind, then; you look on.'
> Away then ran the housemaid and Menlove, and the young footman
> started at their heels. Round the room, over the furniture, under the
> furniture, through the furniture, out of one window, along the bal-
> cony, in at another window, again round the room—so they glided
> with the swiftness of swallows and the noiselessness of ghosts.
> Then the housemaid drew a jew's-harp from her pocket, and
> struck up a lively waltz sotto voce. The footman seized Menlove, who
> appeared nothing loth, and began spinning gently round the room
> with her . . .
> Picotee, who had been accustomed to unceiled country cottages all her
> life, wherein the scamper of a mouse is heard distinctly from floor to
> floor, exclaimed in a terrified whisper, at viewing all this, 'They'll
> hear you underneath, they'll hear you, and we shall all be ruined!'

'Not at all,' came from the cautious dancers. 'These are some of the best built houses in London—double floors, filled in with material that will deaden any row you like to make, and we make none. But come and have a turn yourself, Miss Chickerel.'

The young man relinquished Menlove, and on the spur of the moment seized Picotee. Picotee flounced away from him in indignation, backing into a corner with ruffled feathers, like a pullet trying to appear a hen. (HE 225–226)

Hardy may have learned of, or indeed witnessed, such a scene in a house in London through his Sparks cousins. It is one of the few times in the book that any of its characters break away from their narrative or satirical function and are granted the kind of freedom enjoyed by the sun in the first half of 'Coming Up Oxford Street: Evening'. For it often feels that the constraint and self-consciousness that Ethelberta must marshal in order to prosecute her marital ambitions leaches into the novel as a whole, deadening, like the material used in the best built London houses, Hardy's access to the primary sources of his imagination. Although in many ways a fascinating novel, *The Hand of Ethelberta* is a resolutely guarded and self-conscious performance; and its guardedness and self-consciousness can in turn be read as expressive of the difficulties and anxieties that Hardy himself experienced when performing his own 'London man' persona.

The subtitle that on Stephen's insistence was abandoned for the serial, 'A Comedy in Chapters', clearly signals Hardy's intention to transfer to prose fiction the conventions of stage satires, particularly Renaissance city comedies by such as Jonson and Middleton, or later developments in the mode by Congreve and Sheridan, to whose influence on the novel Hardy draws attention in the *Life* (L 112). Many of the names given the characters evoke these conventions—Menlove, Ladywell, Neigh, Belmaine. *The Book of Snobs* by the *Cornhill's* first editor, Thackeray, lurks also in the hinterland, and in basing Neigh loosely on Stephen, who had paid so handsomely to run the novel, though he seems never to have liked it much, Hardy was somewhat tactlessly insisting that a satirical perspective on London should show neither fear nor favour. If the book channels some of the class animosity that fuelled *The Poor Man and the Lady*, this time Hardy is careful to make sure that, as in Jacobean or Restoration city comedies, nearly all of its characters are viewed on a spectrum that runs from witty derision to humorous caricature. There is no equivalent to Egbert Mayne or Will Strong. One might have expected the scheming heroine to fulfil this role, but she is confusingly presented by Hardy from a range of often contradictory angles, one moment as a gold-digging Becky Sharp, the next as a resourceful and praiseworthy engineer of the rise of her family's fortunes; one moment as a 'poet of the Satanic school in a sweetened form', the next, after a consultation of the political writings of J. S. Mill, as a '*pseudo*-utilitarian' (HE 289). Hardy seems to be spoofing, or perhaps indecisively revolving, a range of Victorian literary and cultural constructions of heroism and womanhood, without allowing Ethelberta to inhabit for long any single genre. And while there are flashes of the kind of interiority that he grants later characters such as Elizabeth-Jane of *The Mayor of Casterbridge* or Grace Melbury of *The Woodlanders*, these tend to be quickly dispersed by Ethelberta's need to make her next move.

Few characters escape what Hardy called in his 1912 preface to the novel the 'artificial treatment' (HE 4) that the book adopts as its dominant mode. This insistence on the artifice that shapes social and literary conventions enables Hardy to expose falsity and selfishness and hypocrisy while resisting the lure of idealistic correctives. Ethelberta's father, it is true, is accorded a sympathy and dignity that his employers would no doubt consider absurd, but Hardy is also at pains to stress that he is more than content with his job as a butler. Sol, his fiery oldest son, is invested with some of Hardy's first protagonist's political radicalism, but by the book's conclusion he has modulated into a rising entrepreneur in the building trade: the sequel tells us that he and Dan have been set up in business in London by Ethelberta (using the money that she acquired by marrying Lord Mountclere) and have 'just signed a contract to build a hospital for twenty thousand pounds' (HE 404). If *The Hand of Ethelberta*, like *The Poor Man and the Lady*, is a social satire that means 'mischief', it is of a very general kind. Its central thrust is not to advocate revolution, but to explore the implications of the improved class mobility to which Lord Mountclere refers when dismissing Ethelberta's anxieties about her lowly connections:

'But my father and friends?' said she.

'Are nothing to be concerned about. Modern developments have shaken up the classes like peas in a hopper.' (HE 300–301)

Indeed, he goes on to predict that Ethelberta's brothers may well end up wealthier than he is.

IV

London is presented in *The Hand of Ethelberta*'s central chapters as much more than just the backdrop to the reversals and uncertainties that characterize its heroine's progress. The city is figured, rather, as the formulator of the limited options available to Ethelberta, and of the terms on which her fate must play itself out. The bleakness of Hardy's diagnosis of these options is vividly encapsulated by the three suitors whom she meets in the capital, who vie with each other not only for her hand, but for the degree of disgust they inspire in the reader: the supercilious Neigh, whose fortune was made in the knackers' business; Ladywell, a nondescript society painter; and Mount-clere, a grotesque old libertine who is forever tittering 'Hee-hee-hee!' Per-haps what tips the balance most decisively in favour of the last of these is the estate that he owns at Lychworth near Knollsea (based on Swanage). It at least allows Ethelberta to escape the dangerous panopticon of the city, which, her quest launched, makes her into an implicitly disposable commodity: 'She is one of those people', observes a guest at one of the parties that she attends, 'who are known, as one may say, by subscription: everybody knows a little, till she is astonishingly well known altogether; but nobody knows her en-tirely' (HE 79). Should her story ever become known 'entirely', as she herself is fully aware, her appeal to subscribers, and consequently her value in the metropolis, would be seriously imperilled.

Proceeding very much in parallel to his heroine, in a manner that can seem almost like a postmodern metanarrative, Hardy dithers between the various options available to him as the artificer of a story about a young woman on the make in London: Is she a victim of social forces or a ruthless adventuress? A romantic lead or a cool and deceitful driver of a hard bargain in the capital's marriage market? Some of Ethelberta's self-doubts result in spells of anguished indecisiveness, as when, after the outing to Cripplegate Church, she longs 'like a tired child for the conclusion of the whole matter, when her work should be over, and the evening come' (HE 206). At other times, however, such as on the morning after the dinner at the Doncastles' at which she was waited on by her father and secretly observed by her sister, her 'restlessness' furnishes Hardy with occasion to punctuate the action with more wide-angled vistas of urban life. Having returned at dawn, she and Picotee clamber onto the roof of the house in Connaught Crescent:

> The restlessness which had brought Ethelberta hither in slippers and dressing-gown at such an early hour owed its origin to another cause than the warmth of the weather; but of that she did not speak as yet. . . . While Picotee was wrapping up, Ethelberta placed a chair under the window, and mounting upon this they stepped outside, and seated themselves within the parapet.
>
> The air was as clear and fresh as on a mountain side; sparrows chattered, and birds of a species unsuspected at later hours could be heard singing in the park hard by, while here and there on ridges and flats a cat might be seen going calmly home from the devilries of the night to resume the amiabilities of the day. (HE 229)

These chattering sparrows and singing birds and homeward bound cats, like the dancing servants of the night before, offer a brief but welcome respite from the constant vigilance and exercise of judiciousness imposed by the novel's central dilemma: how should Ethelberta play her 'hand'? On which of the men pursuing her should she bestow it? At the end of this chapter, in which she and her sister Picotee, the metropolis spread out before them, ponder her variously unappealing suitors, they look up to see that the freshness of dawn has yielded to the polluting routines of another day in the city: 'Tall and swarthy columns of smoke were now soaring up from the kitchen chimneys around, spreading horizontally when at a great height, and forming a roof of haze which was turning the sun to a copper colour, and by degrees spoiling the sweetness of the new atmosphere that had rolled in from the country during the night, giving it the usual city smell' (HE 233). The chimneys of London are imagined creating an alternative sky, a 'roof of haze' that can even alter the colour of the sun.

The transformative effect of London on those who arrive from the country takes many forms in *The Hand of Ethelberta*'s urban chapters, from the corruption of young Joey into a smoking and slang-spouting Cockney who absurdly sets about courting Ethelberta's ex-maid, the much older Menlove, to the specialization in their work that it imposes on Sol and Dan, who are warned in advance by Christopher that the jack-of-all-trades is not in demand in London—if they want to succeed there they must find and 'stick to some principle of specialty' (HE 112). It is wholly characteristic of the perverse spirit permeating the book, a perversity that reflects the changes wrought in Hardy by his own metropolitan experiences, that he should point this out while in the process of deviating, much to the dismay of his publishers, from his own specialty, country life.

The threat of urban poverty so graphically figured by the bachelor whom Hardy met on his first day in the city haunts Ethelberta too: 'We must not be poor in London', she declares to Picotee:

'Poverty in the country is a sadness, but poverty in town is a horror. There is something not without grandeur in the thought of starvation on an open mountain or in a wide wood, and your bones lying there to bleach in the pure sun and rain; but a back garret in Clare Market, and the other starvers in the room insisting on keeping the window shut— anything to deliver us from that!' (HE 172)

Clare Market was a notorious slum between Lincoln's Inn Fields and Aldwych, just a short walk from the offices of both Blomfield and Smith. The fragility of Hardy's financial situation, despite the success of *Far from the Madding Crowd* and the large advance that he received for *The Hand of Ethelberta*, surely informs the fiscal worries of Hardy's heroine, who often comes across as his alter ego. The novel does not delve, as *Desperate Remedies* briefly did, into the world of London's rookeries, but this glimpse at a brutal scenario of the kind depicted in some of Gustave Doré's engravings for *London: A Pilgrimage* of 1872 is disconcertingly vivid for a 'genteel' social comedy. Hardy must have felt under considerable pressure: he had just

married a member of the provincial middle classes who brought with her neither income nor property but enjoyed a well-developed sense of her social
status. All the women whom he had previously courted had worked, and it
was surely a consideration of the difference between their hands and Emma's that generated the odd comparison in chapter 5 of a series of candles to
'the fingers of a woman who does nothing' (HE 46).[11]

Notwithstanding the novel's predominantly jaundiced figuration of
London, some aspects of the conditions of urban domestic servants and
manual labourers are contrasted favourably with those of their rural counter-
parts. Menlove, for instance, firmly insists that she enjoys considerably
more freedom and respect as a lady's maid in the city than she had in the
country: 'We are all independent here', she tells Picotee; 'no slavery for us:
it is not as it is in the country, where servants are considered to be of different blood and bone from their employers, and to have no eyes for anything
but their work' (HE 222). And not long after, in proof of her claim, she is spinning around in the arms of a fellow servant in the main drawing room. In
chapter 43, appalled at the prospect of his older brother marrying the
daughter of a butler, Edgar Mountclere arrives at the premises of Messrs.
Nockett and Perch, builders and contractors, where Sol is employed. Despite
his aristocratic appearance, as he wanders through the workrooms no one
takes any notice of him. Initially the clerk, scenting business, is attentive, but
he at once loses interest on learning that the visit is not a commercial one. In
London, the scene implies, the imperatives of money making have ousted
the culture of deference.

The confusion that this creates in the younger Mountclere, who gets extremely irritated, is emblematic of what Hardy thought of as the modernity
of the novel, its attempt to present in an even-handed satirical way the implications of the shaking up of the classes like peas in a hopper. He had,
however, or so he later decided, jumped the gun: the book came 'thirty
years too soon' (L 111), and there is indeed much justice in his comparison
of its method with the insouciant perversity that later became George Bernard Shaw's stock-in-trade. That does not make *The Hand of Ethelberta* a
success, or indeed a failure. For, like Ethelberta's career, it cannot really be
deemed either: daring, experimental, it 'cleverly', 'ingeniously', sidesteps,
as Ethelberta does, the criteria that make for clear and confident judgement.

Its intertwining of the demands of art and money may be one reason why it is so much more elusive than Hardy's earlier novels. The sum he was paid for it signaled his definitive transformation into a professional writer of fiction, a role that he adopted, and performed punctiliously, and yet that also caused him a degree of unease. During the visit organized by one of the novel's fashionable hostesses, Mrs Belmaine, to the burial place of Milton in St. Giles Cripplegate Church in the City, poetry and finance are brought face to face. The party gathers around the poet's tomb, and Ethelberta, ever the performer, takes out a volume of *Paradise Lost* and begins to read:

> The sentences fell from her lips in a rhythmical cadence one by one, and she could be fancied a priestess of him before whose image she stood when with a vivid suggestiveness she delivered here, not many yards from the central money-mill of the world, yet out from the tomb of their author, the passage containing the words

> > Mammon led them on;
> > Mammon, the least erected spirit that fell
> > From heaven. (HE 200)

A priestly poet, or a Mammon-driven cog in the money-mill? Ethelberta allowed Hardy to act out imaginatively his sense of being torn between contradictory identities. The deceits and ironies and irresolutions that he anatomizes so clinically in *The Hand of Ethelberta* derived from his deepest uncertainties and desires. Further, the novel's exploration of the fault lines between the aesthetic and the commercial, between the autobiographical and the fictive, between upstairs and downstairs, map intriguingly on to the geographical divide that it dramatizes between the country and the city—or, to be precise, between Wessex and London. It is, indeed, probably the closest that Hardy came, until the *Life*, to a prose *apologia pro vita sua*. Did he also hope that it might help smooth Emma's postmarital initiation into the gulf between her antecedents and relations and his? If so, it surely misfired. The highly class-conscious Emma once revealed to a friend that she deeply disliked the novel; it had, she complained, 'too much about servants in it'.[12]

7

Literary London (I)

I

In the copy of Palgrave's *The Golden Treasury* that he received as a New Year's gift from Horace Moule back in 1862, Hardy inscribed the date 'Sept 25. 73' beside Shakespeare's Sonnet 32. According to his custom, Palgrave printed the poem with a title of his own devising—'Post Mortem':

> If Thou survive my well-contented day
> When that churl Death my bones with dust shall cover,
> And shalt by fortune once more re-survey
> These poor rude lines of thy deceaséd lover;
>
> Compare them with the bettering of the time,
> And though they be outstripp'd by every pen,
> Reserve them for my love, not for their rhyme
> Exceeded by the height of happier men. (GT 58)

Four days earlier, Moule had killed himself in his rooms in Queens' College in Cambridge, ending his frequent and prolonged battles with depression and alcoholism by slitting his own throat. Hardy learned of his death on the twenty-fourth and the following day visited Fordington churchyard, where, according to the poem 'Before My Friend Arrived', he made a sketch of the 'white chalk mound, / Outthrown on the sepulchred ground' (CP 821) that was waiting to receive Moule's body. A kindly inquest verdict of 'Temporary

Insanity' at least meant that Hardy's closest male friend could be accorded a church burial.

The various accounts that Hardy gives of his relationship with Moule are all carefully circumspect, while his elegy 'Standing by the Mantelpiece' (sub-headed 'H.M.M., 1873', for Horace Mosley Moule) is enigmatic in the extreme; indeed, it is impossible even to be sure if it is spoken by a man or a woman. The connection between the speaker and the addressee certainly includes an erotic component:

> To-night. To me twice night, that should have been
> The radiance of the midmost tick of noon,
> And close around me wintertime is seen
> That might have shone the veriest day of June!
>
> But since all's lost, and nothing really lies
> Above but shade, and shadier shade below,
> Let me make clear, before one of us dies,
> My mind to yours, just now embittered so.
>
> Since you agreed, unurged and full-advised,
> And let warmth grow without discouragement,
> Why do you bear you now as if surprised,
> When what has come was clearly consequent? (CP 887)

But the poem never divulges exactly what it is that 'has come'. Its *abab* pentameter quatrains evoke so insistently the rhetorical mode of the Sonnets that it seems clear that Hardy was deliberately emulating Shakespeare's fusion of vivid detail with an indeterminate narrative of frustrated love. These intertextual echoes, like the commemoration of the day that he visited Moule's freshly dug grave beside Sonnet 32 in Palgrave's *Golden Treasury*, or the various H.M.M. marginalia made in his copy of Tennyson's *In Memoriam A.H.H.*, emphasize the literary dimension, and pedigree, of the friendship. Moule resembled Tennyson's beloved friend Arthur Henry Hallam in never fulfilling the great expectations invested in him, and this was probably why Shakespeare's Sonnet 32 struck Hardy as an appropriate articulation of his own feelings when responding to his friend's premature death by suicide:

> O then vouchsafe me but this loving thought—
> 'Had my friend's Muse grown with this growing age,
> A dearer birth than this his love had brought,
> To march in ranks of better equipage:
>
> But since he died, and poets better prove,
> Theirs for their style I'll read, his for his love.' (GT 58)

Shakespeare's elaborate self-deprecation is mapped onto Moule's genuine failure to realize his talent and develop into the 'distinguished English poet' that, according to Hardy, he had 'early showed every promise of becoming' (PV 418).

Moule, whom Hardy met in 1856 when Hardy was sixteen and Moule twenty-four, is introduced in the *Life* as 'just then beginning practice as author and reviewer' (L 37). Among his first recommendations was that Hardy read the *Saturday Review*, a weekly newspaper founded in 1855, to which Moule himself contributed. This London-based periodical made Hardy aware of metropolitan and national issues well beyond the scope of local papers such as the *Dorset County Chronicle* and played no small part in shaping his nascent views on politics and culture. Its scepticism towards all established religions was perhaps as significant a factor as the discoveries of Darwin in the waning of Hardy's faith. It was under Moule's aegis that Hardy began engaging in the controversies of the day, such as the furore caused by the seven articles questioning orthodox religious doctrine collected in *Essays and Reviews* of 1860 (L 37). Different as their social and educational backgrounds were, it was from Moule that Hardy first imbibed the notion that he too might have a contribution to make to the debates raging in the pages of London's newspapers and magazines—that he might even become, like his mentor, an 'author'.

Only a handful of letters from Moule to Hardy survive, while none from protégé to mentor escaped the Max Gate conflagrations. Moule is, however, mentioned in the earliest Hardy letter that we have: 'H.M.M. was up, the week before last', Hardy wrote to Mary from 3 Clarence Place on 17 August of 1862: 'We went to a Roman Catholic Chapel on the Thursday evening. It was a very impressive service. The Chapel was built by Pugin. Afterwards we took a cab to the Old Hummums, an hotel near Covent Garden where we had supper. He may come & settle permanently in London in a few months, but is not certain yet' (CL 1:1). If this was their first meeting in the metropolis, it ended up in a suitably literary location, for the Hummums hotel features not only in a ghost story related in Boswell's *Life of Samuel Johnson* and illustrated by Hogarth's 'A Midnight Modern Conversation', but in *Vanity Fair* (George Osborne takes a bath in the Hummums on the night before his marriage to Amelia) and in *Great Expectations*, published the previous year. In chapter 45 Pip suffers suicidal thoughts in the course of a dark night of the soul spent in a 'despotic monster of a four-post bedstead' in a bedroom on the ground floor at the back. He is particularly alarmed by his recollection of a recent story in the newspapers about a guest at the hotel who—in grisly anticipation of Moule's own suicide—'destroyed himself' in the night and was discovered in his bed the next morning 'weltering in blood'.[1]

Although the charismatic but tormented Moule never settled in London— or indeed anywhere—'permanently', he and Hardy did meet on a number of occasions in the course of Hardy's first London residence. They visited the Great Exhibition of 1862 together and shared a love of opera (in a letter of 1867 to Hardy, Moule refers to the sopranos Adelina Patti and Thérèse Tietjens).[2] The trip made to the Church of the Immaculate Conception on Farm Street in Mayfair that Hardy describes in his letter to Mary suggests a readiness on the part of both to use the freedom afforded by the city to look beyond the religious traditions in which they had been raised: the Farm Street church was not just Roman Catholic—it was Jesuit (Gerard Manley Hopkins preached there a number of times in the summer and autumn of 1878), and the service that they attended was an anniversary celebration of Pius VII's bull promulgating the restoration of the Society of Jesus on 7 August 1814. The letter's blithe tone suggests that Hardy had no qualms about letting his family know of his willingness to sample the attractions of Rome. If news of their son's attendance at a Jesuit church also filtered back to Fordington Vicarage, it may well have been viewed as yet more evidence of Horace's compulsion to transgress.

Moule continued to guide Hardy's reading, recommending, for instance, the acquisition of J. R. McCulloch's *Principles of Political Economy*, and giving him, as his 1865 New Year's Day present, *The Thoughts of the Emperor M. Aurelius Antoninus*. In July of 1865, the year after it was published, Hardy read John Henry Newman's *Apologia Pro Vita Sua* because 'H.M.M. likes him so much' (L 50), and further gifts from Moule included Comte's *Positivism* and Goethe's *Faust*. Moule was also happy to offer his protégé advice on composition: 'you must in the end write *your own* style, unless you wd be a mere imitator', he wisely, if uncontroversially, pointed out in a letter of 2 July 1863, while one of six months later explains how to use the subjunctive (DCM). More generally, as a fairly regular contributor of reviews, articles, and poems to magazines and papers such as the *Saturday Review*, *Fraser's*, the *Quarterly Review*, *Macmillan's*, and *The Echo* (London), Moule opened Hardy's eyes to the possibilities, as well as to the realities, of a career in writing. And although he evidently considered his humbly born young friend not quite fit to mix with the Oxbridge-educated types who filled the pages of London's burgeoning literary magazines, Moule was yet able to imagine for him a less elevated niche in the newspaper industry. In a letter of 21 February 1864, one responding, no doubt, to some carping by Hardy on the dreariness of life as an architect's clerk as well as to an exercise in humorous reportage that Hardy had sent him, Moule pushed him to consider setting up as the London correspondent of a provincial newspaper: 'You know the sort of berth I mean—that of a man who sends down a column of condensed London news & talk . . . Your chatty description of the Law Courts and their denizens is *just* in the style that would go down' (DCM). The light-hearted gossip column here envisaged looks forward to the one in the *Wessex Reflector* in which Christopher Julian learns that Ethelberta is indeed the author of 'Metres by Me'. One can't, in retrospect, help noting the satire of circumstance lurking in Moule's suggestion: for it was by doing the opposite, sending up to the capital news of Wessex, that Hardy eventually found his 'berth' in London literary circles.

While Moule did not exactly induct Hardy into literary London, and there was no question of his introducing him into the coteries in which he himself, somewhat irregularly, moved, his involvement in the capital's newspapers and magazines was an important catalyst for Hardy's figuration of himself as a potential writer in his early years in London. The antagonism that develops between Knight and Stephen in the second half of *A Pair of Blue Eyes*, however, indicates some of the uncertainties and complexities of Hardy's relationship with his mentor. If his literary interests and not inconsiderable achievements made Moule into a much-admired role model for Hardy, his erratic behaviour and self-destructive excesses also converted his life into a cautionary tale.[3] The startlingly honest 1866 sonnet 'A Confession to a Friend in Trouble', written at 16 Westbourne Park Villas, rings various fascinating changes on the traditions of the poem of male friendship. Like 'Standing by the Mantelpiece', it summons up Shakespeare's intricately nuanced conjugations of homosociality, yet without allowing the male-friendship sonnet's conventional desire to present a compliment to conquer the primary instinct that the poem conveys—the desire to draw away. And whereas so many of Hardy's early sonnets dramatize a geographical gap between the speaker and the addressee in order to lament it, here London is presented as a welcome refuge from the overwhelming tide of Moule's unnamed 'troubles'.

> Your troubles shrink not, though I feel them less
> Here, far away, than when I tarried near;
> I even smile old smiles—with listlessness—
> Yet smiles they are, not ghastly mockeries mere.
>
> A thought too strange to house within my brain
> Haunting its outer precincts I discern:
> —*That I will not show zeal again to learn*
> *Your griefs, and, sharing them, renew my pain.* . . .
>
> It goes, like murky bird or buccaneer
> That shapes its lawless figure on the main,
> And staunchness tends to banish utterly
> The unseemly instinct that had lodgment here;
> Yet, comrade old, can bitterer knowledge be
> Than that, though banned, such instinct was in me! (CP 11–12)

The emotional as well as geographical distance that the poem charts between Hardy and Moule (who took a job at Marlborough College in Wiltshire in 1865) is delicately reflected in the spatial metaphor through which
the brain's workings are depicted: a thought finds temporary 'lodgment' in
its 'outer precincts', but is 'too strange to house' in its centre. Such subtle
inner discriminations are themselves evidence of the fall into 'bitterer knowledge' that this sonnet enacts: Hardy's guilty understanding that having to
participate imaginatively in Moule's transgressions and miseries has not only
exposed to him the shameful limits of his powers of compassion, but made
him aware of his own potential lawlessness; 'instinct' and 'lovingkindness'
(here called 'staunchness'), the poem confesses, have been thrown into stark
and unsettling opposition.

Moule, it might be said, not only presided over Hardy's late adolescent
and early adult ventures into the literary, first in Dorchester and then in
London; he also furnished him with an example of the kind of uncontrol-
lable waywardness that often serves in Hardy's fiction as a portal into the
tragic—into absorption of the 'bitterer knowledge' that Moule is shown
forcing upon him in 'A Confession to a Friend in Trouble'. The periodic
sprees that led to Moule's leaving so many positions under a cloud are mirrored not only in the catastrophic drunken outbursts of Henchard and
Jude, but in the two-day spell of licentiousness indulged in by Angel Clare
in *Tess*; 'tossed about by doubts and difficulties in London, like a cork on the
waves', he confesses to his bride on the night of their wedding, he had
'plunged into eight-and-forty hours' dissipation with a stranger' (T 243).
Critics have, indeed, found numerous links between the Clares and the
Moules: like Angel, Moule was the black sheep of a pious, high-minded
family, and while it is not known if his sudden disappearances involved 'dissipation with a stranger' as well as prolonged drinking, the transition from
'radiance' to 'twice night' and 'shadier shade' and 'embittered' thoughts in
stanzas two and three of 'Standing by the Mantelpiece' matches the narrative shadowed forth in the dreadful and humiliating disillusionment
awaiting *Tess*'s 'imaginative and ethereal' (T 211) protagonist. Moule, who
was described by his brother Handley as 'shedding an indefinable glamour
of the ideal over all we read', and Clare might both be considered bright
angels who end up suffering a hapless loss of innocence and belief, a fall

into bitter knowledge.[4] In oblique and reticent ways, the novel and Hardy's two poems that are explicitly about his friend record not only the acute distress that Moule endured himself, but the 'trouble' that he caused to all who fell under his spell.[5]

It is pretty much certain that Moule was the 'friend' who is mentioned in Hardy's letter to Tinsley of 14 September 1869 as negotiating on his behalf over the terms on which Tinsley Brothers might agree to publish *The Poor Man and the Lady* (CL 1:10); and it was from Moule that Leslie Stephen learned that Hardy was the author of the anonymously published *Under the Greenwood Tree.*[6] He reviewed both of Hardy's first two novels in the *Saturday Review*, and possibly, as Claire Tomalin suggests, the anonymous piece on *A Pair of Blue Eyes* in the same paper is by him as well (CT 408). Certainly this reviewer's complaints about the 'sprinkling of small oddities of style, and of minor errors of taste' (CH 15) tally with the comments that Moule made on the novel, which he hadn't, he admitted, as yet finished, in his last surviving letter to Hardy, written on 21 May 1873: 'You understand the *woman* infinitely better than the *lady*—' (here anticipating Barrie's strictures on Hardy's attempts to bring 'Society figures' (CH 159) into his novels), '& how gloriously you have idealized here & there, as far as I have got. Yr slips of taste, every now and then, I ought to say pointblank at once, are *Tinsleyan*.'[7] The irony of Moule's adopting a tone in this letter so similar to that of Knight's to Stephen can hardly have been lost on Hardy, and his class sensitivity may well have flared up too on being instructed by Moule that the proper way of titling the man whom Elfride eventually marries should be Spenser Hugo, Lord Luxellian, rather than Spenser Hugo Luxellian, a Lord.

The letter concludes with an affectionate determination to re-establish contact—'I long to meet you again & must & will meet'. Their last London night out together took place the following month. 'June 15. Met H.M.M. at the Golden Cross Hotel {in Charing Cross}. Dined with him at the British Hotel {on Cockspur Street}' (L 96). Hardy was staying at his bolthole in Celbridge Place, where he was joined by his brother Henry for a few days. On the evening of Henry's return to Dorset, Hardy caught a train to Cambridge. Moule was able to keep rooms in Queens' as a base for his current post—one that must have been almost unimaginably dispiriting—of Poor Law Inspector

in East Anglia. This was Hardy's first visit to the university, which, as a result of H. M. M.'s instruction and encouragement, had shimmered like a
mirage—or the lights of Christminster—throughout his early twenties. The
final words of the account in his diary of his stay in Cambridge were transparently added after the event in order to bring out the pathos of their last
hours together. Indeed this entry registers almost as Hardy's elegy for the
friend whose ideas and advice so decisively shaped his early ambitions, whose
reviews helped float his career in literary London, but whose legacy was so
complicated and intractable that Hardy never felt able to articulate it directly
either in poetry or in prose—or at least in the poetry and the prose that survived his ruthless editing of his manuscripts, his journals, and his letters.[8]

June 20. By evening train to Cambridge. Stayed in College—Queens'—
Went out with H.M.M. after dinner. A magnificent evening: sun over
'the Backs'.
    Next morning went with H.M.M. to King's Chapel early. M. opened
the great West doors to show the interior vista: we got upon the roof,
where we could see Ely Cathedral gleaming in the distant sunlight. A
never-to-be-forgotten morning. H.M.M. saw me off for London. His last
smile. (L 96)

II

Shortly after moving from Surbiton to Newton Road in Westbourne Grove
in March of 1875, a shift in quarters that he hoped would enable him to write
the London scenes of *The Hand of Ethelberta* 'as vigorously as possible',
Hardy joined the Copyright Association, which had been founded only three
years earlier. He was also part, on 10 May, of a delegation to 10 Downing
Street led by William Moy Thomas, the association's secretary, whose
lobbying resulted in the setting up by Disraeli of a Royal Commission to
investigate copyright issues in October of that year, both domestic and
international. Of greatest concern to Hardy and his British contemporaries
was the lack of an international copyright agreement in America, where
piracy of works by British authors was routine. The International Copyright Law of 1891 was eventually passed by the U.S. Congress on 3 March of
that year, coming into effect in July—just before serialization of *Tess of the*

d'Urbervilles began in the American magazine *Harper's Bazaar*. As popular in America as it was in Britain, *Tess* became the source of huge U.S. royalties for Hardy.

His early training as an architect with Hicks and his employments with Blomfield and Crickmay had inculcated in Hardy a rigorous professional ethos that he was determined to transfer to the more solitary career of a writer, which lacked the ready-made support and discipline afforded by an office and colleagues. Although while working for Crickmay he had operated in what amounted to a freelance capacity, there were still unnerving aspects to his decision, encouraged by Emma but in defiance of his mother's wishes, to forsake architecture for the more perilous business of novel writing. His decision to join the Copyright Association indicates a desire to see his new career as affording both the social respectability and the financial benefits that pertained to the life of a 'London professional man' (PBE 14). A letter of 4 November 1875 to the American publisher Henry Holt, who issued a number of Hardy's early novels in the United States, captures the kind of methodical accounting practices that Hardy brought to his negotiations with publishers: all details of sales and royalties, he explained, should be set out on a 'systematic basis' (CL 1:40):

> in this manner, that your clerk make out for me every 6 months a tabular statement of sales &c. in a way I could clearly understand—but perhaps a diagram will show my meaning best.

Name of Book	Copies sold in the half year	Retail price of same	10 per cent royalty

Hardy, in other words, was much closer to *The Mayor of Casterbridge*'s disciplined Scotsman, Donald Farfrae, than to its impulsive, short-sighted Michael Henchard when it came to organizing his business affairs.

Serialization, he knew, was the key to financial rewards in this market, and it remained so until the collapse of the circulating libraries in the 1890s. After the failure, however, of *The Hand of Ethelberta* to build on the success that he'd enjoyed in the *Cornhill* with *Far from the Madding Crowd*, Hardy had some trouble finding magazines into which his fiction comfortably fitted. Stephen passed on *The Return of the Native*, as did John Blackwood of *Blackwood's Magazine*, and George Bentley of *Temple Bar*. It was eventually published in the less prestigious *Belgravia*, which was owned by Chatto & Windus, and whose sales, after its sensation-fiction-driven heyday of the 1860s, were in free fall. Hardy received only £20 for each of the twelve instalments, which, even with first-edition rights of £200 from Smith, Elder & Co. and then American rights, meant that the book earned him much less than *The Hand of Ethelberta*. The magazine's prudish editors also forced on him a series of plot changes, and, in the Wessex Edition of 1912, Hardy inserted a note between the penultimate and final chapters of the book explaining that the marriage of Thomasin and Venn had not been part of his original design, but was a concession to the wishes of *Belgravia*'s editors: 'certain circumstances of serial publication led to a change of intent', as he drily put it (RN 440).[9]

The Return of the Native's successor, *The Trumpet-Major*, also rejected by Stephen, first appeared in *Good Words*, a magazine aimed at evangelicals and nonconformists and edited by the Reverend Donald Macleod, who wrote to Hardy on 20 June 1879, six months before the first instalment came out, with a pre-emptive warning: 'We are anxious that all our stories should be in harmony with the spirit of the magazine—free at once from *Goody-goodyism*—and from anything—direct or indirect—which a healthy *Parson* like myself would not care to read to his bairns at the fireside' (DCM). Hardy, alas, failed to anticipate all that might upset what the healthy parson goes on to call 'the susceptibilities of honestly religious & domestic souls', scheduling a meeting between Bob Loveday and his dubious fiancée Matilda for the afternoon of the Sabbath! After due discussion with the reverend at a meeting in London, the penitent novelist agreed to postpone the offending lovers' tryst to the Monday.

The Return of the Native was written in Sturminster Newton in Dorset between 1876 and 1878, a period commemorated in the poem 'A Two Years' Idyll' as the happiest time in the Hardys' married life. 'What seems it now?' opens the poem's final stanza:

> Lost: such beginning was all;
> Nothing came after: romance straight forsook
> Quickly somehow

> Life when we sped from our nook,
> Primed for new scenes with designs smart and tall. (CP 629)

The 'new scenes' here mentioned took place in Upper Tooting, at 1 Arundel Terrace, Trinity Road, also known as 'The Larches', a substantial London-brick end-of-terrace house laid out on four floors (it is now 172 Trinity Road) into which the Hardys moved on 22 March 1878. It was close to Wandsworth Common railway station, with its regular service into Victoria—as well as, more ominously, the Surrey County Pauper Lunatic Asylum (founded in 1840). The suburban streets of the area were still somewhat raw, having been laid out in the previous two decades, as London's suburban railway network expanded. In the *Life* Hardy explains that he 'had decided that the practical side of his vocation of novelist demanded that he should have his head-quarters in or near London', and Tooting must have seemed, like Surbiton, a suitable compromise between the urban and the rural, a place where his 'designs smart and tall' could be realized both imaginatively and practically. The move proved, however, as he goes on ruefully to acknowledge, something of a misjudgement—indeed nearly a fatal one: 'The wisdom of his decision, considering the nature of his writing, he afterwards questioned' (L 121).

Their lease was for three years, but a biographical sketch that Hardy composed for the editor of the American magazine *Boston World* some six weeks after moving in implies that he was attempting to think of himself as a long-term city dweller: 'Mr Hardy first took up his permanent residence in London in 1862', he writes, before stressing the part played by the International Ex-hibition of 1862 and London's public and private galleries in his education—which had been generally 'looked after by an able classical scholar and Fellow of Queens' College, Cambridge' (PV 11). Hardy also gives ample at-tention to his prize-winning architectural essays of 1863, as if he were keen to cite all possible credentials that might boost his profile as a 'London pro-fessional man'. To his friend Charles Kegan Paul he wrote on 21 June 1878 that moving to Tooting was just the opening gambit in what would be a pro-longed residence in the capital: 'I have only settled temporarily in this suburb, to have a foothold from which to choose some permanent spot. We might have ventured on Kensington [where Kegan Paul lived], but for such utter rustics as ourselves Tooting seemed town enough to begin with'

(CL 1:57–58). In this same letter he thanked Paul for supporting his election to the Savile Club (located at 15 Savile Row), whose motto, *Sodalitas Convivium* (friendship through companionship), stressed its ethos of urbanity and sophistication. And so, 'by degrees', as he put it in the *Life*, Hardy 'fell into line as a London man again' (L 125).

While Hardy's three years and three months in Tooting could hardly be labelled a Jamesian 'conquest of London', this was the period in which he set about embedding himself in the literary life of the capital, meeting a wide range of editors and authors, attending literary soirées and publishers' garden parties, and entering, when it seemed necessary, into public justification of his literary practices, as in the letter he published in the *Athenaeum* defending his use of dialect in *The Return of the Native* after their reviewer had ridiculed the language he put into 'the mouth of the modern rustic' (CH 46).[10] He even wrote a review himself, of William Barnes's *Poems of Rural Life in the Dorset Dialect*—a volume published in 1879 by C. Kegan Paul. The diary entries from this period included in the *Life* reflect not only his determination to mingle in social and artistic circles as 'the vocation of novelist demanded' but an undercurrent of unease and embarrassment at his attempts to lead a metropolitan literary life. One entry for 9 June 1879 records his attendance at a Soirée Musicale at the Hanover Square Club to meet members of the Literary Congress and the Comédie Française: 'The whole thing a free-and-easy mix-up. I was a total stranger, and wondered why I was there: many others were total strangers to everybody else; sometimes two or three of these total strangers would fraternize from very despair. A little old Frenchman, however, who bustled about in a skull cap and frilled shirt, seemed to know everybody' (L 130).

When Walter Besant—'a great lover of clubs and societies' (L 136)—persuaded him to become a founder-member of the Rabelais Club in December of 1879, Hardy found himself ill-equipped to join in the virile merriment the club was intended to foster. His account of their first meeting again deftly captures the awkwardness of an occasion intended to be brilliant and memorable yet which signally fails to come to life. The club's inaugural dinner was held at the Tavistock Hotel in Bloomsbury in a 'large, empty, dimly-lit, cheerless apartment, with a gloomy crimson screen hiding what remained of the only cheerful object there—the fire' (L 135):

There was a fog in the room as in the streets, and one man only came in evening dress, who, Walter Pollock said, looked like the skull at the banquet, but who really looked like a conjuror dying of the cold among a common set of thick-jacketed men who could stand it. When I came in Leland turned his high flat façade to me—like that of a clock-tower; his face being the clock-face, his coat swaying like a pendulum; features earnest and energetic, altogether those of a single-minded man. There was also Fred Pollock, girlish-looking; and genial Walter Besant, with his West-of-England sailor face and silent pantomimic laughter. Sir Patrick Colquhoun was as if he didn't know what he was there for, how he arrived there, or how he was going to get home again. Two others present—Palmer [afterwards murdered in the East], and Joe Knight [the dramatic critic], also seemed puzzled about it.[11]

Like many of the urban character sketches or vignettes describing metropolitan social events taken from Hardy's diaries from these years, this damp squib of a dinner is hit off with remarkable pungency and vividness: when after dinner a toast is delivered celebrating those present as 'men who ought to be encouraged', he caustically notes that the 'sentiment was applauded with no misgivings of self-conceit'. Alexander Duffield keeps 'lapsing into Spanish on the strength of his going some day to publish a translation of Don Quixote' (it did in fact appear in 1881) and additionally refuses to drink the health of absent members on the grounds 'that they ought to have been there'. 'Altogether', concludes Hardy, 'we were as Rabelaisian as it was possible to be in the foggy circumstances, though I succeeded but poorly' (L 136).

Hardy worked hard—perhaps too hard—to make a success of his life as a London-based professional author, but, like this would-be Rabelaisian party, his efforts only sporadically caught fire. Not long after his arrival in Tooting, he began making visits to the British Library in order to research background material for *The Trumpet-Major*, and his 'Trumpet-Major Notebook' of 1878–1879 (PN 115–186) reveals him tackling with impressive thoroughness the task of assembling facts and details for the historical novel that he hoped would enable him to recover the market share that he'd lost after the great success of *Far from the Madding Crowd*. The extensive research Hardy carried out in preparation for the composition of *The Trumpet-Major* suggests that the disappointing reception of *The Return of the Native*, which had been dismissed by the *Athenaeum* as 'distinctly inferior to anything of his which we have yet read' (CH 46), may well have dented his faith in his gifts as a 'born storyteller' (L 100), or at least in his ability to support a middle-class wife in a large house in a London suburb without adopting a more calculating approach to the business of novel writing.

Charles Kegan Paul, for one, complained that the novel revealed too obviously that 'the author has had to cram or be crammed for it' (CH 90). There is, of course, no denying the fervour of Hardy's interest in the Napoleonic era: he made frequent visits to Chelsea Hospital to interview the last survivors of Wellington's campaigns, and he and Emma had spent a hot, fatiguing day in June of 1876 tramping over the battlefield of Waterloo.[12] His passion for all things Napoleonic amounted to what might well be called the obsession of his life, and one that eventually resulted in the vast, complex, teeming fabric of *The Dynasts*, which he liked to think was his greatest achievement. Yet elements of both the 'mechanical' (L 154), to use his own term, and winsome pervade his only attempt to fashion from this obsession a commercially successful historical novel. Keen to dispel the notion that he was an unsaleable contrarian, he presented *The Trumpet-Major* to prospective magazine editors as a jolly romp with a happy ending: 'it is', he wrote to John Blackwood, unavailingly, 'above all things a cheerful story, without views or opinions, & is intended to wind up happily'. He made the same pitch, equally unsuccessfully, to J. B. Lippincott, of the Philadelphia-based *Lippincott's Magazine*: 'it is to be a cheerful, lively story, & is to end happily' (CL 1:65).

Cheerfulness is markedly absent from the diary entries that Hardy made in the course of the winter of 1878–1879:

November 28. Woke before it was light. Felt that I had not enough staying power to hold my own in the world.

1879. January 1. New Year's thought. A perception of the FAILURE of THINGS to be what they are meant to be, lends them, in place of the intended interest, a new and greater interest of an unintended kind. (L 127)

Further, he goes on in the same diary entry to reveal that the disturbed and disturbing poem 'A January Night' derived from 'an incident of this new year

(1879) which occurred here at Tooting, where they seemed to begin to feel that "there had past away a glory from the earth". And it was in this house that their troubles began' (L 127–128). The borrowing from Wordsworth's 'Ode: Intimations of Immortality' deftly permits Hardy to skate over details of the rift that opened up between himself and Emma in Tooting, at the same time creating a telling link between himself and the rurally born poet who most powerfully described, in Book VII of *The Prelude*, the threat to the organic imagination and the wholesomeness of the heart's affections posed by prolonged residence in the metropolis.

'A January Night' is the only Hardy poem explicitly dated to his Tooting years, although his residence in South London resulted in a number of others too, such as 'A Wasted Illness' and 'Snow in the Suburbs', as well as one of his very greatest, 'Beyond the Last Lamp', written in 1911 and first published as 'Night in a Suburb' in December of that year in *Harper's Monthly Magazine*.[13] The subtitle to 'Beyond the Last Lamp' tells us that it draws on a scene observed 'Near Tooting Common' three decades earlier—'Though thirty years of blur and blot / Have slid since I beheld that spot, / And saw in curious converse there / Moving slowly, moving sadly / That mysterious tragic pair' (CP 315). The manuscript of the poem is dated 'Sept: 1911'—that is just over a year before Emma died, meaning it was composed at a time when relations between husband and wife had reached their nadir, Emma having retreated by this time to her Max Gate attic. No doubt Hardy did observe the couple in question on Streatham Lane on some wet and dismal evening between 1878 and 1881, but it's also likely that the persistence of the memory relates to the 'troubles' that he and Emma experienced at 1 Arundel Terrace, discovering themselves 'no longer orbed / By love's young rays', while also connecting with their bitter, unshared 'brooding on their pain' in Max Gate thirty years later:

I

While rain, with eve in partnership,
Descended darkly, drip, drip, drip,
Beyond the last lone lamp I passed
    Walking slowly, whispering sadly,
    Two linked loiterers, wan, downcast:
Some heavy thought constrained each face,
And blinded them to time and place.

II

The pair seemed lovers, yet absorbed
In mental scenes no longer orbed
By love's young rays. Each countenance
        As it slowly, as it sadly
        Caught the lamplight's yellow glance
Held in suspense a misery
At things which had been or might be.

III

When I retrod that watery way
Some hours beyond the droop of day,
Still I found pacing there the twain
        Just as slowly, just as sadly,
        Heedless of the night and rain.
One could but wonder who they were
And what wild woe detained them there.

IV

Though thirty years of blur and blot
Have slid since I beheld that spot,
And saw in curious converse there
        Moving slowly, moving sadly
        That mysterious tragic pair,
Its olden look may linger on—
All but the couple; they have gone.

V

Whither? Who knows, indeed. . . . And yet
To me, when nights are weird and wet,
Without those comrades there at tryst
        Creeping slowly, creeping sadly,
        That lone lane does not exist.
There they seem brooding on their pain,
And will, while such a lane remain. (CP 314–315)

'Few people in whom he is interested in the novels', the critic John Bayley has argued, 'possess a proper home'.[14] In this haunting poem about a haunting scene, as in Hardy's descriptions of figures in landscapes in the fiction, specificity of location '(Near Tooting Common)' is allied with a radical sense of homelessness. The ineffaceable impression that the miserable couple makes on the passing poet seems to derive from the suggestion that these 'linked loiterers' are themselves 'blinded' by their unhappiness to 'time and place'. The poem records both, and the weather too, with novelistic fidelity, creating an unbridgeable gulf between the poet who notices such things and the couple's wondrous and tragic indifference ('Heedless of the night and rain') to all outside themselves, an indifference caused by their 'wild woe', which, while it detains them there, also separates them from their surroundings. It is their abstraction from the dreary suburban locale that makes them, and the 'lone lane' near Tooting Common down which they pace, linger so persistently in Hardy's memory. 'Each countenance', he notes—and the observation can be applied as much to the poem as to the faces of the couple that inspired it—'Held in suspense a misery / At things which had been or might be'. These last lines of stanza II make explicit a certain Janus-faced aspect of 'Beyond the Last Lamp', as the couple, and the poem, peer into unhappiness stretching at once back into the past and forward into the future. Suspended, like the soon-to-be-ex-lovers of 'Neutral Tones', in their all-engrossing misery, they become inextricably fused in the poet's mind with the lane and the lamp and the falling rain, as the white sun and ash tree and pond 'edged with grayish leaves' keep recurring to the speaker of the earlier poem. Both poems reveal Hardy's extraordinary ability to compose moving and memorable and richly enigmatic scenarios out of banality, dejection, and disenchantment.

In one of the few entries Hardy made in a notebook that he entitled 'Poetical Matter' that derive from the years 1878 to 1881, he observed: '<u>At Tooting</u>. A pool of water, & beyond it a lamp: drops of rain cause flashes. (1878)' (PM 8). Hardy, as this notebook's editors observe, was at this time 'fascinated by reflections and other light effects' (PM 87), and his terse recording of a scene similar to that of 'Beyond the Last Lamp' is followed shortly after by what is effectively an Impressionist domestic tableau in words, a painterly denotation of the visual effects of warmth and light in a cosy study on a winter evening that brings to mind the contemporaneous depictions of interiors by such as Degas or Monet:

> Shines. 19 Jan. 1879. In the study firelight a red glow is on the polished sides & arch of the grate: firebrick back red hot: the polish of fireirons shines: underside of mantel reddened: also a shine on the leg of the table, & the ashes under the grate, lit from above like a torrid clime. Faint daylight of a lilac colour almost powerless in the room. Candle behind a screen is reflected in the glass of the window, falling whitely on book, & on E's face & hand, a large shade of her head being on wall & ceiling. Light shines through the loose hair about her temples, & reaches the skin as sunlight through a brake. (PM 8)

Hardy here seems to be experimenting with the play of light as in his 'Studies, Specimens &c.' notebook he'd experimented with the sounds of words. Like the domestic scenes that recur in so many French Impressionist paintings, the passage can be read as a hymn to the refined pleasures of bourgeois interiority, both actual and imaginative, and it is no coincidence that Hardy began exploring the aesthetic possibilities of middle-class life indoors once he was himself ensconced in a middle-class house in a suburb of the capital. The near juxtaposition, however, of the entry recording the lone lamp in the rain with that of himself and Emma at peace in their warm study also throws into relief the preoccupation with the meaning of home, and of its opposite, homelessness, that unites Hardy's Tooting poems. It is striking that he presents the golden inner light as triumphantly dispelling the attenuated incursions of the world beyond—'Faint daylight of a lilac colour almost powerless in the room'. For, despite their suburban setting, in these poems the elements can seem as unforgiving and relentless as, say, the storm that menaces Bathsheba's hayricks in *Far from the Madding Crowd*, or the cruel frost through which Tess makes her way from Flintcomb-Ash to Emminster and back.

Although less spectacular, the power of London's weather to oppress is often felt by Hardy as keenly as that of Wessex. He observes in another Tooting entry in his 'Poetical Matter' notebook: 'City scene. Snow & hail:

looked forward under a grove of umbrellas, & saw faces under their shade pushing on through the weather: hard & square faces, whiskered ones, red ones, anxious ones' (PM 8–9). These hapless commuters seem like a posse of animals sheltering from the snow and hail beneath a makeshift umbrella 'grove'. Similarly, in 'Beyond the Last Lamp' Hardy makes sure that we literally hear the rain falling, 'Drip drip drip', on Tooting Common, a relentless drumming like each stanza's repetition of 'slowly', 'sadly'. It makes the 'last lone lamp' that the poet passes seem like a melancholy beacon casting its 'yellow glance' on the watery lane up and down which the lovers are condemned to walk, a frail defence, like the grove of umbrellas, against the 'wild woe' and falling rain that menaces them.

'Snow in the Suburbs' (whose manuscript has the alternative title 'Snow at Upper Tooting' lightly erased, RP 237) similarly dramatizes hostile weather threatening those struggling to survive in the *rus in urbe* of the city's edge-lands—although on this occasion 'lovingkindness' affords some respite for the homeless cat that arrives on the doorstep. Particularly if one assumes, I think justifiably, that the scene is observed through a window, this poem again manifests Hardy's fascination with the relationship between indoors and outdoors:

> Every branch big with it,
> Bent every twig with it;
> Every fork like a white web-foot;
> Every street and pavement mute:
> Some flakes have lost their way, and grope back upward, when
> Meeting those meandering down they turn and descend again.
> The palings are glued together like a wall,
> And there is no waft of wind with the fleecy fall.
>
> A sparrow enters the tree,
> Whereon immediately
> A snow-lump thrice his own slight size
> Descends on him and showers his head and eyes,
> And overturns him,
> And near inurns him,

And lights on a nether twig, when its brush
Starts off a volley of other lodging lumps with a rush.

The steps are a blanched slope,
Up which, with feeble hope,
A black cat comes, wide-eyed and thin;
　　And we take him in. (CP 732–733)

The final line not only testifies to the Hardys' shared affection for animals, particularly cats, but creates a contrast between the baffling, frozen scene outside, in which snow falls upward to the sky and the streets are suddenly mute, and the reassuring domestic comforts still available within. The topsy-turvy changes wrought by the 'fleecy fall', which transforms branches into white webbed feet and almost buries alive the hopping sparrow, allows the 'we' of the poem to come together, in opposition to the indifference and separateness that prevails outside, as rescuers of the foraging cat. If only momentarily, this last line presents 1 Arundel Terrace as more than just a sheltered vantage point from which to observe the winter weather. Like the description of Emma in the lamplight, it turns a house into a home.

'A January Night', on the other hand, a poem subtitled '1879', depicts powerful, malicious, natural—and possibly supernatural—forces invading their domicile from the outside, and something quite different from a hungry cat looking for entry. The poem bears out the claim made by Alexandra Sutherland Orr (the future biographer of Browning) in an article that appeared in *New Quarterly Review* in October of 1879, that Hardy's 'genius' was 'gothic in expression, but largely pagan in spirit' (CH 62):

The rain smites more and more,
The east wind snarls and sneezes;
Through the joints of the quivering door
　　The water wheezes.

The tip of each ivy-shoot
Writhes on its neighbour's face;

> There is some hid dread afoot
> > That we cannot trace.

> Is it the spirit astray
> Of the man at the house below
> Whose coffin they took in to-day?
> > We do not know. (CP 466)

A solidly built corner house in a middle-class and rapidly expanding South London suburb might seem an unlikely site for the elemental threats and mysterious terrors here described as menacing its occupants. The anthropomorphized rain and wind appear to be mounting a deliberate assault on the Hardy homestead in the first stanza, while in the second the battle for supremacy is imagined as being joined even between the ivy-shoots climbing its walls. A later poem called 'In a Wood' savours the irony of a 'city-opprest' seeker after 'sylvan peace' finding the trees that surround him to be 'Combatants all!' (CP 64) in an unending strife that is little different from that waged by the inhabitants of the metropolis he has fled. This scenario itself alludes to a famous passage in *The Woodlanders* that presents an analogy between the deformities afflicting trees competing for survival in the woods around the remote Wessex village of Little Hintock with those to be found 'among the depraved crowds of a city slum' (W 48). Hardy's anxiety during his Tooting years about his own chances of succeeding as a combatant in the urban rat race prompted diary entries such as the one of 28 November 1879: 'Felt that I had not enough staying power to hold my own in the world' (L 127). In 'A January Night' this anxiety seems channeled into fears that verge on the paranoiac. In its last stanza Hardy finds a Gothic emblem for the uncanny 'hid dread afoot' that he senses in the inclement weather of this particular January night, as the 'spirit astray' of his recently deceased neighbour is fearfully pictured, like the smiting rain and snarling, sneezing wind, seeking to infiltrate the house. The 'we' of the poem are united here, not by their shared kindness as in 'Snow in the Suburbs', but by their shared apprehension and distress.[15]

It is interesting to contrast 'A January Night' with 'The Self-Unseeing', a poem set in the cottage in which Hardy grew up in Higher Bockhampton, which also consists of three four-line stanzas rhyming *abab*, although without the contracted last line that brings each stanza of 'A January Night' to such an unnerving, juddering halt. 'The Self-Unseeing' at once recalls and re-creates the ancestral continuity afforded by a house consecrated by use and memory:

> Here is the ancient floor,
> Footworn and hollowed and thin,
> Here was the former door
> Where the dead feet walked in.
>
> She sat here in her chair,
> Smiling into the fire;
> He who played stood there,
> Bowing it higher and higher.
>
> Childlike, I danced in a dream;
> Blessings emblazoned that day;
> Everything glowed with a gleam;
> Yet we were looking away! (CP 166–167)

The vulnerability of the imperilled couple of 'A January Night' can be re-lated to the implicit loss of the links of communal history unconsciously con-necting the generations. The 'dead feet' of Hardy's grandparents exhibit a weird but reassuring livingness that is completely at odds with the disquieting afterlife of the anonymous neighbour whose coffin has just been delivered to a house in Trinity Road. Hardy entitled the chapter in his autobiography describing their first years in Tooting 'Life and Literature in a London Suburb'. Juxtaposing 'A January Night' and 'The Self-Unseeing' prompts the thought that Hardy was at least subliminally aware that his own 'spirit' had gone 'astray', become impossible to 'trace', and was wrongly housed when transplanted to a London suburb so far, imaginatively at any rate, from the 'former door' that opened onto his ancestral identity.

III

The 'hid dread' did not emerge fully from the shadows until the late autumn of 1881. Like his first London residence, this one ended in the complete collapse of Hardy's health. In mid-October of 1880 he and Emma went to Cambridge for a week, where they spent time with Charles, Arthur, and Handley Moule. No doubt the trip reminded Hardy of their brother, of the 'never-to-be-forgotten' morning he enjoyed on the roof of King's Chapel with H. M. M., and of his friend's 'last smile'. A day or so after arriving in Cambridge, Hardy felt 'an indescribable physical weariness' (L 145) take hold of him, and on his return to Tooting on 23 October (the day on which *The Trumpet-Major* was published) he became seriously unwell. A local surgeon suspected internal bleeding, a diagnosis confirmed when they sought a second opinion. Hardy later labeled it a 'bladder inflammation' (CL 4:115), and attributed its onset to prolonged bathing in the English Channel while on holiday in July and August of that year in northern France. Some recent biographers have posited that he was suffering from a bladder or kidney stone, possibly aggravated by typhoid fever (MM 201), or from a severe form of cystitis (CT 184), while Ralph Pite argued in his biography that Hardy's condition was largely due to overwork and anxiety, and could even be seen as 'a form of midlife crisis'.[16]

Happily, given the survival rates of Victorian patients who went under the knife, Hardy opted not for an operation but for a prolonged stay in bed, although one with a peculiar twist: his feet, at first at least, had to be elevated above the level of his head. Whether this helped or hindered his recovery is not easy to judge. The winter of 1880–1881 was an exceptionally harsh one (a diary entry of January 1881 records Emma's discovery that so much snow had seeped into the downstairs passage of the house that 'feet leave tracks on it', L 151). Hardy spent all of it bedbound, not feeling strong enough to venture out of doors until 10 April, when he managed to go for a drive with Emma and his doctor; and it was not until early May that he was able to sally forth alone on foot, taking a walk on Wandsworth Common and reciting to himself some lines from Thomas Gray's 'Ode on the Pleasure Arising from Vicissitude'. In a slightly dryer vein than Gray, who compares a recovered invalid's first experiences of life outdoors to 'opening Paradise', Hardy

noted in 'A Wasted Illness' that 'Old circumstance resumed its former show, /
And on my head the dews of comfort fell / As ere my woe' (CP 152). But the
poem, for all the black humour of its expression of regret that he didn't die
since it only means he'll have to go through the whole ghastly business
again some other time, also records in lurid, phantasmagoric detail his
experience of feeling himself inexorably approaching a very different kind
of door to that of 'A January Night' or 'The Self-Unseeing':

> Through vaults of pain,
> Enribbed and wrought with groins of ghastliness,
> I passed, and garish spectres moved my brain
> To dire distress.
>
> And hammerings,
> And quakes, and shoots, and stifling hotness, blent
> With webby waxing things and waning things
> As on I went.
>
> 'Where lies the end
> To this foul way?' I asked with weakening breath.
> Thereon ahead I saw a door extend—
> The door to Death. (CP 152)

For mysterious reasons it recedes at the last moment, and he slides back
'Along the galleries by which I came, / And tediously the day returned, and
sky, / And life—the same.'

   While Hardy lay ill both Thomas Carlyle and George Eliot passed through
that door, or 'vanished into nescience' (L 152), as Hardy characteristically
put it in his diary, and his own body and possessions underwent various
subtle changes: 'Jan. 31. Incidents of lying in bed for months. Skin gets
fair: corns take their leave: feet and toes grow shapely as those of a Greek
statue. Keys get rusty; watch dim, boots mildewed; hat and clothes old-
fashioned; umbrella eaten out with rust; children seen through the window
are grown taller' (L 152). It was explained to friends that he was 'laid up
with a troublesome malady' (CL 1:84), and he saw only a few intimates such

as Edmund Gosse, the Macmillans, Charles Kegan Paul, and the mathematician George Greenhill. Confined to his room, nursed only by Emma (a decision having been taken to keep his parents and siblings in the dark as to the seriousness of his illness), Hardy stoically ruminated on topics such as adversity, Positivism, Romanticism, style, literary criticism, Matthew Arnold's concept of 'the imaginative reason', and the possibility of writing a Homeric Ballad on the Hundred Days featuring Napoleon as a latter-day Achilles (L 150–152). Astonishingly, although in complete accordance with the professional ethos that governed his literary life in London, he also composed a novel.

A Laodicean is subtitled 'A Story of To-day'. The New York firm of Harper & Brothers had approached Hardy in the spring of 1880 for a serial to run in the opening issues of a new European edition of *Harper's New Monthly Magazine*, for which they were prepared to pay the enticing sum of £100 for each of thirteen instalments. This was the most lucrative offer that he had yet received, and it was readily accepted. The magazine's opening number was scheduled for December, and by the time that he was laid low Hardy had sent off material for the first three issues. Despite the pain, he 'determined to finish the novel, at whatever stress to himself—so as not to ruin the new venture of the publishers and also in the interests of his wife, for whom as yet he had made but a poor provision in the event of his own decease'. Hardy's illness meant, therefore, that at long last, or so it must have seemed to Emma, husband and wife found themselves engaged in a genuine creative collaboration: 'Accordingly from November onwards he began dictating it to her from the awkward position he occupied; and continued to do so—with greater ease as the pain and haemorrhage went off. She worked bravely both at writing and nursing, till at the beginning of the following May a rough draft was finished by one shift and another' (L 150).

Unsurprisingly, the last three-quarters of the novel fail to live up to the extremely promising opening chapters, in which the London-based architect George Somerset meets Paula Power, the daughter of a recently deceased rail magnate and inheritor of an ancient pile, Stancy Castle, not far from Toneborough, Hardy's name for Taunton, the major town of the county that his hero is named after. *A Laodicean* resembles *Desperate Remedies* in being an attempt to front and refract the anxieties and uncertainties of 'To-day' in

relation to Victorian ideas of progress made possible by advances in tech-
nology. Here, in addition to the expansion of the railways, it is improvements
to telegraphy afforded by Émile Baudot's invention in the 1870s of an international telegraph alphabet, known as the Baudot code, as well as developments in the science of photography, that furnish Hardy with the many
convolutions and surprising turns taken by a plot that is almost as sensational
as that of his first published novel.

In 1900 Hardy told the American academic William Lyon Phelps that 'A
Laodicean contained more of the facts of his own life than anything else he
had ever written' (IR 64–65). George Somerset, who, like Egbert Mayne of
'An Indiscretion in the Life of an Heiress', is the son of a painter, is invested
with a more complex set of scruples and with less clear-cut motives and desires than Hardy's earlier architect-heroes—indeed Somerset's 'Laodiceanism' or 'lukewarmness' is mirrored more fully in Hardy's poetry than by
any of his other fictional male protagonists.[17] Somerset is perhaps the only
Hardy hero who might not feel out of place in a novel by Henry James. More
comfortably circumstanced than Mayne or Edward Springrove or Stephen
Smith, he is not driven by the dream of upward mobility that propelled Hardy's youthful alter egos, and his wavering pursuit of Paula Power seems inspired more by a sense of their shared Laodiceanism than the wish to ascend
the social hierarchies at whose apex she, somewhat uncertainly and guiltily,
stands, on account of the vast holdings she inherited from her father, the entrepreneurial John Power. Somerset's father's status as a highly respected
member of the Royal Academy means, unusually for Hardy, that hero and
heroine are more or less social equals: although she is much richer, he is more
artistically sophisticated and, having been brought up in London, introduces
a note of the cosmopolitan to her county set, in which various de Stancys, a
family of decayed aristocrats who once owned Stancy Castle but have since
fallen on hard times, feature prominently.

The Hardy character that Somerset most resembles is Ethelberta, for like
her he participates in the narrative that the novel offers him, without quite
believing in it. As a well-read and well-educated urban professional, he operates with a freedom, and a scepticism, well beyond the scope of Hardy's
earlier architect 'striver[s] with deeds to do' (CP 792). He is, we are told in
the opening chapter, 'a man of independent tastes and excursive instincts,

who unconsciously, and perhaps unhappily, took greater pleasure in floating in lonely currents of thought than with the general tide of opinion' (AL 5). Like his creator, in his early twenties Somerset found himself 'in a mood of disgust with his profession' of architecture, from which he turned to devote himself recklessly to his 'old enthusiasm for poetical literature'. For two years he composed verse 'in every conceivable metre, and on every conceivable subject, from Wordsworthian sonnets on the singing of his tea-kettle to epic fragments on the Fall of Empires'. Like those of the young Hardy, Somerset's effusions met with no success, and he returns, chastened, to his 'legitimate profession', determined to become 'intently practical'. His friendship with Paula promises to lead to his first major commission: the modernization of Stancy Castle.

This project, initiated by her installation of the telegraph that enables her to 'know the latest news from town' (AL 29), foregrounds the relationship between the past and the present that the novel proposes as its main theme. The telegraph wire, threaded through a loophole in the venerable battlements, serves as a symbol for the characters' pressing need to discover a workable blend of the ancient and the modern. Paula's schemes for domestic improvements to her castle are also, however, part of a dialogue between the provincial and the metropolitan. Indeed, on one level the novel can be read as an attempt to respond to Matthew Arnold's repeated association of the provincial with the philistine in his various diagnoses of what was wrong with contemporary English culture. Hardy was irritated by these attacks, observing in his diary in late 1880, just before serialization of *A Laodicean* began, that 'Arnold is wrong about provincialism, if he means anything more than a provincialism of style and manner in exposition. A certain provincialism of feeling is invaluable. It is of the essence of individuality, and is largely made up of that crude enthusiasm without which no great thoughts are thought, no great deeds done' (L 151). Haunting the precincts of crumbling Stancy Castle, Somerset is in quest not only of a suitable helpmeet, but of the 'crude enthusiasm' that lies buried in the past and dwells latent in provincialism—a provincialism encoded in his own name. Whereas previous Hardy architect-heroes had to come to London to do their 'great deeds', Somerset must escape from the city where he grew up to a remote region of Outer Wessex in order to access the 'invaluable' 'provincialism of feeling' that might rescue him from his 'lonely currents of thought', and even propel him to become a successful and important architect, one capable of forging a meaningful alliance between the traditional and the modern, the urban and the rural.

Alas, Hardy's illness meant that many of the most intriguing aspects of the *donnée* inspiring *A Laodicean* ended up only sketchily articulated. Like Stancy Castle itself, the novel is best approached as an uneven ruin—and one self-reflexively laid waste by fire at the end of the book, as if in a wanton fit of authorial exasperation. To complicate matters, *Harper's* demanded 'a predetermined cheerful ending', as Hardy later groused in the 1896 preface to the novel. It is possible, also, that Emma's tastes in fiction played a part in the working out of the various storylines that the novel, ineptly at times, seeks to juggle and intertwine. Writing *A Laodicean* had been, as Hardy later put it in a letter to Edmund Gosse, an 'awful job' (CL 5:237), and as soon as it was off his hands, he and Emma resolved to abandon the attempt to lead a full-time London life. They would make the capital 'a place of sojourn for a few months only in each year, and establish their home in the country' (L 154).

8

❦

Literary London (II)

I

In early March of 1880, some seven months before he fell ill, Hardy renewed his acquaintance with Mrs Procter. They had met at Leslie Stephen's in 1874, while he was at work on *Far from the Madding Crowd*, a novel she fervently admired. 'I can hardly make you understand', she wrote floridly to him on 4 September of that year, 'how one wants the next Number. It is perhaps a taste of Purgatory to wait for the drop of cold water'.[1] Born in the last year of the eighteenth century, Mrs Procter, as Hardy always called her, appealed to him as a literary version of his paternal grandmother, her mind a repository, not of local lore, but of tales of the poets whose work had so overwhelmed him in the course of his first residence in London. He even had her make out a list of all the famous people she had known.[2] Some of these she had met through her husband Bryan Procter (1787–1874), who published poetry under the pseudonym Barry Cornwall, and had been close to Thackeray, Browning, Wilkie Collins, and Thomas Lovell Beddoes. Hardy refers twice in the *Life* to a story that she told him about a visit made to her in the 1820s by Leigh Hunt, who brought with him ' "a youth whom nobody noticed much", and who remained in the background, Hunt casually introducing him as "Mr Keats" ' (L 139/350). His fondness for this anecdote reflects his general fascination with the relationship between literary greatness and ordinariness: 'a worthy man and well-to-do', a Stratford burgher responds in Hardy's poem 'To Shakespeare' (written in 1916 to commemorate the tricentenary of the Bard's death) when asked who is being buried on the day of

Shakespeare's funeral; 'Though, as for me, / I knew him but by just a neighbour's nod, 'tis true'; 'Ah, one of the tradesmen's sons,' his interlocutor replies, 'I now recall. . . . Witty, I've heard' (CP 440). In a similar vein, in 'At
Lulworth Cove a Century Back', the consumptive, Italy-bound Keats is dismissed by a local worthy as 'an idling town-sort': 'So commonplace a youth
calls not my thought', he declares—only to be told in the poem's final lines
that a hundred years later pilgrims will journey to Rome, as Hardy himself
had done, to 'bend with reverence where his ashes lie' (CP 602).

Hardy was conscious that he was rarely the life and soul of a social gathering—and took the precaution of warning Besant that while he was perfectly
willing to attend the festivities of the Rabelais Society, he himself would be
'a mere dummy' (CL 1:63). From his Tooting years on, Hardy made regular
appearances in a range of London literary circles and salons, but never attempted to dazzle or impress in the manner expected of literary lions. There
are many anecdotes told of his unassuming demeanour and conversation on
such occasions, and their tenor can be encapsulated by Douglas Goldring's
account of meeting Hardy at a party held at Ford Madox Ford's:

> I remember seeing a little, quiet, grey old man wearing a red tie, who
> turned out to be Thomas Hardy. I was standing next to Hugh Walpole
> at the back of the room, when he was pointed out to me. The conversa-
> tion among the lion cubs in our neighbourhood was no doubt very bril-
> liant and very 'literary' but suddenly there came the usual inexplicable
> hush. It was broken by Hardy who, turning to an elderly lady by his
> side, remarked, with shattering effect, 'And how is Johnny's whooping-
> cough?' (IR 103)

It is highly unlikely that Hardy intended the 'shattering effect' that Goldring
discerned. Reserved, thoughtful, courteous, softly spoken, always more interested in hearing the stories of others than in talking about himself, Hardy
liked to observe rather than be observed. It is very much in keeping with
his literary London persona that a sketch of him with J. Comyns Carr and
George Lewis in a theatre box that appeared in *The Illustrated Sporting
and Dramatic News* on 7 January 1882 pictures him shielding his face from
the viewer's gaze with his right hand.[3]

Hardy appears to have found Mrs Procter's extravagant language ('the divine Hardy' she calls him in one of her letters) soothing rather than intimidating, and he and Emma soon became frequent visitors to her flat in Queen Anne's Mansions in Petty France, Westminster.[4] She was not only a 'remarkable link' to his most cherished heroes, Keats and Shelley, but to the dominant poets of his own era: Browning was a regular at her Sunday afternoon salons, although he and Hardy never seem to have found much to say to each other, and, shortly after their acquaintance was renewed, she accompanied him to luncheon at Tennyson's temporary residence in Belgrave Street. Hardy's account of his first meeting with the poet whose work he had devotedly copied out in his apprentice years into his 'Studies, Specimens &c.' notebook again draws attention to the 'genial' ordinariness of genius when encountered off the page, in life: 'He was very sociable that day, asking Mrs Procter absurd riddles, and telling Hardy amusing stories, and about misprints in his books that drove him wild, one in especial of late, where "airy does" had appeared as "hairy does"' (L 140). As so often occurs in his descriptions of personages met in London, Hardy secretes a rural simile into the gathering in Belgrave Street: Tennyson's hair and beard, he notes, were 'straggling like briars'.[5] He was struck as well by the Laureate's ambivalent relationship to the capital: 'Tennyson also told him that he and his family were compelled to come to London for a month or two every year, though he hated it, because they all "got so rusty" down in the Isle of Wight if they did not come at all' (L 140). It must have chimed with thoughts of his own, for the following month he wrote a letter to his brother Henry outlining recent investigations that he had made into acquiring a plot of land near Dorchester (Letter of 20 April 1880, CL 1:73).

Another of Mrs Procter's *intimes* was Henry James, caustic reviewer of *Far from the Madding Crowd*. A fortnight after lunch at the Tennysons Hardy expressed astonishment at the notion that she had recently received an offer of marriage from him: 'Can it be so?' (L 140). A joke doing the rounds among Rabelaisians earlier in the year explains his wonder: James was not to be invited to join the club on the grounds that he was insufficiently 'virile' (L 136). But the unvirile novelist was occasionally invited as a guest, and after a Rabelais Club dinner of 1886 Hardy memorably noted his 'ponderously warm manner of saying nothing in infinite sentences'. In this diary entry Hardy also surreptitiously uses James's sense of self-importance to point up his own lack of conceit: James, he records, 'left suddenly in the midst of the meal because he was placed low down the table, as I was. Rather comical in Henry' (L 187).

For someone as shy as he sometimes claimed to be, and to an extent was, Hardy ended up knowing an extraordinary number of people. The majority of those who appear in the biographical index to the *Life*, which runs to sixty double-columned pages, were friends or acquaintances. His years in Tooting were crucial to the expansion of his social and professional network. If life in a London suburb ended up having a deadening effect on his imagination, it also made him into a notable figure on the London literary scene, enabling him to meet many of its key players, and allowing him to gain sustained and firsthand knowledge of the forces that governed the metropolitan literary marketplace. And it was in these years that his critical reputation was firmly established, principally by two extended surveys of his oeuvre to date—that by Alexandra Sutherland Orr published in Charles Kegan Paul's *New Quarterly Magazine* in October of 1879, and one by Charles Kegan Paul himself published in the *British Quarterly Review* of April 1881.

'Well', Hardy wrote in a letter of appreciation to Kegan Paul after reading his long and perceptive account of Hardy's first six novels, 'what can I say? If I have never yet written a good novel your essay should stimulate me to produce one without delay, & indeed will, in a measure: for nothing tends to draw out a writer's best work like the consciousness of a kindly feeling in his critics' (CL 1:89). Kegan Paul's tone throughout is measured and judicious, and he is not afraid to express reservations, about *Far from the Madding Crowd*'s use of melodrama, for instance, or the 'stage revival' (CH 90) aspects of *The Trumpet-Major*. His overall estimate of Hardy's greatness, however, is unambiguous, and seems all the more courageous if one remembers that he is assessing only a decade's worth of writing: 'When George Eliot died', the piece opens, 'it was not unnatural that men should at once ask themselves if she who had been confessedly the greatest living English novelist had left any successor in the true province of literature. The question, floating in so many minds, was answered promptly and decidedly by one journal, which claimed the falling mantle for Mr. Thomas Hardy' (CH 78). It's a claim that Kegan Paul's article not only goes on to substan-

tiate, but to improve upon. Hardy is compared favourably not only with ca-
nonical novelists such as Fielding, Richardson, Scott, Austen, Dickens,
and Thackeray, but with the ultimate gold standard of greatness: Hardy's
characters are 'as real and indestructible' in the minds of his readers, Kegan
Paul avers, 'as those drawn by Shakespeare's mighty hand'—although, he
hastens to add, they perhaps 'lack his perfect art' (CH 79).

What is also striking about this essay is the awareness that it articulates
on a number of occasions of the gulf between the urban consumer of Hardy's
novels and the country life represented in them: 'increasingly is it the case,
that the readers of books are in towns and not in the country' (CH 82), he
observes, and goes on to posit that Hardy's rural fiction might serve to liberate the 'dweller in towns' from prejudices about the 'country labourer',
whom he is prone to consider 'a lout because his speech differs greatly from
his own' (CH 84). In his depiction of rustics Hardy is seen as walking the
same fine line that Shakespeare did, as 'bound to amuse his town audience',
but never 'at the expense of the truth'. Although he may lack the Bard's 'perfect art', the work of Hardy, Kegan Paul intuits, can similarly be made to
intersect with a range of national myths. It is especially interesting to watch
him putting Hardy to use in his construction of a particular dream of En-
glishness that involves the pale and alienated city dweller recovering both
his health and a sense of national pride by first reading Hardy, and then
taking holidays in Dorset. In other words, his essay establishes the template
for figurations of Hardy as enabling both imaginative and then actual recovery
of a connection with an imperiled, pastoral vision of English history. The
crucial first step in this project is the establishing of Hardy's own earthy au-
thenticity. This humbly born novelist, Kegan Paul declares, is 'sprung of a
race of labouring men in a county where the real old families are attached to
the soil'. Needless to say, this much annoyed his class-conscious subject, who,
his effusive thanks out of the way, pointedly insisted in his letter of 18 April
1881 that his ancestors had never been 'journeymen' labourers as Kegan
Paul implied, but always 'master-masons, with a set of journeymen masons
under them' (CL 1:89). Far from taking 'exceeding pride' in the 'dignity of
labour' and his ancestral connections to a race of labouring men, Hardy
was eager to make it clear that his family was a rung above journeymen, and
while 'they have never risen above this level, they have *never* sunk below it'.

Such objections are, of course, beside the point. The middle-class Kegan Paul's essay is not concerned about doing justice to subtle gradations of rank among the rural working classes, but about showing that Hardy is profoundly and ancestrally in touch with English country life and can therefore be relied on as 'an interpreter of the simpler aspects of nature to many who have no time to commune with her, and learn her secrets at first hand' (CH 85). 'Year by year', he continues,

> masses of our people, and they our chief readers, see less and less of simple quiet country scenes. Brick and mortar swallow up our lives, and when we escape from them, it is to the sea or to the mountains, not to lose ourselves in English woods, or wander over the downs and in the green lanes which exist only here, and date from British days, older still than the great Roman roads still to be traced in the west in unexpected places, green across hill and dale. Only a few days since we spoke to a young clerk who had escaped from London on Sunday into one of the loveliest districts of Surrey, and we asked if he had walked through a certain yew-tree grove, the wonder of the neighbourhood. To one country-bred there was something pathetic in the avowal that he did not know a yew-tree nor indeed any one tree from another. (CH 85)

This young clerk, so reminiscent of Hardy's hapless commuter glimpsed in Oxford Street dreaming of 'open ways', would find, Kegan Paul asserts, the description in *Under the Greenwood Tree* of the different sounds made by different trees 'a revelation'.

Reading this in a large suburban house in South London's Tooting, having just finished a novel most of the second half of which concerns the peregrinations around Europe of the fabulously wealthy Paula and her entourage, must have made Hardy wonder if he had not been overlooking what modern creative writing courses would call his U.S.P.—his Unique Selling Point. Certainly Kegan Paul's essay fermented in his mind and influenced his own meditation on representations of 'Hodge' (a generic name for a Dorsetshire labourer) to Londoners in his 1883 article 'The Dorsetshire Labourer', which opens by speculating on the first impressions made by an actual workman in a 'retired district' of Dorset on 'an intelligence fresh from the contrasting world of London' (PV 39).[6] He may well have recalled Kegan Paul's essay often in later life too, as droves of Londoners descended at Dorchester South primed to seek out the originals of Talbothays (Farmer Crick's dairy in *Tess of the d'Urbervilles*) or Wellbridge Mill (where Angel and Tess spend their disastrous wedding night), the boldest of them even prepared to ring the bell at Max Gate in the hope of enjoying afternoon tea with their favourite country-bred author. For, presciently, Kegan Paul's piece concludes with what might well be seen as the first clarion call, or press release, delivered on behalf of the Hardy 'industry': it asks Hardy's readers not only to enjoy his books, but to travel to Dorset, and, in situ, to verify them:

> That Mr. Hardy has taken his place in the true literature of England is to us beyond question. For his sake and for their own we trust the larger public will recognize the fact, and steep themselves in the fresh healthy air of Dorset, and come into contact with the kindly folk who dwell there, through these pages, and then test their truth, as they can, in summer visits to the wolds, hill-sides, and coasts, which their 'native' has described so well. (CH 94)

As the ploughman's lunch was invented by advertising executives in London in the 1950s, so Wessex tourism, it might be argued, was first conceived and disseminated in this eloquent, spirited article written by a literary editor based in Kensington, and published in a London magazine. It is a telling co-incidence that it appeared only a few months before its subject returned to his native county. On 25 June 1881, 'for reasons of health and for mental in-spiration' (L 154), the Hardys moved from 1 Arundel Terrace, Upper Tooting, to The Avenue, Wimborne Minster, Dorset.

II

A mere six months later, however, Hardy wrote to Mrs Sutherland Orr, the author of the first of the extended surveys of his work: 'I seem to see more of London now than when we lived in the suburbs. I very frequently run up, & enjoy those very commonplaces of town life which used to be a weariness'

(CL 7:94). Since it was on the London and South Western Railway's main line, Wimborne offered easy access to the capital. While in 'Lanherne', as the house they rented was called, Hardy kept up attendance at Rabelais Club events, dined regularly with Edmund Gosse at the Savile Club, undertook astronomical research for *Two on a Tower* at Greenwich Observatory, and attended Charles Darwin's funeral at Westminster Abbey on 26 April 1882. Much of the spring of 1883 was spent in London, but in June of that year Hardy finally fulfilled the prediction inherent in the title of his most regionally focused novel to date. The native returned, initially renting Shire-Hall Place in Dorchester itself, while Hardy's brother Henry and their still active father oversaw the building of Max Gate on a plot of ground that he had purchased on the southeastern outskirts of the town.

Yet London was to be an essential part of the Hardys' 'yearly frame', to borrow a phrase of Philip Larkin's. In late spring, from 1884 to 1910, they would move for two, three, or four months into lodgings in the capital, with the exceptions only of the years 1897, when Queen Victoria's Diamond Jubilee attracted so many visitors that they had to settle for a house in Basingstoke from which they commuted up by train for social events, and 1902, which was coronation year, when Hardy was again put off by the crowds. Fran Chalfont, in an impressive piece of research, has identified the various flats and houses that they engaged in the course of these twenty-six years.[7] Among their favourite locations were Bloomsbury—where *Desperate Remedies* opens (1884, 1885, 1886); Kensington (1887, 1888, 1894, 1896, 1898, 1899); and Marylebone (1892, 1905, 1906, 1907). Hardy kept extensive memoranda of those he met at soirées and dinners and crushes each Season, and extracts that he deemed of particular interest were in turn transferred to the *Life*. This is for 16 May 1887:

Met {James Russell} Lowell at Lady Carnarvon's. Also Lady Winifred Byng for the first time since her marriage. Lady Camilla her cousin asked in a roguish whisper if I did not think Winifred looked gloomy. Talked to Lady Rosamund C—{Christie}. She tells me she is in trouble about the colour of her hair; but it is certainly not red as she says. Lady—, whose eyes had a wild look, declares she has not slept for *two months*, since she met with an accident hunting. Lady Marge

W—{Wallop} looked pretty in gauzy muslin—going to a ball, she told
me. (L 208)

Such entries allow one to feel that Horace Moule's suggestion back in 1864
that Hardy become a London gossip columnist for a provincial newspaper
was not, perhaps, altogether wide of the mark.

As in many of the accounts of social events enjoyed during the Season that
get included in the *Life*, the balance between the satirical and the erotic is
delicate and unstable. Hardy veers from safe and trustworthy confidante to
daring admirer, from half-mocking denotations of the speech habits of upper-
class women to enchanted descriptions of their attire, or features. The en-
tangling and disentangling of the libidinous and the aesthetic played out in
his 'Studies, Specimens, &c.' notebook habitually inflects his assessments
of each year's belles: Amélie Rives, an American novelist, is commended as
'a fair, pink, golden-haired creature', but is not, in Hardy's opinion, 'quite
ethereal enough, suggesting a flesh-surface too palpably' (L 230). The sudden
application of painterly terms, as if Hardy were judging a Pre-Raphaelite portrait rather than a woman to whom he was evidently attracted, is one of his
most frequently deployed means of containing and redirecting desire.
While he was at work on *Tess of the d'Urbervilles* (1889–1891), he was particularly drawn to women's mouths: Lady Catherine Milnes-Gaskell has
'quite a "Tess" mouth' (L 249) he observes approvingly, but it was Agatha
Thornycroft, wife of the sculptor Hamo Thornycroft, who proved of particular importance when it came to depicting the 'too tempting mouth' (T 166)
that so entrances Angel: 'Of the people I have met this summer, the lady
whose mouth recalls more fully than any other beauty's the Elizabethan metaphor "Her lips are roses full of snow" (or is it Lodge's?) is Mrs H. T—whom
I talked to at Gosse's dinner' (L 230). Angel makes use of the very same literary comparison when attempting to control his compulsion to kiss Tess:
'To a young man with the least fire in him that little upward lift in the middle
of her red top lip was distracting, infatuating, maddening. He had never before seen a woman's lips and teeth which forced upon his mind, with such
persistent iteration, the old Elizabethan simile of roses filled with snow'
(T 165).[8] There is no purer product than Tess of 'the partly real, partly-
dream country' (PW 9) that is Wessex. The role played in her conception by a

famous beauty at a literary dinner party in London hosted by Edmund
Gosse is one of the most striking examples of Hardy's ability to transpose
the erotic fantasies inspired in him by the sophisticated metropolitan
women whom he met during the London Season to the 'wolds, hill-sides
and coasts', to quote Kegan Paul, of his native region.

The year 1889, when Hardy was staying at 20 Monmouth Road, not that
far from Westbourne Park Villas, was the year when the erotic and the literary began to collide for Hardy in a new manner, or at any rate with a new
explicitness, off the page as well as on it. In the course of that summer in
London he met the twenty-nine-year-old Rosamund Tomson, author of a
volume of verse entitled *The Bird-Bride*, and the first of a series of metropolitan literary women with whom he became infatuated. Not only did she,
like Florence Henniker and Agnes Grove after her, admire his writings, but
her manner encouraged him to believe that she was 'an enfranchised woman',
as he put it in a letter of 16 July 1893 to Henniker, about whom he wishfully
made the same assumption, only to discover that he was again mistaken (CL
2:24). The sexual torture endured by Jude at the hands of Sue owes much to
Hardy's unrequited 'throbbings of noontide' (CP 81) inspired by Tomson and
Henniker. It is transferred also to the unnamed Christminster undergraduate with whom Sue lives for fifteen months in London, whose situation offers a mise en abyme of the frustrations that attended Hardy's pursuit of
these supposedly 'new' women (both were married, although Tomson had
already divorced one husband and was soon to be divorced from her second).
Sue tells the story to an aghast Jude in his lodgings at Melchester, dressed,
appropriately, in his suit while her clothes dry after her night-time escape
across the river from her hated teacher-training college:

> 'We used to go about together—on walking tours, reading tours, and
> things of that sort—like two men almost. He asked me to live with him,
> and I agreed to by letter. But when I joined him in London I found he
> meant a different thing from what I meant. He wanted me to be his mis-
> tress, in fact, but I wasn't in love with him—and on my saying I should
> go away if he didn't agree to *my* plan, he did so. We shared a sitting-
> room for fifteen months; and he became a leader-writer for one of the
> great London dailies; till he was taken ill, and had to go abroad. He

said I was breaking his heart by holding out against him so long at such close quarters; he could never have believed it of woman. I might play that game once too often, he said. He came home merely to die.' (JO 142)

Probing further, even savagely, at Sue's finely balanced mixture of guilt and vanity, he has her go on: 'His death caused a terrible remorse in me for my cruelty—though I hope he died of consumption and not of me entirely.'

Hardy came to realize, or so he later claimed, that Tomson was only interested in him for ignoble, careerist reasons, and accordingly distanced himself: 'Her desire', as he put it in the letter to Henniker, 'was to use your correspondent as a means of gratifying her vanity by exhibiting him as her admirer, the discovery of which promptly ended the friendship, with considerable disgust on his side' (CL 2:24). She appears in his fiction as the 'intellectual, emancipated' Mrs Nichola Pine-Avon of *The Well-Beloved* (WB 301), whom Jocelyn Pierston meets at a London party and for a time believes might be a fresh embodiment of his ideal woman, only to realize that she is neither a true incarnation of the well-beloved nor a truly liberated new woman. In a minor act of revenge, Hardy has, in the 1897 version, Pierston and Nichola overhear an organ-grinder play a song that the sculptor identifies as 'The Jilt's Hornpipe' (WB 226).

After Tomson's early death in 1911 at the age of fifty-one, however, Hardy composed a poem called 'An Old Likeness' and subtitled 'Recalling R.T.', in which he allowed himself to present a more positive account of their flirtatious exchanges and poetic jousting—'Our early flows / Of wit and laughter / And framing of rhymes / At idle times' (CP 670). The poem's highly characteristic premise is that he has come across a painted portrait of her, and although she now 'lies cold / In churchyard mould', he can't stop himself kissing it, and remembering how she conquered him—'took me by storm'—'At a fair season / Of love and unreason'. It is unlikely, if the poem was written in the wake of Tomson's death, that Hardy showed it to Emma (it is undated and was not published until *Late Lyrics* of 1922); for while this indiscreetly prosecuted flirtation may have been a 'bright time' for Hardy, for Emma it was undoubtedly a 'blight-time', to borrow the poem's most memorable rhyme. It heralded both a serious further decline in their connubial relations and the beginning of the 'time-torn' man's more deliberate and wholehearted pursuit of extramarital romance.

Hardy's diary is full of exclamations at the bleakness of urban life: 'April 5 {1889}. London. Four million forlorn hopes!' (L 227). But from the late 1880s until the death of Emma, London was also Hardy's primary site of erotic possibility: 'That girl in the omnibus', he observed in his entry for 29 May 1889, 'had one of those faces of marvellous beauty which are seen casually in the streets, but never among one's friends. It was perfect in its softened classicality:—a Greek face translated into English. Moreover she was fair, and her hair pale chestnut. Where do these women come from? Who marries them? Who knows them?' (L 229). Jocelyn Pierston, the flâneuring sculptor of *The Well-Beloved*, is likewise a connoisseur of the beautiful women to be observed on the streets of London: 'The study of beauty was his only joy for years onward. In the streets he would observe a face, or a fraction of a face, which seemed to express to a hair's-breadth in mutable flesh what he was at that moment wishing to express in durable shape. He would dodge and follow the owner like a detective; in omnibus, in cab, in steam-boat, through crowds, into shops, churches, theatres, public-houses, and slums—mostly, when at close quarters, to be disappointed for his pains' (WB 211). The middle-aged Hardy was probably not quite as intrepid as his artist hero, but he did find in London an escape from both the rigid domestic routines of Max Gate, where Emma's piety was curdling into evangelism, and from reminders of his mother's unforgiving views on the dangers of succumbing to sexual attraction. The huge success of *Tess*, in particular, made Hardy into one of the leading literary celebrities of the fin de siècle—'the popularity of Hardy as an author now making him welcome anywhere', as he put it in his recollections of the year 1893 in the *Life* (L 268).[9] His growing fame gave him an appeal to young women writers that he was keen to exploit. His wooing of both Florence Henniker and Florence Dugdale proceeded on the basis of shared literary interests, and indeed eventually resulted in a number of collaboratively written stories ('The Spectre of the Real' (1894) with Henniker, and 'Blue Jimmy: The Horse Stealer' (1911) and 'The Unconquerable' (posthumously published) with Dugdale).

Henniker was in her late thirties and had already written three novels when Hardy met her in Dublin in May of 1893 and discovered her to be a 'charming, *intuitive* woman' (L 270). The following month they met up in London, where they saw Ibsen's *The Master Builder* together, an almost comically appropriate play for Hardy's excited vision of their future relationship. He gave her an inscribed copy of *Tess* with notes on the originals of the locations used in the book and offered both to instruct her in the principles of architecture and to show her personally around Westminster Abbey. Alas, it fairly quickly transpired that, far from being 'enfranchised' and a believer in Shelleyan free love or Ibsenite transgression, she was hopelessly in thrall to 'ritualistic ecclesiasticism', as he put it in a letter of 16 July (CL 2:23), and he went on to protest, as Jude would do after Sue's return at the end of the novel to her first husband, Phillotson, that 'there are other values for feeling than the ordinances of Mother Church' (CL 2:24). Hardy began work on *Jude the Obscure* in August of 1893 and pointedly gave a middle name to his heroine that connected her with the disappointments that he had suffered that summer: Susanna Florence Mary Bridehead. He revealed to Edmund Gosse after the book was published that 'Sue is a type of woman which has always had an attraction for me—but the difficulty of drawing the type has kept me from attempting it till now' (CL 2:99).

When Jude first starts observing his cousin Sue in Christminster (the Wessex name for Oxford), he finds himself wondering how she acquired the poise and polish that so appeal to him: 'She was quite a long way removed from the rusticity that was his. How could one of his cross-grained, unfortunate, almost accursed stock, have contrived to reach this pitch of niceness? London had done it, he supposed' (JO 84). Hardy's poems about Henniker find a range of ways of conjugating what one of them, 'The Division', calls 'that thwart thing betwixt us twain, / Which nothing cleaves or clears' (CP 221). He tends to represent himself as, like Jude, somewhat out of his depth, confused about what is permissible and what is not, and baffled by her unpredictability. 'A Thunderstorm in Town', which is subtitled 'A Reminiscence: 1893', opens by admiring her 'new "terra-cotta" dress'. Imported from his specialist sphere of knowledge, architecture, his use of the term 'terra-cotta' can be read as implying a secret claim to her, a shared joke deriving from the architectural instruction that he has been giving her, and may even encode a personal allusion—Hardy's 1863 prize-winning essay had been 'On the Application of Colored Bricks and Terra Cotta to Modern

Architecture'. But although he and she have 'terra-cotta' in common, the poor man still can't decide whether or not he has the right to kiss the lady:

> She wore a 'terra-cotta' dress,
> And we stayed, because of the pelting storm,
> Within the hansom's dry recess,
> Though the horse had stopped; yea, motionless
>   We sat on, snug and warm.
>
> Then the downpour ceased, to my sharp sad pain,
> And the glass that had screened our forms before
> Flew up, and out she sprang to her door:
> I should have kissed her if the rain
>   Had lasted a minute more. (CP 312–313)

Thwarted impulse, missed opportunity, capricious weather, and an evasive woman compose many a Hardy mise en scène. In this instance, the wry, would-be-worldly humour of the last lines triumphs over humiliation and disappointment, without, perhaps, entirely suppressing them. Henniker's escape from the hansom can't help seeming a version of her escape from the narrative of adulterous love in which Hardy attempted to ensnare her, although his own belief in, or commitment to, this narrative may itself seem undermined by adjectives like 'snug and warm', which are hardly those of a Byronic libertine. The poem's comedy, almost veering towards a *Punch*-style cartoon, becomes both a means for Hardy to indulge in the fantasy of an adulterous liaison pursued in a private 'recess' insulated from the bustle of the city, and a way to keep himself safe—'snug and warm'—from the complications that would inevitably ensue should he actually kiss her.

Henniker's refusal to play along with Hardy's conception of them as liberated Shelleyan lovers also allowed him to assume the role of the lovelorn martyr, most famously in the vindictive, bitter 'Wessex Heights' of 1896, in which he transforms her—rather unfairly given the long friendship that they went on to enjoy—into a callous trifler with his feelings: 'As for one rare fair woman, I am now but a thought of hers, / I enter her mind and another thought succeeds me that she prefers' (CP 320).

This is also the posture adopted in the more plangent 'A Broken Appointment', prompted by Henniker's failure to show up for a rendezvous at the British Museum (RP 113). In the letter of 20 November 1895 to Edmund Gosse in which Hardy referred to his 'attraction' to the 'type of woman' embodied in Sue Bridehead, he suggests that while there is 'nothing perverted or depraved' in her nature, she has a need 'to withhold herself', which in turn keeps Jude's 'passion as hot at the end as at the beginning, & helps to break his heart' (CL 2:99). Sue's 'weak & fastidious' sexuality maintains its power to inflame, while Arabella's ready availability quickly inspires disgust. 'A Broken Appointment', like *Jude the Obscure*, explores the sublimation of desire, particularly in relation to Hardy's paradoxical experience of the extreme polarities of sex in the city for someone of his particular make-up and standing. If it was 'his mother's spirit' (CP 593), to quote the words of the streetwalker who approaches him in 'The Woman I Met', that kept him chaste when propositioned by one of London's legion of prostitutes, it was the elegant sophistication of the upper-class women to whom he was attracted, and to whom his literary fame granted social access, that rendered them equally unavailable. As 'fastidious' and refined as Sue, whose teenage years in London had 'taken all rawness out of her' (JO 84), Henniker either flees when he is about to kiss her, or avoids meeting him altogether:

> You did not come,
> And marching Time drew on, and wore me numb.—
> Yet less for loss of your dear presence there
> Than that I thus found lacking in your make
> That high compassion which can overbear
> Reluctance for pure lovingkindness' sake
> Grieved I, when, as the hope-hour stroked its sum,
> You did not come.
>
> You love not me,
> And love alone can lend you loyalty;
> —I know and knew it. But, unto the store
> Of human deeds divine in all but name,
> Was it not worth a little hour or more

> To add yet this: Once you, a woman, came
> To soothe a time-torn man; even though it be
>   You love not me? (CP 136)

The disarmingly honest 'time-torn', replacing Hardy's original choice of 'soul-sad', can make the speaker seem closer to the middle-aged and sexually undesirable Phillotson than to Jude; and the appeal of the speaker to 'compassion' and 'lovingkindness' registers as an attempt, like Phillotson's, when he allows Sue to abandon their marriage and go to the cousin whom she loves, to find a way of coping with erotic frustration by evoking larger humanitarian aims. The naked self-pity of its final lines prompts us, however, to wonder how successfully life can be lived on this higher plane, and for how long desire can be content with mere soothing compassion. Such questions are fundamental to *Jude the Obscure*, and on various levels propel its extraordinarily daring and discomfiting narrative. In the creation of Sue, whose evolution he discussed in a number of letters to Henniker, Hardy did full and multifaceted justice to the 'attraction' exerted upon him by metropolitan literary women such as herself and Tomson, as well as to the anguish that they caused him. Although they loved not him, they did prove vital catalysts for one of his most perplexing and original creations.

9

The Well-Beloved

The dialogue between Wessex and London conducted in Hardy's fiction achieved its most stylized and schematically patterned articulation in the last novel that he ever published, *The Well-Beloved*, which was issued in 1897 as volume 17 in Osgood, McIlvaine's edition of his collected fiction. *The Well-Beloved* was a reworking of a serial entitled *The Pursuit of the Well-Beloved* that had appeared five years earlier in twelve weekly instalments (from 1 October to 17 December of 1892) in the *Illustrated London News*. It thus both predates and postdates *Jude the Obscure*, and although it diverges from standards of realism in a radically different manner from that adopted by Hardy in the novel that most upset his critics and his readership, *The Well-Beloved* can be seen as developing out of a similar set of thematic and emotional concerns. This time though, it is the male protagonist who has been transformed by London, and it is the woman—or rather the three generations of women, all named Avice—who embody the 'rusticity' (JO 84) that is an element in the separation of Jude from Sue.

The novel's main character is a sculptor called Jocelyn Pierston. The book is divided into three parts: in the first Pierston is twenty, in the second he is forty, and in the third he is sixty. The son of a prosperous quarry owner on the Isle of Slingers (the Wessex name for Portland), Pierston is presented in *The Well-Beloved*'s opening chapter arriving on the island (which is five miles south of Weymouth and linked by a narrow spit to the mainland) to pay a visit to his father after three years and eight months away. The sculptor looks, we are informed, like 'a young man from London and the cities of the Continent', but we are also told that his 'urbanism sat upon him only as a garment' (WB 179). Another native returns . . . and in this instance his homecoming results in the most outlandish of quests, the lifelong search for the embodiment of the feminine ideal, the 'well-beloved' of the book's title. One way of viewing Pierston's peculiar, and increasingly unsettling, pursuits of the various Avices is as an attempt to cast off his 'urbanism' in order to recover the very distinctive provincialism of the life and culture of the Isle of Slingers. His aims, in this regard, shadow those of *A Laodicean*'s George Somerset, but there is no happy ending awaiting Hardy's final fictional self-projection. Pierston's abject and humiliating failure to unite with the well-beloved, in any of her incarnations, constitutes one of Hardy's most remorseless and painful accounts of the 'border country', to use Raymond Williams's characterization, to which Hardy was consigned by his successful pursuit of a literary career in London and the alienation from his origins that it entailed.[1]

In a letter excerpted in the *Life* Hardy described the novel's narrative, which has a man falling in love in his twenties with one woman, in his forties with her daughter, and in his sixties with her granddaughter, as an exploration of the 'Platonic Idea' (L 304). This allies the three Avices with Sue, and the woman with whom Pierston elopes on a whim, Marcia Bencomb, with the fleshy Arabella. Like the plot of *Jude the Obscure*, that of *The Well-Beloved* is structured around the opposition between sex and love, the bodily and the ideal, but here the locations associated with either polarity are reversed: in *The Well-Beloved* it is provincial Portland or the Isle of Slingers that harbours the unattainable ideal, whereas in *Jude* it was Sue's years in London that rendered her fastidious and refined and ethereal; and it is in London that Pierston impulsively consummates his relationship with Marcia, only to regret it shortly afterwards, as Jude does his seduction by the rural Arabella. *The Well-Beloved* also inverts the social status accorded the antithetical women depicted in *Jude*: the Avices are poor and simple, though Avice III is somewhat more worldly than her mother and grandmother, while Marcia is the wealthy, sophisticated daughter of Pierston's father's chief enemy and rival. Both Pierston senior and Bencomb senior are in the quarrying business, profits from which enable them to educate their offspring, and then launch and support them in London. Pierston's father remains, however, on the island, while the more ambitious Bencomb settles, with his wife and daughter, in South Kensington.

The fact that it was stone from Portland's quarries that was used in the construction of so many famous London buildings, from Somerset House to St. Paul's Cathedral, and that stone from these quarries is still arriving to be used for new buildings in London, is central to the overarching conceit of *The Well-Beloved*. Pierston (himself, as a sculptor, both a peerer into and a piercer of stone) is repeatedly drawn to the Thames-side wharves where stone from his native island is unloaded. In part 1, the youthful artist interrupts his 'professional beauty-chases'—by which Hardy means his walking the streets of London in pursuit of his ideal woman—to cast his eye towards the dock where 'his father's tons of freestone were daily landed from the ketches of the south coast' (WB 211). The sight prompts a suggestive metaphor that subliminally evokes the anxiety present in the very young Hardy's observation that London seems to be advancing across green fields, engrossing the country that surrounds it: 'He could occasionally discern the white blocks lying there, vast cubes so persistently nibbled by his parent from his island rock in the English Channel, that it seemed as if in time it would be nibbled all away' (WB 211). The money sustaining his career as a sculptor of beautiful statues of beautiful women in the capital, we are reminded, is the result of ongoing, systematic depletion of the resources of the Isle of Slingers. The book's conjugation of the Dorset-London axis is delicately invested here with overtones of patrilineal transference: stone quarried from his native region by his own father is transported to London, and is there used in the buildings that surround him on the city's streets that he daily prowls in search of models and inspiration. There is a literal component, therefore, to the unheimlich aura of the book's London, the way it can seem uncanny and familiar at the same time, for some of its most famous landmarks are fabricated from stone that once formed Pierston's distant home. Further, the closeness of his surname (*pierre* meaning stone in French) to the Isle of Slingers's claims to both fame and wealth, its peerless stone, prompts the thought that it is his own substance that is being nibbled away and unloaded in London. The passage resembles the moment in *The Hand of Ethelberta* when the heroine realizes that her stock of stories is finite, and that her career

as a raconteur can last only so long. What Hardy called in the preface to Macmillan's 1903 edition the 'frankly fantastic' nature of the narrative makes
possible an often dizzying range of symbolic, self-reflexive, and interpretive
possibilities.[2]

The middle-aged Pierston of the second section frequents the wharves
more often and more deliberately:

> Nothing now pleased him so much as to spend that portion of the after-
> noon which he devoted to out-door exercise, in haunting the purlieus
> of the wharves along the Thames, where the stone of his native rock
> was unshipped from the coasting-craft that had brought it thither. He
> would pass inside the great gates of these landing-places on the right
> or left bank, contemplate the white cubes and oblongs, imbibe their as-
> sociations, call up the *genius loci* whence they came, and almost forget
> that he was in London. (WB 239)

In the course of one of these visits he notices that a different kind of product
has made its way from the Isle of Slingers to London:

> One afternoon he was walking away from the mud-splashed entrance
> to one of the wharves, when his attention was drawn to a female form
> on the opposite side of the way, going towards the spot he had just left.
> She was somewhat small, slight, and graceful; her attire alone would
> have been enough to attract him, being simple and countrified to pic-
> turesqueness, but he was more than attracted by her strong resemblance
> to Avice Caro the younger—Ann Avice, as she had said she was called.

The first Avice, with whom Pierston grew up and to whom he is briefly
engaged to be married in the first part of the novel, does not visit London,
but her daughter and granddaughter do, and his proposals to both envisage
a wedded life spent together in the capital rather than back on the Isle of
Slingers. In preparation for his marriage to Avice III he even takes 'a new
red house of the approved Kensington pattern' (WB 308), that is of the kind
constructed for Thackeray that became popular in the 1860s. But Pierston
rarely seems convinced that either Avice would thrive there, or that he could

shape them—like a London architect making use of Portland stone—into successful and happy additions to the city. Mrs Kibbs, the wife of the captain on whose boat Avice II arrived, voices the islanders' general distrust of the metropolis: 'I should be afeard o' my life to tine my eyes among these here kimberlins at night-time; and even by day, if so be I venture into the streets, I nowhen forget how many turnings to the right and the left 'tis to get back to Job's vessel—do I, Job?' (WB 240). Her husband, Cap'n Job Kibbs, nods confirmation.

Pierston's attraction to the 'simple and countrified' figure that Avice II makes on the Thames-side quay is at the heart of the satire of circumstance that *The Well-Beloved* explores in such prolonged and excruciating detail: it is in the 'simple and countrified' line of Avices, who all resemble each other, rather than in the vast array of different women of all classes and types whom Pierston can observe and pursue in the salons and streets of London, that the 'implacable Aphrodite' (WB 185) lodges his ineffable Ideal. The impossible love the book charts is Hardy's final exploration in prose of the erotic imagination's perverse compulsion to target and invest in precisely those most likely to frustrate rather than gratify desire. The Avices' 'lack of refinement' (WB 232) makes then ineligible as wives, but only they are made of the right sort of 'clay' from which Pierston's perfect woman might possibly be fashioned: 'It was as if the Caros had found the clay but not the potter, while other families whose daughters might attract him had found the potter but not the clay' (WB 251). In this most self-consciously aesthetic of all Hardy's fictions, however, one that might be subtitled 'A Portrait of the Artist as a Young, Middle-Aged, and Elderly Man', the economy of disappointment and creativity is also firmly established. His fantasies and frustrations are, the narrative insists, crucial to Pierston's powers as an artist: 'Yet he would not', Hardy writes, in what amounts to a self-exculpatory justification of his own sexual restlessness during his Seasons in London in his late forties and early fifties, 'have stood where he did stand in the ranks of an imaginative profession if he had not been at the mercy of every succubus of the fancy that can beset man' (WB 251). Hardy makes it clear, too, that age has no effect on the erotic excitements that drive an artist's imagination, dismissing the assertions of those poets and philosophers who argue that 'love was intensest in youth and burnt lower as maturity advanced' (WB 212).

After a few weeks of residence with the second- and third-generation Caros in the red-brick house that he takes in the capital, in the hope of interesting the youngest Avice, who is forty years his junior, in the life that they might lead together there, Pierston observes: 'There seemed to be something uncanny, after all, about London, in its relation to his contemplated marriage. When she had first come up she was easier with him than now' (WB 310). The uncanny pervades many aspects of the metropolis that *The Well-Beloved* presents, and its London defeats the expectations of the reader and of the novel's characters alike. The 'subjective nature' (WB 174) of the book's extraordinary premise leads to a stylization of the urban that makes it dreamlike and unreal, and certainly closer to the London of other fin-de-siècle fantasies such as Robert Louis Stevenson's *The Strange Case of Dr Jekyll and Mr Hyde* (1886) or Oscar Wilde's *The Picture of Dorian Gray* (1891) than that of Dickens or, from the book's own period, George Gissing. When Pierston and Marcia arrive by train in chapter 6 of part 1, Hardy appears to be about to induct us into the seething urban maelstrom familiar from Victorian fiction and painting: 'Drawing near the great London station was like drawing near Doomsday. How should he leave her in the turmoil of a crowded city street? She seemed quite unprepared for the rattle of the scene' (WB 197). But as Dehn Gilmore pointed out in an essay that develops an interesting comparison between the London of *The Well-Beloved* and the Paris of Impressionist painters such as Manet and Monet, the city Pierston and Marcia move through turns out to be strangely empty, indeed 'something of a ghost town'.[3] The 'rattle' never materializes. A cab is instantly and effortlessly hailed, and they float silently through the depopulated streets, with no mention even made of their cab driver. Directions are given for Bayswater, where Marcia's aunt lives, but after impulsively agreeing to get married in the middle of the journey, they change direction and head for 'one of the venerable old taverns of Covent Garden, a precinct which in those days was frequented by West-country people' (WB 198). Denizens of Wessex, rather than London, are the only members of the population that the chapter allows into a metropolis both homely and unheimlich, and it is hardly a surprise when Pierston sets off to visit his friend, the painter Alfred Somers, to discover that he lives in 'Mellstock Gardens' (WB 199)—Mellstock being Hardy's Wessex name for Stinsford.[4]

While the speaker of 'A Thunderstorm in Town' never quite summoned up the courage to kiss the woman in the terra-cotta dress as the rain beat down on their motionless hansom, Pierston and Marcia manage to come together in the course of their journey across a de-urbanized city—although not until he has answered a strikingly unromantic question, and mounted an equally unromantic argument in favour of their union:

> 'Will you ever be a Royal Academician?' she asked musingly, her excitement having calmed down.
> 'I hope to be—I *will* be, if you will be my wife.'
> His companion looked at him long.
> 'Think what a short way out of your difficulty this would be,' he continued. 'No bother about aunts, no fetching home by an angry father.'
> It seemed to decide her. She yielded to his embrace. (WB 198)

It is as if Hardy feared, and was warding off, the encroachments of realist fiction, with its comprehensible motivations and concerns, onto his Platonic fable. Unexpectedness triumphs time and again in the perverse turns taken by the narrative of *The Well-Beloved*, developing an impish counterpoint to Hardy's working out of Pierston's overmastering, self-repeating obsession. Having informed her father that she is sharing a room in a Covent Garden hotel with the son of his sworn enemy, Marcia expects her father's blessing on a union that will at least save his daughter's reputation: 'but to Marcia's amazement her father took a line quite other than the one she had expected him to take' (WB 206). Her lover in Jersey, from whom she receives a letter telling her that he is ready 'to start for England to claim his darling, according to her plighted troth', must have been equally amazed to receive one back explaining she had 'quite forgotten' their relationship, and was now about to marry someone else—although in the 1897 version she and Pierston are not in fact joined for another forty years, by which time she is so infirm that she can only get to church in a wheelchair.

Wonder and surprise are expressed over and over in the novel—variants on the first term occur nineteen times in the text, and on the second, twenty-four times. London in particular is the site of unpredictability: in chapter 11 of the middle section, Pierston brings Avice II to stay with him in the capital (not knowing that she is already married to the sculptor's much younger namesake, and possibly distant relative, the uncouth Isaac Pierston) and 'to his surprise' (WB 265) finds on arrival that his flat is dark and deserted: his servants have raided his cellar, drunk his wine, and absconded for a holiday, although he had firmly believed they were wholly trustworthy. Later in the chapter he sends Avice out for stamps, only to remember, when she fails to come back after a quarter of an hour, that she knows nothing of London and is probably lost. The incident generates one of Hardy's most evocative descriptions of the streets of London. The passage both reflects his interest in the experiments of late Turner and the Impressionists and anticipates, as Keith Wilson has argued, visions of the city found in works by modernists such as Conrad, Joyce, Woolf, and Eliot.[5]

> The head post-office, to which he had sent her because it was late, was two or three streets off, and he had made his request in the most general manner, which she had acceded to with alacrity enough. How could he have done such an unreflecting thing?
>
> Pierston went to the window. It was half-past nine o'clock, and owing to her absence the blinds were not down. He opened the casement and stepped out upon the balcony. The green shade of his lamp screened its rays from the gloom without. Over the opposite square the moon hung, and to the right there stretched a long street, filled with a diminishing array of lamps, some single, some in clusters, among them an occasional blue or red one. From a corner came the notes of a piano-organ strumming out a stirring march of Rossini's. The shadowy black figures of pedestrians moved up, down, and across the embrowned roadway. Above the roofs was a bank of livid mist, and higher a greenish-blue sky, in which stars were visible, though its lower part was still pale with daylight, against which rose chimney-pots in the form of elbows, prongs, and fists.
>
> From the whole scene proceeded a ground rumble, miles in extent, upon which individual rattles, voices, a tin whistle, the bark of a dog, rode like bubbles on a sea. The whole noise impressed him with the sense that no one in its enormous mass ever required rest.

> In this illimitable ocean of humanity there was a unit of existence,
> his Avice, wandering alone. (WB 268–269)

Hardy had inserted a translation of the last stanza of one of Baudelaire's 'Spleen' poems (the one beginning 'Quand le ciel bas et lourd pèse comme un couvercle') in his 1884 edition of *Les Fleurs du mal*, and certainly this passage in *The Well-Beloved* is imaginatively concordant with the perspectives and techniques developed in the French poet's urban tableaux.[6] It evokes in particular the detached, aesthetic rendering of Parisian scenes found in Baudelaire's *Petits Poèmes en prose* of the 1860s, or indeed in a Baudelaire-influenced novel such as *À Rebours* by Huysmans (both Baudelaire and Huysmans are referred to in Hardy's literary notebooks of the 1880s). Certainly the pictorial precision of the writing communicates, as Wilson notes, a sense of 'epiphanic insight' that allows us to situate the passage in the context of English-language writers' application of French Symbolist modes of depicting Paris to representations of London in the fin-de-siècle and early modernist eras, in particular by such as Oscar Wilde, Arthur Symons, and John Davidson.[7] Pierston's privileged, panoramic viewpoint is that of the observing flâneur, the urban idler, and comes at the cost of realist participation in the life of the streets. His detachment imparts a phantasmagorical atmosphere to the scene that he contemplates, and at the same time conveys a disquieting sense that the modern city is too complex to be understood. Pedestrians are reduced to 'shadowy black figures', and everyday sounds, 'rattles, voices, a tin whistle, the bark of a dog', float free of their sources, become mere 'bubbles', in what is almost a classic manoeuver in decadent urban writing; in Wilde's 'Impression du Matin', for instance, St. Paul's itself looms 'like a bubble o'er the town'.[8]

Hardy's own comment on late Turner in a diary entry of January 1889 expresses exactly the crisis in representation that is shadowed forth by this cityscape, and that, on a more general level, motivated his experimentation in *The Well-Beloved*: 'He first recognizes the impossibility of really producing on canvas all that is in a landscape; then gives for that which cannot be reproduced a something else which shall have upon the spectator an approximative effect to that of the real' (L 226). The 'approximative effect', in this instance, is an urban nocturne at once as vivid and as insubstantial as the 'livid mist' that hangs above the city's roofs; a series of 'abstract imaginings' intended to convey 'the deeper reality underlying the scenic' (L 192).

Despite its abstraction, however, a note of genuine menace also inflects this highly wrought city vista, as it does so many of Baudelaire's. Stark against the evening sky, chimney pots are figured as 'elbows, prongs, and fists', angular reminders of the competition for survival fought out on the streets below. Somewhere adrift on those streets, and the 'illimitable ocean of humanity' that courses through them, is Avice, to Pierston now an imperilled, isolated 'unit of existence'—a formulation impossible to imagine being applied to her, or to her mother or daughter, when on the Isle of Slingers. Pierston sets off in pursuit of his charge, only to find the post office deserted. How is he to find the strayed, vulnerable 'unit' that has now vanished into the unresting 'enormous mass'? Remembering that he told her that if she ever got lost she should avail herself of a cab, he returns to the balcony of his flat, and there, breathless with anxiety, scans the passing traffic: 'The two lamps of each vehicle afar dilated with its near approach, and seemed to swerve towards him. It was Avice surely? No, it passed by' (WB 269). Frantic, he ventures forth again, and on the first 'noisy thoroughfare observed a small figure approaching leisurely along the opposite side, and hastened across to find it was she.'

It soon emerges, in a typical reversal of expectations, that she was neither lost nor threatened. She simply wanted, she explains to Pierston, to see a little of the city:

> 'So when I had got the stamps I went on into the fashionable streets, where ladies are all walking about just as if it were daytime! 'Twas for all the world like coming home by night from Martinmas Fair at the Street o' Wells, only more genteel.'
>
> 'O Avice, Avice, you must not go out like this! Don't you know that I am responsible for your safety? I am your—well, guardian, in fact, and am bound by law and morals, and I don't know what-all, to deliver you up to your native island without a scratch or blemish. And yet you indulge in such a midnight vagary as this!'

'But I am sure, sir, the gentlemen in the street were more respectable than they are anywhere at home! They were dressed in the latest fashion, and would have scorned to do me any harm; and as to their love-making, I never heard anything so polite before.' (WB 270)

While Mrs Kibbs's exaggerated fears of London's sinister 'kimberlins' and its labyrinthine topography make the city seem so hazardous that she insists on remaining on or near her docked vessel, Avice II is naively oblivious of the very real threat posed by the sexual predators roaming its streets, admiring their gentility, and deeming their overtures to be 'polite' 'love-making'. The genuine and dangerous differences between the Street of Wells during Martinmas Fair and Regent Street or Piccadilly Circus after dark fail to register with her; London seems like home, only more 'genteel' and fashionable. 'Well, you must not do it again', expostulates her 'guardian' (the term neatly catches the dubiousness of his own designs upon her), adding, with a glance towards his future education of his artless, unspoiled wife-to-be into the semiotics of London's nightlife, 'I'll tell you some day why'. His schemes are shortly after foiled, however, in a manner that leaves him 'pale and distressed' with shock. Avice II may, in London, be an innocent abroad, but back in the Isle of Slingers she has already followed 'island custom' (that is, had premarital sex), as Pierston and her mother failed to do, and then been married in secret, though not to the man she in fact truly loved, who was a soldier. One wonders if Vladimir Nabokov had this scene at the back of his mind when Lolita reveals her sexual history to a dazed Humbert Humbert on their first night together in The Enchanted Hunters Hotel.

It is in London, too, that Pierston's plans to wed Avice III begin to unravel. Better educated and more refined than her predecessors, the granddaughter is closer to Pierston's social level, but, understandably, a little troubled by the difference in their ages. And she too has a surprise up her sleeve for the sculptor—she is secretly in love with Henri Leverre, a French-speaker brought up on Jersey who also turns out (this being a Hardy novel) to be the stepson of Marcia Bencomb. As the collapse of his hopes of marrying Avice II was preceded by the panoramic aesthetic tableau that unfolds before Pierston on the balcony of his flat, so the turning point in his suit to Avice III is ironically heralded by another example of bravura urban scene painting. In both cases the aesthetic sophistication of the set piece serves to heighten the bathos that soon follows with Pierston's discovery that the Avice in question is not available. The transition in both episodes from a display of dextrous verbal artistry to near-farcical disappointment of erotic hopes can be seen as enacting one of the laws of the fin-de-siècle conception of the artist or dandy figure: he should never attempt to marry. Pierston returns to the rented red house on

> one of those ripe and mellow afternoons that sometimes colour London with their golden light at this time of the year, and produce those marvellous sunset effects which, if they were not known to be made up of kitchen coal-smoke and animal exhalations, would be rapturously applauded. Behind the perpendicular, oblique, zigzagged, and curved zinc 'tall-boys,' that formed a grey pattern not unlike early Gothic numerals against the sky, the men and women on the tops of the omnibuses saw an irradiation of topaz hues, darkened here and there into richest russet. (WB 308–309)

It is 'kitchen coal-smoke and animal exhalations' that generate the artificial urban sublime. Nevertheless, the simile linking the 'tall-boys' (fittings on chimneys) to early Gothic numerals creates a sense of historical continuity between the commuters, the changing fabric of the city, and the complex palette with which Hardy describes the late afternoon light. It puts Pierston in a good mood, and he looks forward to finding 'his prospective wife and mother-in-law awaiting him with tea'; but only the younger Avice is there, and she is crying over a French textbook, the one used by Leverre for the lessons that he gave her in Sandbourne, in the course of which they fell in love. Pierston's four-decades-long conviction of his 'prescriptive rights in women of her blood' (WB 308) soon after receives its coup de grâce, and only a gruesome reunion with a Marcia whose face bears the ravages of 'the raspings, chisellings, scourgings, bakings, freezings of forty invidious years' (WB 332) awaits him.

The Well-Beloved makes use of a similar Wessex-London pattern to that deployed in *A Pair of Blue Eyes*. Elfride's three journeys to the capital that mark the termination of her relationships with each of her three suitors—with

Stephen to get married, to plead for forgiveness with Knight in his chambers, and with Lord Luxellian to die—are mirrored in the three that Pierston makes to the capital with Marcia, with Avice II, and with Avice III, accompanied by her mother. They result, like Elfride's, in disappointment, although not in death, Hardy here seeking to humiliate his protagonist, rather than offer a pathetic or ennobling ending. The humiliation is more grotesque and overt in the 1892 version, which dwells emphatically on the contrast between a large photograph of a blooming Avice III and the now hideous Marcia, who nurses the sculptor after his suicide attempt—'a wrinkled crone, with a pointed chin, her figure bowed, her hair as white as snow', her head 'a parchment-covered skull' (WB 167, 168). So acute is his distress at the sight that Pearston, as he was originally called, seeks again to kill himself, only to be seized by an irrepressible fit of laughter: ' "O—no, no! I—I—it is too, too droll—this ending to my would-be romantic history!" Ho-ho-ho!' (WB 168). Those last 'Ho-ho-ho!'s, it's worth pointing out, are the narrator's.

The irony of the later version is more muted, and involves an explicit rejection of both his quest and his art. His convalescence is spent not on the Isle of Slingers, but in London. As soon as he has recovered enough strength he has Marcia take him to his studio, where, casting a cold eye on his various attempts to model the well-beloved, his accumulated array of Aphrodites and Eves and Freyjas and Nymphs and Fauns, he emphatically pronounces, 'They are as ugliness to me! I don't feel a single touch of kin with or interest in any one of them whatever' (WB 332). And when a subsequent visit to the National Gallery to see the Titians, the Peruginos, the Sebastiano del Piombos inspires neither excitement nor interest, Pierston feels able confidently to declare, 'The curse is removed' (WB 333). With his 'sense of beauty in art and nature absolutely extinct', he bids farewell to London for the last time, retires to the Isle of Slingers, marries Marcia, and performs various charitable deeds, such as paying for water pipes to be installed and for derelict cottages to be pulled down. A Parthian arrow, however, lurks in the novel's final paragraph: 'At present he is sometimes mentioned as "the late Mr. Pierston" by gourd-like young art-critics; and his productions are alluded to as those of a man not without genius, whose powers were insufficiently recognized in his lifetime' (WB 336).[9] With this final swipe at his detractors, Hardy abandoned the writing of novels.

10

<del>o/o/o/</del>

London Streets and Interiors

I

In July of 1926 Hardy was pleased to note the similarity between the concept of love explored in *The Well-Beloved* and that developed in the fifth instalment of Proust's *À la recherche du temps perdu,* the volume in which Proust admiringly discusses Hardy's last two novels (L 466). The comparison might have been pushed further, for both *The Well-Beloved* and *À la recherche du temps perdu* are also romans-à-clef. The various aristocratic women featured in *The Well-Beloved* ostentatiously reveal the humbly born author to be no longer 'a comparative outsider', as he described himself in the covering letter that he sent to Alexander Macmillan accompanying *The Poor Man and the Lady,* to the 'upper classes of society' (CL 1:7). Indeed, the novel shares with Proust's magnum opus and Hardy's own autobiography a pronounced love of name-dropping. By calling, for instance, one of the novel's grandes dames Lady Channelcliffe, Hardy was actively signalling his friendship with her original, Lady Portsmouth (Portsmouth being a city on the English Channel), and perhaps attempting to return a favour: for it was Lady Portsmouth who had initiated Hardy's acceptance into the highest echelons of Society by inviting him as a houseguest to Eggesford House (her country seat in Devon) in March of 1885. Hardy's friend the painter Alfred Parsons (1847–1920) becomes Pierston's friend the painter Alfred Somers, and the description of 'a leading actress', 'a creature in airy clothing, translucent, like a balsam or sea-anemone', who is then compared to 'some highly lubricated, many-wired machine, which, if one presses a particular spring, flies open and reveals its works' (WB 228), is a more or less direct transcription from Hardy's diary of his responses to the arrival of Ellen Terry at a party that he attended at Lady Jeune's in January of 1891 (L 244). The London Society scenes in *The Well-Beloved* replicate the mixture of gossip-column fascination, erotic excitement, and satirical distaste that governs large swathes of the extended reports of each Season that occupy so much of the *Life* from the middle of the 1880s to the outbreak of the First World War.

Not all the entries that he made during his spring and early summer London residences, however, concern the doings of the beau monde. 'In the street outside I heard a man coaxing money from a prostitute in slang language, his arm round her waist. The outside was a commentary on the inside', he observed on 1 March 1888 (L 215). One night in late May of 1894, after a dinner at the Countess of Yarborough's, Hardy was unable to find a cab on account of the cab drivers' strike, and was obliged to return to his South Kensington lodgings on the open top deck of a bus:

> No sooner was I up there than the rain began again. A girl who had scrambled up after me asked for the shelter of my umbrella, and I gave it,—when she startled me by holding on tight to my arm and bestowing on me many kisses for the trivial kindness. She told me she had been to 'The Pav' {The London Pavilion Music Hall in Piccadilly}, and was tired, and was going home. She had not been drinking. I descended at the South Kensington Station and watched the 'bus bearing her away. An affectionate nature wasted on the streets! It was a strange contrast to the scene I had just left. (L 281)

Hardy's early years in London had left him acutely aware of the social and economic forces conditioning the struggle for survival in the city, and on occasion he attempted to formulate some general theory of the effects on the consciousness of Londoners of the ruthlessness of late nineteenth-century capitalism, and even to reckon up the nature of the alienation that it fostered:

> Footsteps, cabs, &c. are continually passing our lodgings. And every echo, pit-pat, and rumble that makes up the general noise has behind

it a motive, a prepossession, a hope, a fear, a fixed thought forward; perhaps more—a joy, a sorrow, a love, a revenge.

London appears not to *see itself*. Each individual is conscious of *himself*, but nobody conscious of themselves collectively, except perhaps
some poor gaper who stares round with a half-idiotic aspect.

There is no consciousness here of where anything comes from or
goes to—only that it is present. (28 March 1888, L 215)

The pressures shaping an urban existence, in other words, promote ego-
tism, foreshorten perspectives, and create a sense of living in an artificial
bubble, although one from which the likes of Hardy's city shopwoman or
his—or Kegan Paul's—city clerk, long to escape. And indeed, ironically, the
appeal of Wessex to an urban readership, as Kegan Paul made clear in his
British Quarterly Review article of 1881, owed much to its vision of a natural
and precious social collective endangered by the expansion of the city's economic might, and its modes of relation and production. The atomization
induced in Londoners by the need to be ever-purposeful, practical, active,
striving, self-serving, is what reduces Avice II to a 'unit of existence' (WB
269) when she is out on the streets of London at night, and prompts Manston in *Desperate Remedies* to see the pedestrians bustling around him on
the Strand as each pursuing a 'solitary trail', 'unconscious of the significant
whole they collectively showed forth' (DR 299). It is only the 'poor gaper',
like Manston or Pierston in flâneur-ing mode, or Hardy himself in the course
of his annual escapes from his Max Gate study 'to the artificial gaieties of a
London season' (L 257), who has time to ponder the traffic on the streets, or
the supply chains that service the city. As on his first trip to London
Hardy observed livestock arrived from the country being herded towards
Smithfield, so a diary entry of 7 July 1888 marks the nocturnal passage of
vegetable carts bringing produce to market: 'One o'clock a.m. I got out of bed,
attracted by the never-ending procession [of market-carts to Covent Garden]
as seen from our bedroom windows Phillimore Place. Chains rattle, and each
cart cracks under its weighty pyramid of vegetables' (L 219).

This snapshot was expanded, three years later, into a central image in a
short story first published in the *Illustrated London News* in December of
1891 and then collected in *Life's Little Ironies* (1894). 'The Son's Veto' makes

particularly interesting use of the iconography of the streets of London, and of the roads that lead to and from the city. It describes the miserable suburban existence of Sophy Twycott, once a parlour maid, but elevated to the gentry after marrying her employer, a vicar much older than herself. Their son, Randolph, is sent away to a famous public school for his education and returns an appalling snob who corrects his mother's grammar. She spends her widowhood watching the street outside the villa in South London that her husband purchased for her shortly before his death. Lame after a fall with a tea tray, poor Sophy is a suburban prose version of Tennyson's Mariana: she finds life 'unsupportably dreary' (LLI 40) and regrets not having married a young market gardener called Sam Hobson who had courted her back in her native Gaymead (the name says it all) in North Wessex. At one o'clock each night, unable to sleep, she stands at her window witnessing the lamplit procession of vegetable carts bound for Covent Garden:

> She often saw them creeping along at this silent and dusky hour—waggon after waggon—bearing green bastions of cabbages nodding to their fall, yet never falling, walls of baskets enclosing masses of beans and peas, pyramids of snow-white turnips, swaying howdahs of mixed produce—creeping along behind aged night-horses, who seemed ever patiently wondering between their hollow coughs why they had always to work at that still hour when all other sentient creatures were privileged to rest. Wrapped in a cloak, it was soothing to watch and sympathize with them when depression and nervousness hindered sleep, and to see how the fresh green-stuff brightened to life as it came opposite the lamp, and how the sweating animals steamed and shone with their miles of travel. (LLI 40–41)

The drama of the story revolves around Sophy's own chances of brightening to life after a man accompanying a wagon laden with potatoes, and scrutinizing the houses as he passes, turns out to be her erstwhile admirer Sam Hobson, hoping at long last to claim her. One morning in June he persuades her to ride up to Covent Garden with him ('There's a nice seat on the cabbages, where I've spread a sack', LLI 43), and, overcoming her protests, he hoists her up into his cart. The 'air was fresh as country air at this hour', and the two talk just as they had in the old days, until day breaks as they approach Central London: 'It grew lighter and lighter. The sparrows became busy in the streets, and the city waxed denser around them. When they approached the river it was day, and on the bridge they beheld the full blaze of morning sunlight in the direction of St. Paul's, the river glistening towards it, and not a craft stirring' (LLI 43–44). The chirping sparrows and the still, sparkling panorama of the Thames and St. Paul's serve to convey Sophy's dawning awareness of the happiness that she might enjoy with Sam should she leave the city and live with him. Shortly after, he reveals his plan to open a greengrocer's shop in Aldbrickham (Hardy's name for Reading) and invites her to be his wife and help him to run his new business.

Alas, 'The Son's Veto' is another cautionary tale exploring the perils of upward mobility. Sophy's inflexibly class-conscious son, who has taken holy orders, will not countenance the marriage of his mother to a greengrocer, maintaining his 'veto' to the bitter end, and even making her swear never to wed her lowly suitor without his permission before a private cross and altar that he has erected in his bedroom in the South London villa. The positions of spectatorship developed in the story are neatly reversed in its final paragraph: while Sophy found 'interest' and 'charm' in the 'semi-rural people and vehicles moving in an urban atmosphere, leading a life quite distinct from that of the daytime toilers on the same road' (LLI 41), Sam Hobson bitterly watches from the door of his fruit and vegetable shop as a very different kind of parade arrives from London and makes its way through the streets of Aldbrickham:

> From the railway-station a funeral procession was seen approaching: it passed his door and went out of the town towards the village of Gaymead. The man, whose eyes were wet, held his hat in his hand as the vehicles moved by; while from the mourning-coach a young smooth-shaven priest in a high waistcoat looked black as a cloud at the shop-keeper standing there. (LLI 48)

It is one of the starkest dramatizations in Hardy's oeuvre of conflict deriving from both class antagonism and the malign aspects of the relationship between the urban and the rural.

II

The unforgiving nature of life in London that 'The Son's Veto' embodies reflects an understanding often voiced in the *Life* of the brutal indifference that prevails in the city towards those who are unable, for whatever reasons, to perform according to its dictates: 'In the City. The fiendish precision or mechanism of town-life is what makes it so intolerable to the sick and infirm. Like an acrobat performing on a succession of swinging trapezes, as long as you are at particular points at precise instants, everything glides as if afloat; but if you are not up to time—' (L 215–216). Hardy had little faith, however, in the kinds of pioneering social changes that the great Victorians such as Carlyle or Dickens or Ruskin felt confident enough to promulgate, identifying himself as neither Tory nor Radical but what he called an 'Intrinsicalist' (L 213), that is, one 'against privilege derived from accident of any kind', but also sceptical of the power of reform to redeem the incorrigible: 'Opportunity should be equal for all, but those who will not avail themselves of it should be cared for merely—not be a burden to, nor the rulers over, those who do avail themselves thereof.' His friend Mary Jeune undertook charity work in the East End of London, and he took a sly delight in noting that 'when she tries to convey some sort of moral or religious teaching to the East-end poor, so as to change their views from wrong to right, it ends by their convincing her that their view is the right one—not by her convincing them' (L 216).

It may have been Mary Jeune's East End visits that prompted the poem 'An East-End Curate', published in *The London Mercury* in November of 1924. Like many of Hardy's comments on London in his journals, the poem's opening lines register the oppression of uniformity inherent in urban living that Hardy found so dispiriting and imaginatively constricting—the triumph, that is, of the 'mechanical' (L 154):

> A small blind street off East Commercial Road;
>> Window, door; window, door;
>> Every house like the one before,
> Is where the curate, Mr Dowle, has found a pinched abode.
> Spectacled, pale, moustache straw-coloured, and with a long thin face,
> Day or dark his lodgings' narrow doorstep does he pace. (CP 713)

Hardy became convinced that, to survive, the Church had, in essence, to abandon belief in the supernatural and to function as a creator of social and cultural cohesion rather than as a promoter of divine truths—this was no doubt one of the reasons why T. S. Eliot disliked his work so intensely. Some of Hardy's Wessex curates, such as Parson Thirdly of *Far from the Madding Crowd* and the poem 'Channel Firing', are invested with a comic ordinariness that endears them to their community and allies them with a tradition of rural church humour stretching back to Sterne and Fielding and Smollett. His only London curate, Mr Dowle, has similarly acquired the colouring of the parishioners to whom he ministers; however evangelical or reforming he may once have been, he has succumbed, like Mary Jeune, to the circumstances that shape the behavior and outlooks of those he must have hoped to convert, becoming, like a chameleon, a barely acknowledged figure on the impoverished streets that he patrols, and has given up trying to improve:

> He goes through his neighbours' houses as his own, and none
>   regards,
> And opens their back-doors off-hand, to look for them in their
>   yards:
> A man is threatening his wife on the other side of the wall,
> But the curate lets it pass as knowing the history of it all.

Only children seem aware of his presence—they 'skip and laugh and say: / "There's Mister Dow-well! There's Mister Dow-well!" in their play'. This doesn't, however, seem to bother him: 'And the long, pallid, devoted face notes not, / But stoops along abstractedly, for good, or in vain, Got wot!' While not villainous in the manner of so many ecclesiastics in Hardy's fiction, such as Randolph Twycott or the scheming brothers of 'A Tragedy of Two Ambitions', this curate is far from being a heroic do-gooder, despite his name. A largely ignored, impotent, neutral figure on the East End streets, he makes an impression only on children mocking him in skipping games, and on a man who notices such things.

It is the social realist in Hardy that captures the interior of the East End curate's 'pinched abode' with such unsparing accuracy:

A bleached pianoforte, with its drawn silk plaitings faded,
Stands in his room, its keys much yellowed, cyphering, and abraded,
'Novello's Anthems' lie at hand, and also a few glees,
And 'Laws of Heaven for Earth' in a frame upon the wall one sees.

Such lines brilliantly illustrate the way that Hardy's poetry incorporates the kinds of detail more often to be found in novels. While not as unrelentingly standardized as the exteriors of the terraced houses that make up the street off East Commercial Road, there is undoubtedly something generic about the trappings of gentility and the emblems of faith with which the curate's room is furnished; not much Heaven is to be found in this particular pocket of Earth, whatever his framed wall-chart proclaims. As with the clerk in 'Coming Up Oxford Street: Evening', there seems to be an element of 'There but for the grace of God'—or should that be 'There but for the inscrutable workings of the Immanent Will'?—'go I!' in Hardy's remorseless itemization of the bleakness of Mr Dowle's life, both indoors and out. Had he followed through on his early longing to go to Cambridge and then enter the church, might he not have ended up as ineffective and disregarded and impoverished as this stooping, solitary man, whose vocational ideals seem powerless in the face of his surroundings? And while the piano, the glees, and the volume of Vincent Novello's collection of anthems might indicate a momentary respite from the indifference of the streets and the dinginess of his domestic arrangements, the various draining adjectives that Hardy applies to the instrument and its covering ('bleached', 'faded', 'yellowed', 'abraded') show shabbiness and entropy invading even music—which is nearly always associated in Hardy with energy and excitement.

Despite the great commercial success of *Tess of the d'Urbervilles*, Hardy never felt able to afford a permanent London residence. The London lodgings that he engaged over almost three decades were drawn on for a number of poems that illustrate the saturnine humour of what 'In a London Flat' (originally titled 'In a London Lodging') calls the 'Phantom Ironic'. In 'At Mayfair Lodgings', for instance, the poet spends a listless night in his rented room, 'undivining' (CP 450) that an ex-girlfriend is breathing her last in the house opposite; 'A Wife in London', one of Hardy's Boer War poems, has a newly-wed receive from her soldier-husband a letter that is

'Fresh—firm—penned in highest feather—/ Pageful of his hoped return' (CP 92) the day after a messenger has delivered a telegram reporting his death. 'In a London Flat' borrows from the pantheon of spirits who preside over affairs in *The Dynasts*, but here shows them taking an interest in less historically weighty affairs:

> 'You look like a widower,' she said
> Through the folding-doors with a laugh from the bed,
> As he sat by the fire in the outer room,
> Reading late on a night of gloom,
> And a cab-hack's wheeze, and the clap of its feet
> In its breathless pace on the smooth wet street,
> Were all that came to them now and then. . . .
> 'You really do!' she quizzed again. (CP 689)

'Let's get him made so—just for a whim!' suggests the Phantom Ironic, amused by her jest. 'O pray not!' pleads the Sprite of the Pities, 'She said it in fun!' Needless to say, when the husband looks towards the bed beyond the folding-doors on the same day of the following year, it is empty, for he is now indeed a widower, and his wife resting 'elsewhere'.

While the lurid ironies that invade these domestic interiors are consonant with Hardy's overall vision of the slaying of joy and the unblooming of hopes, London does often appear to have exacerbated his sense of the complexities and incongruities latent in the relationship between the private and the public. Certainly London's public spaces prompted a number of speculations in both notebooks and poems on the peculiar divide between external performance and inner consciousness; or, to use the terminology deployed in a passage included in the *Life*, between body and soul:

> March 9 [1888]. British Museum Reading Room. Souls are gliding about here in a sort of dream—screened somewhat by their bodies, but imaginable behind them. Dissolution is gnawing at them all, slightly hampered by renovations. In the great circle of the library Time is looking into Space. Coughs are floating in the same great vault, mixing

with the rustle of book-leaves risen from the dead, and the touches of footsteps on the floor. (L 215)

The fusion of the mystical and the quotidian in these reflections evokes the innovative procedures of a great work of the previous decade at least partly composed in the British Library too—Arthur Rimbaud's *Une Saison en Enfer*. Hardy's meditation breaks free from what one assumes was its starting point, the intersection of history and the present moment embodied by readers in a library, and glides, like the souls it so weirdly but matter-of-factly observes, towards a metaphysical moment of vision, one that mixes the abstract and the concrete into a perplexing but subtly wrought whole, evading the constraints of realism—although including prosaic details such as coughs and footsteps—as sinuously as a Rimbaldian prose poem.

Hardy's responses to public London interiors result on a number of occasions in passages that allow one to see with particular clarity the links between his work and that of experimental writers of the kind with whom he is not normally associated. Several months after observing the ghosts haunting the British Museum Reading Room he attended a service at St. Mary Abbots in Kensington. His reflections in his diary on the disjunction between the dutiful behavior of the churchgoers and the monologues that he imagines proceeding inside them offer what amounts to a preview of modernist uses of stream of consciousness:

They pray in the litany as if under enchantment. Their real life is spinning on beneath this apparent one of calm, like the District Railway-trains underground just by—throbbing, rushing, hot, concerned with next week, last week. Could these true scenes in which this congregation is living be brought into church bodily with the personages, there would be a churchful of jostling phantasmagorias crowded like a heap of soap bubbles, infinitely intersecting, but each seeing only his own. That bald-headed man is surrounded by the interior of the Stock Exchange; that girl by the jeweller's shop in which she purchased yesterday. Through this bizarre world of thought circulates the recitative of the parson—a thin solitary note without cadence or change of intensity—and getting lost like a bee in the clerestory. (L 219)

The 'infinitely intersecting' worlds of *Mrs Dalloway* and *Ulysses* and *À la re-cherche du temps perdu* are constructed out of an application of methods in rough accord with that adumbrated in this passage; and the vision it expresses is closer, in turn, to that of Hardy's two most experimental fictions, *The Hand of Ethelberta* and *The Well-Beloved*, both half-set in London, than it is to the Hardy of the Wessex-based novels of character and environment.

III

The distillation of souls from bodies imagined among the readers of the British Library achieves a literal enactment in one of two Hardy poems set in St. Paul's Cathedral. 'In a Whispering Gallery' records the peculiar acoustic effects of the gallery just under the dome of Wren's cathedral. This gallery was one of the London attractions that most excited the young Words-worth before he made his first visit to the capital, and it becomes an impor-tant metaphor in the second edition of Thomas de Quincey's *Confessions of an English Opium-Eater*. De Quincey explains its acoustic properties in a footnote: 'To those who have never visited the Whispering Gallery, nor have read any account of it amongst other acoustic phenomena described in sci-entific treatises, it may be proper to mention, as the distinguishing feature of the case, that a word or a question, uttered at one end of the gallery in the gentlest of whispers, is reverberated at the other end in peals of thunder'.[1] For Hardy it affords an opportunity to juggle his churchiness and his scep-ticism, to linger in the no man's land between his will to believe and his ra-tionally derived agnosticism:

> That whisper takes the voice
> Of a Spirit's compassionings,
> Close, but invisible,
> And throws me under a spell
> At the kindling vision it brings;
> And for a moment I rejoice,
> And believe in transcendent things
> That would mould from this muddy earth
> A spot for the splendid birth

Of everlasting lives,
Whereto no night arrives;
And this gaunt gray gallery
A tabernacle of worth
On this drab-aired afternoon,
When you can barely see
Across its hazed lacune
If opposite aught there be
Of fleshed humanity
Wherewith I may commune;
Or if the voice so near
Be a soul's voice floating here. (CP 522)

Like the passage in the *Life* on the British Museum Reading Room, 'In a Whispering Gallery' juxtaposes the ordinary and the transcendental. It is a 'drab-aired afternoon' ('drab-fogged' was Hardy's original choice), and if God doesn't exist then even St. Paul's is simply a 'gaunt gray gallery' rather than a 'tabernacle of worth'. The Whispering Gallery spiritualizes the voice, allowing it to float free of 'fleshed humanity' and seem to come instead from some invisible compassionate divinity. Hardy's lexical choices interestingly link the urge to believe with romantic notions of poetic inspiration—a 'spell', the 'kindly vision'—and this in turn connects the poet, in his trance of belief, with Hardy's figuration of Paul himself in the poem 'In St Paul's a While Ago' as 'vision-seeing' (CP 716). Paul, more than any other figure in the Bible, even Jesus himself, was invested by Hardy with poetic powers of the most magical kind, and it seems to me possible that Hardy covertly identified with him as an embattled and outspoken figure, derided by his detractors but boldly determined to deliver his vision in the metropolitan 'mart', at whatever cost to himself.

There is certainly an element of Will Strong addressing the crowds in Trafalgar Square in *The Poor Man and the Lady*, or of J. S. Mill's 'personified earnestness' (PV 239) when observed by Hardy making a speech on the hustings, in his figuration of Paul in 'In the British Museum', a poem collected in *Satires of Circumstance* of 1914. Like 'In a Whispering Gallery', it records an encounter with an anonymous fellow-visitor at a venerable site,

or in this case, a fragment of one. For the awestruck labouring man, merely
being in the presence of a stone taken from the temple at the foot of the
Areopagus, where the apostle preached his famous sermon, is cause for
wonder:

'What do you see in that time-touched stone,
        When nothing is there
But ashen blankness, although you give it
        A rigid stare?

'You look not quite as if you saw,
        But as if you heard,
Parting your lips, and treading softly
        As mouse or bird.

'It is only the base of a pillar, they'll tell you,
        That came to us
From a far old hill men used to name
        Areopagus.'

—'I know no art, and I only view
        A stone from a wall,
But I am thinking that stone has echoed
        The voice of Paul;

'Paul as he stood and preached beside it
        Facing the crowd,
A small gaunt figure with wasted features,
        Calling out loud

'Words that in all their intimate accents
        Pattered upon
That marble front, and were far reflected,
        And then were gone.

'I'm a labouring man, and know but little,
        Or nothing at all;
But I can't help thinking that stone once echoed
        The voice of Paul.' (CP 381–382)

Paul served to focus Hardy's lifelong debate over the relationship between the ideals of the spirit and the solid, empirical weight of history and
materiality. To the labouring man the stone, representing an intersection of
the divinely inspired and the earthly, is a moving witness to the appearance
of 'transcendent things' upon 'this muddy earth'. The trancelike state fostered in him resembles the one the spiritualized voice induces in the narrator of 'In a Whispering Gallery': both involve the triumph of language
over matter, of hearing over sight. The stone, at first sight only an unimpressive bit of an old pillar, has been transfigured for the labouring man by the
'intimate' words that 'pattered' upon it, delivered by a Paul strangely resembling Hardy's darkling thrush in the famous poem of that name. For like the
thrush, Paul is 'small' and 'gaunt', though 'wasted' rather than 'frail', and he
flings his soul at the listeners gathered at the Areopagus around 50 AD,
rather than at a rambler leaning on a coppice gate in the last hours of 1900.
Both can be seen as embodiments of the kind of defiant, heroic expression
of belief made impossible for Hardy by his own ingrained Laodiceanism.

A self-reflexive irony, therefore, lurks in Hardy's evocation of Paul as the
thrush's 'ecstatic' urban counterpart in 'In the British Museum'. Like the
bird's song, the labouring man's admiring description of the apostle in
the act of preaching allows the poet to share vicariously in the belief in what
'The Darkling Thrush' calls 'some blessed Hope' (CP 150) without compro-
mising his scepticism. And while there is no indication of where the 'labouring man' comes from, it is worth remembering that Hardy entitled his
1883 account of working conditions in his home county 'The Dorsetshire
Labourer', and the term was one that he more readily applied to the rural
than to the urban working classes. It is perhaps even possible to see the
poem as staging a debate between a version of the pre-London Hardy, an
earnest and innocent rural believer, close both to nature and to his primitive instincts ('treading softly / As mouse or bird'), and the disillusioned,

sophisticated, well-informed post-London Hardy, who still, however, hankers after the simple faith of his earlier self, and is moved by the access to it momentarily afforded by the labouring man's wonder.

This sharing can, of course, only occur while in a trance, when the visual and rational faculties are suspended—'You look not quite as if you saw, / But as if you heard'. But what, after all, Hardy wonders in 'In St Paul's a While Ago', would hardnosed, getting-and-spending Londoners, conscious only of their present desires and needs, make of the apostle should he suddenly appear in their midst, denouncing Victorian materialism and spiritual backsliding, prophesying end times?

> Summer and winter close commune
> On this July afternoon
> As I enter chilly Paul's,
> With its chasmal classic walls.
> —Drifts of gray illumination
> From the lofty fenestration
> Slant them down in bristling spines that spread
> Fan-like upon the vast dust-moted shade.
>
> Moveless here, no whit allied
> To the daemonian din outside,
> Statues stand, cadaverous, wan,
> Round the loiterers looking on
> Under the yawning dome and nave,
> Pondering whatnot, giddy or grave.
> Here a verger moves a chair,
> Or a red rope fixes there:—
> A brimming Hebe, rapt in her adorning,
> Brushes an Artemisia craped in mourning;
> Beatrice Benedick piques, coquetting;
> All unknowing or forgetting
> That strange Jew, Damascus-bound,
> Whose name, thereafter travelling round
> To this precinct of the world,

Spread here like a flag unfurled:
Anon inspiring architectural sages
To frame this pile, writ his throughout the ages:
Whence also the encircling mart
Assumed his name, of him no part,
And to his vision-seeing mind
Charmless, blank in every kind;
And whose displays, even had they called his eye,
No gold or silver had been his to buy;
Whose haunters, had they seen him stand
On his own steps here, lift his hand
In stress of eager, stammering speech,
And his meaning chanced to reach,
Would have proclaimed him as they passed
An epilept enthusiast. (CP 716–717)

Published in *Human Shows* of 1925, 'In St Paul's a While Ago' was first titled 'In St Paul's: 1869' (RP 236). Its origins, then, are in the year when *The
Poor Man and the Lady* was doing the rounds of London publishers, and
some three years after the waning of Hardy's faith, as well as practical difficulties, had led him to abandon his early ambition to emulate Paul and
deliver the word of God in 'eager' speech. St. Paul's Cathedral was, however,
one of the places of worship that he most often visited during his various
residences in London: he records of the summer of 1904 in the *Life* his habit
of attending 'services at St. Paul's whenever he happened to be near the
Cathedral, a custom of his covering many years before and after' (L 345).

The cool interior of the cathedral is presented in the poem's opening
lines as offering a complete contrast to the July heat and 'daemonian din'
of the streets around it. However, the implications of 'daemonian' notwithstanding, St. Paul's is figured more as a museum or tourist site, and even as
a stage for social self-display, than as a holy 'tabernacle of worth' (CP 522).
Hardy's appraisal of its 'chasmal classic walls' is itself knowing and cool—the
potential for the sublime lurking in 'chasmal' ('But oh! that deep romantic
chasm' exclaimed Coleridge in 'Kubla Khan') countered by the architectur-
ally accurate 'classic'. The careful denotation of rays of light spreading fan-

like through 'dust-moted shade' from its 'lofty fenestration' again defuses the
urge towards devotional uplift or meditation on the ineffable. There is certainly no hint of the religious trance that seized the labouring man or the
narrator of 'In a Whispering Gallery'. Hardy's description of the interior
raises issues relating more to appropriate behaviour in historic public places
than to 'kindling vision' (CP 522). The loiterers aimlessly gawping at the
cathedral's commemorative statues remind one of Dickens's Little Dorrit
wondering how she ought to react to all the pictures and famous sights paraded before her eyes on the Dorrits' Grand Tour of Europe. If the 'cadav-
erous, wan' statues and the 'yawning dome' momentarily point towards
fears of mortality, these potentially 'grave' thoughts are again interrupted
by Hardy's penchant for noticing the ordinary—an officious verger moving
a chair, or the dress and antics of other visitors who seem blithely indifferent
to the sacred purpose of the building. The brief taxonomy of types given—
the flaunting Hebe (the Greek goddess of youth), the mourning Artemisia (a
Greek queen who mixed a pinch of her husband's ashes with her daily drink),
Much Ado About Nothing's Beatrice and Benedick—makes the interior into a
social 'mart' in which extravagant self-performance tends to crowd out thoughts
of the Christian belief-system that inspired the 'fram[ing]' of 'this pile'.

It is from the perspective of what *The Dynasts* calls 'The Spirit of the Years'
that Hardy ponders the weirdness of the processes that led from the activities,
remote in both time and place, of a 'strange Jew, Damascus-bound' to the
building, centuries later, of St. Paul's in London—as well as to the assumption of the apostle's name by the thriving market that surrounds the cathedral,
whose commercial values as flagrantly contradict those of Paul's 'vision-seeing
mind' as do the self-displays of Hebe and Artemisia and Beatrice and
Benedick within. The complete conflict between the 'meaning' of Paul's
mission and the mind-sets of those buying and selling in the streets around
is the overall irony towards which the poem moves, and one which is deeply
relished by Hardy in a variety of ways. Paul, it is asserted, would have despised the mercantile values of the market's 'haunters'—but had this or that
caught his eye, being vowed to poverty, he couldn't have bought it anyway;
and were he suddenly to materialize on the steps of the cathedral named in
his honour, his prophecies would be dismissed as the ravings of a lunatic.
Pauline doctrine and capitalism emerge as wholly antithetical, rather than as

complementary as in so much Puritan and Protestant theology, and Paul as a vulnerable and unlikely hero—his stammer here doing the work performed by 'small' and 'gaunt' and 'wasted' in 'In the British Museum'. While the poem is alert to the comedy inherent in all attempts at idealism or spirituality in an age dominated by the 'encircling mart', and the concluding dismissal of the enraptured apostle by the market traders as an 'epilept enthusiast' reduces him to just another urban crazy, the poem's final lines movingly dramatize a complex tension between the imagination and the mercantile, the prophet and the masses. The cold realities of the economic system epitomized by the market are dispassionately balanced by the figuration of Paul excitedly gesturing as he preaches on the steps of his own cathedral, despised and mocked by the Londoners passing by, and yet, in the exalted grip of his divinely inspired vision, bursting into 'eager, stammering speech', courageously, as on the Areopagus, 'facing the crowd' (CP 382).

IV

Hardy's longest London poem also opens with a crowd scene—'A stranger, I threaded sunken-hearted / A lamp-lit crowd; / And anon there passed me a soul departed, / Who mutely bowed'. 'The Woman I Met' (CP 592–594) was published in the *London Mercury* in April of 1921, with its setting and date of composition indicated at its conclusion: *London, 1918*.[2] Hardy's Wessex is as phantom-crowded a region as any in literature, but this ghostly prostitute is his only contribution to the history of urban poetic spectres that arcs from Baudelaire to James Thomson to T. S. Eliot—sections of whose 'The Love Song of J. Alfred Prufrock' Hardy copied into his literary notebook of 1917, with the neutral comment, 'a poet of the vers-libre school' (LN 2:226–227). There is certainly nothing 'vers-libre' about the insistently rhyming 'The Woman I Met', but traces of Dante (whom Hardy read in 1887) that hint at the uses to which he would be put by Eliot in *The Waste Land* and 'Little Gidding' can be discerned in this revenant mutely bowing to a nocturnal urban wanderer. The poem's schema allows past and present to engage in a dreamy dialogue that replicates that of the poet with the woman he met: he is both a 'stranger' in the London crowd, yet also revisiting the streets of his adventures when a 'fresh bland boy of no assurance'; she is a female Lazarus who has 'quitted earth' and is 'yet upon it', back in her haunts of old—indeed they end up as a half-real, half-phantasmagoric version of the couple plodding through the night and rain near Tooting Common in 'Beyond the Last Lamp', although it is through busy Central London that they peregrinate:

> So walked the dead and I together
>   The quick among,
> Elbowing our kind of every feather
>   Slowly and long;
> Yea, long and slowly. That a phantom should stalk there
> With me seemed nothing strange, and talk there
>   That winter night
>   By flaming jets of light.

The layering of the otherworldly and the banal that makes the scenario depicted seem both extraordinary and 'nothing strange' is reflected in Hardy's mixing of hallowed terms from the Nicene Creed ('the quick and the dead') with colloquial turns of phrase such as 'of every feather'—here made even more obtrusive by being rhymed with 'together'. Like so many of Hardy's couples, the narrator and the ghost of the 'tinselled sinner' are 'held in suspense', to use a phrase from 'Beyond the Last Lamp' (CP 315), as they elbow their way through the busy streets of London.

The idea for the poem perhaps derived from an incident of April 1891 recorded in the *Life*: 'Piccadilly at night.—"A girl held a long-stemmed narcissus to my nose as we went by each other"' (L 247). Hardy was, however, over fifty by then, and so by no means a 'fresh bland boy of no assurance'. As 'In the British Museum' develops a dialogue not only between the speaker and the labouring man but between the older and the younger Hardy, so the spectral prostitute of this poem plunges the 'sunken-hearted' man of its opening line into memories of his life as a guileless new arrival walking the city streets as innocently as Avice II:

> In my far-off youthful years I had met her,
> Full-pulsed; but now, no more life's debtor,

> Onward she slid
> In a shroud that furs half-hid.
>
> 'Why do you trouble me, dead woman,
>   Trouble me;
> You whom I knew when warm and human?
>   —How it be
> That you quitted earth and are yet upon it
> Is, to any who ponder on it,
>   Past being read!'
> 'Still, it is so,' she said.

Her outlandish garb vividly transposes the characteristic self-division out of which the poem evolves, his sense of being both old and 'sunken-hearted' and yet in touch with his 'far-off youthful years'. It offers a good example, too, of Hardy's ability to make quasi-allegorical iconography assume a peculiar vivacity, almost a life of its own, through the unquestioning literalness of his imaginative habits: she is a streetwalker, and therefore in furs; she is also dead, and therefore in a shroud. In its unashamed and unselfconscious incongruity the image itself illustrates the relationship between the young Gothic architect and the older writer who had discovered how to make use of the 'Gothic art-principle in which he had been trained', and in particular of Gothic's delight in 'cunning irregularity' (L 323). Sliding onward in her shroud and her furs, as visually distinctive as a medieval emblem, or any of the souls being punished for their sins in Dante's *Inferno*, she demonstrates the 'principle of spontaneity' that Hardy carried over from architecture to poetry, 'straying freakishly', to borrow further from his discussion of the Gothic in his autobiography, into life, where she 'had no business to be'. The puzzled wonder that her appearance evokes in the speaker, she blithely explains, is beside the point—' "Still, it is so," she said'; and although she is no longer 'full-pulsed', or 'warm and human', warmth and humanity leach from these Keatsian adjectives, infusing her with the queer, suspended semi-livingness that animates so many of Hardy's ghosts.

In chapter 2 of the *Life* Hardy 'humorously' alluded to the late development of his sexuality: 'He used to say . . . that he was a child till he was

sixteen, a youth till he was five-and-twenty, and a young man till he was
nearly fifty' (L 37). The unlikely premise of 'The Woman I Met' is given in
the five stanzas of the poem that are spoken by the prostitute: the narrator's
youthful innocence, she explains, amidst the 'town dross' from which she
earned her living, made her fall so deeply in love with him that he became
her 'Cross'. As for many a nineteenth-century literary Magdalen, life on the
streets results in a longing for an unattainable purity, in her case taking the
form of a violent desire for this 'fresh bland boy of no assurance' who would
occasionally nod to her in passing.[3] In his simplicity, however, he proved
not only indifferent to her charms but unaware of her trade—even, she reminds him, after she accosted him directly and presented him with a token
of erotic love, a 'costly flower':

> 'These were my haunts in my olden sprightly
>   Hours of breath;
> Here I went tempting frail youth nightly
>   To their death;
> But you deemed me chaste—me, a tinselled sinner!
> How thought you one with pureness in her
>   Could pace this street
>   Eyeing some man to greet?
>
> 'Well; your very simplicity made me love you
>   Mid such town dross,
> Till I set not Heaven itself above you,
>   Who grew my Cross;
> For you'd only nod, despite how I sighed for you;
> So you tortured me, who fain would have died for you!
>   —What I suffered then
>   Would have paid for the sins of ten!
>
> 'Thus went the days. I feared you despised me
>   To fling me a nod
> Each time, no more: till love chastised me
>   As with a rod

That a fresh bland boy of no assurance
Should fire me with passion beyond endurance,
      While others all
   I hated, and loathed their call.

'I said: "It is his mother's spirit
      Hovering around
To shield him, maybe!" I used to fear it,
      As still I found
My beauty left no least impression,
And remnants of pride withheld confession
      Of my true trade
   By speaking; so I delayed.

'I said: "Perhaps with a costly flower
      He'll be beguiled."
I held it, in passing you one late hour,
      To your face: you smiled,
Keeping step with the throng; though you did not see there
A single one that rivalled me there! . . .
      Well: it's all past.
   I died in the Lock at last.'

A late addition to the long line of Victorian poems about prostitutes that stretches from Thomas Hood and Dante Gabriel Rossetti (whose 'Jenny' was first published in 1848) to the numerous fin-de-siècle evocations of London's 'Papillons du Pavé', to borrow the title of a Vincent O'Sullivan poem of 1896, Hardy's 'The Woman I Met' presents an intriguing contrast to his own earlier contribution to the genre, 'The Ruined Maid', written when he was himself a 'fresh bland boy' in London.[4] The woman's miserable end in the Lock (a hospital a few streets north of Westbourne Park Villas specializing in patients with venereal disease) grounds the encounter in a realism wildly at odds with both the music-hall humour of the earlier poem and the implausible fiery passion that she describes herself conceiving for the innocent young narrator, with whom she seems never to have exchanged a word.

The disparity between the fantasy that the poem propounds of her un-
quenchable love for him and the unflinching details that it offers of a prostitute's life on the streets, 'tempting frail youth nightly / To their death', mirrors the incongruity of her visual appearance, the furs that she wears over
her shroud. As is so often the case in Hardy's best poems, 'The Woman I
Met' avoids establishing an obtrusively purposeful grip on its properties
and narrative. Its blithe lack of consistency extends to the prostitute's im-
putation of the young Hardy's indifference to her charms to 'his mother's
spirit / Hovering around / To shield him'. Are we to think of Hardy's own
mother, Jemima, with her fierce antipathy to the notion of her children
ever marrying or getting embroiled in sexual affairs, or of the Virgin Mary,
as Frank M. Giordano has argued—or is this tutelary spirit more pagan,
less classifiable?[5] The fact that she inspires 'fear' in the prostitute certainly lends the shielding, maternal anima hovering over the boy a visceral
potency that is at odds with either an autobiographical or an allegorical
Christian reading. Like so many aspects of the ghostly prostitute herself,
this spirit, although so briefly glimpsed, establishes herself as a being
weirdly independent of the poem's apparent contexts, requirements, or
concerns.

The woman's speech reaches a climax, though it's perhaps closer to an
anticlimax, that is, similarly ungraspable and unfocused, even enigmatic,
in her presentation of the 'costly flower'. It is not even clear whether or not
he accepts her gift. The note in the *Life* allows one to feel that this stanza
fulfills the raison d'être of 'The Woman I Met', that in it Hardy reaches
the poem's source, yet it does so without bestowing significant light or resolved meaning on the experience that inspired it. The poet smiles, but
without breaking step with the 'throng', and she vanishes in the ellipsis
that precedes the emergence of the shrug of rueful stoicism—'Well, it's all
past'—that attends disasters, great and small, throughout Hardy's poetry
and prose. Her flower and his smile remain disjunct, tokens the poem
presents as contiguous rather than exchanged; the two pass by each other
in silence, without disrupting the flow of pedestrians on the city's streets,
and the dissolve to her miserable death in the Lock allows the dramatic
moment that never quite happened to be dispersed in disappointment and
resignation.

On her return as a ghost, however, they are as free as the spectral Emma and the remorseful poet of 'After a Journey' to 'stalk together' their olden haunts:

> She showed me Juans who feared their call-time,
>   Guessing their lot;
> She showed me her sort that cursed their fall-time,
>   And that did not.
> Till suddenly murmured she: 'Now, tell me,
> Why asked you never, ere death befell me,
>   To have my love,
>   Much as I dreamt thereof?'
>
> I could not answer. And she, well weeting
>   All in my heart,
> Said: 'God your guardian kept our fleeting
>   Forms apart!'

His inability to respond to her question at the opening of the last stanza is the poem's most telling moment: 'I could not answer'. As in 'Neutral Tones', his first great poetic depiction of a couple marooned in an impossible state of cross-purposes, it is the speaker's helplessness, his inability to rise to the occasion, that so movingly compensates for the absence of the dramatic revelation that one might expect from such a *rencontre*. Instead they cruise the streets in a state of shared curiosity, with her presenting an insider's account of her 'trade', for all the world like a farmer or factory owner showing a distinguished guest over the premises. While the poem's pietistic evocation of a guardian God watching over him hardly accounts for the mysterious ebb and flow of their oblique encounters amid the crowds of London, it is worth noting how in her final speech the prostitute attributes to Him a fundamental aspect of Hardy's own muse, which again and again reveals itself as expert at keeping 'fleeting / Forms apart!' Being set on the streets of the city, there is no landscape like that of 'After a Journey' to allow her spirit to assume the role of genius loci, with promise of a further encounter—'nay, bring me here again!' (CP 349). Her departure is lingering but final:

> Sighing and drawing her furs around her
> Over the shroud that tightly bound her,
> With wafts as from clay
> She turned and thinned away.

Returned to the emblematic Gothic status of her initial appearance to him that winter night, with the lurid added detail of her smelling of the grave, she vanishes into the limbo of Hardy's imaginative ghost world, the 'olden haunts' so vividly thronged by composites of fantasy and memory.

Epilogue: Christmas
in the Elgin Room

In 1914, the first year of his marriage to Florence, Hardy made no fewer than five visits to London, or six if one includes the trip to Enfield Parish Church (Enfield being a North London suburb) on 10 February to marry the woman he had surreptitiously wooed in the course of numerous rendezvous in the capital in the last years of Emma's life. Much, however, to the disappointment of his second wife, whose indiscreet letters to such as Rebekah Owen and Sydney Cockerell often complain that life at Max Gate was gloomy and depressing, 1914 proved the exception rather than the rule in the years of wedlock that followed. The war effectively put an end to Hardy's habit of making regular visits to London—although he and Florence did, some three months after hostilities commenced, attend a performance of *The Dynasts*, adapted by Harley Granville-Barker and staged at the Kingsway Theatre, where it ran for seventy-two performances. Hardy composed a prologue and epilogue especially for this dramatization, in which he made the obvious but necessary point that the French were now England's allies rather than their foes. Both prologue and epilogue carefully stress the context of the 'sudden sharp events beneath our eyes' (CP 950) that made this drastically foreshortened stage version of his epic commemoration of the defeat of Napoleon both 'timely and patriotic', as he put it in a letter to Granville-Barker (CL 5:51).[1] The aim of the play was

> To raise up visions of historic wars
> Which taxed the endurance of our ancestors;

That such reminders of the feats they did
May stouten hearts now strained by issues hid. (CP 950)

A great deal of stoutening would need to take place before those issues finally emerged from hiding. To Hardy's despair, the sick battle-god had recovered its 'crimson form' (CP 97), and this 'lurid Deity' (CP 99) relentlessly
mocked Hardy's tentative 'belief in the gradual ennoblement of man' (L 398).
As the second couplet of the bitter quatrain 'Christmas: 1924' put it: 'After
two thousand years of mass / We've got as far as poison-gas' (CP 914).

It was on a brief visit to London made nearly three years after the outbreak
of war that Hardy and Florence most directly experienced combat itself. In
late July of 1917 they spent a couple of nights with J. M. Barrie, who occupied a penthouse flat in Adelphi Terrace, the very building in which Hardy
had worked for Blomfield half a century earlier. Among the guests invited to
meet them for dinner was Arnold Bennett, who in his journal described
Hardy peering from the windows of Barrie's flat at the lights sweeping the
skies in search of the German Zeppelins mounting an air raid on the city,
with a handkerchief (presumably a dark one) covering his head (IR 121). H. G.
Wells and George Bernard Shaw joined the party later in the evening, and
Hardy liked to joke about the number of writers that a single bomb might
have killed had it landed on the illustrious party that the creator of Peter
Pan had assembled in his apartment that night (IR 224).

Some six months after the war ended Hardy attended his final Royal
Academy dinner. Shocked by how many of those whom he'd been accustomed to meet on these occasions had 'disappeared from the scene', he
decided he 'did not wish to go again' (L 421). His last trip to the capital was
made in April of 1920 to attend the wedding of Lady Dorothy Cavendish and
Harold Macmillan, the future prime minister and grandson of the founder
of the firm that had turned down his first three books, but which now owned
the rights to all his works.

Yet Hardy's reluctance to brave the crowds and confusion of the city in
his late seventies and eighties by no means resulted in an old age spent isolated from sophisticated or artistic metropolitan circles: for London, in these
years, came to him. The flow of Wessex pilgrims to Max Gate was rich and
varied, ranging from Hardy-country tourists to American admirers of his

best-selling novels to royalty, although the Prince of Wales (the future Edward VIII), who lunched with the Hardys on 20 July 1923, made little effort to pretend that he was himself an aficionado of the world-famous author: 'My mother tells me you have written a book called *Tess of the d'Urbervilles*', Florence later recalled him remarking; 'I must try to read it some time' (MM 506).

Alternatively, the prince could have gone to see the theatrical version of *Tess* that premiered in Barnes in Southwest London in the autumn of 1925, with the London-born Gwen Ffrangcon-Davies, rather than local girl Gertrude Bugler, who had inspired such jealousy in Florence, in the leading role.[2] In early November it transferred to the Garrick Theatre on Charing Cross Road. Since Hardy's doctor advised against his travelling to the capital, he never witnessed his most famous creation tread the West End boards (although he did see Baron Frederick d'Erlanger's operatic version of *Tess* at Covent Garden in July of 1909). The following month, however, the entire Garrick Theatre cast came down to Dorchester to perform the play for him in the drawing room at Max Gate. The Dorset-London axis that so shaped Hardy's career might be said to have achieved a dizzying consummation in this private performance—especially if one considers Tess's mixed origins in a number of London Society belles as well as in the various more plebeian Dorset beauties, such as a girl glimpsed driving a cart and a Weymouth waitress, cited by Hardy as her inspiration.

Hardy's closest friends among the London literati were Edmund Gosse and J. M. Barrie, who both frequently came to Max Gate for extended stays, as did Sydney Cockerell. Indeed, the many writers drawn by Hardy's fame and hospitality, the flashing, nipping teeth of his cossetted and ill-behaved terrier, Wessex, notwithstanding, allow one to see the drawing room at Max Gate as a veritable literary salon: William Archer, A. C. Benson, Edmund Blunden, John Buchan, Walter de la Mare, John Drinkwater, E. M. Forster, John Galsworthy, Harley Granville-Barker, Robert Graves, George Gissing, A. E. Housman, Rudyard Kipling, T. E. Lawrence, Amy Lowell, John Masefield, Charlotte Mew, John Middleton Murry, Henry Newbolt, Llewelyn Powys, Siegfried Sassoon, George Bernard Shaw, J. C. Squire, Arthur Symons, H. G. Wells, Rebecca West, Leonard Woolf, Virginia Woolf, and W. B. Yeats were all among those who made one or more entries in the Max Gate visitors' book.

Many left accounts of their dapper host—'in trotted a little puffy-cheeked cheerful old man, with an atmosphere cheerful and business-like in addressing us, rather like an old doctor's or solicitor's, saying "Well now—" or words like that as he shook hands' (IR 223), recalled Virginia Woolf in her diary after her visit of July 1926, adding, as if in surprise: 'There was no trace to my thinking of the simple peasant' (IR 224). In conclusion she decided that what most impressed her 'was his freedom, ease and vitality': 'He seemed very "Great Victorian" doing the whole thing with a sweep of his hand (they are ordinary smallish, curled up hands) and setting no great stock by literature; but immensely interested in facts; incidents; and somehow, one could imagine, naturally swept off into imagining and creating without a thought of its being difficult or remarkable; becoming obsessed; and living in imagination' (IR 226). Hardy did on occasion make remarks, particularly when discussing the composition of his novels, that chime with Woolf's not entirely unpatronizing notion that he approached the business of writing without a sense of 'its being difficult or remarkable', but he was also an inveterate reviser. Although Hardy derived, as the editor of the variorum edition of his poetry, James Gibson, notes, 'amusement from belittling his own craftsmanship and giving the impression that his writing was dashed off without much care', his surviving manuscripts in fact reveal him to be both 'conscientious and painstaking', indeed 'meticulous almost to a fault'.[3]

The last poem Hardy published in his lifetime was 'Christmas in the Elgin Room', which appeared in *The Times* on Christmas Eve of 1927. Begun in 1905, returned to in 1926, this poem was not eventually approved, copied, and dispatched until a few weeks before Hardy died. In the *Life*, Florence represents this final piece of literary business as a symbolic end to Hardy's six decades of negotiations with London editors and publishers:

An illness, which at the commencement did not seem to be serious, began on December 11. On the morning of that day he sat at the writing-table in his study, and felt totally unable to work. This, he said, was the first time that such a thing had happened to him.

From then his strength waned daily. He was anxious that a poem he had written, 'Christmas in the Elgin Room', should be copied and sent to *The Times*. This was done, and he asked his wife anxiously whether she had posted it with her own hands. When she assured him that she had done so he seemed content, and said he was glad that he had cleared everything up. Two days later he received a personal letter of thanks, with a warm appreciation of his work, from the editor of *The Times*. This gave him pleasure, and he asked that a reply should be sent.

He continued to come downstairs to sit for a few hours daily, until Christmas-day. After that he came downstairs no more. (L 479)

'Christmas Day in the Elgin Room' is subtitled *'British Museum: Early Last Century'*. The Parthenon sculptures looted by Lord Elgin in the first decade of the nineteenth century were acquired by the British Museum in 1816, but the Elgin Room was not in fact completed until 1832. Hardy's caption suggests that the discontented Greek gods are spending their first Christmas in the 'gloom' and 'cold' of their Borean exile in London.

> 'What is the noise that shakes the night,
> And seems to soar to the Pole-star height?'
> —'Christmas bells,
> The watchman tells
> Who walks this hall that blears us captives with its blight.'
>
> 'And what, then, mean such clangs, so clear?'
> '—'Tis said to have been a day of cheer,
> And source of grace
> To the human race
> Long ere their woven sails winged us to exile here.
>
> 'We are those whom Christmas overthrew
> Some centuries after Pheidias knew
> How to shape us
> And bedrape us
> And to set us in Athena's temple for men's view.
>
> 'O it is sad now we are sold—
> We gods! for Borean people's gold,

> And brought to the gloom
> Of this gaunt room
> Which sunlight shuns, and sweet Aurore but enters cold.

> 'For all these bells, would I were still
> Radiant as on Athenai's Hill.'
> —'And I, and I!'
> The others sigh,
> 'Before this Christ was known, and we had men's good will.' (CP
> 927–928)

The mixture of nostalgia and resignation that the Greek gods feel about their overthrow and transplantation closely resembles Hardy's attitude to the lapsing of his personal Christian beliefs and the transition from faith to scepticism, from belonging to deracination, initiated by his own departure from Dorchester for London on 17 April of 1862. It was, of course, a train rather than 'woven sails' that brought him to the capital, and it is unlikely that such a modest man would have thought to compare the stories, novels, and poems that he 'shape[d]' for 'men's view' with the sculptures of Pheidias—although by the time that the poem was published his works had been granted by the institutions that formulated the cultural values of the age an esteem almost to rival that of the ancient Greek sculptor. His writings had also brought him considerable amounts of 'gold', but in the wistful plaints that he puts into the mouths of the vanquished Greek gods one can still discern the emotions and outlook of the eight-year-old boy so memorably evoked in the first chapter of the *Life*, lying on his back in the sun, feeling its rays streaming through the interstices in his straw hat, and sensing his difference from other boys of his age: 'Reflecting on his experiences of the world so far as he had got he came to the conclusion that he did not wish to grow up'; he would rather, he decided, 'remain as he was, in the same spot' (L 20). Travel in Hardy often leads to catastrophe, and the 'blight' that 'blears' the Acropolitan gods' melancholy afterlives in the Elgin Room of the British Museum inevitably evokes Tess's conversation with Abraham on their ill-fated night journey to Casterbridge:

'Did you say the stars were worlds, Tess?'

'Yes.'

'All like ours?'

'I don't know, but I think so. They sometimes seem to be like the apples on our stubbard-tree. Most of them splendid and sound—a few blighted.'

'Which do we live on—a splendid one or a blighted one?'

'A blighted one.' (T 37)

The death of Prince, the family's horse, in the collision with the mail cart that shortly after follows, leads directly to Tess's transplantation to Trantridge Cross, and her deflowering by her faux-kinsman there.

Hardy's need to convey his sense of 'blight' was rarely detached from a yearning to believe in 'men's good will'. His satisfaction at the fair copying and dispatch of 'Christmas in the Elgin Room' to *The Times*, and at the receipt of the editor's appreciative comments, reproduce in miniature the economy of his writing life. He even managed to respond to a letter from Gosse praising the poem with a scribbled note of thanks written on Christmas Day—his final day 'downstairs'.[4]

On the day Hardy died he summoned up the strength to dictate from his deathbed two caustic epitaphs on an antithetical pair of literary enemies, G. K. Chesterton and George Moore; but the last of his comments that the *Life* records was made 'quite gaily'. That morning he received from the Dorset-born Newman Flower, who had recently become proprietor and managing director of the London publishing firm Cassell & Co., the classic invalid's gift:

An immense bunch of grapes arrived from London, sent by a friend, and this aroused in Hardy great interest. As a rule he disliked receiving gifts, but on this occasion he showed an almost childlike pleasure, and insisted upon the grapes being held up for the inspection of the doctor, and whoever came into the room. He ate some, and said quite gaily, 'I'm going on with these'. (L 480)

Later that evening he asked Florence to read him a particular verse from Edward Fitzgerald's *The Rubáiyát of Omar Khayyám*. Hardy had visited

Fitzgerald's grave in the churchyard of St. Michael and All Angels in Boulge in Suffolk in the spring of 1901 and in the *Life* records reading Fitzgerald's masterpiece during a residence in Campden Hill Road in North Kensington of May of 1887. Fitzgerald's lines combine 'a full look at the Worst', to quote from Hardy's own 'In Tenebris' (CP 168), with a plea for mutual forgiveness, for 'lovingkindness':

> Oh, Thou, who Man of baser Earth didst make,
> And ev'n with Paradise devise the Snake:
>   For all the Sin wherewith the Face of Man
> Is blacken'd—Man's forgiveness give—and take!

NOTES

SELECTED BIBLIOGRAPHY

ILLUSTRATION SOURCES

ACKNOWLEDGEMENTS

INDEX

Notes

Preface

1. Simon Gatrell, *Thomas Hardy's Vision of Wessex* (Basingstoke: Palgrave Macmillan, 2003), 18.

2. Keith Wilson, 'Thomas Hardy of London', in *A Companion to Thomas Hardy*, ed. Keith Wilson (Oxford: Wiley-Blackwell, 2009), 147. See also Michael Slater, 'Hardy and the City', in *New Perspectives on Thomas Hardy*, ed. Charles Pettit (Basingstoke: Macmillan, 1994).

Introduction

1. *Thomas Hardy's Will and Other Wills of His Family* (Mount Durand, Guernsey: The Toucan Press, 1967), 1.

2. Barrie to Lady Cynthia Asquith, 6 June 1920, in *Letters of J. M. Barrie*, ed. Viola Meynell (London: Peter Davies, 1942), 175.

3. Ann Thwaite, *Edmund Gosse: A Literary Landscape, 1849–1928* (London: Secker & Warburg, 1984), 508.

4. *Friends of a Lifetime: Letters to Sydney Carlyle Cockerell*, ed. Viola Meynell (London: Jonathan Cape, 1940), 315–316.

5. Sydney Cockerell's diary, 12 Jan. 1928 (BL); Katherine Hardy's diary, 13 Jan. 1928 (DCM).

6. Basil Willey, *Cambridge and Other Memories 1920–1953* (London: Chatto & Windus, 1966), 55.

7. Michael Millgate, *Testamentary Acts: Browning, Tennyson, James, Hardy* (Oxford: Clarendon Press, 1992), 146.

8. *Friends*, 315–316. Cordial the meeting may have been, but Norris's decision was not as straightforward as Barrie implies. Hardy was the first novelist since Dickens (who

died in 1870), and the first poet since Tennyson (who died in 1892), to be honoured with the offer of interment in Westminster Abbey. Both George Eliot and George Meredith had been denied abbey burials on the grounds that they were not Christian believers. Hardy's own well-known lack of faith inspired considerable unease at the prospect of his burial in the abbey in certain church leaders. To allay their fears, Norris wrote to the Reverend R. Grosvenor Bartelot, the vicar of Fordington (the parish in which Max Gate was located) for an account of Hardy's beliefs. Bartelot admitted that Hardy had never actually attended his church but felt able to assert that his celebrated parishioner had led a life of 'absolute moral rectitude' (quoted in James Gibson, *Thomas Hardy: A Literary Life* [London: Macmillan, 1996], 192), which seems to have been considered good enough. It is unlikely that Norris's predecessor, Herbert Ryle, dean of Westminster Abbey from 1911 to 1925, would have been so easily mollified: in 'The Refusal' (published in *Human Shows*) Hardy had publicly ridiculed Ryle for his refusal to allow a tablet commemorating Byron to be installed in the abbey in 1924 (the centenary of Byron's death).

9. *Daily Mail*, 13 Jan. 1928, 9.

10. Millgate, *Testamentary Acts*, 146.

11. *Daily Telegraph*, 14 Jan. 1928, 11.

12. Although congruent in many ways with Hardy's macabre imagination, there seems to be no foundation to the widely circulated rumour that a cat knocked the biscuit tin off Dr Mann's mantelpiece and dined on Hardy's heart. In some versions of the story a pig's heart was buried in its place, and in others the cat was killed and buried alongside the remnants of Hardy's heart.

13. Charles Lock quotes this passage in his article 'Hardy and the Railway' and interestingly observes:

> The very prosperity of Talbothays Dairy, which contributes so much to its status as an idyllic space, itself depends on the new marketing practices opened up by the railways and, of particular advantage to dairy farmers, by the development of refrigeration in the 1870s. (As wheat prices collapsed in the agricultural depression of the last thirty years of the nineteenth century, dairy farmers alone were spared, and even enabled to prosper.) (*Essays in Criticism* 50, no. 1 [2000]: 51).

14. Since square brackets are often used in the *Life*, my own interpolations in passages quoted from it will be in curly brackets. For details of the composition and publication of the *Life*, see 'Note on Texts' and the introduction to *The Life and Work of Thomas Hardy*, ed. Michael Millgate (Oxford: Oxford University Press, 1984), x–xxix.

15. In a letter of 16 September 1886 inviting the American painter John Alexander to visit, Hardy describes Max Gate, in his grandest offhand manner, as 'only a cottage in the country which I use for writing in' (CL 1:152), while in a letter of 23 October 1890

to the surgeon Sir Henry Thompson he calls it 'a little place in which I do most of my writing' (CL 1:218).

16. Sydney Cockerell's diary, 12 Jan. 1928 (BL).

17. Katherine Hardy's diary, 13 Jan. 1928 (DCM).

1. The Cries of London

1. Mrs T was Agatha Thornycroft, wife of the sculptor Hamo Thornycroft.

2. According to Claire Tomalin, Jemima 'is said to have continued to hanker after the idea of working in London herself even after the marriage' (CT 14). It seems she also considered sending her precocious eldest child there for his schooling. In July of 1922 Hardy confided to Edmund Blunden, who had been educated at Christ's Hospital, which was on Newgate Street near St. Paul's Cathedral, that it was 'a great wonder' that he had not been a pupil of that school himself: 'His mother knew a governor of the School', Blunden explains, 'and a nomination was the natural prospect for him; but the Governor died when he was still very young' (IR 171). Given that Jemima probably came across this governor when she was working as a servant, the 'wonder' that Hardy did not become a Bluecoat boy is possibly not as great as he implies. The anecdote does, however, suggest that Jemima inculcated into her son an awareness of the possibility of residence in London, and of the opportunities offered by London, at an early age.

3. This entry also lies behind the poem 'The Woman I Met' discussed in Chapter 10. The prostitute in this poem attributes the narrator's indifference to her charms to 'his mother's spirit / Hovering around / To shield him' (CP 593).

4. In a letter of 18 November 1909 to Florence Dugdale he commended the actress (Laura Eliza Evans) playing Bathsheba in a production of *Far from the Madding Crowd* staged by the Dorchester Debating and Dramatic Society: 'she gave the real B quite startlingly to me, seeming just like my handsome aunt from whom I drew her' (CL 4:58).

5. The year 1846 was the peak of the Railway Mania: that year Parliament passed 272 acts authorising 4,500 miles of new railway. For a full account of the battles between the various companies looking to expand their networks into Dorset, see J. H. Lucking, *Railways of Dorset: An Outline of their Establishment, Development and Progress from 1825* (Lichfield: The Railway Correspondence and Travel Society/The Dorset Natural History and Archaeological Society, 1968).

6. See Charles Lock, 'Hardy and the Railway', *Essays in Criticism* 50, no. 1 (2000): 50. There are no trains in *Far from the Madding Crowd*, but one is mentioned by the narrator in his attempts to characterize the way that Boldwood responds to Bathsheba: 'Boldwood looked at her—not slily, critically or understandingly, but blankly at gaze, in the way a reaper looks up at a passing train' (FFMC 118).

7. For further discussion of the effect on Dorchester of the choice of the 'central' rather than the 'coastal' route, see Ralph Pite, *Thomas Hardy: The Guarded Life* (London: Picador, 2006), 16–21. For a detailed account of the effect of the arrival of the railways on Dorset rural life, see Birgit Plietzsch, *The Novels of Thomas Hardy as a Product of Nineteenth-Century Social, Economic, and Cultural Change* (Berlin: Tenea Verlag, 2004), 52–76.

8. As Michael Millgate has pointed out, Hardy is here reprising an article by Charles Kegan Paul published anonymously in the *Examiner* of 15 July 1876 entitled 'The Wessex Labourer'. Paul praises Hardy for his descriptions of life in Wessex (although Hardy had only begun to use the term consistently in *The Hand of Ethelberta*, published that year), and observes: 'Time in Dorset has stood still; advancing civilisation has given the labourer only lucifer-matches and the penny post' (MM 168). Hardy and Paul, who had spent twelve years as a vicar in a Dorset village, became good friends after the Hardys settled in Tooting in 1878.

9. *The Letters of Percy Bysshe Shelley, Vol. 1*, ed. Frederick L. Jones (Oxford: Oxford University Press, 1964), 521.

10. Shelley and Godwin stayed in the Cross Keys inn on the night of 30 October 1814.

11. Shelley and Mary Godwin used often to meet, when courting, at the grave of her mother Mary Wollstonecraft in Old St. Pancras cemetery. One of Hardy's tasks when working for Blomfield's architectural practice was to oversee, in the autumn of 1866, the removal of graves and coffins and skeletons from this graveyard to make way for the construction of a new railway line (see Chapter 4).

12. Shelley clearly played a significant role in Hardy's wooing of Henniker. In a letter of 16 July 1893 he reports himself disappointed to find her less receptive than he expected to his Shelleyan ideals of free love:

> I too have been reading 'Epipsychidion'—indeed by mutual influence we must have been reading it simultaneously. I had a regret in reading it at thinking that one who is pre-eminently the child of the Shelleyean [*sic*] tradition—whom one would have expected to be an ardent disciple of his school and views—should have allowed herself to be enfeebled to a belief in ritualistic ecclesiasticism. (CL 2:23)

Sue Bridehead, who is in part based on Henniker, quotes from 'Epipsychidion' as a prelude to allowing Jude to kiss her:

> 'Say those pretty lines, then, from Shelley's "Epipsychidion" as if they meant me!' she solicited, slanting up closer to him as they stood. 'Don't you know them?'
> 'I know hardly any poetry,' he replied mournfully.
> 'Don't you? These are some of them:

"There was a Being whom my spirit oft
Met on its visioned roamings far aloft.

    .   .   .

A seraph of Heaven, too gentle to be human,
Veiling beneath that radiant form of woman . . ."

O it is too flattering, so I won't go on! But say it's me!—say it's me!'
   'It *is* you, dear; exactly like you!'
   'Now I forgive you! And you shall kiss me just once there—not very long.'
She put the tip of her finger gingerly to her cheek; and he did as commanded.
(JO 236)

13. 'Notes of Thomas Hardy's life (taken down in conversation etc.)' by Florence Hardy (DCM).

2. Only Practical Men Are Wanted Here

1. In support of this dating, see Dennis Taylor, 'The Victorian Philological Contexts of Hardy's Poetry', in *Thomas Hardy in Context*, ed. Phillip Mallett (Cambridge: Cambridge University Press, 2013), 235.

2. Hardy was clearly fond of the poem: it is among the nine that he chose for inclusion in the miniature library of Queen Mary's Dolls' House at Windsor Castle (constructed by Sir Edwin Lutyens and completed in 1924).

3. The poem's argument is reprised in chapter 13 of *A Pair of Blue Eyes*, which is set in the London chambers of Henry Knight in Bede's Inn (based on Clement's Inn, just north of the Strand): 'How many of us can say of our intimate *alter ego*, leaving alone friends of the outer circle, that he is the man we should have finally chosen, as embodying the net result after adding up all the points in human nature that we love, and principles we hold, and subtracting all that we hate? The man is really somebody we got to know by mere physical juxtaposition long maintained, and was taken into our confidence, and even heart, as a makeshift' (PBE 124).

4. In the same letter of 1897 Hardy records 'examining several English imitations of a well-known fragment of Sappho' and 'trying to strike out a better equivalent for it than the commonplace "Thou, too, shalt die" &c. which all the translators had used during the last hundred years. I then stumbled upon your "Thee, too, the years shall cover", & all my spirit for poetic pains died out of me. Those few words present, I think, the finest *drama* of Death & Oblivion, so to speak, in our tongue' (CL 2:158).

5. In a letter of 1866 to his sister Mary, Hardy wrote: 'H.M.M. [i.e., Horace Moule] has sent me the "Students' Guide" to the U. of C. [i.e., University of Cambridge]. I find on adding up expenses and taking into consideration the time I should have to wait,

that my notion is too far fetched to be worth entertaining any longer. To look forward 3 years under any circumstances is dreary enough, but when the end of that time only brings with it a commencement of another 3 years (time of residence at C.) and that then almost another year will be taken up in getting a title &c . . . it seems absurd to live on now with such a remote object in view' (CL 1:7). In the *Life*, however, he attributes his decision to relinquish all hopes of entering the church to his loss of faith: 'This fell through less because of its difficulty than from a conscientious feeling, after some theological study, that he could hardly take the step with honour while holding the views that on examination he found himself to hold' (L 53).

6. Sapphics were also used by the Roman poets Horace and Catullus. Hardy clearly came to feel it important that the reader of 'The Temporary the All' be aware of its metre: when he noticed that the subheading was missing from his 1919 *Collected Poems* he composed an erratum slip that he sent to friends: 'Page 5 under the title "The Temporary the All" insert "(Sapphics)"' (RP 287).

7. 'Church "restoration"', Hardy writes in the *Life* of the years 1860–1861, 'was at this time in full cry in Dorsetshire and the neighbouring counties, and young Hardy found himself making many surveys, measurements, and sketches of old churches with a view to such changes. Much beautiful ancient Gothic, and particularly also Jacobean and Georgian work, he was passively instrumental in destroying or in altering beyond identification—a matter for his deep regret in later years' (L 35). See also his 'Memories of Church Restoration', written in 1906 (PW 203–218).

8. 'In May he sent his Presidential Address to the Society of Dorset Men in London, to be read by the Secretary, as he was always a victim to influenza and throat trouble if he read or spoke in London himself, and afterwards on request sent the original manuscript. (By the way, the address never was read, so he might have saved himself the trouble of writing it.)' (L 367).

9. The same tactic is deployed in *The Well-Beloved*: Pierston's friend Somers lives on a street in London called Mellstock Gardens (WB 199), Mellstock being Hardy's Wessex name for Stinsford.

10. In *The Well-Beloved*, Pierston observes the Portland stone from his father's quarry on The Isle of Slingers (the Wessex name for Portland) piled up on wharves on the south side of the Thames (WB 211).

11. For further details, see Fran Chalfont's 'Hardy's Residences and Lodgings: Part One', *Thomas Hardy Journal* 8, no. 3 (Oct. 1992): 51.

12. Robert Gittings, for instance, complains of Hardy's habit of 'loading his novels with untoward digressive references to literature, painting, and architecture', which he attributes to his being 'self-taught' (RG 202).

13. For a full account of the importance of *The Golden Treasury* to Hardy, see Dennis Taylor's 'Hardy's Copy of *The Golden Treasury*', *Victorian Poetry* 37 (1999): 165–191.

14. In 1922 Hardy transcribed the poem and sent it to J.C. Squire for publication in the *London Mercury*'s 'Reprints' series (PV 417–418). 'It is hoped', he wrote, a trifle optimistically, at the bottom of the transcription, 'that this may be printed in any new edition of the Oxford Book of English Verse.'

15. Samuel Smiles, *Self-Help* (London: John Murray, 1958 [first pub. 1859]), 325.

16. The notoriously unreliable Newman Flower claimed that Hardy once told him that he nearly exchanged words with Dickens in a coffee-shop in Hungerford Market: 'Charles Dickens frequently went to the same coffee-shop for his lunch. Hardy watched Dickens perch himself on a high stool at the counter. Many times the urge came to him to speak to one whom he regarded as the master. "Once," he said, "I went up and stood at the vacant place beside the stool on which Dickens was sitting. I had eaten my lunch, but I was quite prepared to eat another if the occasion would make Dickens speak to me. It would be a reward more than fitting for the torment of a second helping. I hoped he would look up, glance at this strange young man beside him and make a remark—if it was only about the weather. But he did nothing of the kind. He was fussing about his bill. So I never spoke to him."' (IR 175). Hardy records lunching at this 'coffee-house' in Hungerford Market in the *Life* (L 44), as well as attending the readings that Dickens gave at the Hanover Square Rooms (L 54) in June of 1863. It seems unlikely that he would not have mentioned this close encounter with the most famous writer of the age if it had actually occurred.

17. Jerry White, *London in the Nineteenth Century* (London: Vintage, 2008), 47.

18. *The Works of William Makepeace Thackeray with Biographical Introductions by his Daughter, Anne Ritchie* (London: Smith, Elder and Co., 1899), 11:xxxv.

19. See Lynda Nead, *Victorian Babylon* (New Haven: Yale University Press, 2000), 161–203, for a full discussion of this 'London ghetto' in the 1860s.

20. There are considerable differences between the version of 'An Indiscretion' that was published in the United States by *Harper's Weekly* and the one that appeared in Britain in *New Quarterly Review*. The *Harper's Weekly* text was probably set from an uncorrected set of *New Quarterly* proofs, to which Hardy then went on to make numerous revisions. In the *Harper's* text, Egbert is 'of no social standing', which was revised for the *New Quarterly* to the less extreme 'of his unequal history'. For a full discussion of the differences between the two texts and their relationship to *The Poor Man and the Lady*, see Pamela Dalziel's edition of *The Excluded and Collaborative Stories* (Oxford: Oxford University Press, 1992), 71–72.

21. 'Amabel' is the only poem dated 1865 (although the manuscript and *Selected Poems* give its date as 1866, RP 97). 'Discouragement' is dated 1863–1867, 'Her Confession' 1865–1867, and the posthumously published 'The Unplanted Primrose' 1865–1867. The first, one of his many sonnets from this period, reflects both the Darwinian perspective of 'Amabel' and the class antagonism of *The Poor Man and the Lady*: 'Her [i.e., Nature's] loves dependent on a feature's trim, / A whole life's circumstance on hap of birth' (CP 829).

22. In their introduction to their edition of the 'Studies, Specimens &c.' notebook (Oxford: Clarendon Press, 1994), Pamela Dalziel and Michael Millgate suggest the title may derive from a character in Charlotte M. Yonge's *The Heir of Redclyffe* (1853) (xiii–iv and 152). This supposition is based on the erased but still partially legible note in pencil on the rear endpaper of this notebook: 'H. of R from Mudie' (SS 89). The other notes, however, in the list of which this forms a part, such as one about 'Mac' (i.e., the publishers Macmillan & Co.) suggest that this list was made several years after the date that Hardy gives for the composition of 'Amabel'.

23. 'Dorp' is an archaic term for a small village.

3. Crass Clanging Town

1. Hardy made a number of sketches and watercolours of London views in his first two years in the capital: one of 'Shoot-up-Hill, Highgate' is dated 1862, one of the sky-line from Westminster Abbey to Big Ben is dated 22 April 1863, and one of St. James's Park is dated 28 April 1863. All are in the Dorset County Museum.

2. As well as the above, Hardy's principal sources for quotations were the fol-lowing: William Barnes, Robert Buchanan, Burns, Byron, Coleridge, Dante (in John Carlyle's translation of 1849), Jean Ingelow, Milton, Shakespeare, Tennyson, and Wordsworth.

3. The volume does contain a lyric beginning 'Absence, hear thou this protesta-tion' given as by Anon. in 1861 but attributed to Donne in the 1891 edition. However, the poem is probably by John Hoskins. Hardy quotes its final stanza in *The Hand of Ethelberta* (HE 319).

4. *Selected Prose of T. S. Eliot*, ed. Frank Kermode (London: Faber & Faber, 1975), 64.

5. For a full discussion of the impact on Hardy of contemporary developments in astronomy, see Pamela Gossin's *Thomas Hardy's Novel Universe: Astronomy, Cosmology and Gender in the Post-Darwinian World* (Aldershot: Ashgate, 2007).

6. Similar interplanetary vistas are explored in the sonnet 'At a Lunar Eclipse', which was composed some time in the 1860s.

7. This scene was based on one in *The Poor Man and the Lady*. In the letter that the publisher Alexander Macmillan wrote to Hardy on 12 August 1868, he commended in particular the 'scene in Rotten Row', declaring it 'full of power & insight' (Letter from Macmillan to Hardy, 10 August 1868, DCM).

8. Philip Larkin, *Collected Poems* (London: Faber & Faber, 1988), 153.

9. Philip Larkin, *Required Writing* (London: Faber & Faber, 1984), 176.

10. Mrs Sarah Headley, Eliza Nicholls's niece, was interviewed by Henry Reed and Richard Purdy in 1955 (MM 559).

11. Larkin, *Collected Poems*, 148.

12. MM 92. The speaker's jealous feelings are closely echoed by those of Cytherea in *Desperate Remedies* when she is seated just behind Edward Springrove and his cousin Adelaide, to whom he is engaged, in church: 'My nature is one capable of more, far more, intense feeling than hers! She can't appreciate all the sides of him—she never will! He is more tangible to me even now, as a thought, than his presence itself is to her!' (DR 205). This is an expansion of the first two lines of the sestet: 'And thus I grasp thy amplitudes, of her / Ungrasped, though helped by nigh-regarding eyes' (CP 16).

13. Chapter 10 of the *Life* includes an extract from Hardy's diary of 1880 in which he describes a saleswoman encountered during a shopping expedition in London with Emma: 'She is a woman of somewhat striking appearance, tall, thin, decided; one who knows what life is, and human nature, to plenitude. Hence she acts as by clockwork; she puts each cloak on herself, turns round, makes a remark, puts on the next cloak, and the next, and so on, like an automaton. She knows by heart every mood in which a feminine buyer of cloaks can possibly be, and has a machine-made answer promptly ready for each' (L 144).

14. See Keith Wilson's 'Thomas Hardy's "The Ruined Maid," Elsa Lanchester's Music Hall, and the Fall into Fashion', *Thomas Hardy Journal*, 15, no. 2 (May 1999): 41–48; and Richard Nemesvari's 'Hardy and Victorian Popular Culture: Performing Modernity in Music Hall and Melodrama', in *The Ashgate Research Companion to Thomas Hardy*, ed. Rosemarie Morgan (Farnham: Ashgate, 2010), 73–76. Jocelyn Pierston in *The Well-Beloved* is a regular visitor to London's music halls and for a time believes his ideal woman to be embodied in 'a dancing-girl at the Royal Moorish Palace of Varieties' (WB 212).

15. Figures from Dagmar Kift, *The Victorian Music Hall: Culture, Class and Conflict* (Cambridge: Cambridge University Press, 1996), 2.

16. Hardy tells us in the *Life* that the mistress of the architect in *The Poor Man and the Lady* is employed as a 'dancer at a music-hall' (L 63).

17. In the *Life* he recalls that during the Season of 1890, he 'had a humour for going the round of the music-halls' (L 237), and devotes a paragraph to considering the physiques and the lives of music-hall dancers.

18. The impact of the theatre on his writing, and his attempts to adapt his own novels for the stage, have been thoroughly explored by Keith Wilson in *Thomas Hardy on Stage* (Basingstoke: Palgrave Macmillan, 1995) and by Richard Nemesvari in *Thomas Hardy, Sensationalism, and the Melodramatic Mode* (Basingstoke: Palgrave Macmillan, 2011).

4. Power & Purpose

1. Seamus Heaney, *Station Island* (London: Faber & Faber, 1984), 34–35.

2. Peter Porter, *Collected Poems* (Oxford: Oxford University Press, 1984), 187.

3. *The Variorum Edition of the Complete Poems of Thomas Hardy*, ed. James Gibson (London: Macmillan, 1979), 717.

4. John Hughes, 'Meter and Context: Hardy's "Neutral Tones"', *Victorian Poetry* 51, no. 1 (Spring 2013): 83.

5. Samuel Hynes, *The Pattern of Hardy's Poetry* (Chapel Hill: University of North Carolina Press, 1961), 136; RG 129; John Bayley, *An Essay on Hardy* (Cambridge: Cambridge University Press, 1978), 72; CT 82.

6. Hughes, 'Meter and Context', 85.

7. R.W. King, 'The Lyrical Poems of Thomas Hardy,' *The London Mercury* (December 1925), reprinted in Graham Clarke, ed., *Thomas Hardy: Critical Assessments*, vol. 2, *The Writer and the Poet* (Mountsfield: Helm, 1993), 207.

8. Bayley, *Essay on Hardy*, 76.

9. A diary entry of 2 July 1865 included in the *Life* is the first indication that Hardy gives of the waning of his belief in a Christian God: 'Worked at J. H. Newman's *Apologia*, which we have all been talking about lately. A great desire to be convinced by him, because H. M. M. {Horace Moule} likes him so much. Style charming, and his logic really human, being based not on syllogisms but on converging probabilities. Only—and here comes the fatal catastrophe—there is no first link to his excellent chain of reasoning, and down you come headlong. Poor Newman!' (L 50–51). The missing 'first link' is the actual existence of God.

10. Hughes, 'Meter and Context', 81–82.

11. His renunciation of poetry in the aftermath of his London years was not in fact complete: 'Song' (eventually published as 'Retty's Phases') is the earliest poetic manuscript of Hardy's to survive and is dated 22 June 1868. In the *Life* he mentions also a lyric entitled 'A Departure by Train', which does not survive, and a plan to compose a narrative poem on the Battle of the Nile (L 59). The brief 'Gallant's Song', published in *Winter Words*, is dated November 1868.

12. Letter from Macmillan to Hardy, 10 Aug. 1868, DCM.

13. Macmillan Papers, 'Macmillan Reader's Reports', BL.

14. Edmund Gosse, 'Thomas Hardy's Lost Novel', *Sunday Times*, 22 Jan. 1928.

15. Brotherton Collection, University of Leeds; also reprinted in Pamela Dalziel, 'Exploiting the *Poor Man*: The Genesis of Hardy's *Desperate Remedies*', *Journal of English and Germanic Philology* 94 (April 1995): 222.

16. Further proof that the lady dies can be found in Macmillan's complaint that Hardy makes her father scrimp on costs for his daughter's gravestone: 'Is it conceivable that any man however base & soul corrupted would do as you make the Hon Foy Allancourt do at the close, accept an estimate for his daughters tomb—*because it cost him nothing?* He had already so far broken through the prejudices of his class as to send for Strong in the hope of saving his daughters life' (Letter from Macmillan to Hardy, 10 Aug. 1868, DCM). Miss Allancourt's first name is not given in any of the accounts of the novel,

but Pamela Dalziel plausibly suggests that it may have been, like that of the heroine of *A Pair of Blue Eyes*, Elfride. The list of jottings on the final page of the 'Studies, Specimens &c.' notebook includes the memo 'use "the lady Elfrid" ' (SS 89). Further, as Dalziel points out, Elfride's surname, Swancourt, echoes that of Allancourt—which may in turn have necessitated the alteration of her surname to Allenville when Hardy came to rewrite *The Poor Man and the Lady* as 'An Indiscretion in the Life of an Heiress' (see Dalziel, 'Exploiting the *Poor Man*', 223).

17. Letter to Edward Clodd, 5 Dec. 1910.

18. Ralph Pite, *Thomas Hardy: The Guarded Life* (London: Picador, 2006), 138.

19. Bayley, *Essay on Hardy*, 71.

20. Charles Morgan, *The House of Macmillan, 1843–1943* (London: Macmillan, 1943), 92.

21. Letter from Chapman & Hall to Hardy, 8 Feb. 1869, DCM.

22. Hardy quoted from this review in one of the last pieces he ever wrote, 'G.M.: A Reminiscence' (PV 467–470).

23. In her 1934 edition of 'An Indiscretion in the Life of an Heiress', Florence recorded that Hardy destroyed the manuscript of *The Poor Man and the Lady* 'some years before his death' (RP 275).

24. In 1879 Hardy met Mary Elizabeth Braddon and declared her 'a most amiable woman' (L 135). Her publisher William Tinsley was also fond of her, naming the villa that he built in Barnes with profits from her work Audley Lodge after her best-selling novel, *Lady Audley's Secret* (1862).

25. As Richard Nemesvari points out in his *Thomas Hardy, Sensationalism, and the Melodramatic Mode* (Basingstoke: Palgrave Macmillan, 2011), we will never know 'precisely what Meredith said to Hardy' (26), or what the older novelist meant by the phrase 'more complicated "plot" '. It is revealing that when recounting the submission of the book to Tinsley Brothers in the *Life*, Hardy's phrasing allows for the possibility that he misconstrued Meredith's advice: 'Why he did not send it to Messrs Chapman and Hall, with whom he had now a slight link, and whose reader, Mr Meredith, had recommended him to write what Hardy *understood to be a story of this kind,* is inexplicable . . . for there is no doubt that Meredith would have taken an interest in a book he had, *or was supposed to have,* instigated' (L 79, my italics).

26. Macmillan Papers, 'Reviews of Manuscripts', BL.

27. Although Manston has to travel down from Liverpool to London for his interview for the stewardship of the Knapwater Estate, the novel makes it clear that his primary residence is London. Cytherea Aldclyffe sends the job advertisement to a London postal address: Wykeham Chambers, Spring Gardens. These chambers are in 'a street not far from Charing Cross' (DR 105).

28. Letter from Macmillan to Hardy, 4 April 1870, DCM.

5. The Hand of E. (I)

1. *Letters of Emma & Florence Hardy*, ed. Michael Millgate (Oxford: Oxford University Press, 1996), 78. In the *Life*, Hardy firmly but implausibly attempts to dissociate himself from the situation and experiences of Stephen Smith of *A Pair of Blue Eyes*, asserting that his own wooing ran 'without a hitch, and with much encouragement from all parties concerned, from beginning to end' (L 76–77).

2. Charles Morgan, *The House of Macmillan, 1843–1943* (London: Macmillan, 1943), 97.

3. William Tinsley, *Random Recollections of an Old Publisher* (London: Simpkin, Marshall, Hamilton, Kent, 1900), 127.

4. Laurence Lerner and John Holmstrom, eds., *Thomas Hardy & His Readers* (London: Bodley Head, 1968), 18.

5. In her memoir *Some Recollections*, ed. Evelyn Hardy and Robert Gittings (London: Oxford University Press, 1961), Emma talks of going, at some point in their courtship years, 'as a country cousin to my brother in London', where she found herself 'bewildered with the size and lengths and distances, and very much embarrassed at going on an omnibus, which seemed a very undignified method of getting about' (60). No date is given for this visit to the capital, and no mention is made of meeting, or being met by, her fiancé there.

6. The Hand of E. (II)

1. In fact, unbeknownst to Hardy, the *Cornhill*'s circulation was rapidly dwindling; during the period that Stephen edited it (1871–1882), its sales dipped from 25,000 to 12,000.

2. In his 'Recollections of Leslie Stephen', written for F. W. Maitland's *The Life and Letters of Leslie Stephen* (London: Duckworth, 1906) and reprinted in *Thomas Hardy's Public Voice*, Hardy again stresses the distance between Higher Bockhampton and London: 'It was at the beginning of December 1872, on a wet and windy morning, when in a remote part of the country, that a letter stained with raindrops arrived for me in a handwriting so fine that it might have been traced by a pin's point' (PV 258).

3. See, for instance, 'Note on the Text' by Suzanne B. Falck-Yi in the Oxford University Press edition (FFMC, xxxi–xxxvii).

4. Hardy stayed at Celbridge Place in June of 1873, when he was joined by his brother Henry; in December of 1873; in April and May of 1874; and from mid-July of 1874 until his marriage to Emma on 17 September.

5. Hardy's script was modified by the dramatist J. Comyns Carr and submitted to John Hare and William Hunter Kendal, the managers of the St. James's Theatre, in the autumn of 1880. Hare and Kendal rejected it, but the following year mounted a produc-

tion of Arthur Wing Pinero's *The Squire*, a play whose main plot elements derived from Hardy's novel. A minor scandal ensued. Comyns Carr's revised version of the script on which he and Hardy collaborated, its title changed back to *Far from the Madding Crowd*, opened in Liverpool in February of 1882, and at the Globe Theatre in London in April of that year. For further details, see Keith Wilson, *Thomas Hardy on Stage* (Basingstoke: Palgrave Macmillan, 1995), 25–28.

6. Emma Hardy, *Some Recollections*, ed. Evelyn Hardy and Robert Gittings (London: Oxford University Press, 1961), 60.

7. *Emma Hardy Diaries*, ed. Richard H. Taylor (Ashington and Manchester: Mid Northumberland Arts Group and Carcanet New Press, 1985), 54.

8. For excellent accounts of Hardy's development of the concept of Wessex, see Simon Gatrell's *Thomas Hardy's Vision of Wessex* (Basingstoke: Palgrave Macmillan, 2003); and Ralph Pite's *Hardy's Geography: Wessex and the Regional Novel* (Basingstoke: Palgrave Macmillan, 2002).

9. In a letter responding to Leslie Stephen's request that he drop the subtitle *A Comedy in Chapters* for the serial, Hardy declared, perhaps somewhat ironically: 'I should certainly deplore being thought to have set up in the large joke line—the genteelest of genteel comedy being as far as ever I should think it safe to go at any time' (21 May 1875, CL 1:37).

10. Cassie Pole moved to London in 1872. She married a man who kept a pub in Shepherd's Market. Hardy's poem 'At Mayfair Lodgings' of 1894 describes her death, which took place that year, and suggests that had she married the poem's speaker, she would not have died prematurely:

> Silently screened from view
> Her tragedy was ending
> That need not have come due
> Had she been less unbending.
> How near, near were we two
> At that last vital rending,—
> And neither of us knew! (CP 451)

11. This is in the *Cornhill* and 1876 edition only. In 1877 Hardy changed it to 'the fingers of a corpse'.

12. Rebekah Owen recorded this comment in the course of a visit that she made to Swanage with Hardy and Emma in September of 1892 (MM 301).

7. Literary London (I)

1. Charles Dickens, *Great Expectations*, ed. Charlotte Mitchell (London: Penguin, 1996), 366–367. For a full account of the Hummums in eighteenth- and nineteenth-century literature, see Cory MacLaughlin's 'The Hummums: Bath, Brothel and Holy Shrine of Literary London', *Literary London: Interdisciplinary Studies in the Representation of London* 6, no. 1 (March 2008), http://www.literarylondon.org/london-journal/march2008/maclauchlin.html.

2. Moule to Hardy, [fragment but probably June 1867], DCM.

3. Moule's *Christian Oratory: An Inquiry into Its History in the First Five Centuries* was published in 1859 (Cambridge: Macmillan), and his *The Roman Republic: Being a Review of Some of the Salient Points in its History, etc.* the following year (London: Bradbury & Evans).

4. H. C. G. Moule, *Memories of a Vicarage* (London: Religious Tract Society, 1913), 35.

5. 'She', subtitled 'At His Funeral', published in *Wessex Poems* and dated 1873, is also often read as relating to Moule, although the accompanying picture is of Stinsford Church rather than Fordington, and the poem's speaker has never been conclusively identified as inspired by an actual 'sweetheart' of Moule's:

> They bear him to his resting-place—
> In slow procession sweeping by;
> I follow at a stranger's space;
> His kindred they, his sweetheart I.
> Unchanged my gown of garish dye,
> Though sable-sad is their attire;
> But they stand round with griefless eye,
> Whilst my regret consumes like fire! (CP 12–13 [where it is titled 'She at His
>   Funeral']).

6. Leslie Stephen's letter of 30 November 1872 to Hardy (the one that was dropped by children and retrieved from the mud by a labourer) opens: 'Dear Sir, I hear from Mr Moule that I may address you as the author of "Under the Greenwood Tree" (RP 336).

7. Moule to Hardy [n.d., but 21 May 1873], DCM.

8. Hardy wrote to Tinsley on 3 October 1871 asking for an extract from Moule's review of *Desperate Remedies* to be used to advertise the novel, and to Macmillan on 14 October to inform them of this positive review (CL 1:13). He made the same request again to Tinsley after Moule's review of *Under the Greenwood Tree* was published on 28 September 1872 (letter of 2 Oct. 1872, CL 1:19).

9. Hardy's note reads in full: 'The writer may state here that the original conception of the story did not design a marriage between Thomasin and Venn. He was to have

retained his isolated and weird character to the last, and to have disappeared mysteri-ously from the heath, nobody knowing whither—Thomasin remaining a widow. But cer-tain circumstances of serial publication led to a change of intent. Readers can therefore choose between the endings, and those with an austere artistic code can assume the more consistent conclusion to be the true one' (RN 440). 'The Distracted Preacher', written in Tooting between *The Return of the Native* and *The Trumpet-Major* and published as 'The Distracted Young Preacher' in *New Quarterly Magazine* in 1879, had a similar note added when reprinted in the Wessex Edition of *Wessex Tales* in 1912: 'The ending of this story with the marriage of Lizzy and the minister was almost *de rigeur* in an En-glish magazine at the time of writing. But at this late date, thirty years after, it may not be amiss to give the ending that would have been preferred by the writer to the conven-tion used above' (WT 223). He goes on to explain that Lizzy would have married Jim the smuggler instead of the preacher, that they would have emigrated to America, and died in Wisconsin between 1850 and 1860.

10. It is worth noting that when asked to expound on his use of Dorset dialect by the English Dialect Society in 1876, Hardy replied: 'The dialect of the peasants in my novels is, as far as it goes, that of this county [Dorset]; but it is necessary to state that I have not, as a rule, reproduced in the dialogues such words as would, from their ap-proximation to received English, seem to a London reader to be mere mispronuncia-tions' (PV 11). The comment suggests how actively he tried to anticipate the responses of an audience composed of 'London reader[s]'.

11. Those mentioned in this paragraph are: Walter Pollock (barrister and author, 1850–1926); Charles Godfrey Leland (American author, 1824–1903); Sir William Frederick Pollock (barrister and author, 1815–1888); Walter Besant (novelist and man of letters, 1836–1901); Sir Patrick Colquhoun (diplomat and author, 1815–1891)); Edward Henry Palmer (orientalist, 1840–1882—he was murdered by robbers in Egypt); and Joseph Knight (drama critic, 1829–1907).

12. 'Quite worn out with the day at Waterloo', Emma observed in her diary the day after (*Emma Hardy Diaries*, ed. Richard H. Taylor [Ashington and Manchester: Mid Northumberland Arts Group and Carcanet New Press, 1985], 93). The *Life* includes numerous accounts of conversations with veterans of the Napoleonic wars, such as this of 27 Oct. 1878: 'Sunday. To Chelsea Hospital and Ranelagh Gardens: met a palsied pensioner—deaf. He is 88—was in the Seventh (?) Hussars. He enlisted in 1807 or 1808, served under Sir John Moore in the Peninsula, through the Retreat, and was at Waterloo. It was extraordinary to talk and shake hands with a man who had shared in that ter-rible march to Coruna, and had seen Moore face to face' (L 127).

13. It seems to me likely that 'No Buyers' and 'A Gentleman's Second-Hand Suit' were also composed from notes or diary entries made in the course of Hardy's Tooting years.

14. John Bayley, *An Essay on Hardy* (Cambridge: Cambridge University Press, 1978), 19.

15. This was not the only occasion during their Tooting years that the Hardys felt some malign person or force was attempting to invade their living quarters. The *Life* records a night they spent in a gloomy room 'painted a bloody red' in a hotel in Le Havre in August of 1880. Remembering that the hotel had been recommended by a stranger whom they had met on the coach from Etretât, and to whom Hardy had unwisely revealed that he travelled carrying bank notes, the couple became convinced that they were in danger. After the departure of the melancholy chambermaid, 'who sighed continually and spoke in a foreboding voice', they searched the room and 'found a small door behind the curtains of one of their beds, and on opening it there was revealed inside a closet of lumber, which had at its innermost recess another door, leading they did not know whither. With their luggage they barricaded the closet door, so jamming their trunks and portmanteau between the door and the nearest bedstead that it was impossible to open the closet. They lay down and waited, keeping the light burning a long time' (L 143). No intruder attempted to rob or murder them, needless to say, and they eventually fell asleep.

16. Ralph Pite, *Thomas Hardy: The Guarded Life* (London: Picador, 2006), 259.

17. The source of the term Laodiceanism is Revelation: 'And unto the angel of the church of the Laodiceans write; "These things saith the Amen, the faithful and true witness, the beginning of the creation of God; I know thy works, that thou art neither cold nor hot: I would thou wert cold or hot. So then because thou art lukewarm, and neither cold nor hot, I will spue thee out of my mouth"' (Rev. 3:14–16).

8. Literary London (II)

1. Letter from Anne Procter to Hardy, 4 Sept. 1874 (DCM).

2. The list contains over one hundred names, split into Artists, Dancers, Music, Actors and Actresses, Literary Men (there are fifty-six of these), and Literary Women. Among the famous writers listed are Godwin, Wordsworth, Coleridge, De Quincey, Hazlitt, Hunt, Lamb, Crabbe, Carlyle, Emerson, Cooper, Longfellow, Beddoes, Thackeray, Trollope, Dickens, and Charlotte Brontë. The ones, she tells Hardy, who were 'the best company' were Sydney Smith, Lord Lytton, and Dickens (DCM).

3. The three are attending a performance at the St. James's Theatre, of Arthur Wing Pinero's *The Squire,* the play loosely based on Hardy's own theatrical adaptation (in collaboration with J. Comyns Carr) of *Far from the Madding Crowd*. Its caption reads: 'Mr Hardy and Mr Comyns Carr are not admiring Mr Stone's acting. They have brought Mr George Lewis to see whether it will be possible to imprison Mr Pinero'.

4. Letter from Anne Procter to Emma Forrest, 5 Jan. 1878, quoted in MM, 175.

5. One of the most striking examples of this occurs in Hardy's description of Pierston making his way through the crush at a London party in *The Well-Beloved*: 'After

ten minutes given to a preoccupied regard of shoulder-blades, black hair, glittering head-gear, neck-napes, moles, hairpins, pearl-powder, pimples, minerals cut into facets of many-coloured rays, necklace-clasps, fans, stays, the seven styles of elbow and arm, the thirteen varieties of ear; and by using the toes of his dress-boots as coulters with which he ploughed his way and that of Lady Mabella in the direction they were aiming at, he drew near to Mrs. Pine-Avon, who was drinking a cup of tea in the back drawing-room' (WB 223).

6. For further discussion of Hardy's essay, see Roger Lowman, *Thomas Hardy's 'The Dorsetshire Labourer' and Wessex* (Lampeter: Edwin Mellen Press, 2005).

7. Fran Chalfont, 'Hardy's Residences and Lodgings: Part Three', *Thomas Hardy Journal* 9, no. 3 (May 1993): 19–38.

8. It is Thomas Campion rather than Thomas Lodge that Hardy and Angel are recalling: 'They look like rosebuds filled with snow' is from the second stanza of 'There Is a Garden in Her Face'. Hardy continued to see Tess in the faces of London society women even after the novel was published: 'Nov. 11 [1893]. Met Lady Cynthia Graham. In appearance she is something like my idea of "Tess", though I did not know her when the novel was written' (L 276).

9. The following year, 1894, he reported: 'Whether because he was assumed to have written a notorious novel or not Hardy could not say, but he found himself continually invited hither and thither to see famous beauties of the time—some of whom disappointed him; but some he owned to be very beautiful' (L 282).

9. *The Well-Beloved*

1. Raymond Williams, *The Country and the City* (1973; repr., London: The Hogarth Press, 1985), 197.

2. *The Well-Beloved* (London: Macmillan, 1903), vi. In the preface to the Wessex Edition of 1912, Hardy changed 'fantastic' to 'imaginative' (WB 174). It is interesting to note that Marcel Proust enhanced the relation between the father's stone quarrying and the son's sculpting when the book is discussed in *The Captive*: 'Do you remember the stonemasons in *Jude the Obscure*, and in *The Well-Beloved* the blocks of stone which the father hews out of the island coming in boats to be piled up in the son's workshop where they are turned into statues'. *In Search of Lost Time: The Captive; The Fugitive*, trans. C. K. Scott-Moncrieff, Terence Kilmartin, and D. J. Enright (London: Vintage, 1996), 430.

3. Dehn Gilmore, 'Vacuums and Blurs: The Related Responses of Thomas Hardy and the French Impressionists to the Modern City', *Literary London: Interdisciplinary Studies in the Representation of London* 2, no. 1 (March 2004), http://www.literarylondon.org/london-journal/march2004/gilmore.html).

4. In *The Pursuit of the Well-Beloved* Pearston's (as he was called in that earlier version) London address is given as Hintock Road, Kensington (WB 36), an allusion to the hamlet of Little Hintock in *The Woodlanders*.

5. Keith Wilson, 'Thomas Hardy of London', in *A Companion to Thomas Hardy*, ed. Keith Wilson (Oxford: Wiley-Blackwell, 2012), 153. Hardy includes a number of fascinating entries on Turner in the *Life*. In January of 1887 he observed: 'The "simply natural" is interesting no longer. The much-decried, mad, late-Turner rendering is now necessary to create my interest' (L 192); and on 9 January of the following year: 'Turner's water-colours: each is a landscape *plus* a man's soul. . . . What he paints chiefly is *light as modified by objects*' (L 225).

6. Cited in Dennis Taylor, 'The Chronology of Hardy's Poetry: Part III', *Thomas Hardy Journal* 18, no. 1 (February 2002): 39.

7. Wilson, 'Thomas Hardy of London', 153.

8. *The Complete Works of Oscar Wilde*, vol. 1, *Poems and Poems in Prose*, ed. Bobby Fong and Karl Beckson (Oxford: Oxford University Press, 2000), 153.

9. For the 1912 edition, to make the attack more pointed, Hardy added 'and journalists' after 'art-critics'.

10. London Streets and Interiors

1. See Wordsworth's *The Prelude*, Book VII, l. 130; and Thomas de Quincey's *Confessions of an English Opium-Eater*, ed. John E. Jordan (London: Everyman, 1960), 89.

2. *London* must refer to its setting rather than place of composition since Hardy didn't visit London at all in 1918. On the manuscript, however, the date is given as 'about 1918', so it is possible that the poem *was* composed in London, but at a different date.

3. For further discussion of the relationship between Hardy's prostitute and the tradition of the Magdalen in Victorian culture, see Frank R. Giordano Jr.'s 'The Repentant Magdalen in Thomas Hardy's "The Woman I Met"', *English Literature in Transition, 1880–1920* 15, no. 2 (1972): 136–143.

4. For further discussion of this tradition, see Peter Robinson's 'The Poetry of Modern Life: On the Pavement', in *The Oxford Handbook of Victorian Poetry*, ed. Matthew Bevis (Oxford: Oxford University Press, 2013), 254–272.

5. Giordano, 'The Repentant Magdalen', 138.

Epilogue

1. For further details, see Keith Wilson's *Thomas Hardy on Stage* (Basingstoke: Palgrave Macmillan, 1995), 85–95.

2. For a full account of this distressing episode, see MM 514–517.

3. *The Variorum Edition of the Complete Poems of Thomas Hardy*, ed. James Gibson (London: Macmillan, 1979), xix. See also Simon Gatrell's *Hardy the Creator: A Textual Biography* (Oxford: Oxford University Press, 1988).

4. 'I cannot resist telling you', wrote Gosse in the last of his many hymns of praise to Hardy, 'how marvellously fine I think your poem in today's *Times*. It is wholly original in form and substance, and of a most arresting quality of style' (Letter from Gosse to Hardy, 24 Dec. 1927, DCM).

Selected Bibliography

Fiction

Desperate Remedies. Edited by Patricia Ingham. Oxford: Oxford University Press, 2003. [1871]

Under the Greenwood Tree. Edited by Simon Gatrell. Oxford: Oxford University Press, 2013. [1872]

A Pair of Blue Eyes. Edited by Alan Manford. Oxford: Oxford University Press, 2005. [1873]

Far from the Madding Crowd. Edited by Suzanne B. Falck-Yi. Oxford: Oxford University Press, 2002. [1874]

The Hand of Ethelberta. Edited by Tim Dolin. London: Penguin, 1996. [1876]

The Return of the Native. Edited by Simon Gatrell. Oxford: Oxford University Press, 2005. [1878]

The Trumpet-Major. Edited by Charles Pettit. Ware: Wordsworth Classics, 1995. [1880]

A Laodicean. Edited by John Schad. London: Penguin, 1997. [1881]

Two on a Tower. Edited by Suleiman M. Ahmad. Oxford: Oxford University Press, 1993. [1882]

The Mayor of Casterbridge. Edited by Dale Kramer. Oxford: Oxford University Press, 2004. [1886]

The Woodlanders. Edited by Dale Kramer. Oxford: Oxford University Press, 2005. [1887]

Wessex Tales. Edited by Kathryn R. King. Oxford: Oxford University Press, 1991. [1888]

Tess of the d'Urbervilles. Edited by Juliet Grindle and Simon Gatrell. Oxford: Oxford University Press, 2005. [1891]

Life's Little Ironies. Edited by Alan Manford. Oxford: Oxford University Press, 1996. [1894]

Jude the Obscure. Edited by Patricia Ingham. Oxford: Oxford University Press, 2002. [1895]

The Pursuit of the Well-Beloved and *The Well-Beloved*. Edited by Patricia Ingham. London: Penguin, 1997. [1897]

A Changed Man and Other Tales. London: Macmillan, 1951. [1913]

Collected Short Stories. London: Macmillan, 1988.

An Indiscretion in the Life of an Heiress and Other Stories. Edited by Pamela Dalziel. Oxford: Oxford University Press, 1994.

Poetry

The Dynasts. London: Macmillan, 1978.

Thomas Hardy: The Complete Poems. Edited by James Gibson. Basingstoke: Palgrave Macmillan, 2001.

The Variorum Edition of the Complete Poems of Thomas Hardy. Edited by James Gibson. London: Macmillan, 1979.

Life, Letters, Notebooks, Miscellaneous Prose

Hardy, Emma. *Emma Hardy Diaries*. Edited by Richard H. Taylor. Ashington and Manchester: Mid Northumberland Arts Group and Carcanet New Press, 1985.

———. *Some Recollections*. Edited by Evelyn Hardy and Robert Gittings. London: Oxford University Press, 1961.

Hardy, Emma, and Florence Hardy. *Letters of Emma & Florence Hardy*. Edited by Michael Millgate. Oxford: Oxford University Press, 1996.

Hardy, Florence. *The Life of Thomas Hardy*. London: Studio Editions, 1994.

Hardy, Thomas. *The Collected Letters of Thomas Hardy*. Edited by Richard Little Purdy, Michael Millgate, and Keith Wilson. 8 vols. Oxford: Oxford University Press, 1978–2012.

———. *The Life and Work of Thomas Hardy*. Edited by Michael Millgate. London: Macmillan, 1984.

———. *The Literary Notebooks of Thomas Hardy*. Edited by Lennart A. Björk. 2 vols. New York: New York University Press, 1985.

———. *One Rare Fair Woman: Thomas Hardy's Letters to Florence Henniker, 1893–1922*. Edited by Evelyn Hardy and F. B. Pinion. London: Macmillan, 1972.

———. *The Personal Notebooks of Thomas Hardy*. Edited by Richard H. Taylor. London: Macmillan, 1978.

———. *Thomas Hardy: Interviews and Recollections*. Edited by James Gibson. London: Macmillan, 1999.

———. *Thomas Hardy's Personal Writings*. Edited by Harold Orel. London: Macmillan, 1967.

———. *Thomas Hardy's 'Poetical Matter' Notebook*. Edited by Pamela Dalziel and Michael Millgate. Oxford: Oxford University Press, 2009.

———. *Thomas Hardy's Public Voice: The Essays, Speeches, and Miscellaneous Prose*. Edited by Michael Millgate. Oxford: Clarendon Press, 2001.

———. *Thomas Hardy's 'Studies, Specimens &c.' Notebook*. Edited by Pamela Dalziel and Michael Millgate. Oxford: Oxford University Press, 1994.

———. *Thomas Hardy's Will and Other Wills of His Family*. Mount Durand, Guernsey: The Toucan Press, 1967.

Biographies

Gibson, James. *Thomas Hardy: A Literary Life*. London: Macmillan, 1996.

Gittings, Robert. *The Older Hardy*. Harmondsworth: Penguin, 1978.

———. *Young Thomas Hardy*. Harmondsworth: Penguin, 1975.

Millgate, Michael. *Thomas Hardy: A Biography Revisited*. Oxford: Oxford University Press, 2004.

Norman, Andrew. *Thomas Hardy: Behind the Mask*. Stroud: The History Press, 2011.

Pite, Ralph. *Thomas Hardy: The Guarded Life*. London: Picador, 2006.

Seymour-Smith, Martin. *Hardy*. London: Bloomsbury, 1994.

Tomalin, Claire. *Thomas Hardy: The Time-Torn Man*. London: Penguin, 2006.

Turner, Paul. *The Life of Thomas Hardy*. Oxford: Blackwell, 1998.

On Hardy and London

Gilmore, Dehn. 'Vacuums and Blurs: The Related Responses of Thomas Hardy and the French Impressionists to the Modern City'. *Literary London: Interdisciplinary Studies in the Representation of London* 2, no. 1 (March 2004), http://www.literarylondon.org/london-journal/march2004/gilmore.html.

Slater, Michael. 'Hardy and the City'. In *New Perspectives on Thomas Hardy*, edited by Charles Pettit, 41–57. London: Macmillan, 1994.

Wilson, Keith. 'Thomas Hardy of London'. In *A Companion to Thomas Hardy*, edited by Keith Wilson, 146–161. Oxford: Wiley-Blackwell, 2012.

Other Sources

Ainsworth, Harrison. *Old St. Paul's*. London: Macmillan, 1968.

Barrie, J. M. *Letters of J. M. Barrie*. Edited by Viola Meynell. London: Peter Davies, 1942.

Bayley, John. *An Essay on Hardy*. Cambridge: Cambridge University Press, 1978.

Chalfont, Fran. 'Hardy's Residences and Lodgings: Part One'. *Thomas Hardy Journal* 8, no. 3 (Oct. 1992): 46–56.

———. 'Hardy's Residences and Lodgings: Part Two'. *Thomas Hardy Journal* 9, no. 1 (Feb. 1993): 41–61.

———. 'Hardy's Residences and Lodgings: Part Three'. *Thomas Hardy Journal* 9, no. 3 (May 1993): 19–38.

Cox, R. G., ed. *Thomas Hardy: The Critical Heritage*. London: Routledge, 1970.

Dalziel, Pamela, ed. *The Excluded and Collaborative Stories*. Oxford: Oxford University Press, 1992.

———. 'Exploiting the *Poor Man*: The Genesis of Hardy's *Desperate Remedies*'. *Journal of English and Germanic Philology* 94 (April 1995): 220–232.

De Quincey, Thomas. *Confessions of an English Opium-Eater*. Edited by John E. Jordan. London: Everyman, 1960.

Dickens, Charles. *Great Expectations*. Edited by Charlotte Mitchell. London: Penguin, 1996.

Eliot, T. S. *Selected Prose of T. S. Eliot*. Edited by Frank Kermode. London: Faber & Faber, 1975.

Gatrell, Simon. *Hardy the Creator: A Textual Biography*. Oxford: Clarendon Press, 1988.

———. *Thomas Hardy's Vision of Wessex*. Basingstoke: Palgrave Macmillan, 2003.

Giordano, Frank R., Jr. 'The Repentant Magdalen in Thomas Hardy's "The Woman I Met"'. *English Literature in Transition, 1880–1920* 15, no. 2 (1972): 136–143.

Gosse, Edmund. 'Thomas Hardy's Lost Novel'. *Sunday Times*, 22 January 1928.

Gossin, Pamela. *Thomas Hardy's Novel Universe: Astronomy, Cosmology and Gender in the Post-Darwinian World*. Aldershot: Ashgate, 2007.

Heaney, Seamus. *Station Island*. London: Faber & Faber, 1984.

Hughes, John. 'Meter and Context: Hardy's "Neutral Tones"'. *Victorian Poetry* 51, no. 1 (Spring 2013): 81–97.

Hynes, Samuel. *The Pattern of Hardy's Poetry*. Chapel Hill: University of North Carolina Press, 1961.

Kift, Dagmar. *The Victorian Music Hall: Culture, Class and Conflict*. Cambridge: Cambridge University Press, 1996.

King, R. W. 'The Lyrical Poems of Thomas Hardy'. *The London Mercury* December 1925. Reprinted in Graham Clarke, ed. *Thomas Hardy: Critical Assessments*. Vol. 2, *The Writer and the Poet*, 206–216. Mountsfield: Helm, 1993.

Larkin, Philip. *Collected Poems*. London: Faber & Faber, 1988.

———. *Required Writing*. London: Faber & Faber, 1984.

Lerner, Laurence, and John Holmstrom, eds. *Thomas Hardy & His Readers*. London: Bodley Head, 1968.

Lock, Charles. 'Hardy and the Railway'. *Essays in Criticism* 50, no. 1 (2000): 44–66.

Lowman, Roger. *Thomas Hardy's 'The Dorsetshire Labourer' and Wessex*. Lampeter: Edwin Mellen Press, 2005.

Lucking, J. H. *Railways of Dorset: An Outline of their Establishment, Development and Progress from 1825*. Lichfield: The Railway Correspondence and Travel Society/ The Dorset Natural History and Archaeological Society, 1968.

MacLaughlin, Cory. 'The Hummums: Bath, Brothel and Holy Shrine of Literary London'. *Literary London: Interdisciplinary Studies in the Representation of London* 6, no. 1 (March 2008), http://www.literarylondon.org/london-journal /march2008/maclauchlin.html.

Maitland, F. W. *The Life and Letters of Leslie Stephen*. London: Duckworth, 1906.

Meynell, Viola, ed. *Friends of a Lifetime: Letters to Sydney Carlyle Cockerell*. London: Jonathan Cape, 1940.

Millgate, Michael. *Testamentary Acts: Browning, Tennyson, James, Hardy*. Oxford: Clarendon Press, 1992.

Morgan, Charles. *The House of Macmillan, 1843–1943*. London: Macmillan, 1943.

Moule, H. C. G. *Memories of a Vicarage*. London: Religious Tract Society, 1913.

Moule, Horace. *Christian Oratory: An Inquiry into Its History in the First Five Centuries*. Cambridge: Macmillan, 1859.

———. *The Roman Republic: Being a Review of Some of the Salient Points in its History, etc.* London: Bradbury & Evans, 1860.

Nead, Lynda. *Victorian Babylon*. New Haven: Yale University Press, 2000.

Nemesvari, Richard. 'Hardy and Victorian Popular Culture: Performing Modernity in Music Hall and Melodrama'. In *The Ashgate Research Companion to Thomas Hardy*, edited by Rosemarie Morgan, 71–86. Farnham: Ashgate, 2010.

———. *Thomas Hardy, Sensationalism, and the Melodramatic Mode*. Basingstoke: Palgrave Macmillan, 2011.

Page, Norman, ed. *Oxford Readers Companion to Hardy*. Oxford: Oxford University Press, 2000.

Palgrave, Francis Turner, ed. *The Golden Treasury of the Best Songs and Lyrical Poems in the English Language, Selected and Arranged with Notes*. Edited by Christopher Ricks. London: Penguin, 1991.

Pite, Ralph. *Hardy's Geography: Wessex and the Regional Novel*. Basingstoke: Palgrave Macmillan, 2002.

Plietzsch, Birgit. *The Novels of Thomas Hardy as a Product of Nineteenth-Century Social, Economic, and Cultural Change*. Berlin: Tenea Verlag, 2004.

Porter, Peter. *Collected Poems*. Oxford: Oxford University Press, 1984.

Proust, Marcel. *In Search of Lost Time: The Captive; The Fugitive*. Translated by C. K. Scott-Moncrieff, Terence Kilmartin, and D. J. Enright. London: Vintage, 1996.

Purdy, Richard Little. *Thomas Hardy: A Bibliographical Study*. Edited by Charles Pettit. London: British Library, 2002.

Robinson, Peter. 'The Poetry of Modern Life: On the Pavement'. In *The Oxford Handbook of Victorian Poetry*, edited by Matthew Bevis, 254–272. Oxford: Oxford University Press, 2013.

Schweik, Robert. 'Hardy's "Plunge in a New and Untried Direction": Comic Detachment in *The Hand of Ethelberta*'. *English Studies* 83, no. 3 (2002): 239–252.

Shelley, Percy Bysshe. *The Letters of Percy Bysshe Shelley,* vol. 1. Edited by Frederick L. Jones. Oxford: Oxford University Press, 1964.

Smiles, Samuel. *Self-Help*. London: John Murray, 1958.

Taylor, Dennis. 'The Chronology of Hardy's Poetry: Part III'. *Thomas Hardy Journal* 18, no. 1 (February 2002): 35–53.

———. 'Hardy's Copy of *The Golden Treasury*'. *Victorian Poetry* 37 (1999): 165–191.

———. 'The Victorian Philological Contexts of Hardy's Poetry'. In *Thomas Hardy in Context,* edited by Phillip Mallett, 231–241. Cambridge: Cambridge University Press, 2013.

Thwaite, Ann. *Edmund Gosse: A Literary Landscape, 1849–1928*. London: Secker & Warburg, 1984.

Tinsley, William. *Random Recollections of an Old Publisher*. London: Simpkin, Marshall, Hamilton, Kent, 1900.

White, Jerry. *London in the Nineteenth Century*. London: Vintage, 2008.

Widdowson, Peter. *Hardy in History: A Study in Literary Sociology*. London: Routledge, 1989.

Wilde, Oscar. *The Complete Works of Oscar Wilde*. Vol. 1, *Poems and Poems in Prose*. Edited by Bobby Fong and Karl Beckson. Oxford: Oxford University Press, 2000.

Willey, Basil. *Cambridge and Other Memories 1920–1953*. London: Chatto & Windus, 1966.

Williams, Raymond. *The Country and the City*. London: The Hogarth Press, 1985.

Wilson, Keith. *Thomas Hardy on Stage*. Basingstoke: Palgrave Macmillan, 1995.

———. 'Thomas Hardy's "The Ruined Maid," Elsa Lanchester's Music Hall, and the Fall into Fashion'. *Thomas Hardy Journal*, 15, no. 2 (May 1999): 41–48.

Illustration Sources

Frontispiece:

'Coming Up Oxford Street: Evening' (*The Nation & the Athenaeum*, 13 June 1925)

Plates:

Hardy's coffin leaving Max Gate for cremation in Woking (© TopFoto)

The urn containing Hardy's ashes in the crematorium at Woking (© TopFoto)

Wreaths in Poets' Corner after Hardy's Westminster Abbey funeral (© TopFoto)

The burial of Hardy's heart in Stinsford (© TopFoto)

Hardy's gravestone in Westminster Abbey (Westminster Abbey Library, © The Dean and Chapter of the Collegiate Church of St. Peter Westminster)

Hardy's illustration for 'Amabel' (*Wessex Poems*, Macmillan)

16 Westbourne Park Villas (Photo by the author, © Mark Ford)

Holywell Street (Reproduced by permission of Historic England)

Sketch of view from Westbourne Park Villas, 22 June 1866 (The Thomas Hardy Archive and Collection, Dorset County Museum)

Sketch of St. James's Park, 28 April 1863 (The Thomas Hardy Archive and Collection, Dorset County Museum)

Hardy's illustration for 'She, to Him I' (*Wessex Poems*, Macmillan)

Eliza Nicholls's photograph of Hardy (c. 1862) (The Beinecke Rare Book and Manuscript Library, Yale University)

The Hardy Tree in St. Pancras Churchyard (Photo by the author, © Mark Ford)

St. Giles Cripplegate Church (© Museum of London)

1 Arundel Terrace, Trinity Road, Tooting (Photo by the author, © Mark Ford)

Sketch of Hardy, J. Comyns Carr, and George Lewis in a box at St. James's Theatre watching Pinero's *The Squire* (*The Illustrated Sporting and Dramatic News*, 7 January 1882)

Acknowledgements

I would like to thank the following: Isabelle Lewis for her maps; Juliette Atkinson, Matthew Beaumont, Simon Gatrell, John Hughes, John Kulka, Virginia Perrin, and John Sutherland for their many useful suggestions; Lady Margot Bright for entertaining me in 16 Westbourne Park Villas; Helen Gibson for her patient assistance on my visit to the Dorset County Museum to inspect the Hardy archive; and Heather Vickers for help in locating pictures. I would also like to pay tribute to the work of Michael Millgate; like so many publications on Hardy, this study is deeply indebted to his pioneering research.

Index